CONSUMERGUIDE™

CONSUMER
BUYING GUIDE
···
2000 Edition
···

CONTENTS _____

INTRODUCTION _____ 6

TELEVISIONS AND TV/VCR COMBINATIONS _____ 8

35- to 41-Inch TV Sets ∘ 32-Inch TV Sets ∘ 27-Inch TV Sets ∘ 20-Inch TV Sets ∘ Front-Projection TV Sets ∘ Rear-Projection TV Sets ∘ TV/VCR Combinations ∘ Satellite Systems ∘ HDTV Set-Top Box

VIDEO ACCESSORIES _____ 42

Universal Remotes

VCRs, DVD, AND LASERDISC PLAYERS _____ 45

VCRs ∘ Digital Video Disc (DVD) Players ∘ Laserdisc Players

CAMCORDERS _____ 64

8mm Camcorders ∘ Full-Size VHS Camcorders ∘ Compact VHS (VHS-C) Camcorders ∘ Digital Video (DV) Camcorders

STEREO COMPONENTS _____ 79

Speakers ∘ Subwoofers ∘ Headphones ∘ Stereo Receivers ∘ Compact Disc Players ∘ Cassette Decks ∘ MiniDisc Decks

STEREO SYSTEMS _____ 125

Home Theater Systems ∘ Mini-/Midi-Systems

CONTENTS

PERSONAL STEREOS _____ 134

Portable CD Players ∘ Personal Radio-Cassette Players ∘ Personal Radio-Cassette Player/Recorders ∘ Personal Cassette Players ∘ Personal Headset Radios ∘ Personal Radios ∘ Personal MiniDisc Players ∘ Personal MiniDisc Player/Recorders ∘ Boom Boxes ∘ Clock Radios

CAMERAS _____ 156

35mm Manual-Focus SLR Cameras ∘ 35mm Autofocus SLR Cameras ∘ 35mm Autofocus Cameras ∘ 35mm Compact Cameras ∘ 24mm Advanced Photo System (APS) Cameras ∘ Instant-Print Cameras ∘ Digital-Still Cameras

TELEPHONES AND ANSWERING MACHINES _____ 181

Feature Telephones ∘ Cordless Telephones (900MHz Models) ∘ Mobile Telephones ∘ Answering Machines

COMPUTERS _____ 193

Home & Small Office Computers ∘ Business/Hi-Powered Computers ∘ Portable Computers ∘ Data Storage Devices ∘ Monitors ∘ Modems ∘ Printers

HOME OFFICE PRODUCTS_____ 221

Desktop Copiers ∘ Scanners ∘ Desktop Fax Machines ∘ Personal Digital Assistants ∘ Multifunction Machines

HOME FITNESS _____234

Exercise Cycles ○ Rowing Machine ○ Treadmills ○ Home Gyms ○ Stair Climbers ○ Ski Machine ○ Total Body Machines ○ Elliptical Machines

HOME IMPROVEMENT _____251

Electric Drills ○ Electric Sanders ○ Circular Saws and Jigsaws ○ Routers ○ Garage Door Openers

SAFETY EQUIPMENT _____264

Smoke Detectors ○ Carbon Monoxide (CO) Detectors ○ Fire Extinguishers

SNOW REMOVAL _____270

Single-Stage Snow Throwers ○ Two-Stage Snow Throwers

LAWN CARE _____276

Lawn Mowers ○ Riding Mowers ○ Lawn Tractors ○ Garden Tractors ○ String Trimmers ○ Blower/Vacs

FOOD PREPARATION _____291

Food Processors ○ Electric Mixers ○ Blenders ○ Toasters ○ Toaster Ovens ○ Juicers/Juice Extractors ○ Steamers ○ Ice-Cream Makers ○ Bread Makers ○ Coffee Makers ○ Tea Kettles

MICROWAVE OVENS _____329

Full-Size Microwave Ovens ○ Family-Size Microwave Ovens ○ Medium-Size Microwave Ovens ○ Compact Microwave Ovens ○ Microwave/Convection Ovens ○ Over-the-Range Microwave Ovens ○ Over-the-Range Microwave/Convection Ovens

CONTENTS

RANGES _____ 343

Gas Ranges ∘ Electric Ranges

REFRIGERATORS AND FREEZERS _____ 360

Refrigerators ∘ Freezers

DISHWASHERS _____ 377

Built-In Dishwashers ∘ Portable Dishwashers

FLOOR CARE_____ 385

All-Purpose Cleaning Machines ∘ Upright Vacuum Cleaners ∘ Powerhead Canister Vacuum Cleaners ∘ Compact Canister Vacuums ∘ Stick and Broom Vacuums ∘ Hand Vacuums

LAUNDRY CARE _____ 399

Washers ∘ Dryers ∘ Combination Washer/Dryer

SEWING MACHINES _____ 412

Computerized Sewing Machines ∘ Noncomputerized Sewing Machines

ENVIRONMENTAL APPLIANCES _____ 417

Ceiling Fans ∘ Air Conditioners ∘ Air Care Appliances ∘ Portable Heaters

BABY EQUIPMENT _____ 430

Portable Cribs and Play Yards ∘ Swings ∘ Nursery Monitors ∘ Car Seats ∘ Strollers ∘ High Chairs

INTRODUCTION

Are you finally ready to buy that full-size stereo system with a CD player? Do you know what the difference is between a carousel and magazine disc changer? Looking to replace your aging television set with a new one? Are you sure you know what "cable ready" means?

In short, do you know how to determine what features you'll want in a product? Then, do you know how to get the most features for your money?

It takes experience and expert knowledge to spend your hard-earned dollars wisely in every facet of today's marketplace. Intelligent choices become more difficult when you consider rapid advances in technology and shifts in the world's economy. These factors can quickly change price, availability, and long-term usefulness, making your buying decisions very confusing.

That's where we at CONSUMER GUIDE™ can help. We recognize the challenge in picking a Best Buy, a product that meets your high standards of quality, performance, and value. Our experts in the major product fields have taken the guesswork and confusion out of making major purchases. CONSUMER GUIDE™ has no affiliation with any manufacturers or retailers, we accept no advertising, and we are not interested in selling products. Our sole purpose is to provide you—the consumer—with the information needed to make informed, intelligent decisions.

In this publication, we have tried to review a wide variety of products to address diverse consumer needs. The products reviewed range from small personal items, such as clock radios, cellular telephones, and automatic-drip coffee makers, to major purchases, such as televisions, refrigerators, computers, and home theater systems. We have not limited the choices to low-end products or top-of-the-line merchandise. We know that a product is only a Best Buy if it meets your needs and budget. Keeping this in mind, we have selected products in a variety of sizes and prices to match the requirements of different shoppers. In fact, this year we have attempted to meet the needs of more consumers than ever. Our Budget Buys, for instance, are affordable products that may not have all the bells and whistles of the top-of-the-line models but are still well constructed and perform well.

Many consumers will find they benefit from exercising patience. When a new product first hits the market, it generally commands a premium price. However, if you wait, instead of rushing right out to make the purchase, you will probably observe that not only does the price come down but changes and improvements will have been incorporated into the product. Prime examples include products such as CD players, personal cassette players, computers, and food processors. These items are much less expensive today than when they first came on the market, and the progression of refinements has been steady.

To make the best use of this book, first review the introductory material at the beginning of each chapter. These introductions contain important information about the product categories, describe product features, and explain the terminology you need to know when you shop. Determine what features will be most useful to you and those using the item. Once you are acquainted with the criteria we use to select products, go on to our product reviews. Items rated Best Buys were chosen for their usefulness, high quality, and overall value. A Best Buy isn't necessarily the least expensive model; it's the highest quality product available at a reasonable price. Recommended selections are also good products, but for one reason or another, they do not measure up to our Best Buy standards.

When you shop, compare prices and models. We provide an Approximate Low Price to serve as your price guide. If a dealer quotes a price close to the Approximate Low Price in this publication, then you know that you are getting first-rate value for your money. **All the prices listed are accurate at the time of printing, but are subject to manufacturer's changes.** In some rare cases, the products are so new that prices were not yet available. All products were checked to make sure that they would be available to consumers in 2000, but product manufacture and distribution is beyond our control.

For additional information and product reviews, visit our Web site at www.consumerguide.com.

TELEVISIONS AND TV/VCR COMBINATIONS

It seems that the American public has a voracious appetite for color televisions. There is also a love affair with bigger and bigger screens above 27 inches. Large-screen and projection TV sales continue to grow, as consumers buy the biggest set that they can (or cannot) afford in pursuit of the best picture quality available.

HOW TO SHOP

How does one evaluate a TV? The obvious criteria are picture quality, brightness, contrast, detail, and lack of signal or video noise. Then combine good sound, a user-friendly remote, and connection options appropriate to your level of use. The colors should be pure and natural. Whenever possible, try to look at programs that offer images you are familiar with for comparison. Try to look at black-and-white images, since these will reveal the quality of the contrast and brightness of the set's picture. DVDs (and laserdiscs and prerecorded VHS tapes) that display the THX logo have been mastered and duplicated to the highest standards and will provide you with an excellent vehicle to evaluate picture quality. You can even do this at your local dealer because they normally have DVD players hooked up to various TVs. Although many major motion pictures already display their THX logo, more and more discs are receiving the THX logo of quality control. Ask your dealer to play one of these discs so you can evaluate the set you are thinking about buying. VHS tapes displaying the THX logo also offer pristine images. Consider checking out images from either DirecTV or EchoStar, for they can also display superior picture quality.

Screen size is a matter of personal preference and budget. Ideally, you should view a TV image from a distance roughly twice as far from the screen as the screen is high. You should also consider TVs with front A/V jacks, which allow easy hook-up to video games and camcorders. Sets 27 inches and above are now the primary sets in most homes. The majority of sets sold are monitor/receiver or tabletop models. These TVs offer the greatest versatility. Models up to 40 inches can be placed into designer cabinets, which are now offered by major furniture companies and specialty manufactuers. Big floor-standing consoles are quickly diminishing, but upright consoles now represent most of this market. Upright consoles take up about the same floor space as a tabletop model, but offer built-in storage for a VCR and videotapes. While 27-inch TVs are popular for the living room/family room, direct-view sets with screen sizes from 30 to 36 inches are selling in record numbers.

Since differences in brand-name televisions are slight, manufacturers have added all sorts of special features to their sets in an attempt to differentiate them. Deciding which television to buy is a matter of matching a set's features with your needs. Except for small LCD mini-TVs and a few portables, virtually all sets include a 181-channel tuner (either quartz or frequency synthesized). Many TVs also offer a feature called either Parental Block or Channel Block. This feature allows parents to program the set so their younger children cannot tune in to certain channels, such as cable channels that offer adult programming.

TVs are becoming more automated. Many sets now offer auto programming, in which you indicate whether your set is attached to either an antenna or a cable system. At the flick of a button, it will automatically tune in all viewable channels. Most sets also include a sleep-timer function, which lets you nod off to late-night television. The set will automatically shut itself off at a preselected interval: 15, 30, 60, 90, or 120 minutes. Other sets can be programmed to turn themselves on at preselected times, either to wake you up or to be sure that you don't miss your favorite show. Many sets now include on-screen help, which includes definitions of features plus explanations on how to accomplish different functions.

HOME THEATER

"Home Theater" is no longer a buzzword. It is becoming a way of life for many people. As more people cocoon and spend time with family and friends at home, everyone gravitates toward the television to watch the latest movie or video. Home theater can be as simple or as complex as you want it to be, as long as you are marrying your television to better audio.

Many people begin their home theater by purchasing a large-screen TV (either direct-view or projection). To get the fullest benefit from home theater, however, you will need various other components, including a hi-fi VCR and a Dolby Pro Logic or Dolby Digital receiver. (For more information on audio equipment, see the chapter on Stereo Components.)

If you want the best possible picture quality, a laserdisc or DVD player may also be in your future. These are the basic building blocks of home theater. The beauty of home theater is that you can buy each component separately or in multiples to enhance your listening and viewing experience. In some cases, a good home theater system can look and sound better than your local cinema.

STEREO SOUND

Stereo sound is a significant feature in TVs today. There are many sets that offer digital sound processing (DSP), Dolby surround decoding, or other sound enhancement options. SRS, for example, is a psycho-acoustic effect that makes the sound emanate from different parts of the room, providing more spacious sound. Spatializer sound offers a similar effect. More than one-third of all TVs sold are now stereo models, and all sets 27 inches and above include stereo as a standard feature.

REMOTE CONTROLS

Most sets include either a basic, standard, universal, or learning remote. A basic remote controls functions such as volume or channel up/down and power on/off. A standard remote is an enhanced basic model with a keypad for direct access that allows you to use on-screen menus and displays. Universal remotes are becoming the most common remote included with televisions. They come with pre-programmed codes for both VCRs and cable boxes. Some brands offer models that are ergonomically designed with keys of different shapes, colors, and sizes. On top of that, a handful of brands include devices with illuminated keys. Learning remotes can be programmed to operate other types of components, such as an A/V receiver or surround processor. If you are trying to tie all your components together, a learning remote might be the best option. However, at best, they can only learn primary functions of each component. Normally, you cannot get into menus from other products to adjust surround settings, for example. A learning remote from an A/V receiver or an aftermarket universal/learning unit provides versatility and access to many functions.

PROJECTION TVs

There are two basic types of projection televisions: front and rear. Although the perfection of these televisions was slow in the beginning, picture quality today verges on exceptional for both types. Projection TVs have become mainstream products, selling approximately one million units annually. Wide-screen has found a home with projection television.

Front-projection TVs need to be viewed in a dark room, lending itself to what some people feel is a true home-theater experience. Units can be either ceiling-mounted or floor-standing. Besides the purchase of the TV itself, a screen is required that will add another $1,200 to $5,000 to the set's purchase price. Front projectors range in screen size from 20 to 300 inches, offering various aspect ratios. To improve picture quality even more, line doublers and line quadruplers are available from the major front-projector manufacturers. These can also add another $10,000 to $20,000 to the package. Front projectors need a dedicated media room just for themselves.

Front LCD projectors are also available, which utilize an LCD wafer and a powerful projector bulb to project an image onto an external surface. The higher the pixel (picture element) count, the better an LCD image will appear on the screen. Remember, though, you need a completely darkened room to enjoy the LCD image. LCD projectors are currently available from only a handful of manufacturers.

Rear-projection models are bigger and brighter than they have ever been, sporting sizes up to 80 inches, up to 1,000 lines of resolution, and brightness topping 500 footlamberts. Rear-projection TVs use CRTs, mirrors, and complex lens systems to project an image onto a translucent screen for viewing. The sets are so bright that they can be viewed in normal room light without appreciable loss of picture quality. Many models include tinted transparent plastic screens that offer contrast as well as protection for their lenticular lens. Rear-projection sets are not the behemoths that they were in the past; their depth, in some cases, has been reduced to approximately 20 inches. Thanks to casters, these sets are easy to move around the room. While wood-tone cabinetry is still found on many models, black cabinets have become the norm.

Projection TVs provide more flexibility in dealing with the considerable variety of aspect ratios since there is no absolute standard for wide-screen image sizes. While tube-projection TVs (both front and rear) use three built-in CRTs (for red, green, and blue), LCD sets have now become somewhat more sophisticated. LCD sets rival their tube counterparts in quality and high resolution, but they need to be viewed in a darkened room. You will also need an LCD set with a high pixel count to offer a seamless picture.

TV/VCR COMBOS

A relatively recent category is the TV/VCR combo, which combines a television set with a VCR. Initially conceived of as a business product, it has found its niche in the home with sales topping two million units annually. While offered in a variety of screen sizes, 13- and 20-inch sets are the most popular. The sets are equipped with either a two-head or four-head VCR and are great for the bedroom or den. Newer models include a stereo TV and hi-fi VCR. While you may not save any money by purchasing a combo, you save in convenience by not having to deal with cables and wires. It is the fastest growing TV/video category.

SATELLITE SYSTEMS

Satellite broadcasting, which fell out of vogue many years ago because of the large dishes (up to ten feet wide) and scrambling by HBO and the other pay services, has made a strong comeback in recent years. This has happened because many people are dissatisfied with their local cable service. While larger dishes have hung on over the years, it has been the introduction of direct-to-home (DTH) satellite broadcasting that is revolutionizing the satellite industry.

Hughes' DirecTV System (formerly DSS) and EchoStar are characterized by a small 18-inch (in circumference) dish, superior picture quality, and CD-like sound. While initially marketed to rural areas and smaller cities, it is now becoming popular in many suburban communities. Previously, these communities had banned large dishes from backyards and subsequently added zoning laws. Now, however, the small dish may be unobtrusively attached anywhere on a dwelling. It only requires a southern exposure free of tall trees to receive signals directly from the satellite. DirecTV can currently receive up to 300 channels (from five satellites). EchoStar also can provide more than 300 channels with similar programming. Satellite equipment can be purchased from several manufacturers. The differences among manufacturers come down to on-screen graphics, remotes, and accessories. Picture quality from all brands is virtually identical, so shop for price and features.

CABLE TERMINOLOGY

A major cause of confusion for shoppers is the term "cable ready." Many people incorrectly believe that a cable-ready set will allow them to receive pay services, such as HBO, free of charge. A cable-ready set only eliminates the need for a converter box to receive basic cable programming. Except for sets 13 inches and smaller, every TV sold today is cable ready. To receive premium channels, which are scrambled, you will probably need the converter box. To this end, many high-end sets offer dual antenna inputs. Through the use of a signal splitter (available from your cable company or Radio Shack), you split the signal before it goes into the cable box. One signal goes directly to your TV and the other to your cable box (in). Then the second signal goes out from your cable box (out) and into the second antenna input of your TV. In this way, all unscrambled programming is available on antenna A, and scrambled/premium services are available on antenna B. As long as your TV has a universal remote, it will control your cable box. Therefore, you do not need your cable company's remote (which is usually supplied at an additional cost).

WHERE TO SHOP

TVs, TV/VCR combos, and satellite systems can all be found in major consumer electronics chain stores across the country, such as Best Buy and Circuit City, and major regional chains such as The Good Guys, Tops, and The Whiz. Many upscale products are found in salon-type consumer electronics establishment. Many up-scale consumer electronics salons are also members of CEDIA or PARA, two custom installer organizations that train their members to understand the needs of their clients. While department stores might carry a product you want, its price might be higher than prices at other retail outlets. On the other hand, discount chain stores such as K-Mart or Wal-Mart might have good buys on many entry-level models and accessories. You can also purchase many products from major retailers that now have a presence on the Web, such as J&R Music World, The Wiz, and Best Buy. However, before you buy on the Web, make sure you've seen the product in person and checked out the kind of image it can display and how easy the remote was to use. Also, get a price from your local retailer as they might still have a better price than the Web (remember, when you purchase items on the Web you have to pay extra for shipping and handling).

FEATURES AND TERMINOLOGY

The following are some of the terms you should familiarize yourself with before you shop for a television.

Audio and Video (Inputs/Outputs): Normally there are more audio outputs than video outputs. More audio and video outputs are desirable as they allow you more versatility in signal switching of multiple VCRs, laserdisc players, and other components. Depending on how you decide to hook up your A/V system, either the TV or your A/V receiver can be used for video switching. Audio and video input jacks are more desirable for hooking up a VCR than putting the signal through your RF antenna connector as they will provide you with better audio and video quality.

Comb Filter: This feature improves resolution and picture quality, and reduces objectionable color patterns. Low-end to midline sets utilize a glass comb filter. High-end sets utilize a CCD or digital comb filter, which greatly enhances resolution.

Component Video (Inputs/Outputs): Also called Color Difference or ColorStream, this is the latest (and superior) input/output to date. While similar to RGB (red/green/blue) connections, it provides superior images of 500 lines of resolution or better. Most DVD players now include component video outputs, which will also be included on most HDTV set-top boxes. Many TV manufacturers are now including these inputs on their mid- to upper-line TVs.

Dual-Antenna Inputs: By having dual inputs, it allows you to switch easily between antenna sources as opposed to using switching devices. This means that your set can accommodate two antenna sources, such as master antenna and cable box or master antenna/cable box and satellite decoder.

External Speaker Jacks: These allow you to attach separate speakers directly to a TV for improved sound quality, or to attach rear speakers that allow you to experience surround sound. The downside to this equation is based on the wattage of your internal television amplifier.

Front A/V Jacks: This jack pack found on the front of a TV (usually hidden under a panel) is a handy feature, especially for hooking up a camcorder or a video game.

Horizontal Resolution: This is the number of horizontal lines that can be displayed on the television. Theoretically, the more lines that can be displayed, the better the picture. Broadcast television has 330 lines, VHS tapes have about 240 lines, S-VHS tapes about 400 lines from a prerecorded video (330 from broadcast), and laserdiscs about 425 lines. On the other hand, when broadcast, satellite or video sources become available with greater resolution, your set will be able to receive an enhanced signal.

Invar: The invar shadow mask gives the picture more brightness and punch. Invar is considered to be a premium feature. When sets are very bright, a side effect called "blooming" occurs. To counteract this bleeding of colors, some manufacturers include the invar shadow mask.

Notch Filter: This filter helps remove a small part of the signal that contains excess color information. By doing so, it helps eliminate some objectionable color effects from less-than-desirable signals. However, by utilizing the circuit, there is a slight loss in resolution of picture.

Parental Lock-out or Channel Block: By punching in a special code (that the parent creates), you can lock out your children or anyone from specific channels on the television, or disable it from being used for a specified time of day or period of hours. It is designed to help parents manage their children's viewing time.

Picture-in-Picture (PIP): Picture-in-picture allows you to view two sources simultaneously. You have the primary picture displayed on the screen. The second is normally a smaller box located in one corner of the screen. To utilize PIP, you need a second video source, such as a VCR. There are both basic and advanced PIP. Advanced PIP allows you to display multiple channels on the screen at the same time (all are frozen except the channel that it is presently scrolling through), change the size or location of the smaller box, or swap back and forth between main and PIP. A handful of high-end models include a second tuner for PIP, thereby eliminating the need to utilize the VCR tuner as the second video source.

Premium Sound Systems: Manufacturers are looking for ways to come up with better sound enhancement systems. RCA and Sony, for example, include SRS (Sound Retrieval System) developed by Hughes in their high-end sets. SRS adds depth and more realistic sound without adding additional speakers. Similar systems have been developed by Toshiba, such as their Cyclone Sub-Bass System with four-channel DSP, and Zenith with SEQ. Recently, some manufacturers are adding Spatializer sound to enhance their audio.

Scan Velocity Modulation: Scan velocity modulation adjusts the rate of horizontal movement of the beam as it "draws" the scan lines, which gives black-and-white picture transitions more punch. This results in a sharper picture.

16:9 Aspect Ratio TV: These sets are designed to provide wide-screen pictures without the letterbox effect (black bars found on the top and bottom of the screen) or greatly reducing it. Sets are available in 28W(ide), 30W, 34W, 55W, 56W, and 57W screen sizes. That's great for letterboxed movies, but for conventional pictures you will either end up with a cropped picture on the top or bottom, black bars on both sides of the picture, or picture-outside-picture on one side. Some projection sets will stretch a standard 4:3 picture to fit the screen, in which case there could be some distortion.

Special Picture Tubes: A recent innovation that has taken the industry by storm is the inclusion of either dark-tint or dark-glass picture tubes. By darkening the face plate, the tube provides greater contrast between black and white. The brands that include darkened picture tubes have had to increase brightness levels so that the picture does not appear too dark. Brightness more than color accuracy is preferred by most consumers. Other advancements include flat screens (or flattened picture tubes; or FST for flat, square tube), sometimes called "SuperFlat" or "FSTPerfect," which offers less distortion on the outer edges of the picture. Some manufacturers use special coatings such as RCA/ProScan and Mitsubishi to help cut down on glare and dust buildup, giving the appearance of a richer picture. Some manufacturers use a combination of techniques to tweak out the highest performance from their picture tubes, for example Panasonic's SuperFlat System, Mitsubishi's Diamond-Vision, Toshiba's FSTPerfect, and Sony's XBR2 Super Trinitron tube. These sets, while costly, offer the viewer a picture with the highest resolution and provide the most lifelike appearance.

Stereo (Watts-Per-Channel): Some manufacturers' literature is a bit deceptive if it indicates that the TV has a 20-watt internal stereo amplifier. This normally means that the set can produce ten watts of stereo per left and per right channels. All sets included in this category include an MTS decoder, which receives and decodes all stereo signals broadcast by the networks or cable channels.

Surround: Many manufacturers include matrix surround sound or other psycho-acoustic effects to enhance the audio. It may also be called ambiance or extended stereo effects. More sets are now including Dolby Pro Logic as a means to enhance the audio quality; you must add rear speakers, however, to obtain the desired effect. A major drawback with these sets is their underpowered amps. Even with five or ten watts-per-channel, it just does not achieve the desired effect. Virtually all sets in this category, however, include variable audio outputs for connection to an A/V receiver. And, we might add, a few sets offer ample wattage. Some sets also include a center-channel input, which allows you to use the TV's internal speakers for the center channel.

S-Video (Inputs/Outputs): Many components besides S-VHS VCRs now include S-video jacks. S-video separates the luminance (Y) and chrominance (C) signals, offering better picture quality than standard video inputs. While increasing resolution, it helps color reproduction and helps reduce jitter during scene transitions. On some televisions, you will find as many S-jacks as you have video inputs. Clearly, to get the most out of your video source, you must use an S-video jack for the highest resolution (if it has one).

BEST BUYS 2000

Our Best Buy and Recommended TV sets and TV/VCR combinations follow. Products within each category are listed according to quality. The unit we consider the best of the Best Buys is listed first, followed by our second choice, and so on. A Best Buy or Recommended designation only applies to the model listed—it does not necessarily apply to other models from the same manufacturer or to an entire product line.

_____35- TO 41-INCH TV SETS_____

Toshiba CN36X81

✓**BEST BUY**

The Toshiba CN36X81 is one of the finest examples of 36-inch TV technology. It is truly HD-ready with progressive scanning built-in. With an HDTV set-top box, this set is 1080i capable. The set includes the FSTPerfect picture tube, which is the flattest and blackest of any 36-inch TV on the market today. Clearly the flagship of its tube TV line, this set claims 880 lines of resolution of sparkling color, thanks to its 3D Y/C digital comb filter, dynamic quadruple focus, and vertical contour correction. The colors are vibrant and lifelike, with sharpness, brightness, and clarity not found elsewhere. Depending on your color preference, the CN36X81 includes adjustable color temperature. Clearly designed to be the centerpiece of a home theater system, this set sports 20 watts of stereo power. Bass presence is enhanced by the use of front surround and sub-bass systems. The set features dual antenna RF inputs, three A/V inputs (with one front and one rear S-video input), two component video inputs (one for a DVD player and one for an HDTV set-top box), and one A/V/S-video output. The front jacks allow for the effortless hook-up of a camcorder or video game. Toshiba now includes component video inputs (besides S-video) to be used with their DVD players, which clearly improve picture quality over S-video. The CN36X81 also features a dual-tuner picture-in-picture. Audio output is fixed or variable for the attachment to an A/V receiver. Besides the rear speaker jacks, external speaker jacks are also included for the attachment of more upscale speakers. There is also a center channel input that can turn the set's internal speakers into the center channel speaker as part of a home theater system. The set features a sleekly designed 37-key illuminated universal remote that will control a VCR, cable box, and one auxiliary component (such as a DVD player or a piece of audio equipment). The new clear-view on-screen menus with icons along the top are straightforward and very easy to use. You can also purchase an optional stand (model #ST3604) for this exemplary set.

Specifications: height, 30¾"; width, 36⅝"; depth, 25⅝"; weight, 178 lbs.
Warranty: 90 days
Manufacturer's Suggested Retail Price: $2,200
Approximate Low Price: not available

RCA F36705

Recommended

Outfitted with RCA's new 36-inch OCS (Optimum Contrast Screen) tube and several step-up picture enhancement features, the RCA F36705 will display up to 790 lines of horizontal resolution. The dark-tint, high-contrast tube displays a clean picture free of video noise and artifacts. Housed in a very stylish black cabinet, the F36705 includes front-firing speakers situated below the screen. Audio performance is rated at five watts per channel, utilizing SRS (sound retrieval system) to increase the spatial presence of sound. A nine-jack panel on the back of the set provides two A/V inputs with one S-video input and one A/V output (both fixed and variable). The set also sports several convenience features such as "sound logic" audio leveler, commercial skip to picture-in-picture, and dual-tuner picture-in-picture. The set receives up to 181 channels and includes GUIDE Plus+ GOLD on-screen program guide, which allows you to see multiday program listings along with descriptions. It also allows for one-button record as long as you have a VCR attached. The F36705 includes an illuminated, ergonomically designed 46-button universal remote with color-coded keys for SAT, VCR, and cable-box control. Lastly, a complete parental control system is included that allows parents to "lock out" specific channels or "lock out" the front panel controls of the set so that it can't be turned on.

Specifications: height, 30⅛"; width, 33⅝"; depth, 24⅜"; weight, 177 lbs.
Warranty: 90 days, labor; 1 year, parts; 2 years, picture tube
Manufacturer's Suggested Retail Price: $1,499
Approximate Low Price: $1,074-$1,399

Sony Wega XBR KV-36XBR250

Recommended

The KV-36XBR250 is part of Sony's new FD Trinitron Wega (pronounced vega) color TV line. Using an FD Trinitron Wega picture tube, it features a completely flat glass screen with a new fine pitch aperture grille. The set produces clear, clean, and bright images free of background video noise. The KV-36XBR250 has a 3D digital comb filter along with scan velocity modulation, which sharpens definition detail with reduced dot crawl and cross-color noise. Convenience features include advanced dual-tuner PIP, trilingual on-screen displays and menus, and XDS (extended data service) reception. The KV-36XBR250 has parental control that will block out two preset channels. Audio is piped though two side-mounted dynamic acoustic chamber (DAC) speakers that are rated at 15 watts per channel. The set includes a center channel input so you can convert all of the set's speakers into the center channel of your home theater system. Audio enhancements include a built-in Dolby Pro Logic decoder and a simulated surround (called TruSurround) and Virtual Dolby. A universal remote will control a VCR or laserdisc player and a cable or Sony DirecTV satellite system box. The KV-36XBR250 set also features dual antenna inputs, three A/V inputs (two S-video), component video inputs (for either a DVD player or an HDTV set-top box), front A/V jacks (behind a drop-down door), and three audio (fixed/variable) and two video (including monitor) outputs. This set includes Sony's S-Link circuitry, which allows other Sony equipment (with S-Link output) to be tethered together. S-Link provides one-button access. For example, if you press the play button on a Sony VCR, it will turn on the Sony TV, change the video input to the proper setting, and start playing. This is an exceptional TV. With component video inputs, you'll be ready for DVD and DTV.

Specifications: height, 29¾"; width, 38⅜"; depth, 24⅞"; weight, 236 lbs.
Warranty: 90 days, labor; 1 year, parts; 2 years, picture tube
Manufacturer's Suggested Retail Price: $2,300
Approximate Low Price: $1,899-$2,049

Hitachi 36SDX88B

`Recommended`

The Hitachi 36SDX88B is a part of a new breed of televisions called the Multi-Media Monitor. It is a 36-inch color TV that offers a solid set of television features and can also be used as a computer monitor. In both modes, it produces a good picture. Using Hitachi's UltraBlack (0.78mm) Digital Pitch Invar picture tube and a digital 3DYC comb filter, the set is capable of delivering up to 800 lines of TV resolution, or 800×600 SVGA resolution, or 1080i (interlaced scan) in HDTV mode (with an HD set-top box). Other video enhancements include Advanced Velocity Scan Modulation and Dynamic Focus. It includes a 181-channel tuner with auto-programming capability and two front-firing speakers rated at ten watts per channel. This set includes BBE Sound, SRS surround sound, and Dynamic Bass. The set features Volume Correction circuitry that lowers the volume of loud commercials or stations. Special convenience features includes the somewhat unique Advanced PIPC (Picture in PC), which lets you display a regular TV image on a computer screen or vise versa. Other convenience features include a child lock that lets you lock out channels, four-event on/off timers, and trilingual on-screen menus. The set includes an RF input, two A/V/S-video inputs, one component video input, front and rear SVGA inputs, and one PC audio input. Outputs include variable audio out, one A/V output, and one PS2 mouse output. The 41-button universal remote features illuminated keys on the bottom half of the unit. The remote will also control a VCR and cable box. Like most 36-inch color TVs today, it is housed in a black cabinet.

Specifications: height, 29½"; width, 34¹³⁄₁₆"; depth, 25"; weight, 163 lbs.
Warranty: 1 year, parts and labor
Manufacturer's Suggested Retail Price: $2,800
Approximate Low Price: $2,699

RCA MM36100 MultiMedia Monitor

`Recommended`

The RCA MM36100 is considered HD-ready and can easily be attached to RCA's DTC-00 HDTV set-top box, which includes built-in DirecTV HD. The exceptional picture quality is due to a new DPP II (Digital Precision Pitch) picture tube, which utilizes FDT (flatter, darker tube) technology and an anti-glare coating. The set also includes an invar shadow mask that gives off 65 watts of picture power, which translates into a very bright picture. Utilizing a three-line digital comb filter, the set is capable of producing 930 lines of horizontal resolution. An adjustable color temperature control makes the colors either cool, medium, or warm. In any mode, the colors are very lifelike and natural because of a wide-band video amplifier, scan velocity modulation, auto kine bias, edge replacement, and auto color circuitry. Also included is special digital video noise reduction circuitry. Thanks to progressive scan, the set is ready for the TV signals of tomorrow. As with virtually every set on the market today, the MM36100 has an auto-programming tuner capable of receiving 181 channels either from an antenna, cable, or DirecTV Systems (formerly DSS). It has two RF inputs. Audio is rated at 7.5 watts per channel from two speakers. Audio is enhanced further by the inclusion of SRS (sound retrieval system), which adds depth to the sound. Convenience features include a dual-tuner picture-in-picture (which allows split-screen viewing) and a 43-button completely back-lit universal remote. Connections include two A/V/S-video inputs, one component video input, two VGA inputs, and one A/V/S-video output. All jacks are gold-plated. VGA-1 is optimized for connection to a computer for reading text. VGA-2 is optimized for video and is the connection to be utilized with RCA's DTC-100 HDTV set-top box. The on-screen displays and menus feature bit-mapped graphics, utilizing a living-room setting with Nipper. They are stunning and easy to use. Lastly, the MM36100 is housed in a black cabinet and takes up no more space than a normal 35-inch set. An optional stand is available.

Specifications: height, 30⁹/₁₀"; width, 33³/₅"; depth, 24³/₁₀"; weight, 190 lbs.
Warranty: 90 days, labor; 1 year, parts; 2 years, picture tube
Manufacturer's Suggested Retail Price: $2,499
Approximate Low Price: not available

32-INCH TV SETS

Philips 32PT70B

✓ **BEST BUY**

The Philips 32PT70B is a full-featured, top-of-the-line 32-inch color TV that is part of their new Philips-only line. Equipped with a 181-channel tuner, the set is a versatile performer. It features a dark-glass flat-square picture tube, a three-line digital comb filter, and noise reduction circuitry, which can display more than 800 lines of resolution. Picture quality is good to very good. The set includes Philips' improved image definition (IID) circuitry, black stretch (that enhances darker portions of the picture), and blue and green stretch (that improve flesh tones). The 32PT70B is equipped with several helpful features such as Multimedia Mode, SmartPicture (which has four settings for optimum video game, sports, movies, and weak station settings), SmartSurf, SmartMute, and advanced dual-tuner picture-in-picture with Double Window (which displays two semi-stretched screens in a letterboxed format). Two five-inch oval side-mounted front-firing speakers, rated at five watts per channel each, frame the set. Audio quality is better than most. To improve sound even further, the 32PT70B has Virtual Dolby, which employs spatial surround sound circuitry to give the sound more ambiance. The set features SmartSound, which keeps your preset sound levels. It also has variable audio output so that you can pipe the sound to a separate audio system. The TV has two A/V/S-video inputs with one component video input. The universal remote will control a VCR, SAT, and cable box. The on-screen menus and displays have a 3-D appearance. This model includes GemStar's GuidePlus+ Gold, which is a superior on-screen program guide that automatically gives you program listings and descriptions with the touch of a button. The set includes VCR Plus+, which means that if your TV is attached to a VCR and you press one-button record, it will automatically tape that channel. Controls are top-mounted, giving the black cabinet a sleek appearance.

Specifications: height, 22⅝"; width, 30⅕"; depth, 18⅖"; weight, 116 lbs.

Warranty: 90 days, labor; 1 year, parts
Manufacturer's Suggested Retail Price: $999
Approximate Low Price: not available

RCA Entertainment Series F32665

✔ BEST BUY

The RCA Entertainment Series F32665 provides very good picture quality at an excellent price. Outfitted with RCA's dark-tint, high-contrast tube, the set includes several upscale video features including a three-line digital comb filter, a wide-band video amplifier, auto color, and dynamic black stretch circuitry. With these video features combined, the set has the capability to display up to 765 lines of horizontal resolution. It receives 181 channels with advanced auto programming. The picture tube displays a very clean picture free of video noise and artifacts. The set is housed in a very stylish black cabinet with front-firing speakers. Audio performance is rated at five watts per channel, utilizing Matrix surround, which makes the action more realistic and enveloping. A nine-jack panel on the set provides two A/V inputs (including one S-video) and one audio output (both fixed and variable). Convenience features include picture-in-picture (PIP), 30-second commercial skip, trilingual displays, and parental control. The F32665 includes an ergonomically designed, illuminated 46-button universal remote with color-coded keys for SAT (or cable box), VCR, VCR/LD, and audio components (RCA only). Continuing this year is GemStar's GuidePlus+ on-screen program guide, which provides multiday program listings along with descriptions and on/off timers. Included with GuidePlus+ is one-button record, which is a handy way to tape programs. A matching optional stand (VS64932) is available for VCR/component storage.

Specifications: height, 29"; width, 30⅛"; depth, 22½"; weight, 120 lbs.
Warranty: 90 days, labor; 1 year, parts; 2 years, picture tube
Manufacturer's Suggested Retail Price: $849
Approximate Low Price: $614-$700

27-INCH TV SETS

Panasonic CT-27G24

✓ BEST BUY

The Panasonic CT-27G24 is a full-featured 27-inch stereo color TV. Utilizing its PanaBlack picture tube, images are sharp, clean, crisp, and show very little video noise. A two-line digital comb filter is employed along with horizontal edge correction to give the set a capability of displaying 500 lines of resolution. Colors are very natural and lifelike, and picture quality is good. This mid-line set includes many desirable features such as picture-In-picture (PIP), front A/V jacks, and parental control (with V-chip). Its 181-channel tuner features auto programming. Panasonic continues to provide TVs and VCRs with exceptional on-screen icon displays and menus that are easy to use via the "action" key. The CT-27G24 uses two bottom-mounted front-firing speakers, which are rated at five watts per channel. Sound quality from this set is somewhat better than average. It features two sets of A/V inputs, one S-video input, and both fixed and variable audio output for hook-up to your hi-fi or home theater system. Included with this package is one of the more sophisticated universal remotes (called the Director Home Theatre), which will control all of the components in your home theater system. This 38-button remote will also control the TV, VCR, cable box, SAT, A/V receiver, CD, Aux, and DVD player. An optional stand (TY-27G22M) with glass doors is available for component placement and tape storage.

Specifications: height, 23⅗"; width, 26⅕"; depth, 21"; weight, 75.5 lbs.

Warranty: 90 days, labor; 1 year, picture tube

Manufacturer's Suggested Retail Price: $450

Approximate Low Price: $359-$399

Philips 27PT40B

Recommended

The Philips 27PT40B is a top-of-the-line 27-inch color stereo TV that offers some interesting and useful features.

Equipped with a 181-channel tuner, the set is a versatile performer. It features a dark-glass flat-square picture tube with black stretch circuitry, which enhances the black portions of the picture. Thanks to its three-line digital comb filter, MagnaVue Plus, and Improved Image Definition (IID), it can display up to 800 lines of resolution. Picture quality is good to very good. The universal remote is nicely styled with an uncluttered look. Useful features include auto clock set, SmartSound, SmartPicture, SmartMute, and SmartSurf. Dual-tuner picture-in-picture (PIP) is included with a feature called "double window," which presents two semi-stretched screens in a letterbox format. The set also includes two side-mounted front-firing speakers, rated at five watts per channel each. Audio quality is better than average, thanks to its Virtual Dolby circuitry, which provides a simulated surround sound. It also has a variable audio output so that you can pipe the sound to a separate audio system. The TV has two A/V/S-video inputs plus one component video input. The 36-button illuminated universal remote will control a VCR and cable box through the blue cursor keys located at the top of the remote. The on-screen menus and displays have a clean, concise 3-D appearance and also include an on-screen help feature that explains all features. This model includes GemStar's Guide-Plus+ Gold, which is a superior on-screen program guide that automatically gives you program listings and descriptions with the touch of a button. The set also includes VCR Plus+, which means that if your TV is attached to a VCR and you press one-button record, it will tape that program for you automatically.

Specifications: height, 23"; width, 30⅖"; depth, 19¹³⁄₁₀"; weight, 83 lbs.
Warranty: 90 days, labor; 1 year, parts
Manufacturer's Suggested Retail Price: $699
Approximate Low Price: not available

RCA F27645
The RCA Entertainment Series F27645 provides | Recommended | an excellent value for the money and takes up very little shelf space.

Equipped with a 181-channel tuner, the set also sports trilingual on-screen menus and displays that are very easy and intuitive to use. Picture quality is very good to excellent, producing up to 680 lines of resolution from its comb filter. Colors are very crisp and lifelike, thanks to its dark-tint high-contrast screen picture tube. Because of its black level expansion circuitry, the brightness and contrast are punched up quite a bit. The F27645 is a stereo set rated at five watts per channel and features one set of A/V/S-video inputs and one variable audio output. Convenience features include commercial skip. GuidePlus+ is a relatively new feature that adds a free on-screen electronic program guide (EPG) that displays up to two days of listings. A VCR blaster is included so that you can one-button record off the program TV by just clicking onto the program that you want to tape and pressing "rec" on the remote. The set also features a 46-button illuminated universal remote that will control the VCR, cable box, SAT, and an audio component. All in all, the F27645 is an excellent value for the money.

Specifications: height, 23¼"; width, 25⅞"; depth, 17¾"; weight, 85 lbs.
Warranty: 90 days, labor; 1 year, parts; 2 years, picture tube
Manufacturer's Suggested Retail Price: $449
Approximate Low Price: $349-$400

Toshiba CZ27V51

Recommended

The Toshiba CZ27V51 is an excellent example of a 27-inch color TV that offers superb picture quality. Using Toshiba's BlackStripe II picture tube, a digital comb filter, and black level expander, the set has the capability of displaying 600 lines of horizontal resolution. Images are sharp and crystal clear, and flesh-tones are very natural-looking. The tuner has the capability of receiving up to 181 channels. Audio is rated at ten watts per channel from bottom-mounted front-firing speaks. Audio quality is assisted by the Front Surround, which adds some ambiance to the sound. Inputs include one RF (antenna), two AV, one S-video, and one component video. One variable audio output is also included.

The 32-button universal remote is nicely laid-out with a blue color-coded keypad. The CZ27V51 includes picture-in-picture (PIP). Since it has only one tuner, you will have to attach it to your VCR so that you can view a second image. You may move the smaller image to either of the four corners, freeze it, or change its size from $^1/_9$ size to $^1/_{16}$ size. You may also swap images to watch two channels at once. The keys on the remote that control your PIP functions also control VCR transport. Convenience features include a 180-minute sleep timer and parental lock, which will "lock-out" up to four channels. Of course, the V-chip is standard equipment.

Specifications: height, 24"; width, 26"; depth, 22⅜"; weight, 73 lbs.
Warranty: 90 days
Manufacturer's Suggested Retail Price: $449
Approximate Low Price: $372-$379

20-INCH TV SETS

Sharp 20L-S100

Recommended

The Sharp 20L-S100 is a reasonably priced 20-inch color TV that offers a solid set of features combined with a very good picture. Utilizing Sharp's High-Focus Dark Tint picture tube, the set features a dark-tint picture tube and a 181-channel tuner with auto programming capability. Picture quality is just fine for a set this size. The set includes two front-mounted side-firing speakers rated at one watt per channel. Dynamic bass circuitry is included to boost bass sound. Convenience features include an on/off timer (called View Timer) and trilingual on-screen displays and menus. The set includes front A/V inputs, which makes it easy to connect a video game console. A 21-button standard remote is included. Like most 20-inch color TVs today, it is housed in a black cabinet.

Specifications: height, 18³/₁₀"; width, 19⅕"; depth, 18³/₁₀"; weight, 44 lbs.

Warranty: 1 year, parts and labor
Manufacturer's Suggested Retail Price: $269
Approximate Low Price: $210-$230

FRONT-PROJECTION TV SETS

Runco DTV-863

✔**BEST BUY**

The Runco DTV-863 is one of the finest next generation of HD-ready front-projection televisions, with the capability of displaying images from 60 inches to 300 inches for the NTSC TV format (PAL and SECAM versions are available). This model is capable of displaying HDTV signals with an optional HDTV receiver (about $5,000 from Runco). Housed in a black cabinet that can be either floor- or ceiling-mounted (a ceiling-mount kit is included), it holds three seven-inch CRT High Performance liquid-cooled tubes, one for red, one for green, and one for blue. The DTV-863 features three lens assemblies with high definition, color-corrected multi-layer coatings and hybrid lens that produce strikingly clear images with very natural color. It includes a separate video processor with a built-in line doubler and a 3D digital comb filter. Depending on the video source, the DTV-863 will display 630p (progressive scan) or 1260i (interlaced per NTSC input frame) lines of resolution. This corresponds to 800×600-pixel resolution. This projector can display HD (High Definition) TV at 1080i (interlaced) resolution using the RGB/Component video input and an HDTV receiver. Brightness is rated at 850 footlamberts, making this among the brightest front projection models available. To adjust the color balance, there are four color temperature control settings that can be customized. This is a model that will properly display wide-aspect ratio movies correctly in 16:9 widescreen (1.85:1). Images that are more severely letter-boxed at 2.35:1 will show smaller black bars at the top and bottom of the screen. The unit includes one each composite video, S-video (separate Y/C), component video, and RGB inputs. It comes with a 12-function remote control for accessing key controls. To help in the setup process, which can certainly be cumbersome on front-projector TVs, this model also features digital auto-assisted convergence. This allows for easy aligning of the crosshairs on all three CRTs to make sure that the projected images are in focus. This set is clearly designed for anyone wanting a true home theater experience.

Specifications: height, 12"; width, 22"; depth, 29"; weight, 92 lbs.
Warranty: 90 days, parts and labor
Manufacturer's Suggested Retail Price: $16,995
Approximate Low Price: $16,765

Vidikron Epoch D-600

The Vidikron Epoch D-600 is an excellent example of a new LCD front projector that is multimedia-capable and HD-ready. It can display images in multiple aspect ratios from 60 inches to 150 inches on any video system. The Epoch D-600 features three 1.3-inch TFT PolySilicon LCD panels. This LCD-HD imager with electronic digital power zoom and power focus has the capability of producing 1280×768 HD-pixel resolution with the attachment of an HDTV set-top box. Vidikron has added several video enhancement features to improve picture quality, such as an Advanced Chroma Decoder (which tries to bring the image closer to film quality and improves color transitions), a multi-dimensional comb filter (which eliminates cross-color artifacts), and a built-in Video Scaler that includes motion compensation for more film-like images. Other video circuits include 10-bit Digital Gamma Correction (for better color reproduction), a Smoothing Circuit (for clean outlines and edges), and center-to-edge uniformity. As with most front projectors, this model is either floor- or ceiling-mountable (ceiling hardware is optional for an additional $399). Depending on the video source, the set has the capability of displaying up to 1080i, 720p, or 480p scan lines from 15kHz to 80kHz, or SVGA/XGA (1024×768) images from a computer. This also allows for multiple aspect ratios. Brightness levels are quite acceptable with the D-600, which is rated at 650 lumens. Like other LCD and Light-Valve front projectors, this model includes a user change-

Recommended

able Metal Halide bulb. The bulb for the D-600 is rated at 2,000 usable hours. Unusual for a front projector, the model includes PIP, so you can display images from RGB and another video source. The Epoch D-600 includes one composite video input, one S-video input, two VGA inputs, one RS232 control, one RGB output, one stereo/audio monitor output, and one 13-pin mouse port. The projector includes two small built-in speakers. A 17-button illuminated remote is also part of the package.

Specifications: height, 6-3/32"; width, 16 9/16"; depth, 1 13/16"; weight, 23 lbs.
Warranty: 1 year, parts and labor
Manufacturer's Suggested Retail Price: $9,495
Approximate Low Price: $9,400

_____REAR-PROJECTION TV SETS_____

Toshiba TheaterWide TW56X81

✔**BEST BUY**

The Toshiba TW56X81 is a 56-inch widescreen rear-projection TV that features a dark-tint, high-contrast screen. It includes three seven-inch PowerFocus HD CRTs with a six-element lens system. A tinted TheaterBright HD acrylic screen offers the illusion of a glass tube set. Utilizing progressive scan technology, a 3D Y/C digital comb filter, and Vertical Contour Correction, the set has the capability of displaying 480p (p=progressive) lines of horizontal resolution at brightness levels of 600 footlamberts. To keep its possible 181 channels in focus, the set includes digital convergence so the crosshairs don't need to be lined up. Other circuitry that help keep images clear and bright are velocity scan modulation, dynamic quadruple focus, color detail enhancement, vertical contour correction, black level expander, picture preference for flesh-tone correction, video noise reduction, adjustable color temperature, and a line doubler. Hooked up to Toshiba's new DST-3000 HDTV set-top box (which includes DirecTV's HD satellite system), the set will receive true High Definition TV from both satellite and networks at 1080i (i=interlaced) lines of resolution. There are two component video inputs (called ColorStream by Toshiba) on this set: one for a DVD player and one for the HDTV set-top box. The set also includes dual-antenna inputs, front A/V jacks, and three A/V (two of which are front and rear S-video) inputs. A DVD player with component video outputs will provide a better image than S-video. Outputs include one A/V and one RF. The TW56X81 sports a smartly designed, illuminated 37-button remote that will control the TV, VCR, cable box, satellite, and DVD player. Audio power is rated at 14 watts per channel for the front speakers, ten watts per channel for the center speakers, and ten watts per channel for the rear speakers, which is a total audio output of 68 watts. The set includes a Front Surround, which is a psycho-acoustic effect that makes the sound seem larger than it is. Bass sounds are improved via its Sub Bass System (SBS), which enhances bass sounds without muffling or distorting them. To round out the audio package, separate center-channel inputs are included, turning the set's audio system into one large center channel for a budding home theater system. Convenience features include dual-tuner picture-in-picture, parental channel lock, and 180-minute sleep timer. This set may be your portal to the next generation of television images.

Specifications: height, 53^{15}/$_{16}$"; width, 52"; depth, 26^{3}/$_{8}$"; weight, 300 lbs.
Warranty: 1 year
Manufacturer's Suggested Retail Price: $4,999
Approximate Low Price: $4,500-$4,699

Panasonic PT-56WXF95

Recommended

The Panasonic PT-56WXF95 is a new rear-projection HD-ready set that combines exceptional performance and great picture with several slick features. This set clearly exhibits the benefits of a screen that offers a 16:9 aspect ratio screen in a rear-projection model. The 56-inch wide set uses three seven-inch CRTs and displays over 850 lines of standard resolution, 480p or 1080i from a High Definition signal (decoded from Panasonic's TU-DST50

HDTV set-top box). It offers several image improvements including built-in progressive scan, velocity scan modulation, and a 3D Y/C comb filter. Together, they produce a picture that is bright, sharp, crisp, and clear. Also included in this model is a dual-tuner, split-screen picture-in-picture (PIP) feature. Audio is rated at seven watts per channel, which is on par with other rear-projection TVs. To further improve the sound emanating from the set's five speakers, the set features Artificial Intelligence Sound. External speaker jacks are also included, so two additional speakers can be hooked up for rear-surround sound, which is perfect for a home theater system. Connections include three A/V/S-video inputs (one front and two rear), one component video input, dual RF inputs, and one A/V output (rear). The component video input can be used for either an HDTV set-top box or with Panasonic's DVD players, which also includes component video outputs. Used in lieu of S-video, these jacks produce a much better image overall, especially for DVD players and set-top boxes. Provided is a special illuminated universal remote with joystick (called The Director) that controls the TV, VCR, SAT, DVD player, and cable box. Because the PT-56WXF95 features a widescreen (16:9) aspect ratio, letterboxed images show less black bars at the top and bottom of the screen, or in the case of films with a 1.85:1 aspect ratio, none at all. Little distortion of the 4:3 image is noticeable, which makes the engineering commendable.

Specifications: height, 55 1/10"; width, 51 4/5"; depth, 26 9/10"
Warranty: 90 days, labor; 1 year, parts
Manufacturer's Suggested Retail Price: $5,999
Approximate Low Price: $4,065-$4,999

RCA Digital
High-Resolution Monitor MM52100

Recommended

The RCA Digital High-Resolution Monitor MM52100 is an HD-ready 52-inch rear-projection TV that offers very good picture quality along with many desirable features. The set includes several step-up video features such as digital focus, custom convergence, and seven-inch digital high resolution CRTs. The optional protective screen (QuikFit SuperShield SSH531) also helps improve contrast. Other video features include a digital 3D Y/C comb filter, scan velocity modulation, auto color balance, wideband video amplifier, video noise reduction, edge replacement dynamic focus, and adjustable color temperature and brightness. The set displays 1280 lines of resolution. It has a brightness level of 320 footlamberts and a maximum viewing angle of 160 degrees. The MM52100 also features progressive scan, which means that if an HDTV set-top box is attached, the set is capable of displaying 1080i signals—true HDTV. With a built-in ten-watt amplifier, each of its two speakers pumps 7.5 watts per channel. SRS (Sound Retrieval System) and matrix surround further enhance sound. The "sound logic" audio leveler is also included. Sound may also be piped to an A/V receiver. The set includes three A/V/S jacks (with auto-sensing S), two SVGA/VGA, one component video input, and one front A/V/S with USB port. Outputs include one switchable audio out. The set also sports dual RF or antenna inputs. The 42-button illuminated universal remote has full RCA DirecTV satellite controllability, and it will also operate two VCRs/LD/DVD and one RCA audio product. Convenience features include dual-tuner picture-in-picture and parental control.

Specifications: height, 52½"; width, 44⅜"; depth, 25"; weight, 278 lbs.

Warranty: 1 year, parts and labor; 2 years, picture tube

Manufacturer's Suggested Retail Price: $3,299

Approximate Low Price: not available

TV/VCR COMBINATIONS

Panasonic PV-M2789

✔ **BEST BUY**

The Panasonic PV-M2789 is a TV/VCR combo that combines a 27-inch stereo color TV and a four-head hi-fi VHS VCR. Using Panasonic's PanaBlack picture tube technology coupled with black level expansion circuitry that further improves and enhances contrast, picture quality is excellent. The VCR section provides for double-fine slow motion, high-speed search, and double-speed playback. The set's tuner is capable of receiving 125 channels and you can program eight events over a one-month period. In terms of convenience features, the PV-M2789 includes auto clock set (with 24-hour program backup) that will automatically keep the correct time, including daylight savings time. A time signal is continuously being broadcast by your local PBS station and received via a special EDS (extended data service) chip. A 24-hour backup program memory is also included to save your future timed tapings. The stereo portion of the TV is rated at two watts per channel from side-firing speakers. Audio is enhanced thanks to the set's internal Spatializer circuitry, which adds depth and ambiance to all sound. The back of the set sports audio out jacks so that the set can be attached to an A/V receiver. Programming could not be easier thanks to Panasonic's proprietary Program Director, which is accessed via a thumbwheel located on the 50-button universal remote. Besides controlling both the TV and VCR portions of the set, the universal remote will also control most cable boxes. Other features found on the PV-M2789 include a real-time counter, an on/off sleep timer, trilingual on-screen icon displays and menus, a VCR lock, an earphone jack, and a front A/V input. New features added include VCR Plus+ for easier taping and a built-in FM radio, making it a very convenient main TV for apartment dwellers. This model includes the V-chip.

Specifications: height, 26"; width, 27⅛"; depth, 21⅜"; weight, 85.8 lbs.
Warranty: 90 days, labor; 1 year, parts
Manufacturer's Suggested Retail Price: $650
Approximate Low Price: $615

JVC TV-20240

Recommended

The JVC TV-20240 is a TV/VCR combo that combines a 20-inch stereo color TV and a four-head mono VHS VCR featuring 19 micron heads. It is housed in a very sleek and stylish silver cabinet with a matching silver 48-button remote. Utilizing JVC's Full Square Dark Tinted picture tube technology coupled with BLE (black level expansion) circuitry that further improves and enhances contrast, picture quality is excellent. The set's tuner is capable of receiving 181 channels and you can program it to record six events over a one-month period. In terms of convenience features, the TV-20240 includes a semi-auto clock set that will automatically keep the correct time, including daylight savings time. Even after power failures, the VCR will always come back to the right time. A 24-hour backup program memory is also included to save your future timed tapings. The stereo portion of the TV is rated at 1.2 watts per channel from front-firing speakers. Programming is relatively easy via the nicely laid-out remote featuring dark gray and powder blue keys. The universal remote will control most cable boxes, along with the TV and VCR. Other features include VCR Plus+, a real-time counter, an on/off sleep timer, trilingual on-screen icon displays and menus, a VCR lock, commercial skip, an earphone jack, and a front A/V input (for the attachment of a game console or a camcorder). New features include quasi-S-VHS playback and EZJECT, which automatically rewinds and ejects all tapes at the touch of a special button on the remote. Like all new TVs, this model includes the V-chip.

Specifications: height, 19⅘"; width, 22½"; depth, 19"; weight, 52.4 lbs.
Warranty: 90 days, labor; 1 year, parts
Manufacturer's Suggested Retail Price: $430
Approximate Low Price: $416

Panasonic PV-DM2799

Recommended

The Panasonic PV-DM2799 combines a 27-inch stereo color TV, a four-head hi-fi VHS VCR, and a DVD video player. Utilizing Panasonic's PanaBlack picture tube technology coupled with black level expansion circuitry for enhanced contrast, picture quality is excellent. The set's tuner is capable of receiving

181 channels, and you can program up to eight events over a one-month period. The VCR provides double-fine slow motion, high-speed search, and double-speed playback. The stereo portion of the TV is rated at two watts per channel from side-firing speakers. Audio is enhanced thanks to its internal Virtual Dolby circuitry. The back of the set sports audio out jacks so that the set can be attached to an A/V receiver. In terms of convenience features, the PV-DM2799 includes auto clock set (with 24-hour program backup). Programming could not be easier, thanks to Panasonic's proprietary Program Director. Accessed via a thumbwheel located on its 50-button universal remote, you simply roll the thumbwheel up or down to reach the desired date and times, then press the thumbwheel to enter it into memory. Other features found on the PV-DM2799 include a real-time counter, on/off sleep timer, bilingual on-screen icon displays and menus, commercial skip, VCR lock, earphone jack, and a front A/V input. New features added include VCR Plus+ and a built-in FM radio. To enhance the audio playback of movies and videos from the DVD player, the set includes both digital coax and digital optical outputs for Dolby Digital and DTS discs.

Specifications: height, 25⁷/₁₀"; width, 27¹/₁₀"; depth, 21⁷/₁₀"; weight, 88 lbs.
Warranty: 90 days, labor; 1 year, parts
Manufacturer's Suggested Retail Price: $999
Approximate Low Price: not available

SATELLITE SYSTEMS

RCA DS5451RB DirecTV

✔**BEST BUY**

Because the DS5451RB features dual LNB, the system is capable of controlling two receivers. The DirecTV system is comprised of an 18-inch satellite dish and an IRD receiver. DirecTV can receive more than 200 channels of network, cable, movie, and pay-per-view channels. The subscription cost is on par with standard cable TV. Because the system is digital, updates and improvements in the system are done at the broadcast center, not via a new set-top box, so your current receiver does not become obsolete. The dish is so small, it can be placed almost anywhere on your dwelling and be unobtrusive. The receiver unit has two antenna inputs, one for the satellite and one for either cable or a rooftop antenna. The DS5451RB has outputs that include two audio, one digital optical, two video, one S-video, and one RF. To receive the best picture possible, you need to employ the S-video output going into your TV or AV receiver (you need an S-video input on your TV). The system has been designed to output its signals to a television and a VCR. Picture quality is superb, displaying about 450 lines of resolution for a seamless picture. DirecTV is virtually free of artifacts, ghosts, haloes, and video noise. Audio quality is on par with CDs. This model also features Dolby Digital output, which enhances the audio even more. The 40-button universal remote comes with an ergonomically designed and color-coded keypad that will let you control the DirecTV receiver, your TV, VCR, cable box, and a DVD player. Besides being very thorough and complete, the new on-screen menu system is pretty slick, using bitmapped graphics. The program guide lists every program that is being broadcast along with a description of each at the top of the screen. You can set spending limits on pay-per-view channels, or lock out specific channels so that children may not watch. The DS5451RB also offers one-button record via StarSight. As long as you've properly attached your VCR (via an included signal blaster), the DS5451RB will automatically record any program you select. DirecTV has been designed for the television viewer who wants the best possible picture and sound and the freedom to choose among many types of programming.

Specifications: height, 2½″; width, 15½″; depth, 14¼″; weight, 27 lbs.
Warranty: 90 days, labor; 1 year, parts
Manufacturer's Suggested Retail Price: $399
Approximate Low Price: $380

Sony SAS-AD4 DirecTV

| Recommended |

The Sony SAS-AD4 DirecTV system is the company's top-of-the-line model, employing a 32-bit microprocessor. Because it includes dual LNB, the SAS-AD4 is capable of controlling multiple receivers. It comes prepackaged with its own 18-inch satellite dish and the IRD receiver. This receiver unit has two antenna inputs, one for the satellite and one for either cable or a rooftop antenna. The SAS-AD4 has outputs that include three audio, one digital optical, two video, one S-video, and one RF. Picture quality is superb, displaying about 450 lines of resolution for a seamless picture using S-video inputs. It's difficult to tell whether the RCA or Sony model has the better picture. The SAS-AD4's remote with built-in trackball navigation system sets this DirecTV system apart. Thanks to the 32-bit microprocessor, response is lightning fast, letting you scroll through hours of programming in a matter of seconds. This universal remote will control a TV, VCR, and cable box. Currently, the SAS-AD4 includes a built-in ten-program event timer that will let you tape up to ten DirecTV programs. Sony also offers a multi-room distribution kit and offers stand-alone DirecTV units. Because this unit features dual LNB, the signal can be easily routed to a second stand-alone receiver. This unit also includes Sony's proprietary S-Link connections for use with other Sony equipment. S-Link lets Sony components communicate with one another so that if you pressed the power button on the SAS-AD4, it would turn on your Sony TV and your Sony A/V receiver and switch to the proper A/V signal input. New to the SAS-AD4 this year is Dolby Digital. If you have a Dolby Digital A/V receiver, you'll be able to receive enhanced audio programming from DirecTV in Dolby Digital sound. Using the digital optical output for all sound from your DirecTV system enhances your aural experience.

Specifications: height, 2⅝"; width, 11"; depth, 9"; weight, 3 lbs. 8 oz.
Warranty: 1 year, parts and labor
Manufacturer's Suggested Retail Price: $400
Approximate Low Price: $235-$350

HDTV SET-TOP BOX

Panasonic TU-DST50 Set Top Box

Recommended

The Panasonic TU-DST50 HDTV Set Top Box is the company's first set-top box able to receive and decode High Definition TV signals (all 18 ATSC digital formats). The receiver unit has one antenna input, and one IEEE1394 connector (to be used with Panasonic's new digital VCR PV-HD1000). Outputs include two audio, two video, two component video, one S-video, and one digital optical (for Dolby Digital). The TU-DST50 converts all standard and High Definition signals into whatever images your set is capable of displaying. To receive the best picture possible, the component video outputs need to be connected to a true HD-ready TV. A new TV that is HD-ready, meaning that it has progressive scan and other digital circuitry built-in, will be able to receive HD broadcasts in HD at 1080i lines of resolution. Non-HD programming will be displayed at either 480i or 480p. Audio quality is on par with CDs. The TU-DST50 also features Dolby Digital output, which enhances the audio even more. To obtain the best possible sound, use the digital optical output. It passes both Dolby Digital surround and regular audio signals. Of course, you'll need an A/V receiver that includes a Dolby Digital decoder and a digital optical input. With digital audio capability, it will sound spectacular. This model includes an electronic program guide that lists every program being broadcast in HD. An illuminated remote, called Director Home Theater, is also included. While clearly designed to work with all Panasonic HD-ready TVs, this set-top box will, in fact, work with any true HD-ready set from any manufacturer.

Specifications: height, 3"; width, 16⁹⁄₁₀"; depth, 12³⁄₁₀"
Warranty: 90 days, labor; 1 year, parts
Manufacturer's Suggested Retail Price: $1,699
Approximate Low Price: not available

VIDEO ACCESSORIES

Accessories are like supporting players in a movie. You just can't have a story with only leads. Accessories is really a hodgepodge category made up of several different types of products. Some are crucial to the enjoyment of your home theater. Some may not be as important to the performance, but are designed to help integrate your components into a living room or family room setting. Some accessories strive to give you better control over your home theater.

BEST BUYS 2000_____

Our Best Buy and Recommended video accessories follow. Products within each category are listed according to quality. The best of the Best Buys is first, followed by our second choice, and so on. A Best Buy or Recommended designation only applies to the model listed—it does not necessarily apply to other models made by the same manufacturer or to an entire product line.

_____UNIVERSAL REMOTES_____

RCA NiteGlo RCU4GLW

✓**BEST BUY**

Ergonomically designed with raised, black-labeled, clear keys, the RCA NiteGlo RCU4GLW features 32 keys laid out into distinct sections. The RCU4GLW is capable of controlling four devices: TV, VCR, cable box, and second cable box or VCR. The function keys are situated across the top, with VCR transport keys directly below. The keypad is in the middle of the remote. The bottom of the remote is shoehorn shaped and rests easily in the palm of either a left- or right-handed person. Because of this design, your thumb automatically rests on the circular channel/volume up/down keys, which are laid out as cursor-type keys. Below them you'll find the power button followed by a Light Bulb key on the bottom. The Light Bulb button activates the NiteGlo feature, which illuminates all of the keys. Powered by four AAA batteries, the NiteGlo RCU4GLW is very easy to program. In its manual, you will find extensive product category lists of virtually every brand of TV, VCR, and cable box. A new feature is a surf button. This key will let you automatically scan through your channels on any of the controlled devices. The RCU4GLW is one universal remote that works well in trying to cut down on coffee table clutter somewhat. Couple that with its easy programming, and the NiteGlo is a hard remote to beat.

Specifications: height, 8"; width, 2"; depth, 0.75"; weight, 8 oz.
Warranty: 90 days
Manufacturer's Suggested Retail Price: $25
Approximate Low Price: $18

Harman/Kardon Take Control TC-1000

✓**BEST BUY**

Harman/Kardon and Microsoft have introduced their sleek and innovative Take Control TC-1000 universal remote. This new intuitive remote sports changeable backlit LCD touch-pad screens for all current and future components in your system. Pre-programmed with complete codes for many types of audio and video equipment, it easily learns the codes from all of your components via a simple Set-Up Wizard. If the remote doesn't have the code for your component in its extensive database, it prompts you to press buttons on your remote so that it can easily learn those functions. With only five permanent keys and one scroll bar (that also acts as the 'enter' key, left- or right-handed people can easily use this remote. This hefty remote (weighing in at 13.4 ounces with four AA batteries) comes with its own PC attachment so that you can unlock additional features, such as creating specialized macros to do several functions at the same time for each component. For example, touching Watch Satellite TV on the keypad or pressing enter on the scroll bar will turn on your TV, A/V receiver, and satellite receiver and switch the inputs on your TV and receiver so that everything is tuned in to the satellite receiver. Then, the keypad on the remote mirrors the one on the satellite's original remote, even letting you access its on-screen guides. Of all of the remotes that we tested, it was the easiest to set up, program, and use.

Specifications: height, 2⅛"; width, 3⅜"; depth, 7½"; weight, 13.4 oz.
Warranty: 90 days, parts and labor
Manufacturer's Suggested Retail Price: $349
Approximate Low Price: $199

Jensen SC-570

Recommended

The Jensen SC-570 is capable of controlling up to seven devices, including a TV, VCR, satellite system, A/V receiver, and DVD player. It is ergonomically designed with raised keys that are placed within different circular groupings. Each ring of cursor keys is devoted to different functions. For example, the top cursor ring is devoted to transport keys for VCR, CD players, and DVD players. The middle ring controls channel and volume up/down. The third ring is devoted to specific menus and input functions, including controlling your home theater's surround. The 39 raised, spongy keys are clearly labeled and easy to read. Set-up was very easy using the 'Enter' and 'Action' keys. The auto codescan lets you scan the codes within memory without having to punch in any numbers. Within a few minutes, seven components' codes were stored in memory. The SC-570 also has a 25-minute memory back-up. As with many universal remotes, it is powered by four AAA batteries. It is very easy to use. You must select the appropriate device key for the device want to use. In other words, if you want to change TV channels, you have to hit the TV button first. Some keys work in both TV and VCR modes, such as channel/volume up/down. In each mode, you can get into the device's on-screen programming and menu system, including PIP for your TV. An added bonus is the sleep timer, which will turn off the TV within a specified time.

Specifications: height, 8⁷⁄₁₆"; width, 2¹³⁄₁₆"; depth, 1¹⁵⁄₃₂"; weight, 5.1 oz.
Warranty: One year, parts and labor
Manufacturer's Suggested Retail Price: $30
Approximate Low Price: $20

VCRs, DVD, AND LASERDISC PLAYERS

More than 20 years ago, videocassette recorders (VCRs) were a rare and exotic commodity found in only a handful of consumer households. Today, they are a basic component found in most home entertainment systems, reaching more than 89 percent of all households in the U.S. And even though other technologies are fast becoming common, VCRs still hold their position as the machine of choice, largely because they are the one technology that allows consumers to record programs unattended.

LASERDISC (LD) PLAYERS

Laserdisc players provide excellent picture and sound for home video; however, they do not record. The list of movies available on laserdisc is extensive; virtually all films are now released on laserdisc. Many are released in special editions that include added footage, interviews with actors and directors, and additional material not previously available on the videocassette version.

Prices of discs are generally competitive with videotapes, but are far less subject to mechanical failure and wear than tapes are. The imminent death of laserdiscs has been rumored for many years, but the quality and economy of the format should ensure its place in the market for the next several years. However, virtually all manufacturers have discontinued their laserdisc players in response to the introduction of Digital Video Disc (DVD). Pioneer is one of the few brands that continues to manufacture combination DVD/LD models.

DIGITAL VIDEO DISC (DVD)

DVD (Digital Video Disc or Digital Versatile Disc) is almost two years old, with sales close to 400,000 in the last year alone. DVD's superb digital audio and video quality has made it a formidable successor to VCRs and laserdiscs. Besides playing movies from a five-inch disc, it will also play CDs. Player prices start at approximately $400 for a basic unit and $600 for a more full-featured model. Close to a dozen manufacturers have DVD players available. DVD movies cost about $25.

DVDs hold promise for the computer industry. As the successor to CD-ROM, it will be known as DVD-ROM. The storage capacity is phenomenal. Data that now needs several discs will be held on one disc. For example, the complete Encyclopaedia Britannica—all 26 or so volumes—along with sound and video clips relating to each entry, could be stored on one disc.

HOW TO SHOP

Buying video components from a specialty dealer usually eliminates hassles and confusion. Specialists do not necessarily charge a higher price than the mass-market superstores, but if they do, they often make it up to you in service. In our experience, home entertainment specialty dealers display a wider selection of equipment in a space more suitable for viewing. They also pride themselves on good, in-store service departments.

However, if you know exactly what you want, you'll be perfectly satisfied with most of the national chain superstores. Keep in mind that superstores often use select models during promotions, selling them at lower prices. Sometimes these models are discontinued or about to be discontinued and the manufacturer wants to unload them. Since there's minimal change from one model year to the next, buying last year's model can be a good value.

BEST BUYS 2000

Our Best Buy, Recommended, and Budget Buy VCRs, DVD, and laserdisc players follow. Products within each category are listed according to quality. The item we consider the best of the Best Buys is first, followed by our second choice, and so on. A Budget Buy describes a less-expensive product of respectable quality that perhaps sacrifices some of the performance and/or convenience features of a Best Buy or Recommended product. Remember that a Best Buy, Recommended, or Budget Buy designation only applies to the model listed—it does not necessarily apply to other models made by the same manufacturer or to an entire product line.

VCRs

VHS VCRs continue to be the preferred format for consumers, largely due to the wide range of movies and other programming available for either purchase or rental. Eventually the future may shift to digital with the introduction of Digital VHS (D-VHS) to record digital images from digital sources (DirecTV and EchoStar/JVC) and DVC (Digital videocassette—an entirely digital format). HDTV will also play a part in this digital revolution, but not until the end of the decade. VHS, as we know it, will continue to dominate the market for many more years.

VCR FORMATS

The most common format for videocassette recorders is VHS, which uses half-inch tape in a cassette shell roughly the size of a paperback book. Hi-8mm is a totally digital format that is technically dazzling and uses a much smaller cassette while producing markedly superior pictures and sound. Regular 8mm tape offers digital images, but does not match the technology of Hi-8mm decks. It should be noted, however, that there are only a handful of 8mm and Hi-8mm machines available, since both formats are primarily used in camcorder applications. You can find combination 8mm/Hi-8mm and VHS decks available from a couple of manufacturers that facilitate editing.

Beta, while in many ways superior to VHS, has virtually disappeared from the marketplace. Sony continues to sell one consumer deck as a replacement model for its installed based (approximately nine million plus) of "betaphiles."

S-VHS VCRs are VHS machines that separate luminance and chrominance signals to give a more detailed image with better definition. Thanks to a lack of prerecorded software, S-VHS never really caught on with the masses, and it continues to represent about one to two percent of total VCR sales. However, with the introduction of DirecTV and EchoStar, we finally have a medium suited for making S-VHS recordings. Obviously, for the almost eight million people who have already purchased satellite systems, S-VHS decks make a good choice for replacing their VCR—they will provide them with the best recorded image currently available.

CHOOSING TAPES

If you are going to record on a tape only once or twice, and only occasionally play it back, standard-grade tapes are perfectly fine. However, if you plan to record and play back the same tape many times, use a high-grade tape. We recommend that you use brand-name tapes; many of the less costly, no-name tapes are made so poorly that they can quickly cause extensive, expensive damage to the heads of your VCR. Most people buy T-120 tapes that record two hours at the fastest speed and six hours at the slowest speed. The longest tape presently available is a T-210 tape, which records 10½-hours at the slowest speed.

HOW TO SHOP

Shopping for a VCR can be a confusing or even intimidating experience. With so many features available in so many different combinations, it can be difficult to make solid comparisons among available machines. Since not every consumer needs or wants every feature, it is important to understand what is available and to know what you want.

WHERE TO BUY

VCRs, DVD players, and laserdisc players can all be found in major consumer electronics chains across the country, such as Best Buy and Circuit City, and major regional chains, such as The Good Guys, Tops, The Whiz, Sound Advice, and Harvey. Many products are available from Web retailers or from major retailers that now have a presence on the Web, such as J&R Music World, The Wiz, and Best Buy. However, before you buy on the Web, make sure you've seen the product in person and have checked out the kind of image it can display and how easy the remote is to use. As well, get a price from your local retailer as they might still have a better price than the Web (remember, on the Web you must pay extra for shipping and handling).

FEATURES AND TERMINOLOGY_____

Auto Clock Set: This feature is found on most brands of VCRs. These models set their own clock thanks to a time signal being sent from your local PBS station. This means you never have to set the clock initially or worry if there is a blackout or a brownout. Once power is restored, the VCR will display the right time.

Commercial Advance: New decks include commercial zapper circuitry that senses the beginning and end of commercials. It records the entire program including commercials. Upon playback, it will automatically fast forward through the commercials and go back to the play mode when the program resumes. This is different from commercial skip, which allows you to view other channels and then returns you to the station you were watching after a preset time of 30, 60, 90, or 120 seconds.

Editing Features: Unless you actually plan on editing your camcorder tapes and making duplicates, you will not need a VCR with sophisticated editing features such as assemble editing, insert editing, or video dubbing. These features can add up to $100 to the cost of the model, and only make the machine more difficult and intimidating to use.

Hi-fi Sound: If you want the best quality sound from your prerecorded movies, you'll need hi-fi. If you're thinking about home theater, you'll definitely need a hi-fi VCR. Hi-fi stands for high fidelity or high quality sound. It is true stereo—not the low-fi sound that was available on VCRs several years ago. Prices for hi-fi VCRs range from approximately $300 to $600. If you are in the market for a VCR, hi-fi is the one upgrade feature that you should consider. All movies and videos are now released with hi-fi soundtracks (encoded with Dolby Surround) as standard.

Index Search: Many VCRs record an electronic index code at the beginning of each recording. To scan your recordings on a tape, press index search. The VCR then stops at each index mark, and plays back a few seconds of the recording. Some VCRs even let you go directly to a specific index mark and start playback.

Jog/Shuttle Control: These special-effect tape advance features allow you to control the speed at which a tape is viewed. Shuttle control allows you to search forward or backward through a tape at a range of fast and slow speeds. Jog control allows you to move the tape forward or backward frame by frame.

Programmability: If you are buying a VCR primarily to record television broadcasts, ease of programming is an important consideration. Except for videocassette players, all VCRs can be programmed to record at least one program. The most rudimentary programming scheme uses a built-in clock timer that you set to start and stop within a 24-hour period. More elaborate programming allows you to record several different programs on different channels for a period of 28 days or more. Other program operations let you record the same program every day or every week. Many VCRs now include VCR Plus+, a simple method of programming by entering a number listed in your channel guide or many newspapers' television guides. Some VCR Plus+ models will also change channels on your cable box via a mouse or blaster, or an infrared transmitter located on the top of the VCR. The inventor of VCR Plus+ is introducing Guide Plus+ Gold, which, if included in your TV, will provide "free" TV listings and one-button programming.

Tape Speeds: Virtually all VCRs let you choose among two or three different recording speeds. Playback speed is automatically set, and even VCRs that record in only two speeds play back on all three speeds. The slow speed allows more recording time on the tape, but the faster speed produces a better quality recording. Since many people record at the slowest speeds, some manufacturers have developed special video heads (19 micron heads) for improved picture quality for recording/playback at the slowest speeds.

Universal Remotes: Many models now feature preprogrammed universal remotes with the ability to control a TV, cable box, and satellite system. A unified remote will control the same brand of TV as your VCR.

Video Heads: To record and play back a tape, you only need two video heads. Additional heads are used for special effects such as slow motion, freeze-frame, and on-screen search. Many manufacturers are tweaking their heads to improve picture quality.

Philips VRA999PH

✓ **BEST BUY**

The Philips VRA999PH is a full-featured S-VHS ET six-head hi-fi VCR with many desirable features. S-VHS ET is a new form of S-VHS that can use normal VHS tape for improved picture playback. Picture quality is excellent on both pre-recorded videos and taped off-the-air programs. It's perfect to use if you have a satellite system and want to get the most out of taped images because it has an S-VHS input. The VRA999PH features VCR Plus+C3, which will even change the channels on your cablebox or satellite receiver. Set-up could not be easier, thanks to its auto clock set feature (called "Plug & Play") that instantly sets the time on the VCR's clock by looking for the time signal sent from your local PBS station. This means the VCR's time will always be correct—even with blackouts/brownouts or daylight savings time changes. This VCR will allow you to program eight events over a 365-day period from its 181-channel tuner. It also features ShowGuard, which protects your timer programming on EPROM in case of power failures. Sporting a very sophisticated, but easy to use, illuminated universal remote, it features keys laid-out in sections, depending on the function. The remote will control your TV and cablebox. Other features include front A/V jacks, high-speed rewind/fast forward, commercial skip, memory rewind/off, repeat play, and auto head cleaner. It offers trilingual (English/French/Spanish) on-screen displays. Philips has added a V-chip and child lock to this VCR so that parents can lock out objectionable TV programming.

Specifications: height, 3⅘"; width, 17¹⁄₁₀"; depth, 12⁹⁄₁₀"; weight, 10 lbs.
Warranty: 90 days, parts
Manufacturer's Suggested Retail Price: $299
Approximate Low Price: $269-$279

RCA VR694HF

Recommended

The RCA VR694HF features the ability to "zap" out annoying commercials. RCA is the first brand to introduce this feature. Called "Commercial Advance," it marks the beginning and end of commercial breaks. Upon playback, the VCR senses those index marks and quickly fast forwards to the end of the segment. RCA's VR694HF features a 181-channel tuner capable of recording eight events over 365 days. Being DirecTV compatible, the tuner can record up to channel 999. One of many features found on this and several RCA VCRs is ShowSaver 24 Memory Protection, which keeps all of your programming saved, even in a power failure, for up to 24 hours. Other slick features include auto clock set with auto daylight savings time, VCR Plus+ with End-time adjustment, AI Picture Control (which optimizes picture quality based on specific tape), front A/V jacks (for the easy attachment of a camcorder), auto head cleaner, child protection system, and XDS Broadcast Data Service. Another feature included is Movie Advance, which quickly jumps to the beginning of a pre-recorded movie by fast-forwarding past the coming attractions. Lastly, the VR694HF comes with a 46-button illuminated universal remote that will control a second VCR/LD/DVD, TV, SAT, and audio equipment. Picture quality is on par with the best VHS decks.

Specifications: height, 3⅝"; width, 17"; depth, 11⅞"; weight, 10.6 lbs.
Warranty: 90 days, parts
Manufacturer's Suggested Retail Price: $299
Approximate Low Price: $180-$199

Sharp VC-H996U

Recommended

The Sharp VC-H996U produces a very good recorded image free from video noise—that's especially true at the EP mode, thanks to its use of 19 micron heads, which improve record/playback performance at the slowest speed. Playback of pre-recorded videos is on par with the best VCRs. Hi-fi performance compared favorably with other models as well. As with most high-end VCRs today, this unit includes a 181-channel tuner and is able to record eight programs over a one-year period. This VCR offers several desirable features such as a jog shuttle ring, complete auto head cleaning system (that cleans your heads when rewinding tapes), and VISS (VHS index search system). To help off-air recording, this model includes VCR Plus+C3 with both cable box and satellite control. This VCR also features auto on, auto play, and auto rewind. The icon on-screen menus, which are trilingual, are very easy to use. A nice touch found on this VCR is its 43-button universal remote that will also control your TV, cable box, and satellite system. There are also front A/V jacks for the easy attachment of a camcorder. Other features include high-speed rewind (360×), quasi S-VHS playback, and a 20-second timer backup. Tamperproof circuitry is also included.

Specifications: height, 3⅝"; width, 14⁹⁄₁₆"; depth, 10⁹⁄₃₂"; weight, 6.2 lbs.
Warranty: 90 days, parts and labor
Manufacturer's Suggested Retail Price: $199
Approximate Low Price: $145-$166

Hitachi VTFX-6400A

Budget Buy

While the Hitachi VTFX-6400A doesn't have a long list of convenience features, it's a terrific hi-fi VCR at a terrific price. The VTFX-6400A produces good recorded images free from most video noise—especially true at the EP mode, thanks to its use of 19 micron heads, which improve record/playback performance at the slowest speed. Playback of pre-recorded videos is on par with many of the better VCRs and hi-fi performance also compares favorably to other models. As with most VCRs today, this unit includes a 181-channel tuner and is able to record eight programs over a one-year period. A handy feature found is a movie return switch that automatically starts playing a pre-recorded tape as it is inserted, then rewinds and ejects it at the end of play. The icon on-screen menus are trilinguall and very easy to use. This model features a 35-button unified remote that will control Hitachi TVs. Other features include high-speed rewind and channel lock, which locks out the VCR from unwanted use.

Specifications: height, 3¹¹⁄₁₆"; width, 14¹⁵⁄₁₆"; depth, 10¹⁵⁄₁₆"; weight, 7.7 lbs.
Warranty: 90 days, parts and labor
Manufacturer's Suggested Retail Price: $129
Approximate Low Price: $119-$124

__DIGITAL VIDEO DISC (DVD) PLAYERS__

Digital video disc (DVD) is a small five-inch disc that will hold a 133-minute movie on one side of the disc, without having to turn it over. Reportedly, 90 percent of all the movies released run 133 minutes or less. Depending on the company that is releasing the film, many discs are dual-layered so that discs containing longer films will not have to be turned over. Each disc, however, clearly states if it is dual-layered.

QUALITY

Touted as the future of home video, DVD has a far superior picture (500 lines of resolution or better) than either Digital Satellite System (approximately 480 lines of resolution), laserdisc (425 lines of resolution), S-VHS (400 lines of resolution), or VHS (240 lines of resolution) formats. Beside playing movies, DVD players will also play CDs. Audio is of digital quality and comparable or superior to CDs. Most discs include Dolby Digital soundtracks that also play back Dolby Pro Logic. You can watch movies in pan-and-scan (action is centered on one image, while information on both sides of the screen is cut off) and letterbox on regular TV, and anamorphic on wide-screen TVs. All discs offer several language/subtitle versions. You can invoke parental control, which will convert an R-rated movie into a PG-13 version, with certain footage or scenes simply not played.

DVD AND DIVX

A formidable challenge for DVD is DIVX, which stands for Digital Video Express. DIVX is the other type of DVD player that has caused a lot of confusion and speculation. While a DIVX player may look like a DVD player, and plays discs that look similar, it is an entirely different type of player. DIVX is a specialized rental form of DVD. DIVX players include special circuitry that decodes and "unlocks" DIVX discs. Players are currently sold only at both Circuit City and The Good Guys chain stores.

Instead of paying approximately $25 to buy a DVD movie, DIVX offers a special rental of $4.50 for 50 hours play. Prior to playing any discs on the machine, you must set up a credit card account with DIVX. You'll also need a telephone outlet for the DIVX player as it needs to be in constant contact with DIVX Central, which will "unlock" your movie for viewing. At the end of the initial viewing period, you can either throw the disc away, keep it for future viewing (paying an additional rental fee), or purchase it. There are two ways to purchase the disc: There is a "Silver" plan, which allows unlimited play within your own home but you cannot play the disc on someone else's DIVX machine without paying an additional rental. Some discs, however, can be made "Gold," which means you can buy it for unlimited viewings on any DIVX machine.

It should be noted, however, that DIVX players play both DVD and DIVX discs, as opposed to DVD players, which cannot play DIVX discs. Also unlike DVD players, DIVX players include a built-in modem; thus you'll need to install another phone jack so you can have your DIVX always attached to it.

FEATURES AND TERMINOLOGY

Audio and Video (Inputs/Outputs): Normally there are more audio outputs than video outputs. More video outputs (and their audio counterparts) are desirable because they allow you more versatility in signal switching of multiple VCR, laserdisc, and DVD players. Depending on how you hook up your A/V system, either the TV or your A/V receiver can be used for video switching.

Chapter Numbers: These numbers are recorded on the discs and are used to indicate sections or chapters (almost like track numbers on CDs).

Component Video (Inputs/Outputs): Also called Color Difference or ColorStream, component video is the newest input and output to date. It provides images that are far superior to S-VHS. Most high-end DVD players include component video outputs, which will also be included on most HDTV set-top boxes. Many TV manufacturers are now including these inputs on their mid- to upper-line TVs. Component video provides 500 lines of resolution or better.

Dolby Digital: This is the next step beyond Dolby Pro Logic, offering 5.1 channels of sound. The player has outputs for the sound audio technique called Dolby Surround Digital, or Dolby AC-3. The rear channel is now stereo, along with a separate channel (the .1) for the subwoofer. This gives the director and sound engineer the ability to localize sound to a specific area or speaker, providing you full stereo surround.

Jog/Shuttle Control: These special-effect tape advance features allow you to control the speed at which a tape is viewed. Shuttle control allows you to search forward or backward through a tape at a range of fast and slow speeds. Jog control allows you to move the tape forward or backward, frame by frame.

Parental Lockout or Channel Block: Designed to help parents manage their children's viewing time, this feature is available on all DVD players. Simply access the on-screen menu system and you can set specific viewing levels for the player. You can override these controls by punching in a personalized code.

S-video (Inputs/Outputs): Many components besides S-VHS VCRs now include S-video jacks. S-video offers better picture quality than standard video inputs. While increasing resolution, it helps color reproduction and reduces jitter at scene transitions. On many televisions, you will find as many S-video inputs as you have standard video inputs. To get the most out of your video source, you should use an S-video jack for the highest resolution.

Universal Remotes: Many models now feature preprogrammed universal remotes with the ability to control TVs and cable boxes. Some are equipped to control satellite systems. A unified remote will control the same brand of TV as your DVD.

Toshiba SD-3109

 ✓ BEST BUY

The Toshiba SD-3109 is one of the best examples of a fourth-generation DVD player. It includes a unique Dual Disc Twin-tray transport system. It permits users to load and play two discs at the same time and play them in succession for uninterrupted viewing of multi-disc DVD titles or for a double feature. Another unique feature found on this player is HDCD decoding for CD playback. This special decoder extends the resolution of HDCD (High Definition Compatible Digital)-encoded discs to a 20-bit level, exceeding the 16-bit standard CD format. In other words, HDCD is a patented process for delivering on CD the full richness and detail of the original microphone feed. The SD-3109 includes a built-in Dolby Digital decoder that allows playback of films with a Dolby Digital soundtrack (as long as its attached to a Dolby Digital-ready A/V receiver). The SD-3109 includes Spatializer N-2-2 sound enhancement, which offers the illusion of multi-channel sound from two speakers, and it is DTS-compatible. It also features a pre-programmed universal remote that will also control a TV and cable box. Outputs include one S-video, one composite video, one AC-3 digital audio, two pairs of analog audio, and one component video (called ColorStream by Toshiba) outputs. A component video output lets you attach this player to newer mid-priced and high-end TVs that feature component video inputs for the best possible resolution.

Specifications: height, 3³⁄₁₆"; width, 16¹⁵⁄₁₆"; depth, 12¹⁄₈"; weight, 8.9 lbs.
Warranty: 90 days, labor; 1 year, parts
Manufacturer's Suggested Retail Price: $499
Approximate Low Price: $400

Sony DVP-C650D

| Recommended |

The DVP-C650D includes all of the desirable features now considered standard on DVD video player, and it also includes a five-disc changer. This player features a dual discrete optical pickup, one for DVD and one for CD. This means that the player has separate lasers optimized for CD (780nm wavelength) and DVD (650nm), which enables stable and accurate playback of both types of discs. The DVP-C650D also features a 10-bit video digital-to-analog converter and a 96kHz/24-bit audio digital-to-analog converter for optimum playback of all types of discs. A built-in Dolby Digital decoder is also included, which allows you to hook-up this player to a Dolby Digital-ready A/V receiver. A built-in circuit automatically looks for the Dolby Digital signal to output. A feature included here (not found on most other players) is Speaker Set-up and Adjustment, including balance, subwoofer levels, and test tones. If you don't have rear speakers, the DVP-C650D includes Digital Cinema Sound that uses Virtual Enhanced Surround (a DSP effect) that offers the illusion of those rear speakers. Besides including two S-video and two composite video outputs, the DVP-C650D also features component video output for optimal video images (as long as it is attached to a television with component video inputs). Other outputs include both optical and coaxial digital outputs. This player comes with a universal remote that controls other brands of TVs and selected Sony A/V equipment. This model includes S-Link. S-Link means that if you press the power or play button on the DVP-C650D, it will turn on your Sony TV and your Sony A/V receiver, and switch everything to the proper inputs. If you're in the market for a new CD changer, buy the C650D instead. You can place five CD discs on the carousel platter for hours of music listening, or five DVDs on the platter for your own film festival.

Specifications: height, 5"; width, 17"; depth, 15⅛"; weight, 11 lbs.
Warranty: 90 days, labor; 1 year, parts
Manufacturer's Suggested Retail Price: $599
Approximate Low Price: not available

JVC XV-D701BK

Recommended

The XV-D701BK DVD player includes a built-in Dolby Digital decoder with 5.1-channel analog outputs, which can be matched-up with a less expensive Dolby Digital-ready A/V receiver. This model is also DTS-compatible. To produce excellent images, the XV-D701BK uses a 10-bit/27MHz video digital-to-analog (D/A) converter. The audio sampling rate has been pushed up to 96 kHz (from the CD standard of 44.1 kHz). This produces exceptional dynamic signal-to-noise ratio of 108db dynamic range. To ensure the best possible audio and video, JVC separates all analog, digital, audio, and video circuits to reduce any possible interference from each other. Indicators on the front panel denote the mode that you are in, from "Resume," "Dolby Digital 5.1," "Linear PCM," or "96 kHz Sampling." The fluorescent display directly above the DVD/CD tray provides track number information and elapsed time. There is also an indicator to denote the number of 5.1 audio channels that are playing. Also included is a slick on-screen display with which you have the option to access all of the menus and still keep watching a video. A headphone jack with volume control is located on the left-hand side of the front panel. JVC provides an illuminated universal remote that will control a TV, VCR, and cable box. Besides including component video and S-video outputs, the XV-D701BK features digital coaxial and digital optical outputs for enhanced listening and viewing. All outputs are gold-plated. To work better with other JVC audio and video products, the XV-D701BK includes the company's AV COMPU LINK interface. This unit is housed in a black cabinet and matches other JVC audio equipment.

Specifications: height, 4⁷/₁₆"; width, 17³/₁₆"; depth, 13¼"; weight, 10.6 lbs.
Warranty: 90 days, parts and labor
Manufacturer's Suggested Retail Price: $700
Approximate Low Price: $379-$450

LASERDISC PLAYERS

A laserdisc is an optical medium for playing video and digital audio recording. Pits cut in the disc are read by a laser beam. Because information can be read from the discs without any physical contact, the acrylic-coated discs will virtually last forever. Laserdiscs also produce excellent image quality with ordinary hookups to your television set. They are capable of producing superb images, with nearly twice the horizontal resolution of standard videotapes when used with TVs that have S-video connections.

WHAT IT OFFERS

Most laserdisc players are combination players, meaning they play multiple types of discs from 5-inch CDs through 12-inch laserdiscs. Many models today provide a separate drawer for CD-only playback. These models utilize a CD Direct input that operates the drawer and disconnects the video circuitry for less interference.

Many laserdisc players offer dual-sided play, which automatically turns the disc over. This process takes about 12 seconds. The unit will either display a blue screen or freeze the last frame of the video until the next scene starts.

Because laserdisc is primarily a medium for people who love movies, many discs are available in letterboxed versions. Letterboxing places black bars at the top and bottom of the screen, retaining the original aspect ratio the director intended. On videocassette, for example, most movies are panned-and-scanned. This means that the action is centered on one image and information on the left and right sides of the screen is cut off.

HOW TO SHOP

Shopping for a laserdisc player can be like looking for a needle in a haystack. With sales down to 10,000 units in 1999 and predicted to continue dwindling, you'll have to search. Quite frankly, if you're a first time buyer, go with DVD. If you have an extensive library of titles and you're in the market for a replacement unit, the combination laserdisc/DVD player offers a terrific value.

WHERE TO BUY_____

Laserdisc players can be found in major consumer electronics chains across the country, such as Best Buys and Circuit City, and major regional chains, such as The Good Guys, Tops, The Whiz, Sound Advice, and Harvey. Many upscale products are found in salon-type establishments such as The Listening Room. Many consumer electronics salons are members of CEDIA or PARA—two custom installer organizations that train their members to understand the needs of their clients. While department stores might carry a product you want, its price may be higher than at other retail outlets. On the other hand, discount chain stores like K-Mart or Wal-Mart might have good buys on many entry-level models and accessories. Many products are available from Web retailers or from major retailers that now have a presence on the Web, such as J&R Music World, The Wiz, and Best Buy. However, before you buy on the Web, make sure you've seen the product in person and have checked out the kind of image it can display and how easy the remote was to use. Get a price from your local retailer as they might still have a better price than the Web (remember, on the Web you must pay extra for shipping and handling).

FEATURES AND TERMINOLOGY_____

Chapter Numbers: These numbers are recorded on the discs and are used to indicate sections or chapters (almost like track numbers on CDs).

Digital Time Base Correction: Time base correction helps reduce jitter at the edges and corners of the picture.

Dolby Digital-Ready: This is the next step beyond Dolby Pro Logic, offering 5.1 channels of sound. The rear channel is now stereo, along with a separate channel (the .1) for the subwoofer. This gives the director and sound engineer the ability to localize sound to a specific area or speaker, providing you full stereo surround.

Random Access: All laserdisc players have the ability to provide random access, allowing you to locate a particular spot on the disc.

Theater Mode: Several seconds are cut from the turnover time of a disc by skipping over side B's table of contents. It will also dim the front panel's illumination.

Types of Discs: There are two types of laserdiscs: CAV (constant angular velocity) and CLV (constant linear velocity). CAV discs spin at a constant speed of 1,800 rpm, with a playing time of 30 minutes per side. CLV discs spin at speeds ranging from 1,800 rpm for the inner tracks to 600 rpm for outer tracks. This permits a playing time of 60 minutes per side.

Pioneer CLD-D606

✔**BEST BUY**

The Pioneer CLD-D606 is one of the last of a dying breed laserdisc-only players. It offers many advanced and useful features, including a 3D digital comb filter and dual side disc play. This laserdisc player features a digital time base corrector (which eliminates noise and jitter from the picture) and other video enhancement circuitry that will make playing back your laserdisc collection a joy. A Dolby Digital RF output pipes the Dolby Digital soundtrack signal (from those laserdiscs that are so encoded) to either an A/V receiver or A/V processor that has a Dolby Digital decoder and RF demodulator built in. The unit includes a digital optical outputs. If you have a DTS decoder included in your home theater setup, you'll be able to pass those signals via the digital optical output (also called Tos-Link). A handy feature included on this model is CD Direct. This means that the unit has a separate drawer in the middle of the laserdisc drawer so that you can load your CDs separately. The remote is easy to use, and features a jog shuttle dial at the bottom of the remote. The front panel is clear, concise, and easy to read, giving you all of the information you need.

Specifications: height, 5³⁄₁₆"; width, 16⁹⁄₁₆"; depth, 15¹⁵⁄₁₆"; weight, 14 lbs. 8 oz.
Warranty: 1 year, parts and labor
Manufacturer's Suggested Retail Price: $760
Approximate Low Price: $550

Pioneer Elite DVL-91

Recommended

The DVL-91 player is a combination unit that plays both laserdiscs and DVDs. Very similar to today's laserdisc players with a separate CD drawer in the middle, the Elite DVL-91 player gives you the ability to play DVDs and laserdiscs. The player includes two S-video outputs, two component video outputs, and two digital audio outputs—one optical and one coaxial (for either AC-3 or DTS). Using Pioneer's 10-bit video digital-to-analog converter, picture quality is quite good. Video dynamic range is increased 6 dB. On the audio side, the player uses a 20-bit digital-to-analog conversion system capable of decoding DVD stereo audio tracks using high sampling rates up to 96 kHz. Pioneer's Hi-Bit circuitry looks to improve signal resolution and extremely low noise from standard 16-bit audio CDs. The player has separate color-coded trays for laserdiscs and CDs/DVDs. Like most upscale laserdisc players, the DVL-91 has a dual-sided play mechanism, Digital Time Base Correction, and Digital Field Memory, which enhances special effects and stills. It uses the same 10-bit video and 20-bit audio digital-to-analog conversion systems. The DVL-91 uses a somewhat standard remote control. The DVL-91 also includes Variable Digital Noise Reduction, which digitally processes the chrominance (C) and luminance (Y) signals for improved picture clarity. Other enhancement features include Pioneer's Legato Link circuitry, which restores high frequencies filtered out of the digital signal during recording and, in turn, provides for a cleaner analog output. While it might seem pricey, the DVL-91 is a powerhouse combining state-of-the-art video technology of both DVD and laserdisc. If you have a laserdisc library and don't want to abandon the format, but want to buy into DVD, this is the player for you.

Specifications: height, 5½"; width, 16⁹⁄₁₆"; depth, 18¼"; weight, 19 lbs. 3 oz.
Warranty: 2 years, parts and labor
Manufacturer's Suggested Retail Price: $1,800
Approximate Low Price: $1,600

CAMCORDERS

The camcorder, which combines a video camera and a videocassette recorder in one unit, records live action on tape for near-instantaneous playback. Even the least expensive camcorders incorporate a variety of useful features with satisfactory performance. As the sales boom of the late 1980s faded, prices for basic models fell, reaching new lows in 1997. Sony, Panasonic, JVC, Sharp, Canon, and Hitachi manufacture nearly all camcorders on the market, no matter what brand name is on the unit. Thus, you might be able to save a few dollars by comparing two similar (sometimes identical) models sold under different brand names.

ZOOM LENSES

Manufacturers use increasingly longer (more powerful) zoom lenses as enticements to buy more expensive models. In reality, they serve little purpose. An 8-power zoom lense is about the maximum necessary for steady shooting with a compact handheld model, and a 12-power lens is the maximum for shoulder-supported full-size models or those with effective electronic image stabilization. However, virtually all models sold today come with a 16- or 18-power zoom as standard. Only if you have firm support, such as with a monopod or tripod, can you effectively use a zoom lens greater than 12-power. Digital zoom, in which the camcorder electronically magnifies the picture, causes graininess and picture distortion, making it nearly useless for serious shooting. Despite this fact, there are models with high magnifications upward to 200-power.

VIEWFINDERS

Many models now come with color LCD viewfinders, which have improved somewhat since they were first introduced several years ago. While it's nice to see what you're shooting in color, these viewfinders are usually dimmer and lower in resolution than their black-and-white counterparts. Manufacturers have, however, improved the pixel count and beefed up the brightness levels. If you opt for a color viewfinder, choose a model with at least 100,000 (or 100K) pixels, preferably more. A color viewfinder adds about $100 to the camcorder's cost, which is somewhat excessive to the benefit derived.

A recent feature that replaces the viewfinder on some camcorders is a 2.5- to 4-inch color LCD screen. This allows shooting from a variety of positions without holding the camcorder directly to your eye. It's also convenient for playback away from a TV set. The drawback is that the LCD screen may wash out in bright sunlight. Sony, RCA, Panasonic, and JVC offer the screen as a "stealth" option that folds into the camcorder body while you continue shooting using the standard black-and-white viewfinder.

CAMCORDER FORMATS

The market share among the three different camcorder (8mm, VHS, and VHS-C) formats has somewhat stabilized. Both 8mm and VHS-C continue to do well, but full-size VHS continues to decrease in popularity. DVC, the newest format, has grown about five percent in the last year.

The VHS and 8mm formats are electronically compatible. This allows you to connect your 8mm camcorder to your VHS VCR and copy your 8mm videos onto VHS tape. Front-panel input jacks for this purpose are becoming nearly standard on VHS decks. Input jacks have previously been placed on the back panels. You can also connect your 8mm camcorder directly to your TV for viewing as well. Many TVs also sport front A/V jacks just for this purpose.

Digital Video (DV): These camcorders, introduced a couple of years ago, offer superior audio and video quality. While somewhat pricey, DV offers the highest quality currently available. With cassettes slightly larger in size than a matchbox, these camcorders digitally record and process information. This means that there is virtually no loss of picture quality after dubbing to another format or your computer. These camcorders use a 570,000-pixel, 1/3-inch CCD image sensor to create high quality recordings. PCM digital audio offers equally superior digital audio, which is several notches above VHS hi-fi. The standard DV cassette uses metal tape and records for 60 minutes. Power is provided by lithium batteries that are slightly larger than AA batteries and have no battery "memory effect."

8mm: The cassettes for the 8mm format are roughly the size of audiocassettes, though slightly thicker, and they use 1/3-inch-wide tape, which is narrower than the 1/2-inch VHS video format. By using metal tape to increase recording density, 8mm tapes reproduce an image comparable to VHS or slightly better. Camcorders that use this format are compact and lightweight, with many models weighing less than 1 1/2 pounds. A standard 8mm camcorder records up to 2 1/2 hours on a single tape in SP. Many models offer both SP and LP recording capability.

Hi-band 8mm (Hi8): This format offers the same resolution as S-VHS (about 400 lines), but Hi8 records with slightly less color noise, making the picture quality subtly better than S-VHS's. Standard 8mm tape will record and playback on Hi8 machines, but tapes recorded on Hi8 will not playback on conventional 8mm machines. Hi8 camcorders require special tape formulations: a premium metal evaporated tape (Hi8-ME) and the improved metal particle tape (Hi8-MP). Both are more expensive than standard VHS tape. Hi8-ME offers superior performance, but it is difficult to manufacture, costs appreciably more, and is more difficult to find. New Hi8-MP formulations narrow the performance gap and work as well for everyday shooting. Hi8 camcorders, like S-VHS, include S-video jacks for maximum signal transfer quality to a TV or an S-VHS VCR. However, most of the Hi8 advantage can still be realized through ordinary cables.

VHS: This format has the longest recording capacity of all formats. VHS can record up to 10 1/2 hours on a T-210 tape using the slow, extended play (EP) speed; however, picture and sound quality noticeably degrade. The bulky size of the VHS cassette with its 1/2-inch-wide tape requires a relatively large, often heavy camcorder. Full-size VHS is the only format that can be played back directly in home VHS VCRs. Camcorders without the hi-fi option record low-fidelity audio.

VHS-C: This format is a variation of the VHS format that uses cassettes about one-third of the size of regular VHS cassettes. The signals recorded on VHS-C are fully compatible with full-size VHS. This allows VHS-C cassettes to record and play back on any VHS VCR when placed in an adapter supplied with nearly all VHS-C camcorders. VHS-C tapes record for a maximum of 40 minutes at the standard play (SP) and two hours at the low quality extended play (EP) speed. Like full-size camcorders, VHS-C camcorders without the hi-fi option record low-fidelity audio.

Super VHS (S-VHS): This format uses a specially formulated, much more expensive tape along with superior electronics. This tape records up to 400 lines of resolution—close to laser disc in video quality—and far outperforms conventional VHS (240 lines). It also substantially improves the video quality of the slow EP speed, making it more acceptable for ordinary recording.

HOW TO SHOP

Shopping for a camcorder can be a confusing or even intimidating experience. So many features are available, and in so many different combinations, that it can be difficult to make solid comparisons between machines. Because not every consumer needs or wants every feature, it is important to understand what is available and to know what you want. Picture quality between models in similar categories varies only slightly, but the feel and operational ease differ substantially. Shop for a camcorder as you would for a pair of shoes. Try it on for comfort, and try it out for ease of use. Many of the smaller models have diminutive buttons that are hard to use for someone with larger hands. Make sure the buttons and controls feel comfortable. Remember, this is the model that you're going to carry around when filming on vacation.

WHERE TO BUY

Camcorders can be found in major consumer electronics chains and camera stores across the country, such as Best Buy and Circuit City, and major regional chains such as The Good Guys, Tops, The

Whiz, Sound Advice, and Harvey. Many upscale products are found in salon-type consumer electronics establishments such as The Listening Room. Many upscale consumer electronics salons are also members of CEDIA or PARA—two custom installer organizations that train their members to understand the needs of their clients. While department stores might carry a product you want, its price may be higher than at other retail outlets. Discount chain stores like K-Mart or Wal-Mart might have good buys on many entry-level models and accessories. You can also purchase many products from the Web—many major retailers, such as J&R Music World, The Wiz, and Best Buy, now have a presence on the Web. However, before you buy on the Web, make sure you've seen the product in person and checked out the kind of image it can record and how easy it was to use. Get a price from your local retailer as they might still have a better price than the Web does (remember, on the Web you have to pay extra for shipping and handling).

FEATURES AND TERMINOLOGY_____

Aperture Designation: This refers to the maximum opening of the iris—in other words, to the greatest amount of light that can be admitted. The designation is given as an f-stop rating, such as $f/1.6$. The smaller the f-stop number the larger the aperture and the more light that will pass through the lens. In all camcorders, the iris automatically adjusts. Some camcorders offer a manual adjustment as well.

Autofocus: This feature focuses the lens and keeps it focused even as the distance between the camcorder and the subject changes. Some camcorders also permit manual focusing. Each manufacturer uses a proprietary autofocus system with varying degrees of speed and accuracy. Although most companies employ some form of computerized through-the-lens (TTL) system, the simpler infrared system sometimes works better. Be sure to try out the autofocus system when evaluating the camcorder.

Automatic (or Continuous) White Balance: This keeps the color of the video image true to life under varying lighting conditions, from outdoor to indoor and fluorescent to incandescent. An inaccurate white balance can result in a picture that is too pink or too blue.

Character Generators: These allow you to add the time, date, titles, and other written information to the images that you are recording.

Fade In/Fade Out: This feature automatically fades the image from, or to, a black (or white) screen.

Flying Erase Head: This is mounted on the spinning video head drum rather than in a stationary position along the tape path. Because it spins with the other heads, a flying erase head allows you to make smooth transitions when you stop and start the tape between scenes, eliminating noise bursts. The flying erase head is particularly desirable if you want better quality in edited tapes.

Image Stabilization: This is a generic term for reducing unwanted camcorder motion caused by shakes and jitters. It has become a standard feature in recent years. Some companies use a digital electronic system that slightly fuzzes the picture to reduce the unwanted motion. Others compensate by rapidly moving the lens, calling it optical image stabilization. Having reviewed a large number of camcorders, we question the overall benefit of this feature. Effectiveness of image stabilization will vary from brand to brand, however.

Imager (or Imaging Device): This solid-state device collects light and transforms it into an electrical signal. A high-speed shutter alters the method that the camcorder uses to collect light from its CCD (charged-coupled) imaging device. This results in the equivalent of allowing less light into the camcorder. A high-speed shutter permits operation at speeds up to $1/40,000$ second. Most camcorders on the market today have a shutter range from $1/60$ to $1/4,000$ second, which is adequate for most people. Unless you plan to shoot sporting events, a high-speed shutter is probably not an essential feature.

Lux: This refers to a unit of measurement that gauges the amount of light falling on a photo subject. Many camcorders have a low-light rating of around 10 lux, which is similar to the amount of light cast on an image about 12 feet from one 60-watt lightbulb. Although sensitive camcorders can deliver a picture at 1 lux, you are most likely to get a good image with 80 lux. The best color and depth of field require several hundred lux. For many years, manufacturers have played a lux war game with each claiming the lowest lux level with no real standard in place for measuring lux. There is now a standard in place—EIA-639. New literature will state lux as "measured by the EIA standard." This will mean that brand A's 3 lux will be equivalent to brand B's 3 lux if they both state their lux "as measured by the EIA standard." Minimum illumination tells you the minimum amount of light, stated in lux, necessary to record a clear picture.

Pixel: Short for "picture element," a pixel is one of the tiny points (or dots) that make up a video image. The higher the pixel count, the more detailed the image. But because the size and type of imaging devices vary, comparing pixel counts between different devices doesn't always determine which can yield the most detailed image.

Program Auto Exposure (or Program AE): This feature offers different modes of preprogrammed exposures depending on your shooting and lighting conditions. These modes alter the shutter, iris, and white balance to different settings; for example, snow, twilight, sepia, and sports (high-speed shutter). Usually found on a dial located on the side of the camcorders, these settings can easily be changed to suit your lighting or special effects needs.

Resolution: This is the ability to produce fine detail in a video picture. It is usually measured in horizontal lines. Vertical resolution, less frequently used, is a more stringent measure. A good video monitor produces more than 500 lines. Television broadcasts have about 340 lines, and satellite systems more than 450. Conventional VHS reproduces 240 lines and 8mm close to 300.

Superimposer: A superimposer is a digital memory function that can store images or titles. At the push of a button, you can superimpose the stored image over the picture currently being recorded.

BEST BUYS 2000

Our Best Buy and Recommended camcorders follow. Within each category, camcorders are listed by quality; the item we consider the best of the Best Buys is first, followed by our Recommended choices, and so on. Remember that a Best Buy or Recommended designation applies only to the model listed; it does not necessarily apply to other models made by the same manufacturer or to an entire product line.

8MM CAMCORDERS

Canon ES290

✔ BEST BUY

The Canon ES290 employs slick camcorder technology in Canon's FlexiZone autofocus system, which allows you perfect focus and exposure of your subject. Thanks to FlexiZone AF/AE, you keep your subject in focus at all times even if your subject moves to the left or right of center. Through the use of a joystick style controller situated in the back middle of the camcorder, you center in on your subject. You invoke FlexiZone by pressing the FlexiZone button on the top back of the camcorder. Telephoto zooms were fairly rock solid. Canon's four-mode Program Auto Exposure adjusts the camcorder for a variety of shooting conditions: Portrait, Sports, Spotlight, and Sand & Snow. Also included are Digital Effects such as Art, Sepia, Black and White, Negative Conversion, Mirror-half/Mirror-full, Mosaic, Pastel, Emboss, Color Key, and 16:9 (widescreen). The 0.55-inch color viewfinder has a solid 113,000-pixels, offering a fairly bright image. Audio is above normal quality, offering AFM sound. The ES290 also features two Custom keys that allow you to store up to eight functions, such as settings and titles, in memory for easy retrieval during taping. A helpful feature found on this camcorder is Battery Refresh, which completely drains the battery of power. This way, this model's batteries will not suffer from memory loss over time. This battery holds a two-hour charge. The maximum recording time is 2½ hours. All in all, this full-featured entry-level model can't be beat.

Specifications: height, 3⅞"; width, 4⅛"; depth, 8⅛"; weight, 1 lb. 9⅜ oz. without tape and battery
Warranty: 1 year, parts and labor
Manufacturer's Suggested Retail Price: $499
Approximate Low Price: $400

RCA ProV730

Recommended

The RCA ProV730 offers several compelling features at a reasonable price, including a three-inch color LCD display panel (113,000 pixels) that folds out of the left side of the camcorder. The camcorder uses a standard NiCad battery, which holds 60 minutes on one charge and fits onto the back of the unit. The ¼-inch, 250,000-pixel CCD imager is coupled with an 18×zoom. It includes an f/1.4 to 2.6 lens with a focal range of 4.0mm to 60mm. Date, time, tape remaining, battery, and zoom gauges are displayed within the viewfinder. Also included is an 11-button mini remote, which stores within the battery compartment. The camcorder features a built-in lens cover. The ProV730 also includes a flying erase head for seamless edits, a Scene Select AE recording dial with nine recording modes, 16:9 recording model, eight Quick Titles, a one-page Titler, manual exposure control, and an automatic head-cleaning system.

Specifications: height, 4⅜"; width, 4⅞"; depth, 8⅞"; weight, 1.9 lbs. without tape and battery
Warranty: 90 days, labor; 1 year, parts
Manufacturer's Suggested Retail Price: $599
Approximate Low Price: not available

Hitachi VM-H855LA

Recommended

The Hitachi VM-H855LA is one of the best examples of an 8mm camcorder at a reasonably affordable price. The Hi8mm format offers superior resolution in a hand-held camcorder, but with a third of the weight and bulk of a standard VHS camcorder. Using a ¼-inch, 470,000-pixel CCD imager coupled with an f/1.4 lens, the VM-H855LA produced videos that were sparkling—even down to two lux. The flying erase head helps with seamless edits that are free of video noise. The VM-H855LA uses a lithium ion battery, which allows up to three hours of recording time. To keep recorded images solid, the camcorder includes electronic image stabilization (EIS), called Advanced StablePix by Hitachi. It worked fairly well, but there is an ever-so-slight loss of picture quality when EIS is employed. The camcorder features a black-and-white viewfinder, which was OK. Sound quality is somewhat better for an 8mm camcorder overall. The camcorder includes a fold-out three-inch color LCD monitor featuring 90,000 pixels. While not as bright as some such LCD screens, it performed well. A built-in speaker is included for video playback. Other features include Cool Shots, which is a five-mode programmed auto exposure. This is handy because you can change the camcorder's internal setting to match your shooting environment, such as sun, sand, snow, or sunset. The 16-bit DSPIII controls the entire auto exposure system, controlling auto exposure, auto white balance, auto iris, and auto backlight.

Specifications: height, 4¾"; width, 3¹¹⁄₁₆"; depth, 8⁵⁄₁₆"; weight, 1.9 lbs. without tape and battery

Warranty: 90 days, labor; 1 year, parts

Manufacturer's Suggested Retail Price: $700

Approximate Low Price: not available

_____FULL-SIZE VHS CAMCORDERS_____

Hitachi VM-7500LA

✔ **BEST BUY**

The Hitachi VM-7500LA has been downsized from previous models by a good two inches. In lieu of a color viewfinder, this model sports a fold-out three-inch color LCD screen located on the lower left-hand side of the camcorder. A built-in speaker is also included. It's perfect for playing back recently shot videos or popping in a movie to keep the kids occupied. Its slimmer width for a full-size model also makes this camcorder more manageable. The viewfinder is slightly larger than most at 0.6 inch, which is especially great if you wear glasses. Automatic operation assures the best videos in most shooting situations. As with Hitachi's full-size models, this camcorder clock/calendar comes preset. It automatically switches between standard and daylight savings time on the correct days. The date and time will automatically record on the tape if you desire. Convenience features include a five-way digital fader (white, wipe, zoom, color wipe, or black and white), Cool Shots (a form of programmed auto exposure), and a two-line/one-page titler with auto trigger. The blank search feature finds the end of the previous recording, eliminating gaps and overlaps before new recordings, even if you remove and re-insert a tape. It comes with a standard two-hour battery.

Specifications: height, 8⅜"; width, 4¾"; depth, 13⅛"; weight, 4.1 lbs. without tape and battery
Warranty: 90 days, labor; 1 year, parts
Manufacturer's Suggested Retail Price: $400
Approximate Low Price: not available

RCA CC4392

✔ **BEST BUY**

The RCA CC4392 is a full-size VHS camcorder that takes good videos with a minimum of fuss and bother with its full-range autofocus system. RCA has fully automated the camcorder with programmed automatic exposure and automatic white balance for ease of use. It includes a two-page titler to record captions on your videos, and it will record the date and time on your videos if you choose. For convenience, the 0.55-inch color electric viewfinder tilts and slides so you can position the camcorder's EVF more comfortably (for either left- or right-eye viewing). New this year is a three-inch LCD color display that folds out from the body. As well, the camcorder also features a four-watt color enhancement light that helps provide illumination in low lighting conditions. Program auto exposure (AE) is also included as well as DSP3 digital signal processing for more accurate colors. Otherwise, this model is as basic as they come, omitting even a flying erase head. It provides all of the features you need to take good videos at a reasonable price. If you desire a full-size camcorder, look no further than the RCA CC4392.

Specifications: height, 8⅛"; width, 4½"; depth, 13⅛"; weight, 4.7 lbs. without tape and battery
Warranty: 90 days, labor; 1 year, parts
Manufacturer's Suggested Retail Price: $599
Approximate Low Price: $500

COMPACT VHS (VHS-C) CAMCORDERS

Panasonic PV-D209

✔**BEST BUY**

The PV-D209 includes all the essential features for shooting good videos and is designed to be easy to use. The camcorder automatically sets recording parameters for optimum videos. The model includes a 0.5-inch color viewfinder with 120,000 pixels, which is quite bright. Not only will the PV-D209 date- and time-stamp your videos automatically if you desire, the clock automatically toggles between daylight and standard time on the appropriate day. A flying erase head virtually eliminates video noise when starting and stopping recording. Graphical tape and battery gauges in the viewfinder, rather than numbers, show tape remaining and battery charge levels. An auto titler is built in, with greetings for ten holidays. The high-speed shutter has a range of ⅟60 to ⅟10,000 of a second. The camcorder now comes with a color-enhancement light. The PV-D209 offers everything you need to shoot great videos at a great price.

Specifications: height, 4.62"; width, 4"; depth, 7.12"; weight, 1.9 lbs. without tape and battery
Warranty: 90 days, labor; 1 year, parts
Manufacturer's Suggested Retail Price: $450
Approximate Low Price: $400

JVC GR-AXM910 DualCam

Recommended

The JVC GR-AXM910 is a VHS-C camcorder that also doubles as a digital still camera and includes many numerous upscale features, including a three-inch, 110,000-pixel LCD color monitor and a built-in auto light. The viewfinder itself measures 0.55 inch. If the scene becomes too dark, the built-in three-watt auto light will turn on automatically. A flying erase and four video heads are standard. To help shoot better videos, the GR-AXM910 includes a seven-mode Program AE (auto exposure) with special effects that automatically sets focus, white balance, shutter speed, and iris for particular taping conditions. The GR-AXM910 has an RS-232 PC terminal for image transfer to your computer, letting you manipulate images with Photo CD software. Convenience features include a built-in character generator that lets you create 18-character messages and offers instant titles with eight preset messages. Editing features include a random assemble edit that lets you re-order scenes within the camcorder for transfer to another tape. A neat feature is digital insert edit, which lets you insert a digital still image onto your VHS-C tape. A 12-button mini remote is included to facilitate the editing process. Other creative editing functions that can be accomplished include animation, audio dubbing, and time-lapse. Within the color viewfinder, there are displays for battery indicator, zoom meter, time elapsed, special effects, and calendar (day/date/time). Mono sound is standard for VHS-C. This camcorder does have a built-in speaker next to the three-inch LCD monitor. A ten-second self timer, DSP, and fader also come standard with the camcorder. Battery power will last about 60 minutes, unless you are shooting with the auto light. The camcorder includes image transfer and retouch software, including Picture Navigator and Mr. Photo.

Specifications: height, 4¹¹⁄₁₆″; width, 3⅝″; depth, 7³⁄₁₆″; weight, 1.7 lbs.

Warranty: 90 days, labor; 1 year, parts

Manufacturer's Suggested Retail Price: $850

Approximate Low Price: $585

__DIGITAL VIDEO (DV) CAMCORDERS__

JVC GR-DVL9500

Recommended

The JVC GR-DVL9500 is a top-of-the-line digital video (DV) camcorder with a 3.8-inch fold-out color LCD screen and a color viewfinder. The camcorder weighs in at about 1.7 pounds equipped with battery, tape, and hand strap. This unit is smaller than most other camcorders. The DVL9500 can be easily attached to a computer via an IEEE-1394 cable. This makes it very easy to manipulate images in cyberspace. Besides shooting normal video, the DVL9500 also lets you to take digital still pictures. The DVL9500 features 480 lines of vertical resolution with progressive scan CCD and progressive color filter. The top-mounted 0.55-inch color viewfinder (with 112,000 pixels) moves upward for ease of use. The model also features high-speed recording and Pro Slow playback at one-tenth the normal speed. The DVL9500 uses extensive on-screen menus and displays. All can be seen and accessed within the viewfinder or through a fold-out 3.8-inch LCD color monitor. Two back-mounted silver dials control the operation and special effects modes. There are nine different digital effects and 11 scene transitions. The DVL9500 comes with its own software for post-production, including JLIP Video Capture, JLIP Video Producer, and three Presto! titles (Mr. Photo, Photo Album, and ImageFolio). Along with its built-in RA edit (random assemble editor) feature and a 23-button multi-brand remote, you can create your own home movies. This unit uses a lithium ion battery that slips into the camcorder body, and lets you tape for one hour. Besides shooting in the standard 4:3 mode, you can also tape in the cinema mode of 16:9 for playback on a widescreen TV or in letterbox format on a standard 4:3 TV.

Specifications: height, 3¾"; width, 2⅞"; depth, 5"; weight, 1.5 lbs. without battery and tape
Warranty: 90 days, labor; 1 year, parts
Manufacturer's Suggested Retail Price: $2,000
Approximate Low Price: $1,610

Canon Elura

Recommended

The Elura offers several neat and innovative features here-to-fore not found on either DV camcorders or digital cameras. The Elura can capture both full motion audio and video and digital still images. Using their "Progressive Scan Digital Motor Drive," the Elura records high-resolution still images of fast moving subjects at a rate of 30 frames per second (fps). The Elura offers a Photo Mode and a Normal Movie Mode. The Photo Mode turns the hybrid DV camcorder into a virtual digital SLR camera. The microphone stays active for a voice annotation for each image. The Normal Movie Mode is designed for shooting full motion video for playback on television. This camcorder uses PCM digital stereo sound for excellent audio quality. Included within the camcorder, you'll find one-touch dubbing, A/V insert, and audio dubbing. The Elura also includes an analog line-in jack for dubbing your 8mm or VHS-C tapes onto DV. There are seven programmed auto exposure modes: Easy Recording, Auto, Sports, Portrait, Spotlight, Sand and Snow, and Low Light. There are also Digital Effects in the form of various fades, wipes, and special effects, plus 16:9 widescreen. This model uses a lithium ion battery that allows for one hour and 50 minutes of recording time. In addition to its color viewfinder, the Elura also features a foldout 2.5-inch LCD screen. Within the screen, you can display up to sixteen pictures and choose the speed in which the images are captured. A full-featured remote is also included. To extend your recording time, the Elura also features an LP recording mode that increases recording time to 90 minutes with a 60-minute DV tape. An added bonus is that each Elura comes pre-packaged with Digital Origin's "EditDV Unplugged" editing program on two CD-ROM discs.

Specifications: height, 5"; width, 2⅜"; depth, 4¼"; weight, 1 lb. 4.8 oz.
Warranty: 1 year, parts and labor
Manufacturer's Suggested Retail Price: $1,799
Approximate Low Price: $1,480

STEREO COMPONENTS

Home music systems, as separate entities from radios and record players, arrived in stores about 50 years ago. Originally they were the domain of hobbyists and serious audiophiles only. Since that time, however, home music systems have evolved from being complicated and costly to accessible and affordable. In the process, performance has also dramatically improved, making today's stereo components an exceptional bargain.

HOME THEATER SYSTEMS

Purists think of stereo components as strictly for music, but the rest of us also enjoy the delights of the home theater experience. With the right components you can re-create the movie theater experience at home. In fact, even on a reasonable budget you can enjoy better sound at home than at the local multiplex movie theaters. The recipe is simple: Start with a 32-inch (or larger screen) TV and add a quality sound source, such as a hi-fi VCR or DVD player. Combine these with a multi-channel receiver equipped with Dolby Pro Logic (or the newer, more impressive Dolby Digital) and five speakers (you may also want to add a subwoofer for low frequency effects). Wire it together in an hour or less and get ready to challenge the local movie house for sonic supremacy.

Nearly all manufacturers now design the majority of their audio components to be used in home theater systems. All but the most basic audio receivers switch video sources, and many display their settings on your TV screen. Generally, the more money you spend the more versatility you'll have. Most companies market complete home-theater packages, either assembled from existing components or as custom designed systems, often at a discount over separate components. The system typically includes a five-channel AM/FM receiver (with Dolby Pro Logic or Dolby Digital), the necessary five speakers, and perhaps an optional powered subwoofer. Ideally, the system should include a matched trio of speakers for the left, center, and right front channels, plus another pair of matched speakers for the left and right surround channels. The surround speakers don't necessarily have to be as large as the front ones, but they should sound similar, even if they sacrifice some bass. (In Dolby Pro Logic the two surround speakers reproduce the same mono signal, while in Dolby Digital they are stereo.) Try to include a subwoofer, as it provides the "oomph" for music and the boom and bang for movies.

In the past year Dolby Digital surround sound rapidly overtook its predecessor, Dolby Pro Logic. Originally called AC-3 when introduced in 1996, Dolby Digital provides a dramatic upgrade in sound quality and realism over the analog Pro Logic. Initially, receivers and processors featuring Dolby Digital were so expensive they could not be included in this guide. However, with dramatic price decreases we can include several high-performance and moderately-priced receivers and processors.

While you still pay a significant premium for Dolby Digital, we feel it's justified. However, be aware that even if you own a Dolby Digital receiver, you can only enjoy its benefits if you have Dolby Digital sources, such as DVD and laser disc players. Nonetheless, Dolby Digital receivers also include Pro Logic, so you still can enjoy surround sound from VHS tapes, satellite, stereo TV broadcasts, and DVDs lacking Dolby Digital soundtracks. Direct-to-home satellite systems (such as DSS and Primestar) and the new digital television systems (DTV and HDTV) provide extremely high quality audio, and offer further incentives to consider home theater. All these innovations—plus the ever improving audio quality of CDs and Mini-Discs—justify a good stereo component system now more than ever.

QUALITY AND COST

Over the past 50 years, technology continued to raise the performance level of audio and video components while lowering the prices. For example, the first CD players introduced just 17 years ago cost $1,000. Now you can enjoy a far better sounding player for about $125.

The dramatic fluctuations in the exchange rate between the dollar and the Japanese yen have forced Japanese companies to increase productivity through automation or by manufacturing off-shore in countries with cheaper labor costs. This has caused a subtle decline in the quality of some gear. When the yen increased in value against the dollar, companies eliminated features or kept the same models in the line for two or three years. At the time of this writing, the value of the dollar has dramatically increased over the yen, making for better values on the market than ever before.

HOW TO SHOP

In this guide we offer Best Buy, Recommended, and Budget Buy ratings as guideposts to a satisfying sound system. Most important, however, use your ears. Bring your favorite CDs to the store. You should always make an effort to listen before you purchase any audio components. Buy only from a dealer that permits a "no questions asked" return period of at least seven days. Remember, speakers will always sound different in your home than they do in the store. Room acoustics determine the sound of speakers as much as the speakers themselves.

Until a few years ago, most people bought two-channel stereo systems. Now most people purchase multi-channel home theater systems. Home theater systems include a receiver with five channels of amplification connected to five speakers (and sometimes a powered subwoofer), a multi-channel encoded video source (either Dolby Pro Logic from a VHS hi-fi VCR or Dolby Digital from a DVD player or DSS satellite transmission), and conventional two-channel sources, such as a CD or tape player. In many systems, a DVD player doubles for video and audio, because it also plays CDs. A good home theater system will serve music-only sources as well as the dramatic sonic effects and dialogue of movies and music videos. Even two-channel music sources often sound better heard through five speakers.

Most multi-channel receivers can retrieve the original ambience of the recording or synthesize a surround effect. If you're sure that you'll never use a system for home theater, you can concentrate your budget on two expensive stereo speakers rather than five moderately priced home theater speakers. But premium two-channel receivers are a vanishing breed.

Buying stereo components instead of a prepackaged or all-in-one system lets you upgrade your equipment at any time without discarding the entire system. If you can't afford all the components you want, or the quality of components you desire, begin with a good stereo or multi-channel receiver, a pair of speakers that offer optional matching center and surrounds, and a budget CD or DVD player. This setup will serenade you with high fidelity AM/FM stereo radio, play prerecorded music, and even work with your TV and VCR as a basic home theater system.

People logically express concerns about obsolescence. Unlike the computer industry, audio and video maintains its currency for many years, often decades. Today some people play CDs through the receivers and speakers they purchased during the 1970s. LPs enjoyed a 35-year run, and new turntables and phono cartridges remain available to play them today. CDs, now in their seventeenth year, continue going strong. Although a new "super CD" (also known as DVD-Audio) became available in 1999, it is unlikely to eclipse the CD we all know and love. Generally, it takes a decade for a new technology to surpass an old one, so you can expect a minimum of ten years, or a possible maximum of 20 or more years, before you need to apply the word "obsolete" to most audio equipment.

WHERE TO BUY

Buying a system from a specialty dealer usually eliminates hassles and confusion. Most specialty dealers deliver the system and set it up in your home. Specialists do not necessarily charge a higher price than the mass-market superstores; but if they do, they often make it up to you in service. In our experience, home entertainment specialty dealers display a wider selection of equipment in a space more suitable for listening. They also pride themselves on good, in-store service departments. But if you know exactly what you want and feel confident about installing it, you'll be perfectly satisfied with most of the national chain stores, or ordering off the Internet.

When you shop at a specialty dealer and purchase the entire system from that dealer you will often receive a system discount of

5 to 15 percent. Don't be shy about bargaining. The dealer might throw in better speaker wire or a CD cleaner to sweeten the sale. Superstores often use select models during promotions, selling them at lower prices. Sometimes these models are discontinued or about to be discontinued and the manufacturer wants to unload them. Sometimes the chain simply bought too many of them. Because there's minimal change from one model year to the next, buying last year's model can be a good value. However, be alert for major technological changes, such as the shift from Dolby Pro Logic to Dolby Digital. Be careful of the "bait-and-switch," in which you ask for the advertised model and the salesperson attempts to sell you a different and usually more expensive (or more profitable to the store) model.

WARRANTIES

Extended warranties reward the dealer with almost pure profit. The big superstores promote extended warranties as a means to increase profit margins on discontinued equipment. Most audio equipment will long outlive the extended warranty. If equipment fails, it's usually in the first few weeks, well before expiration of the manufacturer's warranty. Leave nonmechanical equipment, such as a receiver, powered up continuously for the first few weeks you own it. Also, use your tape player or CD player extensively during its first few weeks. If the equipment does not fail by then, it probably will not die before the end of its natural life expectancy. Over the past few years, many extended warranty firms failed before the equipment they insured, leaving buyers holding a worthless piece of paper.

PRECAUTIONS

Purchase a surge protector. Jolts of electricity quickly fry integrated circuits, unlike the rugged tube equipment of the early days. A lightning strike two miles from your home can possibly zap your equipment. Most power companies regularly send unexpected jolts down the line as they switch loads or suffer equipment failures. A good surge protector costs between $20 and $50; however, you can spend as much as $200 for a deluxe six-outlet model that protects outdoor antenna cable, cable company cable, and phone lines. The better models come with free insurance policies. Consider a quality surge protector essential to the longevity of your home theater system.

Never ground your equipment to anything but the third hole of your electrical outlet. If you ground your system to water pipes, the earth, or anything else, it could act as a magnet for lightning or electrical faults and not only blow out your gear but possibly set your home on fire.

Avoid placing speakers too close to a television unless they are specifically designed for this kind of placement with magnetic shielding. The magnetic field of regular speakers can distort the TV picture, and permanently damage the picture tube.

Keep all your equipment well-ventilated. Heat causes premature equipment failure. Never obstruct ventilation slots or holes, and if you stack components, try to leave at least one inch of breathing room between them. A small, quiet cooling fan mounted near your components may extend their life expectancy.

When making connections, removing or installing components, or swapping speakers, always turn the power off. You can blow out your speakers from plugging cables in and out with the power on. Just one strand of speaker wire touching the adjacent terminal can blow the receiver's fuse(s), or in rarer cases, the entire power output section of the receiver.

Heed the instruction manuals' warnings about no user-serviceable parts. Most components consist of a power supply and a board full of chips and transistors permanently soldered in place. You cannot diagnose or replace anything by poking around inside because you may cause more damage or give yourself a nasty electrical shock.

BEST BUYS 2000

Our Best Buy, Recommended, and Budget Buy picks for stereo components follow. Products are listed according to quality. The best of the Best Buys is listed first, followed by our second choice, and so on. A Best Buy, Recommended, or Budget Buy designation applies to only the model listed—it does not necessarily apply to other models made by the same manufacturer or to an entire product line.

SPEAKERS

More than 365 speaker companies flood the market with multiple models, from those constructed in garages to those constructed in large factories. Every few years someone announces a radical new speaker technology, but generally, the tried-and-true speaker designs offer the best sound for the money. Because speakers are material and labor intensive (rather than technology intensive), their prices typically do not decline like other audio components. While discerning the differences among electronic components taxes your concentration, you can relax and still tell speakers apart. Always insist on the right to return speakers that fail to meet your expectations.

HOW TO SHOP

Because speakers are so integral to sound, they retain a respected position when choosing stereo components. Like choosing a favorite singer, judging speakers is a subjective task. Speakers will determine your choice of receiver, since some speakers require more power than others, and some receivers and speakers make a better match than others. Thus, the advice of friends, reviews, and the recommendations here should serve only as a starting point. Take care in choosing speakers by spending ample time listening.

Spend some time positioning your speakers. Speakers dramatically interact with room acoustics. What sounded stunning in the store may sound tinny, muddy, or boomy at home. You can alter this slightly by where you place them in your room—even a few inches closer to or farther from a wall can make a difference. The speakers should form a triangle with your normal listening position. The front of the speakers should always be precisely in the same plane, although they may be angled slightly inward. Taking the time to experiment will reward you in the long run.

The size of the speaker enclosure and the number of speakers inside it (woofers, midranges, tweeters) do not always correlate with sound quality. Always look for solid, dense, well-made cabinetry. We base our speaker ratings on the quality of construction, reputation, and listening tests.

HOME THEATER SPEAKERS

Home theater speakers share many of the desirable attributes of the stereo speaker pair, except there are five placed appropriately around the room. You can enjoy fairly small speakers when you include a subwoofer in the system to reproduce deep bass.

Home theater makes its own demands. First, all of the speakers should sound the same, even if some are larger or smaller than others. This is called "timbre matching," which means the speakers should have the same tonal quality and balance, even if some of the speakers reproduce more extended frequency response than others. The surround speakers may be smaller, but they should retain the same sonic characteristics as the rest of the system. One quick way to determine if the speakers are timbre-matched is to listen to the applause from a live recording. No one speaker should draw attention to itself with a different sound quality. One recommendation is to buy the entire home theater system speakers from a single manufacturer.

Traditionally, and in most of our listings, the surround speakers are smaller than the left and right front speakers. Dolby Digital now sends a greater amount of bass to the surround channels, so future home theater speaker systems may include somewhat larger surround channels. Since many people refuse to let speakers dominate their rooms, it is unlikely they would want surround speakers that match the front speakers in size.

Most companies magnetically shield the three front channel speakers. Many people usually place them in close proximity to a TV screen. Speakers normally generate powerful magnetic fields that can distort the TV picture if they are not shielded. Incidentally, the magnetic fields of unshielded speakers can also mildly erase magnetic tapes, so don't place tapes near the speakers.

Place the center channel speaker either directly above or below the TV screen. The surround speakers generally should be placed high on a side wall, not necessarily on the rear wall behind you. The surrounds should be above and just slightly behind where you sit. Try not to point them directly at your ears, since you don't want to localize the sound as though it's coming from the speakers. As with stereo speakers, experimenting with the placement of four of the five home theater speakers (the center channel offers limited options, although you can tilt it up or down) can pay off in the long run.

FEATURES AND TERMINOLOGY

Acoustic Suspension Speakers: Sometimes referred to as air-suspension speakers, acoustic suspension speakers are most common among bookshelf-size speakers. A tightly-sealed enclosure forces the speaker to fight the air within. This causes them to be less sensitive to power than most ported speakers, therefore requiring more amplifier power to produce a given level of sound. A well-designed acoustic suspension system reproduces tightly controlled bass.

Construction Quality: The crossover network consists of resistors, capacitors, and coils that divide the incoming sound from the receiver into appropriate frequency ranges, ensuring that the bass goes to the woofer and the treble to the tweeter. You cannot tell the actual sound or construction quality of a speaker system just by the size of its components and the material from which they are manufactured. An 8-inch woofer sometimes reproduces better bass than a 12-inch woofer, and paper occasionally surpasses space-age plastics and metals in the quality of a speaker cone and the sound it reproduces. The thickness, materials, and construction of the speaker enclosure, or cabinet, can influence the system's sound as much as the drivers. When shopping for speakers, keep an eye out for a solid enclosure that shows minimal resonance when you rap your knuckles on it.

High-efficiency Ported Systems: Also known as ducted or reflex systems, these highly-sensitive (sensitivity has replaced the term efficiency when referring to how much sound a speaker produces from a given amount of power) systems are common among large speakers. Ported systems often require less power from the amplifier (or amplifier section of your receiver) to produce a given level of sound when compared to acoustic suspension speakers. Ported speakers take advantage of the port's resonance to amplify the bass frequencies acoustically.

Power and Ratings: Different speakers take advantage of different physical properties to produce sound. For example, large floor-standing speakers can reproduce throbbing sound levels with as little as 20 watts of power, whereas compact bookshelf models often require twice that much power to reproduce the same sound level, if they can play that loudly. Too much power can damage speakers, but speaker ratings and amplifier ratings don't always tell the whole story. Speakers rated at 100 watts maximum may safely be powered by a 300-watt amplifier, but if you force all 300 watts into the speaker, the sound will cause you pain and damage the speakers. Too little power can also damage a speaker. If you try to play a low-powered amplifier too loudly it can distort the sound waves, and this distortion can destroy a speaker.

Speaker Impedance: Speaker impedances are commonly listed from 4 to 8 ohms, with some ranging from 2 to 16 ohms (this is a technical description of the amount of inductive resistance the speaker offers to the flow of electrical signals). Under normal circumstances, impedance bears no relation to sound quality, but many receivers need a minimum of 4 ohms to work properly. A good receiver may work with 2 ohms, but other receivers or amplifiers will automatically shut off or blow a fuse. If you intend to use two pairs of speakers in parallel from the same terminals, choose speakers rated at least 8 ohms. Also note that speaker impedance ratings are nominal, meaning that a speaker may actually fall below its rated impedance at some frequencies.

Woofers, Tweeters, and Other Speaker Elements: The woofer is the largest speaker component (or driver). It reproduces bass notes and often the lower midrange sounds as well. The tweeter is the smallest component and reproduces higher sounds (treble and upper midrange). The tweeter is the most fragile component because of its fine wires, and it is the most prone to failure. Many speaker systems include one or more midrange speaker components that reproduce the range of sound between the woofer and the tweeter—the range of the human voice. A midrange component is not essential for good sound, although most larger systems include them.

STEREO SPEAKERS

NHT SuperOne

✔ **BEST BUY**

The NHT SuperOne is no misnomer. It ranks as the Mighty Mouse of speakers, producing a super sound from a super-compact size. NHT began by manufacturing small speakers, and though it now builds floor towers, it keeps returning to small speakers to see just how good it can make them. This two-way acoustic suspension speaker uses a 6½-inch woofer with a one inch fluid-cooled soft-dome tweeter. NHT magnetically shields the speaker for use near video equipment. While it won't reproduce the lowest organ notes, it does a surprisingly good job on the lowest piano notes, and the rest of the keyboard as well. Its natural tonal balance will please even demanding listeners. Small speakers generally produce a good stereo image because of their small baffles. The SuperOnes excel in this important attribute. The voices and instruments sound like they're playing not only between, but also in front of and behind the plane of these speakers. To achieve their impressive bass, the SuperOnes sacrifice some sensitivity, requiring a minimum of 25 watts. However, they'll accept plenty of high power. NHT offers the SuperOne in high gloss black or white laminate. NHT also designed customs stands ($100) and custom wall-brackets ($90) for these speakers.

Specifications: height, 11⅔"; width, 7¼"; depth, 8½"; weight, 10 lbs. each
Warranty: 1 year, electronics; 5 years, parts and labor
Manufacturer's Suggested Retail Price: $175 each
Approximate Low Price: not available

Polk RT400

`Recommended`

The Polk RT400 could be regarded as the basso profundo of our listings. It provides ample natural bass without obscuring the rest of the frequency spectrum. We placed it a couple of feet away from the walls and there was still plenty of bass. You can hear even more bass if you place the speakers closer to a wall. The RT400 benefits from a joint research project between Polk Audio and Johns Hopkins University into eliminating speaker-cone resonances. The reduction of resonances in this speaker results in its clear sound and its ability to reproduce bass without muddiness. The RT400 consists of a 7½-inch woofer and a one-inch soft-dome tweeter in this two-way system in an enclosure large enough for the ample bass. Polk complements the system with low-diffraction removable grilles and easy-to-use binding posts for the speaker wires. Polk spends its money on the sound. The tower enclosures are finished in black-ash vinyl. Magnetic shielding permits placing the RT400 very close to your TV without creating picture distortion.

Specifications: height, 36½"; width, 9⅓"; depth, 10¼"; weight, 35 lbs. each
Warranty: 5 years, parts and labor
Manufacturer's Suggested Retail Price: $449/pair
Approximate Low Price: $400

Bose 201, Series IV

`Budget Buy`

The Bose 201, Series IV represents a further upgrade of the best-selling 201 speakers. Bose sells a lot of 201s because, like Henry Ford, it perfected mass production without sacrificing quality. Bose sells the 201, Series IV in mirror-imaged pairs, so that the two-inch fluid-cooled tweet angles from a corner of the enclosure to a broader listening area. This radiates high frequencies over a wider area and lets the good stereo image be enjoyed over a wider area. This satisfies the Bose criteria of "direct/reflecting" sound. A 6½-inch woofer in the ported enclosure provides satisfying bass with as little as 10 watts of power. The 201, Series IV reproduces appealing sound at a price nearly everyone can afford. The flared port reduces air noise. Injection-molded plastic end caps, foam grilles, and a black or rosewood vinyl finish provide a contemporary look.

Specifications: height, 9½"; width, 15⅛"; depth, 6¾"; weight, 21.75 lbs. total
Warranty: 5 years, parts and labor (transferable)
Manufacturer's Suggested Retail Price: $198
Approximate Low Price: $178

HOME THEATER SPEAKERS

Atlantic Technology System 170

✔ **BEST BUY**

The System 170 once again confirms that Atlantic Technology knows how to design a home theater speaker system that makes people of modest means feel wealthy. The company continues a winning streak of speakers in the $1,500 price range that deliver impressive, realistic sound. Atlantic Technology invests in the interior of these speakers rather than their cabinet finishes. The System 170 looks like basic boxes in black. We especially like the use of the dipole surround speakers, similar to those used in more expensive THX-certified speakers. The surrounds, which are basically triangular with one apex chopped off, face speakers in nearly opposite directions. This diffuses and spreads the sound, improving the surround illusion. The center channel is nearly identical to the main left and right speakers, ideal for maintaining the same timbre. It also has a treble level control for taming the shrillness of some movie soundtracks. Each of the three front speakers uses a pair of four-inch coated composite molded graphite woofers and a one-inch silk dome tweeter. A 150-watt amplifier powers the muscular 12-inch subwoofer. Beneath their humble exteriors, these speakers are gems that will do justice to James Bond or Gustav Mahler.

Specifications: height, main left and right: 13½"; center: 6¹⁄₁₀"; surrounds: 10⅕"; subwoofer: 20½"; width, main left and right: 5½"; center: 13¹⁄₁₀"; surrounds: 9¹⁄₁₀"; subwoofer: 13⅕"; depth,

main left and right: 6½"; center: 6⁷/₁₀"; surrounds: 5⅕";
subwoofer: 13⁴/₅"; weight, main left and right: 7.6 lbs. each;
center: 8.4 lbs.; surrounds: 7.1 lbs.; subwoofer: 42.75 lbs.
Warranty: subwoofer: 1 year, parts and labor; speakers: 5 years,
parts and labor
Manufacturer's Suggested Retail Price: $1,396
Approximate Low Price: not available

Energy Take 5 with e:XL-58 subwoofer

✔ **BEST BUY**

The Energy Take 5 home theater speaker system has
generated a great deal of favorable comments. Energy builds the
system from four of its Take 2 mini-speakers, a Take 1 center channel speaker, and the ES-8–powered subwoofer. To lessen the load
on the mini-speakers, the subwoofer handles all the sound below 90
hertz, which is about where a baritone voice ends. The subwoofer
automatically turns on when you play your system, and its built-in
limiter reduces its gain when distortion threatens. Energy designs the
system to work in a variety of configurations and with a variety of receivers. Although the Take 2 speakers look simple, they consist of
high-tech components such as a 3½-inch carbon/graphite midrange
and upper bass driver and ¾-inch Hyperdome tweeter. They are
mounted to a special non-resonant synthetic material front panel,
which is then bolted to a rigid cabinet. They are also magnetically
shielded, meaning you can place the speaker as close to the TV as
you desire. Since Energy uses the same speakers, front and back, as
well as the same internal components in the center channel speaker,
the timbre matches perfectly all the way around. Whether playing
music or movies, the Take 5 system reproduces a natural sound with
good ambience and convincing images. The sound is clear, and
often seems effortless. While Energy forgoes novel shapes and
styles, the enclosures in gloss black or matte white have their own
subtle elegance.

Specifications: height, Take 2 satellites: 6¾"; Take 1 center channel: 4"; ES-8 subwoofer: 15⁷/₈"; width, Take 2 satellites: 4"; Take 1

center channel: 10⅜"; ES-8 subwoofer: 9⅞"; depth, Take 2 satellites: 5⅜"; Take 1 center channel: 5⅜"; ES-8 subwoofer: 10⅞"; weight, 43 lbs., complete system
Manufacturer's Suggested Retail Price: $800
Approximate Low Price: $620

Bose Acoustimass 10, Series II

Recommended

The Bose Acoustimass 10, Series II is the ideal home theater speaker system for those without the space for home theater and for those unwilling to sacrifice decor for sound. Five magnetically shielded pairs of tiny speaker cubes, each housing a 2½-inch speaker, provide the front and surround channels. A compact woofer/subwoofer, about the size of an airline carry-on suitcase, called the bass module, reproduces the bass. Bose employs its proprietary Acoustimass design using three 5¼-inch speakers inside the box to achieve surprising bass. The module contains the crossover that separates the sound, sending the mid and high frequencies to the cubes. Because bass is omnidirectional, this bass module can be placed almost anywhere in the room, or even in the basement firing upward through a grate in the floor. You can twist each pair of cubes to vary the spaciousness of the sound. If you aim one of the pair at the wall it creates reflected sound, which broadens the sound field. The speaker cubes come in black or white, and Bose offers optional wall-mounting brackets, table stands, or floor stands. The white speakers against a white wall seem to disappear. When used with a good-quality receiver or amplifier, the sound will impress you with breadth, depth, and quantity.

Specifications: height, cube arrays: 6¼"; bass module: 14"; width, cube arrays: 3"; bass module: 22"; depth, cube arrays: 4"; bass module: 7½"; weight, 44 lbs.
Warranty: 5 years, transferable
Manufacturer's Suggested Retail Price: $1,099
Approximate Low Price: $1,000

SUBWOOFER

Although there's no specific agreement on the definition of a sub-woofer (many companies refer to the woofer as the subwoofer), most experts agree that it must produce full sound levels below 50 hertz and descend to at least 30 hertz while still producing a significant sound level. For reference, the lowest male bass voice sings at about 80 hertz, and the lowest note on a grand piano is about 27 hertz (some organs go as low as 20 hertz, which you feel more than hear). Most subwoofers begin at 80 hertz (although most allow you to select 120 hertz as their cutoff point). That means subwoofers do not, and should not, radiate sound above these frequencies.

HOW TO SHOP

Although the size of the speaker driver in a subwoofer may hint at its effectiveness, larger is not automatically better. Sophisticated enclosure designs, the design of the driver, and electronic sleight-of-ear in the amplifier will allow a 10-inch subwoofer to sound as good as a 12- or even 15-inch model.

Bass is omnidirectional, which means you cannot tell where the sound comes from. For example, hearing bass in mono does not dilute the stereo or surround effect. You can hide the subwoofer from view and still experience its bass. We say "experience" because low bass is felt as much as it is heard. Bass also requires prodigious amounts of energy and can rattle room surfaces and contents. The one thing that should not rattle is the subwoofer itself. You should look for subwoofers with an amplifier that produces a minimum of 100 watts. Subwoofers should also be placed a considerable distance from the main speakers.

Velodyne CT-120

✓BEST BUY

In the audio world, Velodyne is synonymous with subwoofer. The CT-120 represents one of Velodyne's most afford-able subwoofers. (The CT in the model number stands for "classic theater" series.) The CT-120 uses a 12-inch woofer with a rein-forced fiber cone, powered by a 120-watt amplifier that is able to produce 270 watts of peak power. Special circuits prevent distortion and speaker damage. The CT-120 has plenty of boost down to 25 hertz with excellent accuracy. You can adjust the speaker's upper frequency limit and phase, and also bypass the speaker's internal crossover if your receiver has a subwoofer output. The speaker turns on automatically when it senses a signal from your system.

Specifications: height, 18"; width, 15"; depth, 18¾"; weight, 60 lbs.
Warranty: 2 years, parts and labor
Manufacturer's Suggested Retail Price: $599
Approximate Low Price: $530

HEADPHONES

Like speakers, headphones are best judged according to how they sound. The general criteria for good headphone performance include a full bass response with accurate tonal definition, and balance from the midrange frequencies up to the highest frequencies.

A comfortable headset is also an important consideration. Weight and fit should be carefully considered. There are three basic designs for headphones. Circumaural phones cover your entire outer ear and block out all external sound. Supra-aural phones do not completely block out external sound. Open-air phones rest lightly against the outer ear and usually have a foam pad that separates the actual phone from your head. This allows almost all outside sounds to be heard while you're wearing them. As a general rule, circumaural phones provide the most bass, whereas open-air phones usually provide the least bass.

NOISE-CANCELING HEADPHONES

This new technology enhances the pleasure of headphone listening. Extremely small microphones inside the headphones pick up ambient noise and feed it to a special amplifier in a small box or bulge in the headphone cord. This amplifier changes the phase of the noise and turns it into "antinoise," which is sent back to the earpiece. When the noise and antinoise meet, they cancel out, reducing the ambient noise that you hear. This reduces distractions and allows playing music at a lower volume, which protects your hearing. The phones can also be used to just reduce noise without listening to music, such as when flying on airplanes.

We strongly recommend against using noise-canceling phones when cycling, jogging, or in any activity where you must hear warnings. Noise-canceling phones range from large, elaborate, effective $1,200 models designed for pilots to ineffective $100 models. We've chosen models that meet our criteria for suitable headphones with the added bonus of noise cancellation.

Sony MDR-65

The lightweight, open-air-design MDR-65 headphones rest comfortably on the ear with their soft ear pads on gimbal-mounted ear cups. The wide, molded headband with its gentle cushion further adds to the comfort of these headphones. At only 2½ ounces, they feel like they're floating on your head. When it comes to sound, however, the MDR-65 is a heavyweight, with full, well-balanced sound from mid-sized diaphragms using powerful neodymium magnets. For convenience, a sturdy, nearly 6½-foot-long single cord (rather than the cumbersome yoke design) connects the phones to your stereo. This unit can be used with either a personal stereo or home components, because the gold-plated mini-plug comes with a screw-on adapter for standard ¼-inch jacks.

Specifications: weight, 2½ oz.
Warranty: 1 year, exchange
Manufacturer's Suggested Retail Price: $50
Approximate Low Price: not available

Grado Labs SR60

The Grado SR60, praised by audio enthusiasts, easily compares with headphones costing five times as much. The large foam pads sit comfortably on the ears without sealing out external sound. The six-foot straight cord is sturdier than most other headphones' cords. Grado also supplies a gold-plated ¼-inch plug adapter, so you can use them with home stereo components. Because of their high sensitivity, they work with the lowest-output stereos and make even weak portables sound their best. These headphones sound exquisite with clear, crisp treble; deep, authoritative bass; and transparent vocals. Although larger and heavier than most headphones, they are not a burden on the head. These are the kind of headphones you wear by choice, not necessity. Grado is a small company and the SR60 might be difficult to locate. However, the company has been in business for many years and nationally distributes its products.

Specifications: weight, 7 oz.
Warranty: 1 year, parts and labor
Manufacturer's Suggested Retail Price: $69
Approximate Low Price: $60

Koss QZ2000 Quiet Zone

Recommended

Koss begins with its very good PortaPro lightweight headphones as the basis for the noise-canceling QZ2000 Quiet Zone. The comfortable, medium-density foam earpieces rest directly on the ear, supported by a single metal headband. The physical design only modestly blocks external noise, but the active noise cancellation dramatically reduces noise between 30 hertz and 1,000 hertz (the area of most annoying noise, such as aircraft or bus engines). The titanium nitride coating on the headphone diaphragms aids in reproducing crisp, clear high frequencies when listening to music. A small black box, about half the size of a pack of cigarettes, contains the electronic circuitry for noise cancellation. A green LED indicates that active noise cancellation is on; a red LED warns of weak batteries. The QZ2000 operates on a pair of alkaline AA batteries that last for 60 hours or more. The headphones completely collapse for carrying in the supplied vinyl pouch. Although we consider the noise cancellation a very desirable feature, it adds about $100 to the cost of the basic PortaPro headphones.

Specifications: weight, 2⅖ oz.
Warranty: 1 year, parts and labor
Manufacturer's Suggested Retail Price: $200
Approximate Low Price: $150

Sennheiser HD525

Recommended

Sennheiser was an innovator on the open-air headphones field a decade before Sony unveiled its Walkman-style open-air phone, and the Sennheiser HD525 continues and improves upon this tradition. These well-made headphones come with a Kevlar reinforced 10-foot cord that uses high-grade, oxygen-free copper wire. They use powerful neodymium magnets in their earpieces for plenty of sound from a very light-weight transducer. The large foam cushions rest comfortably on the ear, and although the plastic headband is relatively narrow, ample padding allows it to rest comfortably on your head. The sound is very smooth, with exceptionally wide frequency response and impressive depth. The HD525 terminates in a mini-plug and comes with an adapter for the larger standard ¼-inch jacks. These phones feel both rugged and flexible, which bodes well for extended life.

Specifications: weight, 7.5 oz.
Warranty: 2 years, parts and labor
Manufacturer's Suggested Retail Price: $129
Approximate Low Price: $80-$100

STEREO RECEIVERS

Originally conceived as a space- and cost-saving combination of a radio tuner and stereo preamplifier/power amplifiers, today's receiver usually includes five amplifiers instead of two, digital signal processing (DSP) to alter and enhance the sound, and Dolby Pro Logic and/or Dolby Digital surround sound decoders for home theater. (All Dolby Digital receivers contain Pro Logic.) The package remains the same size or is smaller than it was back at the receiver's conception.

Preamplifiers were originally created to amplify the weak signal from a phonograph cartridge. Today, the universality of CDs, as well as production cost-cutting, has resulted in some receivers without the phono stage of the preamp. If you still play vinyl, be sure to select a receiver with a phono input. The power amplifier provides the muscle that pumps up the electrical signal to power the speakers.

To fully enjoy the home-theater effect, the power of each of the front channels must be the same, and the surround channels should each have at least half of the front-channel power. (We occasionally make an exception to this rule if the receiver is otherwise exemplary in performance.)

Video producers encode surround channels on stereo hi-fi VHS tapes, laser discs, DVDs, and many TV and satellite broadcasts. Surround sound processors can also extract ambience from many music sources, such as CDs, which may pleasantly enhance the sound.

TECHNOLOGY

Digital signal processing (DSP) lets you make subtle or major changes to the sound with a minimum of distortion. DSP can simulate the sound of different listening environments, from jazz clubs to arenas, because it can add echoes and reverberation to the sound. DSP can also spread two-channel sound among five speakers or simulate surround sound from only two speakers, although it is not as effective or impressive as having a multichannel home system.

Dolby Labs, the company that set the standards for noise reduction, also dictates surround sound decoding with its analog Pro Logic and Dolby Digital. On the latest generation of laser discs and DVDs, Dolby upgraded surround sound with its new digital system. Dolby Digital normally provides five discrete channels, plus a low-frequency effects channel, commonly called the subwoofer channel. Retrieving four channels from two in the Pro Logic analog matrix system requires considerable electronic fudging, which can compromise sound quality, while the discrete Dolby Digital system involves fewer compromises. Pro Logic, virtually standard on all but the most basic receivers, adds only a few dollars in cost. Dolby Digital adds about 20 percent.

FEATURES_____

Manufacturers fill most receivers with far more features than any normal listener needs or will ever use. Fortunately, these features add little to the price. When shopping, don't let dozens of buttons and flashing lights beguile you. Radio station presets offer great convenience. Some receivers go overboard with 40, although most cities don't have that many radio stations. Once again, it costs the manufacturer no more to include 40 presets than 20. We list the most essential features in our reviews.

The sonic differences between receivers vary, but tend to be slight when compared with speakers. It is best that you use your ears and listen and compare. We don't discuss sound extensively in our receiver reviews because of the slight differences and the lack of good subjective terms for these differences.

TWO-CHANNEL STEREO RECEIVERS

Stereo (two-channel) receivers face extinction as sure as the 8-track. Generally audiophiles who want a dedicated music system purchase separate preamplifiers, power amplifiers, and tuners rather than receivers. Manufacturers learned how to build receivers with five channels of amplification for a little more than what it cost to build a receiver with two channels. (They also realized that if you bought the five channel receiver, they could sell you five, more profitable, speakers.) Remember that even a multichannel home theater receiver can play just two stereo channels. If you simply want a music system, the stereo receivers we list offer a remarkable value. They come without a plethora of unnecessary features and deliver solid, basic performance.

Technics SA-EX110

✔ **BEST BUY**

It's a difficult call as to whether to classify the Technics SA-EX110 a Best Buy or Budget Buy. It has a bargain price, and a slightly higher distortion level than the Sony that follows. However, its reliability edges it slightly ahead of the Sony. Its five inputs still include a phono input, and the lone video input is strictly for audio from a video source. Even its styling resembles the Sony, with a large volume knob and smaller knobs for bass, treble, and balance. The understated front panel with its red and blue fluorescent display contains a minimum of confusing clutter. However, direct-access tuning is only available from the supplied remote control, which is designed to control any Technics/Panasonic audio/video component. You can program 30 radio station presets. Technics' proprietary Class H+ amplifier circuitry provides a generous 100 watts, with some reserve for musical peaks. The Class H+ modular design also simplifies servicing should it ever be necessary. The frequency-synthesized FM tuner delivers very respectable performance. Technics includes a headphone jack for private listening. The receiver includes provisions for connecting two pairs of speakers. The design of the SA-EX110 places performance above frills.

Warranty: 1 year, parts and labor
Manufacturer's Suggested Retail Price: $150
Approximate Low Price: $130-$150

Sony STR-DE135

✓ **BEST BUY**

The STR-DE135 is the last two-channel receiver in Sony's product line and, like its predecessors, represents an exceptional value at an economical price. The STR-DE135 produces 100 watts per channel using discrete output transistors rather than integrated circuits. To keep the noise level low, separate transformers power the audio sections and the blue fluorescent display. The five inputs no longer include a phono input. However, you can buy a stand-alone phono preamp if you still have a turntable and plug that into one of the high-level inputs. The reasonable quality, frequency-synthesized tuner in this model matches, in most respects, the tuners in Sony's most expensive receivers. Direct-access tuning makes listening to your favorite station a snap. Just tap in the radio station's frequency on the numeric keypad of the supplied Sony audio/video system remote or the front panel. Direct-access, or the auto-set feature, makes quick work of setting the 30 possible station presets. The use of knobs, a large one for volume and smaller ones for bass, treble, and balance, simplifies operation of the STR-DE135. Sony includes a headphone jack for private listening and a bass boost to compensate for loss of bass at low listening levels. You can switch between two pairs of speakers with front panel buttons. The modest styling, rewarding performance, and ease-of-use make this receiver a good choice.

Warranty: 2 years, parts and labor
Manufacturer's Suggested Retail Price: $200
Approximate Low Price: $150

DOLBY PRO LOGIC RECEIVERS

Dolby Pro Logic receivers currently dominate the receiver market—they've never been more affordable. Within a couple of years they may be as rare as two-channel stereo models are today, thanks to the arrival of the superior Dolby Digital. All of the Pro Logic receivers we list are upgradable to Dolby Digital with an external adapter. Do not buy a receiver that lacks the requisite audio inputs on the rear panel for connecting an adapter.

Technics SA-AX730

The Technics SA-AX730 five-channel home theater receiver contains enough power and features to please any home theater enthusiast. The SA-AX730 produces 100 watts for each of the five channels. The receiver handles both 8-ohm and 4-ohm speakers, and has a bit of extra power for loud volume peaks. Technics' proprietary enhanced Class H+ amplifier design makes this possible at such an affordable price. The extra power for the surround channels means stunning reproduction of movie soundtracks with the unit's Dolby Pro Logic decoder. Technics uses higher quality capacitors in the SA-AX730 than in last year's model, which it claims improve sound quality, although it probably is not noticeable in casual listening. It adapts to and synthesizes a variety of surround modes, as well as theater, hall, and club ambience. It contains all the necessary test modes for setting up Pro Logic, and variable surround delay time for adjusting the system to your room and listening position and a subwoofer output for adding a subwoofer. The forward-looking design of the SA-AX730 contains six audio input jacks for use with DVD players or digital TVs that contain built-in Dolby Digital decoders. Thus you can have immediate Dolby Digital, or any other future multi-channel theater system, by simply buying an appropriately equipped player or adapter. The receiver can handle three audio/video and four audio inputs. You can plug a phono turntable into one of the audio inputs. We particularly like this unit's help function. Pushing a single red button activates the multicolor fluorescent display, which tells you why you're not hearing anything, and holding it down returns all settings to "normal" and switches on the FM tuner. Pushing a memory button helps the unit remember your preferred settings. The respectable frequency synthesized FM tuner is the same as that found on most other Technics receivers. Direct access from the home-theater remote control simplifies setting the tuner's 30 radio station presets. Even with its myriad features, the front panel remains reasonably uncomplicated, although the display puts on quite a light show, displaying the relative volume levels of the five channels. Technics supplies a 44-key pre-programmed universal audio/video remote control. Note that Technics' more expensive model is sonically similar, but includes Dolby Digital.

Warranty: 1 year, parts and labor
Manufacturer's Suggested Retail Price: $300
Approximate Low Price: $230-$250

JVC RX-558VBK

| Recommended |

The JVC RX-558VBK Dolby Pro Logic surround sound receiver cuts the frills, but still manages good performance at an affordable price. It produces 100 watts per channel for the front three channels and 50 watts for the rear surround channel. It is Dolby Digital-ready, with five discrete rear-channel inputs. Besides the built-in Dolby Pro Logic processor, JVC offers four digital acoustics processor (JVC's terminology for digital signal processing, or DSP) sonic environments, such as concert hall or theater. If you want to use the RX-558VBK as simply a two-channel receiver, JVC's 3D-PHONIC Virtual Dolby Surround can create an impressive surround effect from just two speakers. Although not true surround sound, the illusion might tide you over until you have the funds or space for the surround speakers. JVC continues to incorporate increasing amounts of digital technology in many of its formerly analog products. The receiver switches three audio and two audio/video inputs. You can preset 30 FM and 15 AM radio stations. The universal remote is well laid-out and reasonably easy to use. Although there's a large, easy-to-grasp, motor-driven volume knob, all other operation requires pressing buttons and tapping the four large cursor keys arranged in a cluster near the volume knob. The tuner section is about average, which these days is more than satisfactory for most listeners. Overall, the RX-558VBK makes a good entry for an affordable home theater system.

Warranty: 2 years, parts and labor
Manufacturer's Suggested Retail Price: $230
Approximate Low Price: $190-$200

DOLBY DIGITAL RECEIVERS

Dolby Digital receivers provide equal power on all five channels. There are probably fewer sonic differences between Dolby Digital decoders than Pro Logic decoders. Since manufacturers endow their best models with Dolby Digital we find most Dolby Digital receivers deliver excellent sound.

The system reproduces six channels, but not all of them are equal; thus you may see the nomenclature Dolby Digital 5.1. Technically, the .1 is designated the "low frequency effects" (LFE) channel, which means it is not a full-range channel and only carries the lowest frequencies intended for the subwoofer. Although you will appreciate the benefits of a subwoofer, it's presence is not necessary to fully enjoy the five other channels of the Dolby Digital system. Those channels also contain plenty of bass, so you won't miss all the thrills and chills.

Sony STR-DE835

✓BEST BUY

Sony loads the STR-DE835 with sound and features. All five channels deliver 100 watts in 8- or 4-ohm speakers. Sony uses both 24-bit and 32-bit digital signal processing (DSP) to offer a whopping 27 acoustic environments. The 32-bit DSP power enables Sony's proprietary Digital Cinema Sound system, based on measurements and knowledge gleaned from its Sony Pictures Studios in Hollywood in optimizing the movie theater experience for the home. Virtual 3D processing compensates for the difference between the many speakers used for surround in movie theaters and the two used in the home. The Dolby Digital processing offers all the adjustments inherent in the system, including the ability to match bass output to your speakers. This year's model adds DTS as well. To input the Dolby Digital from your DVD player or Digital TV, there are both optical and coaxial digital inputs. There are seven analog inputs, including a phono input. There are even dual subwoofer outputs, and a special surround output for optional wireless surround speakers that Sony sells. This is an important feature, as some DVD players have only one or the other. Sony puts all of its effort in the home theater area. The rest of this receiver, such as phono preamplifier and tuner, are identical to Sony's least expensive surround sound models. There are 30 radio station presets and you can direct-access tune by using the numeric keypad on the front panel or remote control. The remote control is quite advanced and unusual. The two-way pre-programmed universal remote contains an LCD screen that duplicates some of the information from the front-panel LED. You can group stations by musical category and see the category displayed on the remote. The surface layer of the remote is simple and logical. The lower layer contains the lesser used (and more confusing) controls. A large front panel knob controls volume, and a jog dial simplifies rapid cycling through different functions.

Warranty: 2 years, parts and labor
Manufacturer's Suggested Retail Price: $480
Approximate Low Price: $330-$400

COMPACT DISC PLAYERS

The compact disc rapidly evolved from a technological novelty to a fact of life. In less than two decades, it vanquished the analog phonograph record and the cassette to become our primary way of buying music. A small clique of audiophiles still worship the LP, but now most CDs surpass the sound quality of LPs and analog tapes. Most obviously, the laser-scanned CD eliminates the annoying noise and hiss of analog recordings, not to mention the clicks and pops of vinyl records. If you hear hiss on some CDs, it originates from the analog master tape recording (some CDs originate from analog masters, although most are now digitally mastered). Inaudible distortion and flat (uniform) frequency response contribute to CD's popularity, along with the disc's incredible convenience and ease of use. Furthermore, CDs contribute no wow or flutter (distracting speed variations and inaccuracies that cause a wavering of pitch) to the sound.

CD changers dominate the market, far overshadowing sales of single-disc players. Unlike LP changers, CD changers play without compromise and they cause no additional wear to the discs. Since changers sell for only a small premium over single-disc players there is little reason not to choose a changer. Only in the audiophile realm do single-disc players hold their own.

CAROUSEL CD CHANGERS

Carousel CD changers load discs on a large tray and rotate them into playing position. The mechanism lifts the disc from the tray and places it on a turntable inside the unit where the laser scans it. This permits the tray to rotate while the disc plays, allowing you to change discs. There are minimal differences between models. They compete on how fast they can change discs, but the differences between brands are not much more than one second or two. The original carousel changers used a hinged lid that you lifted to access the CDs. This prevented stacking the changer beneath other components. Contemporary models all use a drawer system. Carousel changers, introduced about a decade ago, prove impressively reliable.

MEGA CD CHANGERS_____

A recent development in the CD market, mega-changers store anywhere from 50 to 200 discs. Increasingly, manufacturers allow you to daisy-chain two or three changers to create mammoth 600-disc changers. Change time from one disc to another on the opposite side of the changer takes about ten seconds; some changers operate faster than others.

Nearly all models reserve one slot for impromptu disc loading, so that you don't have to unload one disc to listen to a new one. Manufacturers allow you to categorize discs loaded in the mega-changer by music type or family member or both. Many also provide notebooks or albums for storing the CD booklets. Many now display CD text, or allow you to enter your own titles and artists.

SINGLE-PLAY CD PLAYERS

Sony CDP-XA20ES ✔ BEST BUY

The Sony CDP-XA20ES single-play CD player strongly resembles Sony's most expensive player in basic technology and features for roughly one-quarter the price. The difference is that the CDP-XA20ES is not as ruggedly built and does not use the same hand-selected parts. You lose more status than sound. While we admit that the CDP-XA20ES costs more than most single-disc players, we think people desiring a single-play machine are more interested in high performance than low price. The CDP-XA20ES represents a longer-term investment than players in the $200-$400 range because of its significantly better construction quality. For example, the CDP-XA20ES uses an anti-resonant frame-and-beam construction in a rather substantial chassis to resist vibration and shock. The fixed-pickup laser tracking keeps the laser stationary while the disc moves beneath it on a motor-driven sled. This reduces vibration and increases stability, resulting in fewer digital errors. The CDP-XA20ES employs eight advanced current-pulse digital-to-analog converters, which cancel distortion when their outputs add together. The 8x-oversampling, three-stage, feed-forward digital filter with 20-bit outputs greatly reduces noise and distortion. This player takes CD distortion to virtually its lowest possible level. One interesting new feature is a knob, which Sony calls a "jog dial," that you twist or spin to select tracks, rather than pressing numbered keys. Once you become used to the jog dial, pressing keys seems cumbersome. Of course, you'll also find the rest of the features you'd expect on a pricey CD player, including keys on the remote control that offer 12-key direct access. You can program 32 tracks, aided by the 15-track music calendar on the fluorescent display. There are six play modes and eight repeat modes, along with computerized time editing and peak search for optimal cassette recordings. Digital outputs enable flawless recordings to MiniDisc or CD recorders.

Warranty: 5 years, parts and labor
Manufacturer's Suggested Retail Price: $700
Approximate Low Price: $599

Technics SL-PG480A

Budget Buy

Just because the Technics SL-PG480A rates as a Budget Buy doesn't mean you sacrifice sound or performance. It could just as easily have been rated a Best Buy. If the SL-PG480A runs true to previous Technics models, it should last an impressively long time for a budget model. Technics uses its recently upgraded MASH one-bit digital-to-analog converter technology, now called S-Advanced MASH Class A, for low distortion and noise. This technology is coupled with Technics' amazingly effective digital servo that keeps the laser focused on the disc, even on imperfect or warped discs, reducing digital errors and mistracking. The player skips between the first and last track with lightning speed. The player includes a Peak Level Search for setting recording levels. You can program 20 tracks, and the player will automatically cue for taping. The multi-function fluorescent display shows track numbers and various timings. It includes the expected random and repeat play functions. The player responds quickly to your commands and sounds good. It even includes a full-function remote control.

Warranty: 1 year, parts and labor
Manufacturer's Suggested Retail Price: $150
Approximate Low Price: $130

CAROUSEL CD CHANGERS

Technics SL-PD8

✓**BEST BUY**

The Technics SL-PD8 five-disc carousel CD changer continues an unbroken string of Technics hits. The company's nearly totally automated factory consistently turns out well-made, surprisingly durable CD players. Technics was one of the innovators of carousel changers, and many generations later has refined it to near perfection. Technics has cut down cost without noticeable compromises in performance. This year's model sells for the same price as last year's model. Bi-directional Quick Disc Rotation reduces change time from one disc to another to about seven seconds. It complements the Technics' lightning-fast ability to skip from the first to last track on a disc. You can swap four discs while one plays. It even has a pitch adjustment, a rarity on CD players. An easy-to-read disc location display clearly shows how many discs are loaded and which is playing. The disc selection buttons have two-color LED indicators. Technics provides a plethora of playing choices, including full random play, single-disc random play, or a Spiral play, which plays all the first tracks from each disc, followed by the second, third, fourth, and so forth. You can even program the changer to delete tracks in the random mode. Similarly, the repeat mode can also repeat individual tracks, discs, or programmed sequences. The ID scan mode samples the loudest, and presumably more recognizable, portion of each track. Direct disc and track access keys, logically arrayed in "telephone style" on the front panel and the wireless remote, make 32-track programming from any or all of the loaded discs easier. The Edit Guide feature computes optimum track arrangement for taping. Technics backs up all these features with good sound from its proprietary MASH single-bit digital-to-analog converters. Its advanced digital servo accurately controls the laser pickup for low digital errors. This feature and a decent suspension allow the player to resist minor shocks and vibration. Technics incorporates an optical digital output.

Warranty: 1 year, parts and labor
Manufacturer's Suggested Retail Price: $170
Approximate Low Price: $150

Onkyo DX-C540

✔**BEST BUY**

Onkyo wisely decided that if five discs were good, then six discs were better when designing the DX-C540 carousel changer. It handles six discs as well as other players that only change five discs. In the process, Onkyo's Accupulse Quartz System single-bit digital-to-analog converters with Fine Pulse Conversion System 8x oversampling digital filters provide natural-sounding music. You can change three of the six discs while one plays. You can program 40 tracks from among the six discs, assisted by a 20-track music calendar on the fluorescent display. The "drawer-under" layout keeps the player's highly legible, four-mode display visible while changing discs. Or you can select one of the six repeat modes or random-shuffle play. The Next Selection control permits choosing the next track to be played without interrupting the track currently playing. Playing or programming tracks is easy with the direct-disc and track-access buttons on the front panel and supplied remote. The player's Music File will remember your favorite tracks on up to 202 discs. Not only will the peak-level search find the loudest portion of the disc for setting recording levels, but it will repeat the segment until you complete the level setting.

Warranty: 1 year, parts and labor
Manufacturer's Suggested Retail Price: $320
Approximate Low Price: $285

Denon DCM-370

Recommended

We chose the Denon DCM-370 five-disc carousel CD changer for its solid construction and performance. It includes

110

fewer features than competing models, thus lowering it to Recommended status. This changer uses a premium American-made digital-to-analog converter with a 20-bit 8x oversampling digital filter. This arrangement produces clear, clean sound. However, what sets this changer apart is that it's one of the first to include HDCD decoding, a technology that improves CD sound and is encoded on an increasing number of CDs. A rival company demands $500 for a changer with HDCD. Denon's digital servo keeps the laser focused on the disc even when playing imperfect discs or when the player experiences minor shock and vibration. There's a coaxial digital output that enables upgrading the player with an outboard digital-to-analog converter (although the quality of the D/A in this player makes that rather senseless). The digital output can be used for direct digital recording to MiniDisc or a CD recorder. Denon offers three-mode random play and five-way repeat, plus intelligent disc scan that lets you automatically sample the discs. If you're throwing a party, you can have music all night in the players continuous-play mode. A digital attenuator (volume control) lets you connect the DCM-370 directly to a power amplifier if you desire maximum sound quality. The blue fluorescent display provides disc, track, and timing information, along with a 20-track music calendar. Denon keeps the button count to ten on the front panel.

Warranty: 2 years, parts and labor
Manufacturer's Suggested Retail Price: $299
Approximate Low Price: $250

Technics SL-PD6

The Technics SL-PD6 five-disc carousel changer is **Budget Buy** basically the same as the Best Buy SL-PD8 without a few of the features, such as the Edit Guide taping convenience and ID scan. Bi-directional Quick Disc Rotation reduces change time from one disc to another to about seven seconds. It complements the Technics' lightning-fast ability to skip from the first to last track on a disc. You can swap four discs while one plays. An easy-to-read disc-location display clearly shows how many discs are loaded and which disc is playing. The disc selection buttons have two-color LED indicators. Technics provides a plethora of playing choices, including full random play, single-disc random play, or a Spiral play that plays all the first tracks from each disc, followed by second, third, fourth, and so on. You can even program the changer to delete tracks in the random mode. Similarly, the repeat mode can also repeat individual tracks, discs, or programmed sequences. You can program 32 tracks on this changer. Technics backs up the features with good sound from its proprietary MASH single-bit digital-to-analog converters. Its advanced digital servo accurately controls the laser pickup for low digital errors. This feature and a decent suspension allow the player to resist minor shocks and vibration. It even includes an optical digital output. The only inconvenience that drops this from Best to Budget Buy is the lack of a remote control, although direct track access is still available from the telephone-style keypad on the front panel.

Warranty: 1 year, parts and labor
Manufacturer's Suggested Retail Price: $150
Approximate Low Price: $130

MEGA CD CHANGERS

Pioneer PD-F908
✔ **BEST BUY**

The Pioneer PD-F908 101-disc changer performs its duties with aplomb. The PD-F908 is basically a 100-disc changer with a single-disc slot in its roulette rack mechanism. You can group CDs into three categories in Pioneer's CD File Custom Mode. An unusual feature is "previous disc scan," which samples ten seconds of the last 20 discs to which you've listened, starting with the most recent. Hi-Lite Scan plays back a minute or so of the first track on each disc or the each track on every disc, or just tracks and discs selected for Best Selection Memory. You create this memory by pressing the Best Selection key while listening. The player memorizes up to 20 tracks. You can program 36 tracks, and play any or all discs in random mode and a quartet of repeat modes. Convenience doesn't compromise sound. Pioneer uses its proprietary one-bit Direct Linear Conversion along with digital filters for good sound. The PD-F908 includes an optical digital output.

Warranty: 1 year, parts and labor
Manufacturer's Suggested Retail Price: $250
Approximate Low Price: $175

Kenwood CD-3260M

Recommended

The Kenwood CD-3260M 200-disc changer not only performs well, but it might be the most attractive mega-changer on the market. Its smooth, curvaceous, platinum-colored front panel contains only seven keys and a jog shuttle knob, along with the power button. You can change 199 of the discs while one plays. The unit displays CD text if the CD is so encoded, and you can label 20 tracks per disc, plus you can name 210 of your favorite discs. The CD-3260M comes with a mind-boggling 26 music categories, and it still permits you to define 8 of your own categories. Direct disc access is possible from the front panel, and direct track access from the supplied remote. You can program 32 tracks. Kenwood uses basic one-bit digital-to-analog converters with 8x oversampling digital filters for respectable sound. The player includes a digital audio output. Although it comes with a basic remote, when used with one of Kenwood's fancy LCD system remotes it will display information and text on the remote.

Warranty: 1 year, parts and labor
Manufacturer's Suggested Retail Price: $300
Approximate Low Price: not available

Technics SL-MC4

Budget Buy

The Technics SL-MC4 60-disc changer is similar to our Best Buy. It sounds the same, and the mechanism is similar, although the Technics has fewer features. It still can zip from one disc to any other disc in 11 seconds or less. The SL-MC4's optical disc-detection system scans the disc compartments every time you turn the power on, memorizing empty slots, thus reducing change time. The front panel flips down, revealing the CD slots, and you can replace or rearrange any of the other discs while one plays. A single-play slot lets you insert and play a CD without finding an empty storage slot or removing an already-loaded disc. You can electronically group discs into one of 14 musical categories, such as rock, jazz, country, and dance. A disc can be in more than one category. The SL-MC4 displays CD text if the record company has included it on the disc, or you can add your own electronic disc titles. You can program 32 tracks, even while a disc plays. A convenient telephone-style keypad in the center of the front panel makes selecting discs, tracks, and programming easy. You can select random play from a single disc or all the discs within a group. The SL-MC4 also offers repeat play of a track or disc and ID scan, which plays the loudest and most recognizable passage from each song on a disc. Technics backs up these features with good sound from its proprietary MASH single-bit digital-to-analog converters and noise-shaping digital filters. Its advanced digital servo accurately controls the laser pickup for low digital errors. This feature and a decent suspension allow the player to resist minor shocks and vibration. The SL-MC4 comes with a 37-key full-function remote control and an attractive portfolio to hold the booklets from the jewel boxes.

Warranty: 1 year, parts and labor
Manufacturer's Suggested Retail Price: $180
Approximate Low Price: not available

CASSETTE DECKS

Cassettes could whimsically be called "the people's format." They are cheap, easy to use, and universal. Since being introduced by Philips in the early 1960s as a low fidelity dictation medium, cassettes matured into a true high fidelity contender by the 1980s, thanks to Dolby noise reduction and improved tape formulations. However, the ever-increasing portability of CDs, along with the newer digital Mini-

Disc format, pose formidable challenges to the cassette. Manufacturers noting decreased interest in cassette decks released the fewest new models in 1998 since the format took off in the 1980s, and the new models that did arrive contained fewer features, such as the Dolby S noise reduction.

SINGLE-TRANSPORT CASSETTE DECKS_____

We list single cassette decks solely for people serious about recording. We chose decks that offer the maximum fidelity and flexibility. There remain a few ultimate single decks with prices over $1,000, but we cannot justify this in the age of digital recording. The decks listed here make great recordings at a reasonable price and have the features that help you get the most from your recordings. Dolby B and C noise reduction and HX-Pro headroom extension are mandatory, and Dolby S is preferred for serious recording. Decks should have at least two motors. Real-time tape counters that show you how much actual tape time you've been recording or how much time is left on the tape are a desirable feature. All decks should smoothly and assuredly handle tape and never jam.

DUAL-TRANSPORT CASSETTE DECKS_____

Dual-transport cassette decks became the rage a decade ago when people began duplicating tapes, and they nearly eclipsed single-transport cassette decks. They offered a bargain since each transport could share common parts, making the cost only one-third to one-half more than a single deck. A good dual-transport deck should have many of the same features as a good single deck. In addition it should have auto-reverse on both transports. We think that dual-transport decks should offer the added utility of being able to record as well as play on both transports. This permits more than three hours of virtually uninterrupted recording, or making two copies of a third source (such as a CD) simultaneously. Many of the decks we list include this feature. All dual-transport decks can high-speed copy tapes in half the normal playing time. However, even on the best decks, high-speed copies lose more fidelity than copies made at standard speed.

TAPES

Always buy brand-name tapes. The brands we recommend include Fuji, JVC, Maxell, Sony, and TDK. Some companies add a bit more zing to the treble with certain tapes, such as TDK tapes that end in an X (SA-X) or Maxell tapes that end in an S (UD-XLIIS).

FEATURES AND TERMINOLOGY

Bias, Equalization, and Level-setting Adjustments: These adjustments are not available on all cassette decks; however, some tape decks offer fine-tuning controls that allow you to adjust for slight differences in the bias of recording tapes. Other decks control adjustments with microprocessor chips. These circuits test the tape and adjust for the optimum bias, equalization, and sensitivity to provide the best performance from a tape.

Distortion: Distortion is quoted by tape deck manufacturers at a -20 dB recording level, which is lower than the level at which most people record. (A few specs quote a more realistic 0 dB level.) Many manufacturers advise recording peaks as high as +5 dB.

Frequency Response: Frequency response is sometimes improved at the expense of distortion and signal-to-noise ratio. But achieving the true hi-fi range of 20 to 20,000 hertz may not mean the overall quality is better, since most humans (especially as they get older) cannot hear much above 15,000 hertz and few instruments other than a grand pipe organ produce tones that go much below 30 hertz. When comparing the frequency responses of two different machines, be sure the response of each machine is accompanied by a tolerance, usually stated as plus or minus a certain number of decibels (dB); otherwise the frequency response statement is meaningless.

Noise Reduction Systems: Even with the very best cassette tape used in a superior cassette recorder, you will probably notice some tape hiss, or noise, when playing back your recordings. Hiss, which occurs where the human ear is most sensitive (in the upper midrange and treble), is especially noticeable during playback of softer musical passages. Although several noise-reduction technologies competed during the cassette's early days, Dolby noise reduction proved the most viable. Different levels of noise reduction from Dolby Laboratories are now standard on all cassette decks. Dolby A is a very expensive professional noise-reduction system not used in consumer cassette decks.

Dolby B reduces high-frequency (treble) noise by 5 to 10 decibels; this is equivalent to perceiving about a 50-percent reduction in high-frequency noise. Tapes recorded in Dolby B can be played back on non-Dolby players with only a slight sonic aberration.

Dolby C reduces both midrange and high-frequency noise by about 10 decibels, but it sounds as if it reduced noise twice as much as Dolby B. It also slightly lowers distortion on high-frequency peaks. While Dolby C-encoded tapes can be played back with some success using Dolby B, they sound unpleasant when played back on machines lacking any Dolby decoding.

Dolby S reduces noise throughout the audible range and as much as 20 decibels in high frequencies. It also significantly reduces distortion. Dolby S is the consumer version of the Dolby SR professional noise-reduction system. Dolby requires a basic standard of quality for cassette decks equipped with Dolby S. Tapes recorded on these decks approach digital sound quality, with dramatically low noise and distortion. Dolby S cannot eliminate speed variations such as wow and flutter. Dolby S tapes can be played back through Dolby B or C with reasonable success. Although its full benefits won't be realized, the sound quality is acceptable.

Dolby HX-Pro is a headroom expansion (HX) system that, unlike noise-reduction systems, is single-ended. That means it works only during recording and needs no decoding on playback. Dolby HX-Pro adjusts the recording current, or bias, to allow higher levels of high frequencies on the tape, while lowering distortion. A by-product of this is a subtle reduction of noise. A cassette deck with HX-Pro will greatly assist your efforts to make superior tape recordings. It is now becoming standard on all but the least expensive cassette decks.

Signal-to-Noise Ratio (S/N): S/N ratios often use the -20 dB recording level as a reference. Choose a deck with better than 60 dB S/N ratio when the Dolby noise reduction is switched off. To enjoy the best sound from the tape deck you have selected, use the brand and type of tape recommended by the manufacturer, or have a technician adjust the machine for your favorite type of tape. Avoid bargain-brand tapes—not only will they lower sound quality, they can potentially damage the machine.

3-Head Cassette Decks: These decks have one head for erasing, one for recording, and a third for playback. This arrangement provides the same sort of rapid off-the-tape monitoring capability found on professional open-reel machines. Using a separate head for each function also improves performance by permitting the use of specialized heads for record and play.

Wow and Flutter: A measurement of tape-speed fluctuation, wow and flutter is usually listed as a percentage, followed by the acronym WRMS. For example, a wow-and-flutter specification might read 1/10% WRMS. Look for the lowest percentage available within your budget limitations.

SINGLE-TRANSPORT CASSETTE DECKS

Sony TC-KE500S

✔**BEST BUY**

The Sony TC-KE500S is a high-performance, full-featured single-transport cassette deck. However, this is a three-head deck, which permits tape monitoring while recording, and the specialization of the tape heads for maximum fidelity. In addition to the expected Dolby B and C noise reduction and HX-Pro headroom extension, it includes the less common Dolby S, the ultimate consumer noise-reduction system. This lets you record tapes with very wide dynamic range and impressively low noise. You can play back tapes recorded with Dolby S on machines with Dolby B; although you lose the benefits of Dolby S, the tape still sounds pretty good. Unfortunately, this is one of the last decks on the market with

Dolby S. We regret that this deck lacks automatic tape tuning, which adjusts the deck's electronics to the specific tape on which you wish to record. You can manually adjust the bias, a task most people will skip. The two-motor transport with full-logic controls features high-speed fast forward and rewind. Sony keeps the cassette rigidly seated with a ceramic cassette holder and reduces vibrations with a Sorbothane cassette stabilizer. The real-time tape counter reads in minutes and seconds.

Warranty: 1 year, parts and labor
Manufacturer's Suggested Retail Price: $360
Approximate Low Price: $305

Denon DRM-740

Recommended

The Denon DRM-740 single transport cassette deck combines the features we demand from a single deck (from which we expect more than a double deck) at a reasonable price. It has the obligatory Dolby B and C noise reduction and HX-Pro headroom extension. Unfortunately, Denon dropped Dolby S, the ultimate consumer noise-reduction system, which was on a previous year's model. Nonetheless, the DRM-740 enables recording tapes with very wide dynamic range and impressively low noise. Denon provides a manual bias fine-tuning control to match the deck's electronics to specific tapes, but we suspect most users will skip this feature. The three-motor, microprocessor-controlled, full-logic mechanism handles tapes smoothly. The DRM-740 includes music search, memory stop, and the ability to automatically return to where you started recording if you make a mistake and want to record over. Wide fluorescent record-level indicators, along with a large record-level setting knob, aid in setting levels. A real-time tape counter is part of the display, letting you know tape times in minutes and seconds. The headphone jack has a volume control.

Warranty: 1 year, parts and labor
Manufacturer's Suggested Retail Price: $399
Approximate Low Price: $275

DUAL-TRANSPORT CASSETTE DECKS

Sony TC-WE835S

✔**BEST BUY**

The Sony TC-WE835S dual-transport cassette deck with Dolby S noise reduction and four motors is truly a Best Buy. It costs $100 less than last year's model with most of the same features, performance, and functionality. As indicated by the model number, the TC-WE835S incorporates Dolby S noise reduction in addition to the standard Dolby B and C, and HX-Pro headroom extension. The TC-WE835S also includes real-time tape counters, along with pitch control and Sony's high-speed winding mechanism. Unlike Sony's single-transport deck, this deck auto-calibrates, tuning its electronics to match the specific tape on which you record. Both dual auto-reverse decks record and play on both transports, enabling sequential recording and parallel recording. The TC-WE835S uses two motors and two heads in each transport for smooth, steady tape handling and good fidelity. Full-logic, feather-touch controls provide easy operation, and further assure good tape handling. Auto-record level control optimizes levels for lowest noise and distortion. You can program these decks to play songs in any order you choose. The TC-WE835S promises durability, as it has two motors for each transport. The headphone jacks lack volume controls.

Warranty: 1 year, parts and labor
Manufacturer's Suggested Retail Price: $300
Approximate Low Price: $250

Technics RS-TR575

✔**BEST BUY**

The Technics RS-TR575 stands out as an exceptional value among dual-transport cassette decks. All that's missing on this high-performance deck is a headphone jack and more colorful markings to differentiate the controls. Its forte is sound quality, made possible not only by proper design, but also by one of the most accurate automated tape-calibration circuits on the market. The RS-TR575 precisely adjusts its electronics for whatever tape you place in the machine. This noticeably improves fidelity. This deck plays and records (and automatically calibrates) on both transports, for parallel or serial recording. It loads tape automatically, like a VCR, and handles tape rapidly and smoothly. Each transport's dual-motor design contributes to making it one of the fastest-winding decks on the market, at nearly twice the speed of many others. (Rewinding a C-60 takes 50 seconds.) The feather-touch, full-logic controls quickly translate your commands to accurate responses. The deck includes Dolby B and C noise reduction as well as HX-Pro. The twin electronic real-time tape counters let you know where you are on the tapes in minutes and seconds. Sound quality and operation are exemplary for a deck in this price range. We only wish Technics would add Dolby S.

Warranty: 1 year, parts and labor
Manufacturer's Suggested Retail Price: $270
Approximate Low Price: $240

Onkyo TA-RW544

Recommended

The Onkyo TA-RW544 dual-transport cassette deck delivers solid performance with all essential features. Since both auto-reverse decks record and play, you can make serial and parallel recordings. The deck comes with Dolby B and C noise reduction and HX-Pro headroom extension. The deck uses four motors and handles tape swiftly and smoothly. The electronic counter is part of the fluorescent display, but it does not indicate real time. The headphone jack lacks a volume control. You cannot custom tune the electronics to the tape. However, even without these features, this deck makes a good-sounding tape and is blissfully simple to operate.

Warranty: 1 year, parts and labor
Manufacturer's Suggested Retail Price: $350
Approximate Low Price: $299

MiniDisc DECKS

In 1998, dozens of new MiniDisc (MD) models from nearly a dozen companies appeared on the market, perhaps an indicator that MD's time has arrived. For a number of years only Sony and Sharp marketed MD in the United States. Ahead of its time when introduced seven years ago, MD may yet become a successful format.

Many critics, and subsequently most of the public, leapt to the conclusion that Sony intended MD to replace CD. It took awhile for Sony to realize MD was the ideal replacement for the cassette, not the CD. The MD is to the CD what the cassette was to the LP: a highly portable, recordable medium.

HOW IT WORKS

This innovative technology digitally records (and rerecords) up to 74 minutes in stereo (the same amount that is stored on a CD) on a 2½-inch disc encased in a protective caddy like a computer diskette. The player uses a laser and a magnetic head, similar to a tape head, to record on the disc. MD is as easy, if not easier, to use as a CD, with nearly instant access to desired tracks, and programming capability. Recordable MDs perform some of the same tricks as computer diskettes, permitting nonsequential recording on any blank space on the disc. You can also reorder selections on the MD without rerecording or programming, as well as electronically label discs and tracks.

All MD players use a "shock-resistant memory" to perform their computerlike functions and improve portability. These memory chips store from 10 to 40 seconds of sound. Shake or jar the player and the music just keeps playing. This makes MD a more effective portable medium than CD.

THE FUTURE OF MD

Because of initially high prices and failure to understand the format, minuscule MD sales nearly doomed its existence. However, the Japanese public now enthusiastically embraces MD, making it wildly successful in its homeland. Europeans also are showing interest. Many broadcasters in the United States have replaced tape cartridge machines with MD. This increasing success has resulted in falling prices for the players and discs, and holds some hope for acceptance of the format here.

Sony MDS-JE530
✔ **BEST BUY**

Sony leaves few features off its MDS-JE530 Mini-Disc deck, yet it sells at an exceptionally low price. The MDS-JE530 sells for $60 less than last year's model, yet has the same features and better sound quality. To ensure its sound quality surpasses analog tape and will rival CD, Sony uses its latest Hybrid Pulse 24-bit digital-to-analog converter and newest generation of the ATRAC compression algorithm, "Type R," which makes MD possible. It uses an improved 24-bit analog-to-digital converter for recording, verses last year's 20-bit analog-to-digital converter. The deck has one optical digital input and one optical digital output, along with the standard analog inputs and outputs. It even uses a sampling rate converter, so it will accept the direct digital output of CD or DAT. Sony also provides a digital input level control, a rarity among digital recorders, which lets you optimize levels in the digital domain. While casual recordists best leave this feature alone, serious recordists will find it very useful. The MDS-JE530 includes all the unique features of MD, such as being able to combine, divide, move, and selectively erase tracks. You can even undo a mistake. Sony uses the MD memory, which gives you a six-second reprieve if you hear a song come on the radio you want to tape. Assuming the deck is on, you can start recording six-seconds into the song, and still capture the whole song to disc. The two-line display shows disc and track titles. You can enter your own titles by scrolling through the alphabet using the jog dial, which speeds up an otherwise arduous task. The same jog dial assists in automatic music search, letting you skip forward or back to your favorite tracks. Not only does this deck record up to the normal 74-minute maximum in stereo, but it will record up to 148 minutes in mono. A timer switch enables unattended recording or play when used with an external timer. The unit includes a headphone jack with volume control. Sony supplies a remote control.

Warranty: 1 year, parts and labor
Manufacturer's Suggested Retail Price: $300
Approximate Low Price: $285

Denon DMD-1000

Recommended

Denon is one of the few companies other than Sony to have experience with MiniDisc, and the DMD-1000 demonstrates that. Denon has made MD decks for radio stations, as well as a previous consumer model. Denon stresses its digital expertise with the DMD-1000 using its proprietary Enhanced Dual-Bit Delta Sigma 20-bit analog-to-digital converters in the recording stage, and its Advanced Super Linear Converter for digital-to-analog in playback. In another enhancement, Denon includes both optical and coaxial digital inputs along with an optical digital output, and the standard analog inputs and outputs. The sampling rate converter enables recording from any digital source, such as CD or DAT. Another Denon attribute is its Disc Recovery function, which salvages most of the recording time that normally is lost bit by bit as an MD is edited and rerecorded. Of course, the DMD-1000 includes MD features, such as combining, dividing, moving, and selectively erasing tracks. You can even undo a mistake. Should you be in a rush to record you can set the deck to begin recording as soon as you insert a disc. Denon allows you to electronically label discs and tracks. You can record the standard 74 minutes in stereo, or 148 minutes in mono. You can program 25 tracks, or select random or repeat modes. Although somewhat more expensive than the entry-level MD decks, the DMD-1000 comes strongly Recommended.

Warranty: 1 year
Manufacturer's Suggested Retail Price: $499
Approximate Low Price: not available

STEREO SYSTEMS

Sometimes you just can't decide among the array of stereo components available and would rather purchase your sound system as a single package. Most manufacturers market a wide array of complete systems in an equally wide range of prices. The packaged system, once called a "rack system" because it came in a rack inside of a cabinet, now comes in many monikers. Many still come in a cabinet. The advantage of a single-brand system is that you know that the manufacturer designed all the components to work optimally together, and often it represents a good value. (However, some manufacturers cut corners on these systems in ways not always evident, reducing the actual value.) Usually the systems come prewired, or require minimal wiring, making installation and setup a breeze. For people who desire music and/or movie surround sound without electronic involvement, these systems offer a satisfying alternative.

BEST BUYS 2000

Our Best Buy, Recommended, and Budget Buy stereo systems follow. Products within each category are listed according to quality. The item we consider the best of the Best Buys is first, followed by our second choice, and so on. A Budget Buy describes a less-expensive product of respectable quality that perhaps sacrifices some of the performance and/or convenience features of a Best Buy or Recommended product. Remember that a Best Buy, Recommended, or Budget Buy designation only applies to the model listed—it does not necessarily apply to other models made by the same manufacturer or to an entire product line.

HOME THEATER SYSTEMS

Home theater systems still offer an array of choices for you to make concerning which components will serve your purposes. This includes whether you want just stereo or a complete home theater system. These days you'll search extensively to find a system that includes a phono turntable, even as an option. Multiple-CD changers now occupy the space originally given to single-disc players on all but the entry-level systems. Logic connections between components simplify operation. For example, the system automatically switches from radio to CD when you load a disc, or from CD to tape when you load a cassette. Most system interconnect the CD player and tape deck to simplify taping CDs. Usually the biggest compromises of a complete home theater system are the speakers, because most electronic manufacturers do not excel at speakers. Other sacrifices might include a cassette deck without Dolby C noise reduction, which is acceptable. Manufacturers often included features you don't need and will rarely, if ever, use, such as equalizers. Buying a complete system reduces the complexity of home theater, and frequently lowers the cost of admission. Complete home theater systems are becoming increasingly common and may replace basic stereo systems in a year or two.

Pioneer D4500K

✔ **BEST BUY**

Pioneer builds the full-size D4500K from separate components, which include its VSX-D498 receiver, CT-W103 dual-transport auto-reverse cassette deck, PD-F908 101-disc CD changer, and GR408 equalizer. The system includes Dolby Digital, making it a good value, especially at $200 less than the comparable system last year. Of course, you will have to add a DVD player or one of the forthcoming digital TVs to take advantage of this feature. Although built from separate components, Pioneer wires everything together and mounts it in a tall black cabinet that matches the height of the front three-way tower speakers with massive 15-inch woofers. It is also about the height of a 50-inch rear-projection TV, which Pioneer also will gladly sell you. Pioneer provides center channel and surround speakers. The VSX-D498 produces 70 watts for all five channels and has all the controls and flexibility of a stand-alone model. (It produces 100 watts per channel in two-channel stereo.) You can preset 30 radio stations. The tuner section is average, but does an acceptable job in most urban/suburban areas. Like its competitors, Pioneer has cheapened the cassette deck from last year's model in order to offer a more attractive price. The CT-W103 cassette deck includes Dolby B noise reduction. One transport records and plays, while the second only plays. We have selected the PD-F908 CD changer as a Best Buy; this unit is basically a 100-disc changer with a single-disc slot in its roulette-rack mechanism. You can group CDs into three categories in Pioneer's CD File Custom Mode. An unusual feature is "previous disc scan," which samples 10 seconds of the last 20 discs you've listened to, starting with the most recent. Hi-Lite Scan plays back a minute or so of the first track on each disc or each track on every disc, or just tracks and discs selected for Best Selection Memory. You create this memory by pressing the Best Selection key while listening. The player memorizes up to 20 tracks. You can program 36 tracks, and play any or all discs in random mode, and a quartet of repeat modes. Pioneer provides a seven-band equalizer, which is of questionable value. We think equalizers, although impressive looking and fun to play with, are largely ill-used or unnecessary. Altogether, Pioneer offers a pretty stunning system for the price with plenty of power, performance, and flexibility, and the bonus of Dolby Digital.

Warranty: 1 year, parts and labor
Manufacturer's Suggested Retail Price: $1,280
Approximate Low Price: $899

Sony R-4900

✔**BEST BUY**

The Sony R-4900 full-size system stands tall, about 40 inches. This complete Dolby Pro Logic surround system is Dolby Digital ready, meaning there are discrete audio inputs for all five channels on the back of the receiver. Sony builds the system from three independent components, including the STR-SE491 receiver, which produces 100 watts for each of the five channels. It has plenty of flexibility with six inputs and digital signal processing (DSP) for re-creating various acoustic environments such as movie theater or concert hall. The tuner section stores 30 radio station presets. The TC-WE471 dual-transport auto-reverse cassette deck records and plays on one transport and only plays on the other.

Both include Dolby B noise reduction and the recording transport uses HX-Pro headroom extension. Its piano key mechanical controls are a bit clunky, but Sony has economized on the cassette deck to improve the receiver. The deck is easy to use and still maintains decent tape handling. The CDP-CX681 CD changer handles a whopping 200 discs. You can divide them into groups by music type or family member. The jog dial on the front panel instead of number keys expedites finding your favorite disc or track and programming, or you can use the supplied full-function universal remote control if your prefer the number keys. The keys on the remote glow in the dark. You can program 32 tracks, and choose among three play and two repeat modes. The three-way main front speakers include a 12-inch woofer made from a special material that Sony claims improves bass response and lowers distortion. Sony houses the system in a black, wood-grain cabinet with a large glass door. You can choose the same system with Dolby Digital decoding built-in and a 300-CD changer as the R-5900 for $200 more.

Warranty: 1 year, parts and labor
Manufacturer's Suggested Retail Price: $950
Approximate Low Price: $830

Technics SC-S2250

Budget Buy

Technics always packs as much value into a product as technologically possible, and the SC-S2250 exemplifies this. The black cabinetry for this system is basic, but the components are not. Technics builds the system around the SA-G78 five-channel receiver with an equal 80 watts to all channels and Dolby Pro Logic decoder. That's ten watts more per channel than last year's model. It even comes with a pair of video inputs, so you're all set to connect your VCR, DVD player, or TV. You can preset 30 stations on the tuner. Beneath the receiver is a seven-band stereo graphic equalizer with enough red and green LEDs for Christmas. The LEDs show you the effects of your adjustments. Below the equalizer, Technics installs an auto-reverse dual-transport RS-TR180 cassette deck. Both transports play and one records, and both have Dolby B noise

128

reduction. The recording deck also has Dolby HX-Pro headroom extension. The decks gently power eject cassettes and have an electronic tape counter. Many people will find the automatic record level control a recording convenience. Finally, the system includes the SL-MC59 60+1-disc mega CD changer. You can load a single disc without removing one of the 60 discs. Like all Technics CD changers, this unit changes discs with impressively high speed. Changing discs is easy with the loader carriage, which slides out. The CD changer lets you divide your discs into 14 different subject groups and supplies a notebook for filing the CD booklets. It uses Technics MASH one-bit digital-to-analog converters. You can program 32 tracks, and it offers the standard array of random and repeat modes. The left and right front channel SB-A28 three-way speakers have 12-inch woofers and special tweeters that widely disperse the sound. Technics magnetically shields the speakers. The center and surround speakers are substantially smaller conventional boxes. Technics supplies a universal remote control. While the manufacturer's suggested retail price might seem high for a Budget Buy, common discounting of Technics systems places this well in budget territory. We believe it comes close to being a Best Buy.

Warranty: 1 year, parts and labor
Manufacturer's Suggested Retail Price: $900
Approximate Low Price: not available

MINI-/MIDI-SYSTEMS

Though small speakers struggle to produce the volume and bass of full-size speakers, they are closing the gap thanks to advances in electronics and small speaker design. Some manufacturers offer in-between, or midi-systems, which make it easier to include mega-CD changers and somewhat larger speakers. Mini-systems tend to make more compromises, such as including cassette decks without any noise reduction. Mini- and midi-systems restrict swapping, upgrading, or adding components. Most include only a single additional input. For people who desire music or movie surround sound without electronic involvement, these systems offer a satisfying alternative.

Aiwa XR-M88

✔**BEST BUY**

The Aiwa XR-M88, which Aiwa classifies as an ultra-mini system, combines the essentials with ear pleasing sound in an extremely handsome package at a modest price. The system comes in two halves that can be stacked or placed side by side. The system has a decent receiver, single-disc CD player, and single-transport cassette deck, along with matching two-way magnetically shielded speakers. The speakers radiate sound in an unusually wide pattern. Aiwa calls it 180-degree dispersion. The receiver produces 16 watts per channel, and includes Aiwa's proprietary BBE system, which adds punch to the sound, sometimes making it seem like it leaps from the speakers. There's also a preset graphic equalizer with rock/pop/jazz settings, and a three-position bass boost. You can preset 32 radio stations on the tuner. The top-loading CD player operates smoothly. You can program 20 tracks, and there are random and repeat play functions. The auto-reverse cassette deck, with its full-logic, feather-touch controls, comes with Dolby B noise reduction. A music sensor helps you locate your favorite selections on the tape. The styling is unusually handsome and conservative, without a surfeit of flashing lights. The electronics and speakers stand well under a foot high. Aiwa supplies a full-function remote control.

Warranty: 1 year, parts and labor
Manufacturer's Suggested Retail Price: $400
Approximate Low Price: $299

Denon D-M10

✔**BEST BUY**

We consider the Denon D-M10 a Best Buy, even though it is expensive, for two reasons. It's the only mini-system of which we know that comes with excellent speakers from a speaker specialist. It also comes with the option to add a matching MiniDisc deck. The three component D-M10 consists of the UDRA-M10 stereo receiver with 40 watts per channel, the UCDM-M10 three-disc CD changer, and the DRR-M10 single-transport cassette deck. The Mission 731i shelf speakers grace the fine electronics. The

731i speakers are similar to our highly rated Mission 701 speakers. The 731i is a two-way system with a 5¼-inch specially treated paper cone woofer and a one-inch silk dome tweeter. This year, Denon ups the power to 100 watts per channel without increasing price, further improving the system's value. The receiver has three audio inputs and a pair of audio outputs. The tuner section includes 40 radio station presets. A clock/timer permits unattended recording. The CD changer offers 20 track programming and random and repeat play. The cassette deck uses an unusual and elegant drawer loading mechanism. The deck incorporates Dolby B and C noise reduction, along with HX-Pro headroom extension. It will synchronize with the CD changer for easy CD recording. The music search feature locates your favorite selections on the tape. The optional DMD-M10 MiniDisc recorder ($499) offers 25 track programming, as well as random and repeat play. It incorporates all of the titling and versatile editing features inherent in the MiniDisc format. It matches the other M10 components and comes with its own remote control. Denon provides a universal remote as well. This system sounds distinctly better than the average mini-system, and is quite possible the best sounding stereo mini-system on the market.

Warranty: 1 year, electronics; 5 years, speakers
Manufacturer's Suggested Retail Price: $999
Approximate Low Price: $899

JVC MX-J30
✔ BEST BUY

The JVC MX-J30 mini-system fits nearly anywhere, providing music in home or office. It packs ample sound with plenty of flexibility into a very compact package. The MX-J30 combines a three-CD changer, AM/FM stereo tuner, cassette deck, amplifiers, and matching speakers finished in dark silver. We particularly like the concept of the changer, which loads each CD in a separate drawer, providing instant access to each disc. It uses JVC's standard one-bit digital-to-analog converter with 8× oversampling. You can program 20 tracks from any or all of the discs with the aid of a 16-track program chart, or you can have the player random play from any or all the discs. The digitally synthesized tuner has 45 presets (15 AM and 30 FM) that you can set or have the tuner set automatically. The dual auto-reverse cassette transports have full-logic electronic controls, but lack Dolby B noise reduction. It works in conjunction with the CD changer to record CDs. The amplifier section produces a mammoth 100 watts per channel, which is a lot of power from such a compact unit, and has three preset "live surround" modes that change the character and ambience of the music. There's also an auxiliary input, for such components as a hi-fi VCR. The fluorescent display includes a clock timer for auto shut-off in the sleep mode and wake-up. JVC supplies a full-function remote control. The custom matched speakers reproduce impressive sound.

Warranty: 1 year, parts and labor
Manufacturer's Suggested Retail Price: $280
Approximate Low Price: $240

Sony LBT-S3000

Recommended

The Sony LBT-S3000 midi-system offers a pleasing combination of features for its price. It consists of a receiver/equalizer, five-disc CD changer, and auto-reverse dual transport cassette deck. The amplifier produces a substantial 70 watts per channel. Sony presets five equalization settings on the equalizer with a 12-band spectrum analyzer. The latter puts on quite a light show. If you like disco, the "groove effect" will set your heart pounding. The Matrix Surround Sound provides the illusion of sound coming from all around when you sit in the right position. It basically expands the sound field, even if it doesn't actually surround you. You can preset 20 FM and 10 AM stations on the tuner. The CD changer uses one-bit digital-to-analog converters with a $4\times$ oversampling digital filter. You can program 32 tracks, and can exchange one disc while another is playing. The CD player includes time edit to optimize taping, and synchronizes with the cassette deck for one button recording. The jog shuttle dial speeds up and simplifies programming and skipping to your favorite tracks. There's an optical digital output. You control the cassette deck by touching the full-logic, feather touch controls. The deck plays on both transports and records on one, and offers Dolby B noise reduction on both. A clock timer permits using the system as a fancy clock radio. The two-way speakers contain seven-inch woofers and 2½-inch tweeters. Sony supplies a full-function remote control. If the bass of the LBT-S3000 is insufficient for you, the nearly identical step up LBT-W300 includes Sony's Direct Radiating Superwoofer and 100 watts per channel for about $200 more.

Warranty: 90 days, labor; 1 year, parts
Manufacturer's Suggested Retail Price: $250
Approximate Low Price: not available

Panasonic SC-AK27

Budget Buy

The Panasonic SC-AK27 produces about 60 watts per channel, and funnels that power separately to each of the tweeters and woofers, plus the 5½-inch "Super Woofer." The five-CD changer uses a vertical parking system, which moves each disc tray to the rear after it's loaded and then up and down. You can program 32 tracks, or choose among random and repeat play modes. It uses Panasonic's one-bit digital-to-analog converters. The tuner can store 24 radio station presets. The dual-transport cassette deck records on one transport and plays on both. To lower cost, Panasonic eliminated Dolby B from its systems this year. Panasonic jazzes up the SC-AK27 with a modern front panel with a dual-layer fluorescent display, which puts on an impressive, if garish, show. There are also various equalization and ambience modes. Panasonic supplies a full-function remote control. A clock timer allows you to use the system as a deluxe alarm clock. You can enjoy plenty of music with respectable sound on this economical mini-system. The SC-AK27 comes with Energy Star certification for using negligible power in the standby mode.

Warranty: 1 year, parts and labor
Manufacturer's Suggested Retail Price: $269
Approximate Low Price: $230

PERSONAL STEREOS

The personal stereo forever changed the way we listen to music—elevating FM above AM radio, raising cassettes above records, and ultimately raising CDs above cassettes. Personal stereo prices range from about $20 for a basic tape player to about $400 for the most elaborate tape player/recorder or CD player. Most personal stereos cannot be serviced and come with short 90-day replacement warranties. Manufacturers manage to keep lowering prices by not only eliminating features, but also reducing durability. Depending upon your usage, don't expect more than a year or two of entertainment from most personal stereos.

HOW TO SHOP

Most personal stereos within a broad price range sound similar, and differences appear largely in cosmetics and features. To keep prices enticing, features such as auto-reverse and Dolby B in tape players, and programming options and digital outputs in CD players migrate to top-of-the-line models. Several companies market four or even five variations of the same basic chassis with different features, such as rechargeable batteries, car adapter kits, and metallic versus plastic cases.

Bring a favorite tape or disc with you when shopping to test the product. Shake the player, whether it be tape or CD. Listen to how it responds to shock. Hold the player and feel if the controls are convenient and easy to use. Try on the headphones to be sure they fit and that they are comfortable on your head. Testing radios poses somewhat more difficulty, since the buildings in which many stores are located interfere with reception.

WHERE TO BUY

Because sonic differences are slight, warranties short, and service rarely an issue, we recommend shopping for personal stereos mainly by price. Thus, large discount chain stores usually offer the widest variety and best prices on these products. Also, large chain stores are usually pretty good about exchanging defective products or warranty replacement. If you are certain of the model you want after reading our reviews, on-line shopping is also a good bet, since personal stereos are light, so shipping charges are low.

FEATURES AND TERMINOLOGY_____

Analog Tuner/Digital Tuner: An analog tuner uses conventional circuitry with a tuning knob or thumbwheel and pointer to show you the frequency to which you are tuned. A digital tuner, more accurately a synthesized tuner, permits using a digital frequency readout and presetting radio stations for touch tuning. Neither system is inherently better as far as sound quality.

Auotmatic Music Search (AMS): This feature allows jumping forward or backward by a desired number of tracks to hear a specific selection. It is sometimes called auto-search or random music search.

Electronic Shock Protection, Anti-shock Memory, or Electronic Anti-shock System (EASS): These features employ computer memory chips that act as an audio buffer. The chips store sound during normal play, and when the laser mistracks from shock or vibration, the chips supply sound from memory until the laser resumes tracking. The disc spins faster than normal to supply sound to the memory buffer quicker than the buffer supplies audio to following stages of the personal CD player. Using this feature shortens battery life considerably, since it requires additional power. It still may not be sufficient to prevent audible mistracking when using a CD player while actively jogging, but it should work for walking, bicycling, and other less jarring activities.

Mega Bass, XBS, or DSL: These are circuits that artificially boost bass to provide a more throbbing sound in headphones. Because many headphones accompanying personal stereos lack good bass response, these circuits may somewhat compensate. However, the bass boost might also muddy sound and increase distortion.

NiCd, NiMH, or Li Batteries: NiCd, or nickel-cadmium, is the oldest and most common of rechargeable battery types. It is also the least desirable. It does not store as much power as disposable batteries

135

and needs to be recharged frequently. It also deteriorates if not discharged and recharged properly. The cadmium in nickel-cadmium is highly toxic and environmentally hazardous. NiMH, or nickel metal-hydride (sometimes just nickel hydride), is a newer and superior alternative to nickel-cadmium. Although double the price, it lasts longer, holds a charge better, is less subject to deterioration from abuse, and is less toxic in landfills. Li, or lithium-ion, is the most advanced rechargeable battery available. It holds a charge much better and lasts far longer than either NiCd or NiMH, and because of this it can be made smaller and lighter than other rechargeable batteries. It can be discharged and recharged without any special procedure or precautions. The most advanced lithium batteries can power a personal stereo up to ten times longer than NiCd. However, Li batteries cost four to ten times more than NiCd.

BEST BUYS 2000

Our Best Buy, Recommended, and Budget Buy personal stereos follow. Products within each category are listed according to quality. The item we consider the best of the Best Buys is first, followed by our second choice, and so on. A Budget Buy describes a less-expensive product of respectable quality that perhaps sacrifices some of the performance and/or convenience features of a Best Buy or Recommended product. Remember that a Best Buy, Recommended, or Budget Buy designation only applies to the model listed—it does not necessarily apply to other models made by the same manufacturer or to an entire product line.

PORTABLE CD PLAYERS

Panasonic SL-S360
✔**BEST BUY**

The Panasonic SL-S360 represents a nearly ideal combination of features, performance, and price. The silver-colored, heat resistant polycarbonate body withstands wear and tear. A pair of large buttons on each side of the LCD display on the front-top of the unit make operation easy. A very large button on the front right side fully opens the top cover and ejects the disc so you don't have to fumble to change CDs. Panasonic uses its proprietary MASH one-bit digital-to-analog converters for good sound, and the unit includes S-XBS (super extra bass) for those listeners who just can't get enough bass. You can program 24 tracks, choose random play, and repeat a single track or all tracks. The player will resume playing where it left off when powered down. It will also turn itself off automatically. Panasonic builds in 40 seconds of anti-shock memory, which should be sufficient to keep the sound playing smoothly in all but the most violent activities. It plays for 25 hours from a pair of alkaline AA batteries. Rechargeable nickel-hydride batteries are an option. Panasonic supplies an AC power adapter and comfortable on-ear headphones with a wide plastic headband. Panasonic model SL-S361C is the same model with car adapter kit for $20 more; SL-3600I is also the same model supplied with CD jogger case that can be strapped around the waist for $10 more.

Specifications: height, 1 3/32"; width, 5 1/16"; depth, 5 11/16"; weight, 7.5 oz.
Warranty: 90 days, labor; 1 year, parts
Manufacturer's Suggested Retail Price: $90
Approximate Low Price: not available

Sony D-E441   ✔ BEST BUY

The Sony D-E441 personal CD player is somewhat behind the Panasonic in value, but is still a well designed, satisfying player. Sony offers the polycarbonate case in silver or blue metallic finish. Large, slightly recessed buttons on the rounded, beveled front corners make operation easy. Additional buttons surround the center top front LCD. A one-bit digital-to-analog converter translates the digital bits into good analog sound. Sony's Mega Bass, coupled with its Groove Sound, can provide throbbing, headshaking bass. The D-E441 comes with 20 seconds of electronic shock protection, enough for most activities. You can program 22 tracks, and there are ten playback modes, including random play and various repeat modes. Resume play begins playing on the disc where it stopped when the player was turned off. The two-position automatic volume limiter system protects your hearing while maintaining volume output at levels below the distortion threshold. The D-E441 plays for 16 hours on a pair of alkaline AA batteries. Sony supplies on-ear headphones with a plastic headband wide enough for reasonable comfort. The model D-E445 is the same player supplied with nickel-cadmium rechargeable batteries for $20 more.

Specifications: height, 1″; width, 5″; depth, 5¾″; weight, 7.75 oz.
Warranty: 90 days, labor; 1 year, parts
Manufacturer's Suggested Retail Price: $120
Approximate Low Price: $100-$117

Panasonic SL-S202

Budget Buy

The Panasonic SL-S202 personal CD player delivers good sound for more sedentary people on the go. It contains most of the features of Panasonic's more expensive models, but only three seconds of basic anti-shock memory. Its black, heat-resistant polycarbonate body contains an LCD in the top front middle, with a pair of large control keys on either side. Panasonic uses its proprietary MASH one-bit digital-to-analog converters for good sound, and the unit includes XBS (extra bass) for those listeners who want more bass. You can program 24 tracks, choose random play, and repeat a single track or all tracks. The player will also resume playing where it left off when powered down. It also will turn itself off automatically. A hold switch prevents accidentally operating the controls. The SL-S202 plays for ten hours on a pair of alkaline AA batteries. Panasonic supplies a decent set of on-ear headphones with a plastic headband, and an AC power supply.

Specifications: height, 1³⁄₃₂″; width, 5¹⁄₁₆″; depth, 5¹¹⁄₁₆″; weight, 7.8 oz.
Warranty: 90 days, parts; 1 year, labor
Manufacturer's Suggested Retail Price: $60
Approximate Low Price: $55

PORTABLE CD PLAYERS WITH RADIO

Aiwa XP-R100

✔ **BEST BUY**

The Aiwa XP-R100 combines a good CD player with an AM/FM stereo radio. Control keys surround the LCD in an oval at the top rear of the silver polycarbonate case, each key logically positioned and sized for easy operation. Aiwa uses a basic one-bit digital-to-analog converter for respectable sound. The CD player comes with ten seconds of shock-resistant memory. Bass lovers will appreciate the DSL (dynamic super linear bass). You can program 24 tracks, and the radio has 30 radio station presets for its digitally synthesized tuner. You can play CDs for about 12 hours on a pair of alkaline AA batteries or listen to the radio at least three times longer. The player has two-mode repeat play (one track or the entire disc). You can recharge optional nickel cadmium batteries inside the player. The player comes with an AC power supply. Aiwa also supplies its unusual Swoops neckband headphone. The design, which wraps around your neck, is supposed to preserve your hairstyle and hold the in-ear phones in place. Active users may appreciate this, but others may find it awkward.

Specifications: height, 1⅛"; width, 5⅛"; depth, 5⁹⁄₁₆"; weight, 8.8 oz.
Warranty: 90 days, parts; 1 year, labor
Manufacturer's Suggested Retail Price: $110
Approximate Low Price: $90-$100

Sony D-F411

Recommended

The Sony D-F411 is somewhat more deluxe than the Aiwa XP-R100, but also more expensive and slightly larger and heavier. However, it comes with conventional on-ear headphones supported by a wide plastic headband. For simple operation, a pair of buttons flank each side of the large LCD on the top front edge of the player. Sony finishes the heat-resistant polycarbonate case in silver. The 20 seconds of anti-shock memory coupled with digital signal processing makes the player immune from all but the most intense shock. The player uses Sony's basic one-bit digital-to-analog converter. If Mega Bass isn't enough to keep your ears throbbing with bass, there's Sony's "Groove Sound Position," which adds even more bass. You can program 22 tracks, and there are ten play modes, such as random play and various repeat modes. The digitally synthesized radio has 24 FM radio station presents and six AM radio station presets. Sony's dual position Automatic Volume Limiter System (AVLS) helps protect your hearing while reducing distortion. A lock switch prevents accidental triggering of control keys, and the player can pick up where it left off playing on a disc when powered down. The D-F411 plays CDs for about 14 hours on a pair of alkaline AA batteries and at least three times longer when playing the radio. The player also can charge the optional nickel-cadmium batteries with the supplied AC power supply.

Specifications: height, 1¼"; width, 5¼"; depth, 6"; weight, 9.2 oz.
Warranty: 90 days, parts; 1 year, labor
Manufacturer's Suggested Retail Price: $160
Approximate Low Price: not available

PERSONAL RADIO-CASSETTE PLAYERS

Panasonic RQ-E20V

✔**BEST BUY**

    The Panasonic RQ-E20V personal radio/cassette player performs very well, includes the most desirable features, and operates very economically. The auto-reverse tape player handles tape smoothly. Four mechanical buttons on the spine operate the tape player. Five soft-touch keys on the face select the radio station presets on the digitally synthesized tuner. However, those five keys can select from a 20 station memory. You can select between normal/city FM sensitivity, which reduces overload in strong signal areas. The AM tuner selects between North American and European tuning increments, allowing the RQ-E20V to function almost anywhere in the world. A clear LCD read-out on the face shows a variety of information beyond merely tuning frequency. Pressing a large button adjacent to the display shows battery life. A switch locks the controls to prevent accidentally triggering the radio or tape player. Panasonic provides comfortable on-ear headphones supported by a wide plastic headband. You can add bass to the those phones by switching in the XBS Extra Bass circuit. The most amazing facet of the RQ-E20V is that it plays tapes for up to 26 hours on a single alkaline AA battery, and Panasonic supplies four batteries with the unit and also includes a belt clip.

Specifications: height, 4⅜"; width, 3¼"; depth, 1³⁄₁₆"; weight, 5.7 oz.
Warranty: 90 days, labor; 1 year, parts
Manufacturer's Suggested Retail Price: $45
Approximate Low Price: $40

Sony WM-FX323

Recommended

The Sony WM-FX323 is a very basic, solid performer among radio/cassette players. Sony builds it with an old-fashioned analog AM/FM stereo tuner, manual tuning knob, and horizontal ruler-style dial. The WM-FX323 does come with a few niceties beyond auto-reverse, such as auto shut-off, the ability to properly adjust for metal/chrome tapes, and Sony's Mega Bass for bass-hungry listeners. There's also an FM local/distant switch that should help eliminate overload in strong signal areas. Sony's Automatic Volume Limiter System (AVLS) helps protect your hearing and reduce distortion. The unit plays tapes for up to 13 hours or FM radio for up to 30 hours on a pair of alkaline AA batteries.

Specifications: height, 4⅝"; width, 3½"; depth, 1⅜"; weight, 7.25 oz. (with batteries)
Warranty: 90 days, labor; 1 year, parts
Manufacturer's Suggested Retail Price: $45
Approximate Low Price: $30-$36

Aiwa HS-TA164

Budget Buy

There's not much to write about the Aiwa HS-TA164 radio/cassette player, except that it works and provides good value for very little money. You tune its analog tuner with a ruler-style tuning dial at the top of the unit. A large window in the center shows you the cassette that's playing. It stops automatically at the end of a side. You can select the proper playback for normal or chrome/metal tapes. The HS-TA164 plays tapes for up to 18 hours on a pair of alkaline AA batteries—an impressive figure for a unit in this price range. The HS-TA164 comes in black, silver, green, or blue. It comes with Aiwa's most basic headphones.

Specifications: height, 4⁷⁄₁₆″; width, 3¹¹⁄₁₆″; depth, 1½″; weight, 4.2 oz.
Warranty: 90 days, parts and labor
Manufacturer's Suggested Retail Price: $17
Approximate Low Price: $15

PERSONAL RADIO-CASSETTE PLAYER/RECORDERS

Aiwa HS-JS479

✔BEST BUY

The HS-JS479 makes few compromises for those who want great playback performance and good recording performance. A major convenience is auto-reverse that functions in both the record and play modes, so you can make a 90-minute, virtually uninterrupted recording. It records as well as plays in stereo on normal or chrome-type tapes and comes with built-in stereo microphones. In many situations, a stereo recording is more intelligible. The HS-JS479 plays back with Dolby B noise reduction, a rarity among headphone stereos these days. Four mechanical buttons along the spine control tape motion, and feather-touch keys on the face operate the AM/FM stereo radio. We like the six large preset keys. You can manually select your 30 favorite radio stations or let the HS-JS479 do it for you. The digitally synthesized tuner functions almost anywhere in the world. Aiwa's "multi-sound processor" gives you some flexibility in adjusting the tone. The unit plays tapes for up to 22 hours on a pair of alkaline AA batteries. It comes with Aiwa's basic on-ear headphones.

Specifications: height, 3½"; width, 4½"; depth, 1⁷/₁₆"; weight, 6.5 oz.
Warranty: 90 days, labor; 1 year, parts
Manufacturer's Suggested Retail Price: $90
Approximate Low Price: not available

Sony WM-GX322

| Recommended |

The Sony WM-GX322 actually contains a pair of small stereo speakers, along with a separate tie-clip-size stereo microphone and a little stand. It records and plays in stereo. There is also a handy pitch control to speed up or slow down the tape during playback. The WM-GX322 is also economical to operate, with a pair of alkaline AA batteries powering playback for 22 hours (or radio listening for 30 hours). You can record from the internal radio for eight hours on a set of batteries. The conventional AM/FM stereo tuner has a fairly spacious horizontal tuning dial. A local/distant switch optimizes reception for urban/non-urban listening. Large mechanical push buttons operate the tape mechanism for reliable fail-safe control. The auto-reverse, auto-shutoff tape player records on normal or chrome tapes. Three Mega Bass settings should satisfy even the most bass-hungry listeners. The automatic volume limiter systems reduces dynamic range and distortion, while protecting your hearing. Sony supplies good-sounding, comfortable on-ear headphones supported by a wide plastic headband.

Specifications: height, 3½"; width, 4½"; depth, 1⅛"; weight, 8.3 oz.
Warranty: 90 days, labor; 1 year, parts
Manufacturer's Suggested Retail Price: $90
Approximate Low Price: not available

___PERSONAL CASSETTE PLAYERS___

Aiwa HS-GS292

The Aiwa HS-GS292 is remarkably deluxe for its low price. The silver-colored player features auto-reverse and a normal/ chrome-metal switch for proper sound from all tapes. Aiwa incorporates its multi-sound processor as a large rotary switch on the face of the player. You can select what Aiwa considers preferred tonal balances for jazz, rock, pop, or classic. Four mechanical buttons on the player's spine control tape operation. The cassette lid lock holds the tape firmly in place to reduce distortion from vibration. There's even a jack for an optional AC power adapter. You can play tapes for up to 24 hours on a pair of alkaline AA batteries, adding further economies to this economical player. Aiwa provides its most basic on-ear headphones.

Specifications: height, 3½"; width, 4½"; depth, 1¼"; weight, 4.2 oz.
Warranty: 90 days, labor; 1 year, parts
Manufacturer's Suggested Retail Price: $20
Approximate Low Price: not available

Panasonic RQ-P35

The Panasonic RQ-P35 is as basic of a personal cassette player as you can find, but it does maintain the quality of other Panasonic products. The player automatically stops at the end of the tape. You can switch in the XBS extra bass system for more bass through the comfortable on-ear headphones, supported by a wide plastic headband. The attractive styling includes a large round window for viewing the cassette. Panasonic provides a detachable belt clip. Panasonic does not state its playing time on its pair of alkaline AA batteries, but you can expect at least ten hours.

Specifications: height, 4⁷⁄₁₆"; width, 3⁷⁄₁₆"; depth, 1⁵⁄₁₆"; weight, 4.6 oz.

Warranty: 90 days, labor; 1 year, parts
Manufacturer's Suggested Retail Price: $25
Approximate Low Price: not available

_____PERSONAL HEADSET RADIOS_____

Sony SRF-H2

✔**BEST BUY**

The Sony SRF-H2 AM/FM stays on your head because of its double headband. You won't mind the tenacity because it's extremely lightweight and has reasonably comfortable on-the-ear cushions. A flexible short-whip antenna resists breaking, yet it pulls in stations loud and clear. The reflective yellow tip on the antenna is a safety feature that increases visibility, which is especially useful when jogging at night. The SRF-H2 has a local/distant switch for optimizing FM reception. The unit operates for about 74 hours on a single AAA alkaline battery (25 hours on a regular battery).

Specifications: weight, 4.2 oz. (with battery)
Warranty: 1 year, parts and labor
Manufacturer's Suggested Retail Price: $28
Approximate Low Price: $26

Aiwa HR-SP75

Recommended

The Aiwa HR-SP75 stays planted firmly on your head while jogging because of its wide dual headbands. Its AM/FM digitally synthesized tuner can automatically set its 20 station presets (ten AM and ten FM). You tune by touching the buttons arrayed on one of the earcups. There is an LCD that helps with tuning, which also serves as an exercise monitor that shows calories/distance. (One problem with older models of some digital tuning headsets was the lack of a display.) For safety, Aiwa builds in a light reflector. The super bass circuit pumps up the bass if you can't get enough, although these are pretty good headphones that will reproduce a wide range of sound.

Specifications: weight, 6.7 oz.
Warranty: 90 days, labor; 1 year, parts
Manufacturer's Suggested Retail Price: $60
Approximate Low Price: $40-$50

PERSONAL RADIOS

Sony SRF-85

✔ **BEST BUY**

This AM/FM stereo model has a local/distant switch to optimize FM reception. It includes Sony's Automatic Volume Limiter System to protect your hearing and improve audibility in noisy environments. Sony provides ultra-light, in-the-ear headphones. A belt clip and swiveling armband/handgrip keep the SRF-85 glued to you whether you're relaxing or jogging. The SRF-85 uses the old-fashioned mechanical tuning, which we prefer because the feather-touch buttons of the digital models can accidentally activate when you put the radio in a pocket or purse. It operates on a single AA battery.

Specifications: height, $3^7/8''$; width, $2^5/8''$; depth, $3^1/32''$; weight, 3.4 oz.
Warranty: 1 year, parts
Manufacturer's Suggested Retail Price: $35
Approximate Low Price: $34

Aiwa CR-LD100

Recommended

The aluminum finished Aiwa CD-LD100 is one slick little AM/FM stereo radio, and little is the operative term. About the size of a pack of chewing gum, the radio is based on a digitally synthesized tuner. It has a whopping 45 radio station presets, accessed by using a pair of keys beneath the LCD on the unit's face. Aiwa even includes its dynamic super linear bass, which should satisfy bass lovers. The LCD also shows battery life. It operates over 40 hours on a single alkaline AAA battery. Reception is quite good for such a small radio. Aiwa supplies tiny in-ear headphones. Admittedly, these may be uncomfortable for some listeners, but they make sense with such a small radio.

Specifications: height, 1 13/16"; width, 3 1/4"; depth, 25/32"; weight, 1.6 oz.
Warranty: 90 days, labor; 1 year, parts
Manufacturer's Suggested Retail Price: $60
Approximate Low Price: not available

_____PERSONAL MiniDisc PLAYERS_____

Sony MZ-E33

✔ **BEST BUY**

The Sony MZ-E33 brings the cost of MD playback down. The MZ-E33 is smaller and lighter than preceding models, and plays over twice as long on a single battery. The player offers nearly all of the benefits of MD: ten-second shock resistant memory, nearly instant random access, and an LCD on the headphone cord remote, which shows disc and song title, track number, battery life, and play mode. The MZ-E33 includes Mega Bass for bass lovers. MD is a wonderfully portable medium because of its small, robust discs, which hold 74 minutes. All the controls are touch buttons. It plays nine hours from a single alkaline AA battery, and Sony offers a rechargeable nickel-hydride battery that can fit in the same battery compartment as the standard alkaline battery. The rechargeable battery can power the unit for about six hours. This handsomely designed player sounds very good, certainly better than the best cassette portables, although no better than a CD portable. Sony supplies folding headphones and a carrying case. The MZ-E33 comes in champagne gold, black, or blue.

Specifications: height, 3 5/8"; width, 3 1/8"; depth, 3/8"; weight, 4 oz.
Warranty: 90 days, labor; 1 year, parts
Manufacturer's Suggested Retail Price: $250
Approximate Low Price: $200

Sharp MD-S301

✔ **BEST BUY**

The Sharp MD-S301 promises eight hours of playing time by using more advanced lithium-ion batteries, which are supplied with the player. The MD-S301 will attract attention with its metallic silver and blue finish. A front-loading mechanism allows sliding the disc in through a slot like a floppy disk. Although the MD-S301 contains only ten seconds of shock resistant memory, it should play through all but the worst shock and vibration. The LCD screen on the supplied remote control, which looks like a wristwatch, displays titles, artist names, tracks, and times encoded on the MD. Sharp includes its X-bass extra bass circuit for listeners desiring heavy bass. Sharp provides comfortable on-ear headphones, an AC power adapter, and a carrying case.

Specifications: height, 3$\frac{3}{32}$"; width, 3$\frac{7}{16}$"; depth, 3$\frac{1}{32}$"; weight, 7 oz. (with battery)
Warranty: 90 days, labor; 1 year, parts
Manufacturer's Suggested Retail Price: $250
Approximate Low Price: not available

__PERSONAL MD PLAYER/RECORDERS__

Sony MZ-R37

✔ **BEST BUY**

The Sony MZ-R37 has light-touch control keys that are next to the LCD along the edge of the unit, although you'll most likely find yourself using the supplied wired remote control, which permits editing and titling. MD permits you to electronically label discs and tracks. The LCD screen shows all the standard data available with MD. The MZ-R37 includes an optical digital input with a sampling rate converter, allowing you to record from any digital source along with the expected analog input and a microphone input. An ample 40-second memory buffer makes the player sonically immune to shock and vibration. The supplied nickel-cadmium rechargeable batteries provide 2$\frac{1}{2}$ hours of recording time or 4$\frac{1}{2}$ hours of playback. You can swap the rechargeables for a pair of alkaline AA batteries, which provide about double the times of the rechargeables. If you wish to sacrifice stereo for longer record/playing time, the MZ-R37 will record/play 148 minutes in mono. The unit incorporates Sony's Mega Bass and automatic volume limiter system, which reduces dynamic range and distortion while protecting your hearing. Recordings made with the MZ-R37 sound very good and should please all but the most demanding audiophiles. Sony supplies the AC adapter/recharger, carrying pouch, and collapsible headphones.

Specifications: height, 3″; width, 4¼″; depth, ¾″; weight, 6.6 oz.
Warranty: 90 days, labor; 1 year, parts
Manufacturer's Suggested Retail Price: $350
Approximate Low Price: $250-$299

Sharp MD-MT821

Recommended

Barely larger than the MD itself, the MD-MT821 records for almost eight hours and plays for about 11½ hours per charge. Snap on the external battery pack holding a single alkaline AA battery and those times skyrocket to 11 hours of recording and 16 hours of playback. This player/recorder accomplishes all of MD's editing and titling functions, and displays titles on the remote control's large illuminated LCD. Sharp incorporates an ample 40 seconds of memory to insure shock and vibration don't interfere with sound quality. The unit's optical digital input works with an internal sampling rate converter. You can set the unit to record time markers at specified increments (three, five, or ten minutes) to make finding selections easier. When you insert a disc and close the clamshell lid, the disc begins playing automatically. Sharp supplies a pair of comfortable on-ear headphones, AC power adapter, and optical digital connecting cable.

Specifications: height, 3¹/₁₆″; width, 3¼″; depth, ¹³/₁₆″; weight, 6 oz.
Manufacturer's Suggested Retail Price: $400
Approximate Low Price: $200-$256

BOOM BOXES

BOOM BOXES WITH CDs

Panasonic RX-DS19

✔ **BEST BUY**

If excellent sound is a priority, then consider the Panasonic RX-DS19. The CD player section uses a "Front-Open CD Tray," which is located in the lower middle of the boom box. A blue backlit LCD display is located directly above the drawer. You can program 24 tracks for random-access programming and repeat play. There are two four-inch full-range speakers with 3-Dimensional Sound, Diffusers, and "Sound Virtualizer" circuitry. For high-powered sound, it also includes XBS (extra bass system). To improve sound quality even further, the speakers are housed in an acoustic separator cabinet with bass relief ports that also adds to its futuristic appearance. The top-mounted cassette deck features soft-touch controls, auto stop, pause control, and a soft-eject system. An added bonus is the basic remote that allows you to adjust volume, tune in radio stations, and operate the CD player. There is no numeric keypad, however. Eight D batteries power the RX-DS19 for easy on-the-go play, or you can use the AC power cord for at-home play.

Specifications: height, 5¾"; width, 19⁵³⁄₆₄"; depth, 10²³⁄₆₄"; weight, 7.8 lbs.
Warranty: 1 year, parts and labor
Manufacturer's Suggested Retail Price: $100
Approximate Low Price: $90

Aiwa CSD-EL33

Recommended

Sound is of prime importance on this model, which pumps a solid 2.5 watts per channel from its two bass reflex speakers. The speakers add some ambiance to the music selections along with the Bass Boost and Q-surround sound (a psycho-acoustic effect that adds height, width, and depth to the music). A three-position T-Bass is also included to offer the user even more bass sounds. The single-play CD player features a one-bit D/A converter with $8\times$ oversampling. It has continuous 20-track play with repeat function options. It uses a slide-out drawer, which is located in the lower middle of the unit below the green LCD display. The CSD-EL33 also features a digitally synthesized tuner with 30 station presets. A large green LCD screen offers easy-to-read screens and a music calendar. The tape deck is top-mounted. Power is provided via the AC adapter or eight C batteries.

Specifications: height, 7"; width, 7½"; depth, 9⅞"; weight, 9 lbs.
Warranty: 1 year, parts and labor
Manufacturer's Suggested Retail Price: $140
Approximate Low Price: $120-$136

Sony CFD-V177

Recommended

The Sony CFD-V177 provides excellent sound from its top-mounted CD player and single-play cassette deck. The CD player portion features twin D/A converters and $8\times$ oversampling. It also includes a four-way disc repeat mode: single track, all tracks, 20 Track RMS (random music search), and shuffle play with CDs. It has 20 Track programmability. The top-mounted single-well stereo cassette deck provides for direct recording from either CD or tuner. There is synchronized CD/cassette dubbing, which starts the CD as you press record on the cassette. An analog tuner portion provides both AM/FM bands. Radio tuning is very easy through a handy sideways-mounted thumbwheel. There is an LCD display located directly in the upper center section of the boom box. For improved bass, the CFD-V177 includes the MegaBass system. Each speaker enclosure includes a four-inch full-range speaker. The CFD-V177 operates on either AC power or six D batteries.

Specifications: height, 6½"; width, 16½"; depth, 10"; weight, 8 lbs. 12.5 oz.
Warranty: 1 year, parts and labor
Manufacturer's Suggested Retail Price: $110
Approximate Low Price: $60-$68

RCA RT-7945

Recommended

RCA offers a truly unique portable CD boom box that features a four-inch active matrix color LCD TV. The single-play CD player features a one-bit D/A converter with 8× oversampling. It has continuous 20-track play with repeat one/all and random-play functions. Besides a standard headphone jack, this model also sports A/V inputs. Sound emanates from twin four-inch full-range dynamic front-mounted speakers. Two antennas are included: one AM/FM and one TV (dipole VNF/FM). The Bass Boost helps add oomph to the sound. There is no cassette deck. The RT-7945 also features a digitally synthesized tuner with five station presets. To power this model, you can use the detachable AC line cord or nine D batteries for on-the-go play. The RT-7945 offers the best of both worlds (audio and video) at a fair price.

Specifications: height, 7⅞"; width, 20⅞"; depth, 9⅞"; weight, 8.2 lbs.
Warranty: 1 year (limited)
Manufacturer's Suggested Retail Price: $300
Approximate Low Price: $250

Sharp QT-CD114

Budget Buy

Sharp's QT-CD114 has very few frills, but offers basic playback of either a single CD or single cassette at a very reasonable price. The QT-CD 114 offers 16-bit linear D/A conversion with 4× oversampling. It includes an analog AM/FM tuner with a rotary dial located on the top right of the unit. While not as precise as digital tuning, the analog tuner is able to capture most stations easily. Other function controls and a small LCD display are situated between the two speakers. This model features two four-inch full-range speakers that are front-mounted and covered by metallic mesh speaker grills. Power is rated at two watts per channel. The sound quality is fair to good. For sound with more bass, X-Bass circuitry is included. Eight D batteries power the QT-CD114 for easy on-the-go play. For at-home play, an AC power cord is included. A headphone jack is also included for private listening.

Specifications: height, 6¹⁄₁₆″; width, 18¹⁵⁄₁₆″; depth, 10″; weight, 7.1 lbs.
Warranty: 1 year, parts; 90 days, labor
Manufacturer's Suggested Retail Price: $60
Approximate Low Price: not available

BOOM BOXES WITHOUT CDs

Panasonic RX-FT530

✔ **BEST BUY**

The Panasonic RX-FT530 is a compact portable stereo with big boom-box sound. The pleasing sound quality comes from the dynamic bass boost (DBB). The two-way four-speaker system provides excellent sound reproduction. A bonus is two tiny tweeters. This model features a dual cassette deck that allows you to record from either AM or FM bands, or dub from another tape. Deck A includes auto-reverse, and Deck B features auto-record level control. High speed dubbing is included on Deck B as well. To facilitate recording, there is one-touch recording. This model includes automatic replay play so that it will play the tape on Deck A and then automatically switch to play the tape in Deck B. There is AM and FM stereo tuning via a rotary analog dial. This model features an electronic tape speed control that monitors specific tape functions. The unit is powered by six D batteries or an included AC power cord.

Specifications: height, 6³⁄₁₆″; width, 22⁵⁄₁₆″; depth, 6⁵⁄₁₆″; weight, 6 lbs.
Warranty: 1 year, parts and labor
Manufacturer's Suggested Retail Price: $80
Approximate Low Price: not available

Aiwa CS-P77

Budget Buy

The Aiwa CS-P77 is a simply elegant portable stereo system featuring a single mid-mounted cassette deck. This model is housed in a stylish silver titanium cabinet with an arched carrying handle that is visually appealing. The play/record tape system gives this model lots flexibility. A digital tuner with AM (featuring AM Wide) and FM bands is also included. Tape transport controls are top-mounted for ease of use. Other controls surround the LCD display in the center of the portable. A Stereo LED indicator is featured so that you know if an FM broadcast is in stereo. A microphone is also built-in. For private listening, a headphone jack is included. Otherwise, there are two full-range speakers to pump the sound. To enhance the audio somewhat, Q Sound is included, which gives the sound a bit of a boost. The unit is powered by four AA batteries or an included AC power cord. For a small, easy to carry portable stereo, sound quality is much better than average.

Specifications: height, 3⅝"; width, 10⅞"; depth, 2⁵⁄₁₆"; weight, 1.4 lbs.
Warranty: 90 days, parts and labor
Manufacturer's Suggested Retail Price: $60
Approximate Low Price: $40

CLOCK RADIOS

Panasonic RC-6099

✔**BEST BUY**

Panasonic understands the essence of a clock radio—and it shows in the RC-6099. A bright green, dimmable clock display and lighted linear radio dial make the radio easy to use under any lighting condition. Rather than jarring you awake, the volume gently increases when the alarm goes off. An earphone jack permits late-night listening without disturbing your bedmate, but should you fall asleep with the earphone in, the buzzer alarm will still function. The radio has two alarms with indicators on the display. It has the usual sleep timer and snooze functions found on nearly all clock radios. You can easily set the clock and alarm times with the forward, backward, and fast buttons, which provide a choice of speed in either direction. A battery backup keeps the clock running and sounds the alarm in the case of a power failure, and an indicator shows when the power has failed. A mechanical rotary volume control allows setting the volume with the radio off. A three-inch speaker provides good, although not outstanding, sound quality. If this radio continues the Panasonic tradition, it will operate nearly forever. The RC-6099 comes in a compact black or white cabinet.

Specifications: height, 2⅜"; width, 9⅛"; depth, 6⅙"
Warranty: 90 days, labor; 1 year, parts
Manufacturer's Suggested Retail Price: $35
Approximate Low Price: not available

Proton Clock Radio RS-330

✔ **BEST BUY**

The Proton RS-330 uses a 3.5-inch speaker with a five-watt amplifier for very pleasing sound quality. We particularly like the photo cell that adjusts the large clock display to the brightness of room lighting—or you can manually adjust brightness to your taste. In the dark, the clock remains just bright enough to read without becoming a night-light. The digitally synthesized tuner has 24 presets. The RS-330 has dual alarms: radio or buzzer. The radio gently fades up the volume so as not to shock you awake. Sleep timer and snooze alarm are standard. The front panel control buttons are back-lit so you can see them in a dark room. A capacitor, rather than a battery, maintains time and alarm settings in the event of a power failure. The capacitor will not sound the alarm and may not keep the settings for as long as a battery, but should work fine during most normal power outages. Time and alarm setting is easy with forward and backward buttons. Proton lays out the controls logically for ease of operation, and uses manual knobs for volume setting and "loudness," which balances the frequency response for volume level, providing a richer sound at low levels.

Specifications: height, 6"; width, 10⅝"; depth, 3⅓"
Warranty: 90 days (limited)
Manufacturer's Suggested Retail Price: $160
Approximate Low Price: not available

CAMERAS

A trip to the camera store can be bewildering to someone unfamiliar with cameras. Row upon row of gleaming chrome and shiny black cameras, of all different sizes and prices—how do you choose? The process isn't hard if you first determine exactly what you want to do with the camera.

Before buying a camera, first determine the types of photos you'll be taking and the degree of personal involvement you want to have in the process. Shop for a camera that will best suit your needs. Even some less expensive cameras provide sophisticated systems to automate your photography.

TYPES OF CAMERAS

Single Lens Reflex (SLR) Cameras: With this type of camera, you are looking through the same lens that will form the image on the film; this is the most precise viewing method available. Most SLR cameras feature interchangeable lenses, and this is one of the reasons to consider an SLR. Lens choices range from wide angle and telephoto to a wide variety of zooms and close-up or "macro" lenses. The major brands of SLR cameras also have extensive accessory systems that let you tackle almost any photographic task. Whether it's special lenses and flash units for close-ups of tiny insects, an intervalometer for recording a time-lapse series of a flower opening up, or a high-speed motor drive that permits taking up to ten pictures per second for fast-action series, the SLR is the most versatile and adaptable form of camera. Another variation, the ZLR (zoom lens reflex), has a permanently attached zoom lens. While slightly less versatile, it is a good choice for traveling because it avoids a lot of separate components that might get lost or stolen.

Viewfinder Cameras: With this type of camera, you view scenes through an optical window adjacent to the lens. This method is not as precise as an SLR, but is fine for everything except close-ups. All cameras reviewed here other than SLRs fall into this general category. Within this category are five subtypes of cameras:

Autofocus Viewfinder Cameras: This type of camera, as the name implies, automatically focuses the lens for maximum sharpness in your photo.

Fixed-focus Viewfinder Cameras: Also called "focus-free," the lenses on this class of camera are set at the factory for a distance that will deliver the greatest range of sharp focus on objects from just a few feet from the camera to distant landscapes. This type of lens is found mostly on economy models.

Rangefinder Cameras: This type uses manual focusing to bring a split image in the viewfinder together as one image. Today these are only available as expensive professional models.

Single-use Viewfinder Cameras: Also referred to as "disposable" cameras, these are merely inexpensive fixed-focus cameras, usually featuring a plastic lens that is preloaded with film. When you're finished taking pictures, you drop the entire camera off for processing. These are great for use in environments that would damage a good camera, such as at the beach, in the rain, and even underwater with some models. The results are surprisingly good for album-size prints.

Instant-print Cameras: Polaroid makes the only instant-print cameras available in the U.S. They use only Polaroid film, which is more costly per print than 35mm or APS film. However, there's no denying the appeal of having a fully developed color or black-and-white print in hand in a matter of seconds or minutes after taking the photo. Polaroid cameras have been popular with partygoers for decades, and probably will be for the foreseeable future.

HOW TO SHOP

If a camera that is featured here appeals to you but is a bit too expensive, or perhaps lacks a particular feature you're looking for, keep in mind that there is often a companion model just above or below the one reviewed. You might save money by deleting an unnecessary feature.

WHERE TO BUY_____

Cameras are carried by several types of retail stores. You might have to shop around to find the exact model you're looking for. The discount stores often have good prices, but they carry smaller selections. Camera specialty stores will have more knowledgeable help, and are often the only place to find some of the more upscale camera models, though you will generally pay a little more at these shops. Look for sales and manufacturer rebates.

FEATURES AND TERMINOLOGY_____

Auto Fill-flash: This is an automatic flash mode on the camera that decides when and if daylight fill-flash is needed and the amount of flash light to deliver.

Daylight Fill-flash: In bright sunlight, the sunlit and shadow sides of a person's face vary greatly in brightness. Our eyes compensate for the disparity, but film does not, resulting in inky-black shadows. You can overcome this contrast difference by firing the camera's flash unit, which brightens the shadows for a more pleasing rendition. You can manually adjust the flash intensity on some cameras, or have the camera deal with it for you (see Auto Fill-flash).

Exposure Compensation: This is a means of overriding a camera's automatic film speed setting, letting you modify the exposure for tricky lighting conditions, such as backlighting or for special effects. not available on economy models.

Film Speed: The more sensitive to light a type of film is, the "faster" it is said to be. This rating is expressed by ISO (International Standards Organization), followed by a number, such as ISO 100. This example is considered to be a medium-speed film; ISO 400 is a fast film and ISO 25 is a slow film. Fast films let you take pictures in lower light levels or set higher shutter speeds to freeze fast action. Slower films are sharper, important if you regularly have enlargements made. Slower films also have better color saturation. Picture quality will be best with films of ISO 200 or less, as a grainy appearance increases with film speed.

Focal Plane Shutters: Most commonly found in 35mm SLRs, this type of shutter consists of either a cloth curtain or metal blades located just in front of the film. They let you change lenses without fogging the film.

Hot Shoe: This is a fitting on the camera that will accept an accessory flash unit without the need for a connecting cord. Most camera makers today offer dedicated—or proprietary—hot shoes when they have such a fitting. A dedicated hot shoe requires a flash made by the camera maker, or made specifically for that brand of camera, for proper operation.

Lenses: In different camera formats, what is called the "normal lens" will be different. This "normal lens" approximates the angle of view seen by the human eye. For a standard 35mm camera this is a lens of about 45mm focal length. Lenses with shorter focal length than the normal lens are referred to as telephoto. A zoom lens is a lens that can vary its focal length, which varies the angle of view as well as the magnification. There has been some confusion concerning focal length now that the new Advanced Photo System (APS) cameras have been introduced. These new cameras use a film that is only 24mm wide, as opposed to the standard 35mm. This smaller film means the "normal lens" is also smaller, so a "normal lens" for an APS camera is about 28mm.

Lens Aperture: Also commonly referred to as the "f-stop," this is a mathematical ratio of the size of the lens opening relative to the focal length of the lens. Lens designations are most often expressed by the focal length in millimeters and the maximum aperture (largest opening), such as a 50mm f/2.8 lens. The f-stop is usually marked on the lens. This is important because the larger the lens opening, the more light can get through. A lens that lets a lot of light through (referred to in photographic jargon as a "fast" lens) lets you take pictures in dimmer light without using a flash. This type of lens also lets you use faster shutter speeds in all light conditions (for better action-stopping photos). Faster lenses are more expensive, though. F-stops run in a sequence that might seem backward at first, but all you really need to remember is, the smaller the number, the more light gets through. For example, a lens with a maximum aperture of f/2 lets more light through than a lens of f/5.6.

Leaf Shutters: Most commonly used in the popular "point-and-shoot" cameras, these are located within the body of the lens. They are found in cameras without interchangeable lenses.

Red-eye Reduction Mode: We've all seen photos of people or animals with glowing red eyes. This occurs under dim lighting conditions when the pupils of the eyes are wide open. Light from a flash is reflected off the back of the eyeball and back to the camera lens, resulting in the "red-eye" appearance. A camera's red-eye reduction feature fires several short, rapid bursts of light before the actual exposure is made. This closes the pupils down somewhat and reduces the red-eye phenomenon. Note that the term is "reduction," not necessarily elimination. The effect is worse when subjects are staring directly at the camera; it will help if you can photograph them at a slight angle.

Self-timer: This is a timer within the camera that lets you get into the picture with the camera mounted on a tripod; ten seconds is the usual delay before the shutter fires. Some cameras have an infrared remote control that lets you fire at any time after you've gotten into position in front of the camera.

Viewfinder Display: Most cameras provide some degree of exposure information in the viewfinder. This can be as basic as red or green lights, with their obvious implications, or a sophisticated LED or LCD readout of shutter speed, aperture, flash status, and other information.

BEST BUYS 2000

Our Best Buy, Recommended, and Budget Buy cameras follow. Products within each category are listed according to quality. The best of the Best Buys is first, followed by our second choice, and so on. A Best Buy, Recommended, or Budget Buy designation only applies to the model listed—it does not necessarily apply to other models made by the same manufacturer or to an entire product line.

35mm MANUAL-FOCUS SLR CAMERAS

The 35mm SLR (single-lens reflex) camera is probably the most widely used professional camera. Manual-focus SLR cameras are particularly suitable for amateur photographers who want focus and exposure controls to master the images they create.

Pentax ZX-M

✔ **BEST BUY**

The Pentax ZX-M has a good array of features and access to the extensive selection of Pentax lenses and accessories, making this camera a Best Buy. Included is an array of exposure controls designed to handle a wide variety of photographic applications. A built-in film winder advances the film at two frames per second; advance to frame one when loading and film rewind are also automatic. The Pentax ZX-M includes a feature that is absent on most cameras in this price range: the depth-of-field preview button, which allows closing the lens down to taking aperture before taking the picture. Exposure compensation is possible over a ±3 f-stop range, making it easy to deal with backlighting or to intentionally over- or under-exposure a picture to enhance the mood of a scene. The fastest shutter speed available is $\frac{1}{2,000}$ second, which helps freeze fast action. Flash synchronization is at $\frac{1}{100}$ second or slower. A 12-second delay self-timer enables you to get into your own pictures. Film speed is set manually over a range of ISO 6 to 6400. The viewfinder displays all exposure information, including flash-ready (also displayed on an LCD panel atop the camera). The focusing screen is of the combination split image/microprism type. Data imprinting is available with the optional Data Back FJ. Compatible lens mounts are Pentax KAF2, KAF, KA, and K.

Warranty: 1 year
Manufacturer's Suggested Retail Price: $280 (body only)
Approximate Low Price: $155-$172

Minolta X-700

Recommended

This electronically governed camera provides programmed or aperture-priority automatic operation with Minolta's MD-series lenses, and aperture-priority auto with MC-series lenses. Exposure modes available are fully programmed auto ("P"), for point-and-shoot simplicity; aperture-priority auto ("A"), for occasions when you want to control the extent of near-to-far sharpness; and metered manual ("M"), when you want total creative control. The focal-plane shutter offers electronically controlled, stepless speeds from $1/1,000$ second to 4 seconds in "P" and "A" modes, and fixed speeds from $1/1,000$ second to 1 second and Bulb ("B") in "M" mode. The electromagnetic shutter release locks if battery voltage drops too low, preventing wasted shots. Exposure metering is TTL, center-weighted averaging type. Flash metering is also TTL/OTF (off the film), for highly accurate flash pictures (flash synchronization is at $1/60$ second). Film speeds from ISO 25 to 1600 are manually set. Exposure compensation can be set over a ±2 f-stop range, for backlight situations or to allow for lens filters. LED exposure indicators are visible in the finder, as is a flash-ready signal. Viewfinder meter display is activated by slight pressure on the shutter release button. Film advance is via a thumb-wind lever; accessory motor winder and motor drive are available. The X-700 is a good choice for anyone wanting to maintain control over focus and several exposure options.

Warranty: 1 year
Manufacturer's Suggested Retail Price: $427 (body only)
Approximate Low Price: $248-$280

Contax Aria

Recommended

The smallest and lightest Contax SLR ever made, the Aria uses metal components in the image-forming path where alignment is critical, and engineered plastics in other areas of the 16.2-ounce camera body. The built-in motor drive transports the film at three frames per second in continuous mode. You have three choices of exposure modes: center-weighted averaging, good for average scenes; five-segment, evaluative metering, wherein the camera's computer weighs each segment individually to create a well-balanced bias; and spot metering, which reads a small central area of the viewfinder, the best choice for lighting conditions with a lot of contrast that might otherwise fool the camera. Other standard Contax features include custom (user-set) functions, automatic exposure bracketing, auto exposure lock, and depth-of-field preview. Top shutter speed is $1/4,000$ second, with flash synchronization at $1/125$ second. An optional D-9 Data Back adds multifunction capabilities, and can imprint exposure and dating information. A new, lightweight Zeiss Vario-Sonnar 28-70mm zoom lens has also been introduced with the Aria buyer in mind, and it features a macro mode for easy close-ups.

Warranty: 3 years
Manufacturer's Suggested Retail Price. $0.49 (body only)
Approximate Low Price: $589

Olympus OM2000

Budget Buy

The Olympus OM2000 is a good camera for beginners. Even though the OM2000 is an entry-level SLR, it draws its optical talent from a fine line-up of Olympus Zuiko lenses. Lens choices range from a 16mm fisheye to a 1000mm telephoto, with just about anything else you'd ever need in between. The metering system of the OM2000 consists of both center-weighted averaging and spot metering modes, which offer a good degree of creative control over exposure. The shutter's top speed is $1/2,000$ second, with $1/125$ second as the top flash synchronization speed. The shutter is entirely mechanical, which means it won't stop functioning due to dead batteries (only the meter requires batteries). The film advance lever locks the shutter release when pushed fully into the body, preventing accidental exposures. Other features include a ten-second self-timer, a battery check button, depth-of-field preview button (located on the lenses), and a multiple-exposure lever for superimposing two or more frames. Unlike most cameras in its price range, the camera body is die-cast aluminum. This unit is packaged as a kit, which includes the camera body, a 35-70mm f/3.5-4.8 Zuiko zoom lens, and a case, thus qualifying it as a Budget Buy.

Warranty: 1 year
Manufacturer's Suggested Retail Price: $418 (OM2000 Kit, with f/3.5-4.8 lens)
Approximate Low Price: $210-$240

35mm AUTOFOCUS SLR CAMERAS

When autofocus SLRs first appeared, most professionals shunned them. Today, it's hard to find a pro without one. Improved accuracy and reliability are the main reasons for their popularity.

FEATURES

Today's sophisticated, motor-driven autofocus SLR camera tracks fast-moving subjects much more quickly and precisely than can be done manually. In a programmed-auto mode, these cameras are nearly as simple to operate as a point-and-shoot camera, with the advantage of having interchangeable lenses. However, most photographers who invest in these complex machines do so to take advantage of their wide-ranging capabilities, plus their versatile lens and accessory systems.

Adaptable to any task from the family vacation to involved scientific-industrial imaging, this class of camera can be configured for any photographic task from sky diving to scuba diving. Most of the better models let you turn off the autofocus and auto exposure facilities when creative manual control is desired or necessary. All but the top-end pro models now have built-in pop-up flash units. While no substitute for a more powerful and versatile shoe-mount unit, they are great for informal shots. These cameras place no limits on your picture-taking possibilities.

Pentax ZX-5N

✓ **BEST BUY**

The Pentax ZX-5N is compact and lightweight, fits the hand well, and sports a retro silver and black finish. The controls are mainly large, easy-to-comprehend dials. The small LCD panel displays the exposure counter and confirms the selected exposure program, flash status, film speed, and battery condition. All necessary exposure data is visible in the viewfinder; a panorama format mask can be employed when desired, and the viewfinder eyepiece is adjustable over a range of -2.5 to +1.5 diopters. Metering modes available include 6-segment, multi-pattern, which serves well for widely varying lighting conditions; center-weighted averaging; and spot, for when you don't want areas surrounding your subject to influence the reading. Program modes include Programmed AE, which makes all the decisions for you; Metered Manual, for when you need full creative control; Aperture-Priority AE, for when you need to control the depth-of-field; and Shutter-Priority AE, for when you need either an action-stopping high shutter speed or a blur-inducing slower one. The built-in, pop-up "Smart Flash" handles auto fill flash, and has a slow-shutter sync setting for nighttime or interior pictures without the background coming out black. Other features include auto bracketing, electronic depth-of-field preview, and 12-second self-timer. Pentax's fine line of lenses (including power zooms) and accessories make the ZX-5N a prime contender for your camera-buying dollar.

Warranty: 1 year; 5 years at additional cost
Manufacturer's Suggested Retail Price: $700 (body only)
Approximate Low Price: $360-$500

Canon EOS Rebel 2000

Recommended

Canon's EOS Rebel, in its various incarnations, has been the world's best-selling 35mm SLR for quite a while. The latest update, including a restyle, is the EOS Rebel 2000. The smart new silver and black trim has a thoroughly modern look, and its popular price in relation to the substantial list of features should only enhance its standing. The major new enhancements are relative to the autofocus (AF) system and the exposure metering scheme. The AF system now has a 7-point, wide-area sensor array, along with a revised focusing algorithm for increased AF speed and more accurate focusing point selection. Either of two AF modes, One-Shot AF or AI-Servo AF for tracking moving subjects, is selected automatically by the camera. There is an AF-assist beam for low-light conditions. You can also focus manually, with electronic confirmation. Another important addition is a depth-of-field preview, which lets you check the zone of sharpness before you take the picture. There are eleven picture-taking modes that let you tailor the camera's operation to any subject. Shutter speeds are $1/2,000$ second to 30 seconds (flash synchronization at $1/90$ second). Other features include multiple exposure capability, AE lock, ten-second self-timer, camera shake warning, full-information viewfinder, and LCD data panel. The built-in pop-up flash is weighted at the selected focusing point. Fill-flash and red-eye reduction are featured. Film loading, wind, and rewind are motorized automatically. Body weight is 11.7 ounces, and two CR2 lithium batteries are required. The Canon EOS Rebel 2000 is very compact and provides access to Canon's extensive line-up of EF-series lenses.

Warranty: 1 year
Manufacturer's Suggested Retail Price: $450 (body only)
Approximate Low Price: $255-$269

Nikon N60

The N60 offers both simplicity of operation and █Budget Buy█ an adequate array of features, so it doesn't feel like a stripped-down model. The body chassis is made of zinc alloy, and the exterior is finished in attractive silver and black. Operating the camera can be as simple or sophisticated as you desire. The N60's new Auto-Servo autofocus (AF) system can detect whether your subject is stationary or in motion and senses the direction of movement. Use the General-Purpose Program for point-and-shoot ease, or go with the Vari-Program modes for more effective handling of challenging subjects or lighting situations. The camera offers Portrait, Landscape, Close-up, Sport, and Night Scene modes. The camera's 3D Matrix Meter uses a 6-segment sensor. An AF-assist illuminator makes AF operation possible in nearly any low-lighting conditions.

Film loading, advance (1fps), and wind/rewind are automatic and motorized. AE and AF locks are provided for off-center subject situations. Matrix-balanced fill-flash helps erase harsh shadows with outdoor portraits. Shutter speed range is $1/2{,}000$ second to 30 seconds. Film speeds from ISO 25 to 5000 are set automatically. Self-timer duration is ten seconds. The camera includes a two-button reset feature that lets you quickly cancel special settings, reverting to the camera's default settings; this can prove handy when shooting conditions change suddenly. Body weight is 20.3 ounces.

Warranty: 1 year
Manufacturer's Suggested Retail Price: $420 (body only)
Approximate Low Price: $279-$320

_____35mm AUTOFOCUS CAMERAS_____

The 35mm leaf-shutter autofocus (AF) camera is popular because it makes shooting high-quality 35mm film easier. An AF camera does more than automatically focus the lens. It also loads the film, advances it after each exposure, and rewinds it at the end of the roll.

FEATURES_____

Many AF cameras come with a sophisticated meter that activates a built-in flash under difficult lighting conditions, such as backlighting, to balance the lighting intensity between the subject and the background. Some have lenses of fixed focal length, while others offer zoom lenses for wide angle to telephoto effects. Many now have special red-eye reduction features, compact design, and a panorama format that can be selected at will.

Minolta Freedom Zoom Supreme EX Date

Minolta's Freedom Zoom Supreme EX Date is a feature-laden camera that offers a lot for a medium-priced model. It has a silver-metallic finish and an almost retro styling that will appeal to many prospective buyers. A rubber grip area ensures a secure hold. The zoom lens has an extended 39mm to 125mm range; this covers a lot of picture-taking territory. The lens also has a close-up mode that focuses down to 17.7 inches. You can set the camera to a fully automatic mode for effortless picture taking or choose three other modes for subject-specific situations. A zoom-integrated, dual-segment metering scheme is used, and spot metering of small areas is possible. The built-in, retractable flash offers auto-flash operation (with or without red-eye reduction), manual fill-flash, flash off, and slow shutter synchronization. Film speed range is ISO 25 to 3200. Self-timer delay is ten seconds, and an accessory infrared remote release (included with the camera) provides instant or two-second-delayed release. Film loading, wind, and rewind are automatic; rewind can be set for manual triggering. The camera can imprint several combinations of date and time information on your photos. Weight without the battery is 9.7 ounces; to conserve battery power, the camera turns itself off after eight minutes of inactivity.

Warranty: 1 year, parts and labor
Manufacturer's Suggested Retail Price: $355
Approximate Low Price: not available

Canon SureShot 85 Zoom

Recommended

The SureShot 85 Zoom has a 38-85mm f/4.2-8.7 zoom lens that is suitable for a wide range of subjects. The zoom action is controlled with two buttons on the front of the camera. The lens focuses as close as two feet for good close-up capability. A 3-point, 280-step AF system identifies the subject precisely, even if it isn't centered in the frame. A large mode dial on top of the camera facilitates selection of Auto Flash mode (with or without red-eye reduction), whereby the flash fires whenever the camera deems it necessary; Flash On; Flash Off; Self-Timer; and Real-Time (RT) mode. A built-in lens cover opens and closes automatically when the camera is turned on or off. An LED indicator in the viewfinder displays the frame counter and battery condition; a green LED signals that it's okay to shoot, and an orange one indicates the flash is ready. A viewfinder mask automatically activates upon switching to panorama mode. Film ISO range is 25 to 3200. Motorized film loading, wind, and rewind are automatic. The weight is 7.6 ounces without the battery.

Warranty: 1 year
Manufacturer's Suggested Retail Price: $195
Approximate Low Price: not available

Pentax IQ Zoom 115M

Recommended

The IQ Zoom 115M has a 38mm to 115mm f/3.9-10.5 zoom lens with a power zoom control. This is a more than adequate focal length range for the majority of picture opportunities. Autofocus (AF) range is from 2.1 feet to infinity. The AF system used is a phase-matching passive 5-point type that provides quite a degree of flexibility as to subject placement within the picture. Exposure control is fully programmed automatic, with a multi-metering scheme. Normal shutter speed range is $1/300$ second to 2 seconds; switching to Bulb mode extends this from $1/2$ second to 5 minutes. Focus and flash status indicators are visible in the viewfinder; an external LCD panel displays the frame counter, battery condition, and flash mode, along with self-timer (ten second delay) and remote control data. The viewfinder eyepiece is adjustable from -3 to +1 diopters. Switching to panorama mode automatically masks the viewfinder accordingly. The built-in auto-flash fires any time—lighting conditions dictate in auto mode, but it can be turned off or set to fire every time for flash-fill, and red-eye reduction is available. Film wind to frame one is automatic, as are wind and rewind; mid-roll rewind is possible. Film ISO range is 25 to 3200. An optional infrared remote control, which has a three-second delay, is available.

Warranty: 1 year
Manufacturer's Suggested Retail Price: $350
Approximate Low Price: $199

Nikon Fun Touch 5

Budget Buy

If you want a stylish, reliable, 35mm point-and-shoot autofocus (AF) camera, but don't want to spend a lot of money, then you should consider the Nikon Fun Touch 5. It offers a good, basic list of features at an attractive price. The lens is a 29mm f/4.5 wide angle. The single shutter speed is $\frac{1}{125}$ second, adequate for all but fast action subjects. The built-in flash has three modes: Auto Flash (fires when necessary), Anytime Flash (fires every time), and Flash Off. It also has a red-eye reduction feature. The AF system operates over a range of 4.3 feet to infinity. A focus lock lets you maintain focus for your subject while repositioning for an off-center composition. Film loading, wind, and rewind are motorized and automatic, and mid-roll rewind is possible. Film ISO range is 100 to 400, which might be a drawback if you want to use the new ISO 800 films to extend your low-light picture-taking opportunities. The Fun Touch 5 uses two AA batteries, which makes replacement uncomplicated in foreign locales. Weight is 5.8 ounces without batteries.

Warranty: 1 year
Manufacturer's Suggested Retail Price: $60
Approximate Low Price: $39-$50

35mm COMPACT CAMERAS

These cameras have fixed (single) focal length and "focus-free" lenses, which provide sharp pictures from a few feet away to infinity. Most feature simple auto-exposure systems designed for color negative films, and many offer a built-in automatic flash as well. Despite their simplicity of operation and relatively low cost, these cameras are capable of taking excellent photos.

Fujifilm Auto 10

✓ **BEST BUY**

The Fujifilm Auto 10 features a 29mm f/5.6 wide-angle lens, which is great for situations in which you want to capture a wide area in the photo but can't back up far enough. The zone of sharp focus is from 4.9 feet to infinity. The shutter speed is $1/125$ second, which will handle most situations other than fast action. The built-in flash fires automatically in low light, and has a range of 9.8 feet with ISO 100 film. Film loading, wind, and rewind are motorized and automatic. The oversized viewfinder is a help for those who wear glasses. Two AA batteries are required, and the camera weighs 6 ounces without batteries. The Auto 10's foolproof simplicity makes it a Best Buy.

Warranty: 1 year
Manufacturer's Suggested Retail Price: $60
Approximate Low Price: not available

Minolta F15BF

| Recommended |

The carefree operation of a "focus free" camera is an attraction to many people who just want good pictures without having to become involved in the photographic hobby. The Minolta F15BF fulfills all the requirements for simplicity and reliability typical of this class of camera. Anyone who wears eyeglasses will appreciate the large, bright, magnified viewfinder. Indeed, the viewfinder shows images approximately three times larger than most other cameras in its class, and is particularly appropriate for far-sighted people. The lens is a 35mm medium wide angle. A concealed lens cover protects the lens automatically when the camera is switched off. The built-in flash fires automatically as dim lighting conditions dictate, and has a red-eye reduction feature to help eliminate that deer-in-the-headlights look common to pictures of people taken in dimly lighted interiors. Film loading is motorized and automatic, as are wind and rewind.

Warranty: 1 year, parts and labor
Manufacturer's Suggested Retail Price: $41
Approximate Low Price: not available

24MM ADVANCED PHOTO SYSTEM (APS) CAMERAS

The Advanced Photo System (APS), developed by a number of international camera and film manufacturers, has been in existence for about four years now. It is designed around a smaller size film and cassette, which at first glance resembles a 35mm film cassette. However, the APS film employs an impressive array of new technologies, all with the ultimate purpose of giving you better pictures and more ways of putting them to use in your daily life.

FEATURES

Film loading couldn't be simpler; just drop the cassette into the camera and close the film chamber. The camera automatically winds the film to the first frame, eliminating the bothersome threading of 35mm-film leader. The film features a clear magnetic coating, similar to audio recording tape but optically transparent, which records exposure and format selection data from the camera. This information is in turn read by the processing machinery at the film lab, resulting in more precise adjustments of color and density during the printing stage.

Depending on the camera model, a variety of information, such as date, time, exposure data, or special titles and messages, can be imprinted on the back of your prints. You can choose from three different formats, including panoramic. The format choice is indicated on the film, so if you change your mind later, you can have any picture printed in any format at a later date. Your film is returned with an index print, containing small thumbnail images of every picture on the roll, making filing and negative selection a breeze.

Some cameras also let you switch film types in mid-roll, such as from color to black-and-white. Upon reloading the partially exposed cassette, the camera remembers where you left off and automatically advances the film to that frame. Some companies even offer APS scanners that let you view your pictures on a TV or import them into your computer to incorporate them into various kinds of documents. These options offer more user control over the end product than any other film-based camera system. APS prints cost a little more to process than 35mm, but your options are limited only by your imagination.

Rollei Nano 60

✓ **BEST BUY**

Rollei, long famous for its medium-format professional cameras, now has a very compact Advanced Photo System (APS) camera, the Nano 60. Measuring a mere 3.8"×2.3"×1.4", the stylish aluminum camera is handy to keep with you at all times for capturing those unexpected picture opportunities. The lens is a German-designed 28-60mm f/4.0-8.0 zoom with first-class imaging characteristics. Zoom action is powered, controlled via a thumb-operated rocker switch. An electronically controlled program shutter offers speeds from $1/400$ second to $1/3$ second. The active infrared autofocus (AF) system has a working range from infinity down to approximately two feet, and has a focus lock feature for recomposing off-center subjects. The built-in flash offers auto-flash (fires when necessary), fill-flash, slow-sync flash (for capturing background details in night flash scenes), red-eye reduction, and flash off. A camera-back LCD panel displays exposure data, date and time, title imprinting, frame counter, and battery condition. The power source is one 3V lithium battery (CR2). Weight without the battery is 7 ounces. This camera's effortless operation, high style, and quality optics earn it a Best Buy rating.

Warranty: 3 years
Manufacturer's Suggested Retail Price: $350
Approximate Low Price: $245

Minolta Vectis Weathermatic Zoom

Recommended

Inclement weather presents unusual opportunities for out-of-the-ordinary pictures. Unfortunately, most cameras can't handle being rained or snowed on. An exception is the Minolta Vectis Weathermatic Zoom. This Advanced Photo System (APS) camera shrugs off rain with impunity, and you can take it snorkeling or diving down to a depth of 33 feet. The Weathermatic's 30-50mm f/4-6.4 zoom lens is equivalent to 38-63mm lens in 35mm format. The camera is the first in its class to provide underwater autofocus (AF) capability, made possible by its passive phase-detection AF system. AF focusing range is 1.3 feet to infinity (1.7 feet to infinity underwater, due to the refractive difference of water). The large, high-eyepoint viewfinder makes viewing easy, whether with eyeglasses on land or when wearing goggles underwater. Strap and accessory ports let you clip the camera to a backpack or belt, or wear it on your arm underwater. Exposure is programmed automatic, with center-weighted averaging metering. Film speed range is ISO 100 to 3200. As with all APS cameras, film loading is drop-in automatic, date imprinting is standard, and you have a choice of three picture formats, switchable at any point in the roll. The self-timer has a ten-second delay. One 3V lithium battery (CR2) is required. Weight without battery is 12 ounces. The camera housing is yellow (for good visibility underwater), with a charcoal gray rubber trim.

Warranty: 1 year
Manufacturer's Suggested Retail Price: $427
Approximate Low Price: $279-$320

Nikon Pronea-S

Recommended

With a satin-silver finish and form-follows-function ergonomics, the futuristic Pronea-S encompasses all of the convenience and quality-enhancing APS attributes, along with access to the huge selection of 35mm-format Nikon lenses and accessories. The lenses designed specifically for the Pronea-S (a 30-60mm IX Nikkor zoom is standard) are smaller and lighter than their 35mm counterparts, but there are many special-purpose lenses that are only available in the 35mm format line. Focus can be achieved via autofocus (AF) or manually. In AF mode, the camera automatically selects either Single Servo AF or Continuous Servo AF according to whether the subject is moving or stationary. Moving subjects automatically activate the Focus Tracking feature; an AF lock is also provided. An AF illuminator permits autofocusing in dim lighting conditions. Exposure modes include General-Purpose Program, Auto-Multi Program, Shutter-Priority Auto, and Aperture-Priority Auto. Vari-Program modes include Portrait, Landscape, Close-up, and Night Scene. 3D Matrix exposure metering is used with IX Nikkor, D-type AF Nikkor, AF-S, and AF-I Nikkor lenses; 6-segment Matrix metering is used with non-D-type AF Nikkors. The electronically controlled shutter has speeds from $1/2,000$ second to 30 seconds ($1/125$-second flash synchronization). Time exposures are possible with an optional remote control. Active exposure information is displayed in the illuminated viewfinder, with a camera-back LCD panel showing complete data. The built-in pop-up flash provides coverage for 24mm or longer lenses. Automatic balanced fill-flash, slow sync, red-eye reduction, and flash off are available. Film ISO range is 25 to 800. Two CR2 lithium batteries are required. All standard APS features are available (drop-in film loading, three picture formats, date/time imprinting, etc.), plus Mid-Roll Change (good for changing film speeds when lighting conditions warrant). Body weight is $11 1/2$ ounces (16 ounces with standard 30-60mm zoom lens), making it the smallest, lightest interchangeable-lens AF SLR camera made.

Warranty: 1 year
Manufacturer's Suggested Retail Price: $520 (with lens)
Approximate Low Price: $367-$370

Fuji Endeavor 60 AF

Budget Buy

For anyone looking for an uncomplicated, economical Advanced Photo System (APS) camera, the Fuji Endeavor 60 AF merits investigation. With point-and-shoot simplicity, it offers a choice of three picture formats (the viewfinder is masked accordingly), foolproof drop-in loading (the film cartridge will fit into the film chamber only the correct way), auto advance and rewind, and convenient index prints with every roll of processing. Once loaded, the film chamber can't be opened accidentally, preventing light-fogged film. The lens is a 24mm f/6.3. The shutter has a single speed, $^1/_{125}$ second, adequate for all but fast action subjects. The active infrared autofocus system focuses from 2.6 feet to infinity. The built-in flash is effective to 11½ feet with ISO 200 film, and offers fill-flash and red-eye reduction. The camera can be powered by either a pair of AAA batteries or a long-life CR2 lithium battery. Weight without batteries is 4.8 ounces. The camera has a satin silver finish, and features smartly modern styling.

Warranty: 1 year
Manufacturer's Suggested Retail Price: $100
Approximate Low Price: not available

INSTANT-PRINT CAMERAS

Instant-print cameras are only available from Polaroid in the United States. Consumer models produce color prints that self-develop within a few minutes. Although the cost per print is higher than with 35mm and APS, these cameras offer the advantage of providing immediate gratification for those who can't wait to see the pictures they've taken.

Polaroid I-Zone Instant Pocket Camera

Recommended

The I-Zone capitalizes on the popularity among youths of trading collectible stickers by offering films that produce either miniature photos (.95"×1.14") or photo stickers; each film provides twelve pictures or stickers. The lens is focus-free, and the shutter speed is $^1/_{100}$ second. A built-in flash makes indoor portraits a breeze, from 2 to 8 feet away. Two AA batteries are required. The camera is kid-sized (6"×1¾"×1¾") and kid-friendly in operation. It is offered in your choice of bright red, green, or blue, as well as Bugs Bunny, Taz, Tweety, and Barbie versions that feature three-dimensional character molds of the popular children's icons. Additionally, adults may find the sticker film handy for adding quick and easy photo ID to convention badges and other similar uses.

Warranty: 1 year
Manufacturer's Suggested Retail Price: $25
Approximate Low Price: not available

Polaroid Pop Shots

Recommended

This is the first instant-print, single-use camera, which comes pre-loaded with film for ten 4.4"×2.5" pictures. Since a Pop Shots camera doesn't need to be sent in for processing, Polaroid has instituted a mail-in recycling program for the empty cameras. The cameras come with a pre-paid return mailer, and purchasers who return their Pop Shots for recycling are automatically entered in a prize sweepstakes and receive a $2 coupon off their next Pop Shots camera. The compact (6"×4"×2"), lightweight (9 ounces) camera has a sleek, funky, modern design. It is black and red with operating instructions printed right on the camera. The camera's single-element 90mm fixed-focus (focus-free) lens can take portraits as close as three feet away. Maximum flash range is seven feet. A manual ring-pull arrangement propels the film through a roller system for picture development. Pop Shots is a fun addition to Polaroid's line of "social catalyst" cameras.

Warranty: 1 year
Manufacturer's Suggested Retail Price: $20
Approximate Low Price: not available

DIGITAL-STILL CAMERAS

A few years ago, you had only two choices in digital-still cameras: good quality and extremely expensive or reasonably priced but poor quality. Today, consumer digital cameras offer a favorable combination of quality, versatility, and affordability. It is simple to import your pictures into your computer for use with computer graphics. You can take a picture and within minutes send it to friends, relatives, or business associates. You can also view your pictures on a TV or print them out as regular photos with either a special printer or via your color inkjet printer.

QUALITY

Instead of film, images are captured by a CCD and then stored on one of various removable magnetic storage media, usually referred to as a "card." Unlike film, the exact number of pictures obtainable per card can vary considerably, depending on the resolution and degree of compression chosen. The higher the quality (resolution), the fewer pictures per card.

While digital cameras share many similarities with film cameras, there are some terms specific to digital. Before making a purchase, decide whether you will use a digital camera in conjunction with your computer and be sure of the camera's compatibility with your computer's operating system. Adapters are also available.

FEATURES AND TERMINOLOGY

CCD: The charge-coupled device, often referred to as a "chip," is the light-sensitive device that captures the image when you press the shutter release.

Compression: A means of storing a greater number of images on a given card size or disk. There are several file formats used, but JPEG and TIFF are common examples. Compression is a trade-off of quality for storage space. Uncompressed images are the highest quality, but severely limit the number of pictures per card. Many cameras let you choose the degree of compression applied.

Equivalent Focal Length: Because a CCD is much smaller than a frame of 35mm film, and therefore requires lenses of much shorter focal length to produce the same coverage (magnification) as a lens on a 35mm camera, manufacturers usually specify what the equivalent lens would be on a 35mm camera.

NiMH Batteries: Nickel metal hydride rechargeable batteries, the optimal batteries for use with digital cameras.

Optical Zoom: A true, lens-based zoom. Optically zoomed images are much sharper than digitally zoomed images.

Storage Media: A magnetic equivalent of film, this is usually referred to as a "card" that stores the pictures as they are taken. Spare cards can be carried. Unwanted pictures can be erased, freeing space for new pictures. Some examples of these cards include PCMCIA (types I and II), CompactFlash, and SmartMedia. Some Sony cameras use common 3.5-inch computer disks.

Nikon Coolpix 700

 BEST BUY

The Nikon Coolpix 700's autofocus lens is a fixed 6.8mm (38mm equivalent in 35mm format), but 4-step (1.25×; 1.6×; 2×; 2.5×) digital zooming, plus macro (down to 3.5 inches) is included; fish-eye and wide-angle adapter lenses are optional. There are three aperture settings: f/2.6, f/3.8, and f/8.0. Three TTL exposure-metering modes are provided: 256-element Matrix, spot, and center-weighted. Exposure control is programmed automatic, with ±2 EV of manual exposure compensation possible when desired. ISO equivalent is 80. The high-speed continuous shooting feature is capable of up to two frames per second. Shutter speeds are 1/750 second to 1 second. Tone curve (contrast and brightness) settings are user-selectable. Images can be saved as uncompressed TIFF files, or in any of three JPEG compression modes. An 8MB CompactFlash card comes with the camera and can store up to 128 images at maximum compression and minimum resolution, or one image at maximum resolution, uncompressed. Cards with up to 64MB capacity are available. There is both an optical viewfinder and a 1.8-inch LCD monitor. Modes for the built-in flash include auto, off, fill-flash, red-eye reduction, and slow-sync. An auto-power-save feature turns the camera off after 30 seconds of inactivity; this feature can be reset to 1, 5, or 30 minutes. The camera interfaces with a computer using a serial port. Platforms supported are Windows 95, Windows 98, Windows NT 4.0 or later, and Mac OS 7.5.1 or later. Four AA batteries (supplied) are required; an AC adapter is optional. Dimensions are 4.5×2.6×1.5 inches, and the camera weighs 9.5 ounces without batteries. This camera's 2.11-megapixel capability allows for greater enlargements of your pictures at photo-realistic quality.

Specifications: minimum requirements (PC), Windows 95, Windows 98, Windows NT 4.0 or later; (Macintosh), Mac OS 7.5.1 or later
Warranty: 1 year
Manufacturer's Suggested Retail Price: $599
Approximate Low Price: $499-$585

Olympus D-340R

Budget Buy

This 1.3-mega-pixel camera is available for less than $500, and it isn't a stripped-down model by any means. The autofocus lens is 5.5mm (36mm equivalent in 35mm format) with an f/2.8 maximum aperture. A 2× digital telephoto mode extends the lens range. The 1.8-inch LCD display activates automatically in 2× tele mode, providing through-the-lens composition in a digital SLR simulation. The built-in intelligent flash has four modes: auto low light, fill flash, red-eye reduction, and forced off. You can select either 100 or 200 ISO rating equivalent. In burst mode, the camera captures ten shots at $\frac{1}{2}$-second intervals and writes the photos to the camera's D-RAM internal memory. Pictures can be stored as uncompressed TIFF files for maximum picture quality, or at three degrees of compression for greater picture capacity (an 8MB card can hold 2 images without compression or 120 at maximum compression). The D-340R uses SmartMedia memory cards of up to 16MB capacity (an 8MB card is supplied with the camera); images so captured can be directly transferred to any Macintosh or PC on 3.5-inch disks with the help of the Olympus FlashPath adapter. You can also print pictures directly to the Olympus P-330 photo printer without a computer. Camera power comes from 4 AA batteries (supplied); an AC adapter, rechargeable batteries, and a battery charger are optional. A software bundle for PC and Macintosh computers is included, as is a video connection cable for TV or VCR. The D-340R measures 5×2.6×1.8 inches and weighs 9 ounces. This camera's strong complement of features versus its modest price make it a Budget Buy.

Warranty: 1 year
Manufacturer's Suggested Retail Price: $499
Approximate Low Price: $339-$400

TELEPHONES AND ANSWERING MACHINES

Telephones are getting smarter, smaller, more streamlined, and more stylish. Even tabletop corded phones have a futuristic look. Basic corded phones offer some of the same capabilities that high-priced, multi-featured models had just a few years ago. The good news is you can ignore the features you don't need and choose a phone based on the features that make your life easier.

HOW TO SHOP

Shopping for a phone or answering machine is easy. Just make a list of features you'd like to have, and consider or eliminate models on that basis. Don't forget color choices if basic black will be a problem in the setting you want to use the phone in.

Features to consider are corded or cordless, frequency, security, single or multiple lines, the availability of caller ID, and whether or not you want a built-in answering machine. Don't forget that caller ID, while an attractive option, is also a service you need to subscribe to (and pay for) from the local telephone company. A phone that offers a caller ID display won't display the desired information unless you've subscribed to the service.

WHERE TO BUY

If possible, look at different phone models before making your purchase. Many of the cordless 900MHz models are available in warehouse chains such as Costco and Sam's Club. Business oriented models are frequently on display at larger office supply stores, including chains such as Staples and Office Depot. Evaluate the models you're interested in based on how they feel when you use them and whether you feel that the controls are sufficiently clear. When you find the models you deem most suitable, comparison shop on the Internet for the best price.

FEATURES AND TERMINOLOGY_____

Caller ID/Call Waiting: A supplement to caller ID service, which lets users see who is calling without having to interrupt the current call.

Caller ID Memory/Log: Remembers the last calls made to your phone. Some phones can also move stored numbers into permanent speed-dial memory.

Flash: This sends a brief signal that duplicates a quick press of the telephone's switch hook—without the chance of accidental disconnection. Flash is useful if you subscribe to optional phone company services such as call waiting and conference calling.

Hearing-aid Compatible: These phones are designed to provide normal conversation for people who wear hearing aids. Most phones are hearing-aid compatible.

Hold: Retains the call, but both parties are on mute.

Last-number Redial: A common feature. A press of this key dials the last number called on the specific phone you're using.

Mute: The mute key stops transmission of sound. The other party cannot hear noises at your end of the conversation while the mute key is pressed.

900MHz: 900MHz technology, used with cordless phones, is more secure, provides clearer communication, and has better range than traditional 47MHz. The 900MHz phones come in three varieties: analog (good range but poor security); digital (better clarity, range, and security, but can be blocked by obstructions); and Digital Spread Spectrum, or DSS, (best clarity, range, and security).

Speakerphone: A microphone and a speaker are built into the phone, so you can have a conversation without picking up the handset.

Speed-dialing Memory: Most phones have some type of speed-dialing memory; higher-end phones have keys set aside just for speed-dialing. These memory keys usually have enough space for 16 or 24 digits each, and are designed to hold phone numbers frequently dialed. Some phones also allow programming pauses—you would use this if you must dial 9 to access an outside line.

Three-way Conference: Found on several two-line phones, this allows the user to connect a second user through the speakerphone using the second line, thus enabling a three-way conversation with the caller on the other end of the line.

BEST BUYS 2000

Our Best Buy and Recommended telephones and answering machines follow. Products within each category are listed according to quality. The item we consider the best of the Best Buys is first, followed by our second choice, and so on. Remember that a Best Buy or Recommended designation only applies to the model listed—it does not necessarily apply to other models made by the same manufacturer or to an entire product line.

FEATURE TELEPHONES

Casio Phonemate TC-945

✔**BEST BUY**

The Casio Phonemate TC-945 is not much larger than a standard corded feature phone. It has a base unit with a keypad on which the handset rests. This base unit has two-line speakerphone capability, so even if you leave the handset in another room, you can still answer and place calls on either of the two lines using the speakerphone. An LCD display panel shows you the status of each line. The 900MHz wireless handset is also a two-line unit, with a flashing LED that indicates which line a call is coming in on. The base unit also contains a digital answering machine, with 24 minutes of message recording capability that can answer both phone lines. You can record two separate greetings, one for each line. If the TC-945 is busy answering a call on one line, and the second line rings, the caller on the second line hears a digitally synthesized voice that tells them their call will be answered shortly. Once the TC-945 is done recording the first call, it plays the appropriate greeting, then records a message on the second line. You can play back all the messages when you return, or play back each line's messages separately.

Warranty: 1 year (limited)
Manufacturer's Suggested Retail Price: $179
Approximate Low Price: not available

Casio Phonemate IT-380 E-Mail Link Telephone

`Recommended`

If you've ever wished you could check your e-mail without the bother of booting up your PC, now you can with the Casio Phonemate IT-380 E-Mail Link Telephone with Digital Answering Machine. The telephone, which is compatible with the popular POP3 e-mail protocol, works with many popular Internet Service Providers (ISPs), including AT&T, Compuserve, Mindspring, and Prodigy. It doesn't work with America Online or MSN (the Microsoft Network). The IT-380 is a high-quality telephone with a hands-free speakerphone and 20-number autodial. It also has a built-in digital answering machine with 14 minutes of message recoding capacity, and you can record two different greetings and switch between them.

Warranty: 1 year (limited)
Manufacturer's Suggested Retail Price: $149
Approximate Low Price: not available

Brother Quattro Starter System CTS-400-SS

`Recommended`

The Quattro is a four-line system that offers the features many small businesses want and need. Caller ID is available, as long as you subscribe to this service, and you can mix up to 12 corded and cordless handsets in the system. The deluxe corded speakerphones offer a caller ID display and 18 speed-dial keys. The cordless handsets greatly resemble a small cellular phone, also provide caller ID, and can access any of the four lines. Setting up the system isn't hard, but there are a lot of pieces to connect. Each cordless handset comes with its own charger, and you'll probably need a power strip to accommodate all of the small power supplies, since each unit has its own. The starter system includes a single speakerphone, one handset, a caller ID unit, and a cordless base unit. You can purchase additional phones and handsets separately.

Warranty: 1 year, parts and labor
Manufacturer's Suggested Retail Price: $899
Approximate Low Price: not available

CORDLESS TELEPHONES (900MHz MODELS)

Cordless phones are much clearer, more secure, and operate at longer distances than before. When shopping for a cordless unit, check how long the battery remains charged. If it needs to be recharged frequently, the convenience is greatly diminished. Another important feature is the pager, which helps locate a misplaced handset quickly. Also, some cordless phones come with an intercom feature, which allows you to talk from the phone to the base. If security is an issue, consider a spread-spectrum phone. These use a technique that changes the operating frequency several times a second, so that no one outside can eavesdrop on your conversation.

Casio Phonemate CP-750

✔ **BEST BUY**

The Casio Phonemate CP-750 is a 900MHz cordless phone that incorporates caller ID. It's not an expensive unit at $60, so some of the features that you'll find in higher-priced units, such as a base with its own keypad or speakerphone, are missing from this model. But the handset, which includes a handy clip so you can wear it on your belt, has some nice features, including a three-line LCD display that shows the phone number and name of the caller. The handset can store up to 50 calls, so you can find out who called even if you don't have an answering machine. You can also store another 20 numbers for the autodial, and use the LCD to page through to the number you wish to dial. The CP-750 incorporates Casio Phonemate's Modem Monitor, which prevents you from accidentally disconnecting an online session or incoming call. And if a call has been received and logged into the caller ID log while you were out, a light illuminates on the base and an indicator shows on the handset, reminding you to check.

Warranty: 1 year (limited)
Manufacturer's Suggested Retail Price: $60
Approximate Low Price: not available

Casio Phonemate MA-240

✔**BEST BUY**

Unlike many 900MHz phones, the handset of the MA-240 doesn't charge in the base station, so you can position the compact transceiver base almost anywhere, as long as its small fold-up antenna isn't blocked by metal. Two jacks and included modular cable make it easy to connect to two different phone lines. The phone handset looks much more like a cellular phone than typical 900MHz units. The MA-240 uses a long-lasting Nickel Metal Hydride rechargeable battery and comes with a handy belt clip. Small as it may be, the handset offers a caller ID display that saves up to 30 calls. You can also speed-dial any of ten numbers you have stored in the handset. With the handset, you can answer either of the two lines, conference call using both lines, or transfer the call to another handset. One feature we liked a lot was the MA-240's ability to communicate between handsets connected to the same system. This intercom facility is great when you have multiple handsets scattered among family members or a large office.

Warranty: 1 year (limited)
Manufacturer's Suggested Retail Price: $199
Approximate Low Price: $179

Microsoft Cordless Phone System MP-900

✔**BEST BUY**

The Microsoft Cordless Phone System, which combines a full-featured 900MHz cordless telephone to a computer interface, is a bit of a departure for the vendor. The MP-900 is a system where the phone can be used normally to make and receive calls when the PC is turned off. With the computer on, however, the Call Manager software, an integral part of the system, can match caller ID (if you subscribe) to a database to screen your calls. If you don't answer, the software/PC combination provides a sophisticated voice messaging system that can even page you and let you know there's a message waiting. Voice commands to dial by name are available using the handset, and there's even a "message" button on the handset that lets you access and scroll through messages recorded on the PC. Getting the best use out of the Microsoft Cordless Phone System, however, requires you pay close attention to the manual, though there is a separate quick setup guide that helps.

Warranty: 1 year (limited)
Manufacturer's Suggested Retail Price: $80
Approximate Low Price: not available

Panasonic KX-TC1710B

Recommended

Panasonic's KX-TC1710B is a 900MHz cordless phone with some enhanced features. Its base station has its own keypad and speakerphone, so you can place calls without needing the handset. The handset is a typical 900MHz model, though it incorporates an LCD display on the rear of the unit, which displays caller ID information. The handset can remember the last 50 caller ID numbers and names, and can store ten speed-dial numbers. The base station can store up to five speed-dial numbers. Unlike many cordless phones, the KX-TC1710B works nicely with the voice mail services offered by many phone companies. If you subscribe to this service and receive a call that's answered by the service, a small LED indicator on the base station lights up and an icon appears on the LCD panel on the handset. You can program your access number to easily retrieve your messages with the press of a key. The KX-TC1710B is somewhat expensive for just a cordless telephone, and it has none of the answering machine features that you'll find in other models offered at this price. But we did like the easy-to-use LCD panel on the handset, and we feel that the KX-TC1710B is a higher-end model that offers a good, if not exceptional, value.

Warranty: 1 year, parts and labor
Manufacturer's Suggested Retail Price: $120
Approximate Low Price: $92-$100

MOBILE TELEPHONES

Mobile phones used to be classified by size, but adapters and other accessories now make the difference between a lightweight slim phone and a car phone plugged into a cigarette lighter. The first mobile phones were analog, with different rate plans that probably included a free or low-cost phone. Then carriers began offering the more advanced digital service. The latest technology—digital PCS cellular—sounds less like a radio. Instead, the sound can have a slightly mechanical quality. The digital signal can carry much more information than the analog signal can, so the carrier can offer extras, such as caller ID, pagerlike messaging, and call forwarding. PCS phones cost a bit more, and they are usually not offered free with a service commitment, but their built-in security means eavesdroppers are much less likely to monitor your calls. So far, analog networks still cover more ground than PCS networks, but the gap is closing. Dual-mode phones, which operate as a digital phone when a digital network service is available, but switch to analog mode when roaming where no digital service yet exists, are a good compromise.

Qualcomm QCP-820

✔**BEST BUY**

Qualcomm Corporation designed the basic chips that are used in many of the digital CDMA-type cellular telephones on the market. So we're not surprised to find the standard array of digital cellular features such as caller ID, call waiting, 99-number phone book, and voice-mail capability built into the QCP-820. A dual-mode CDMA digital and analog phone, the QCP-820 also offers dual NAM capability. That means you can use the same instrument with two different cellular numbers. Unlike many cellular phones, the QCP-820's battery is built into the phone, so it's not easily or casually replaceable (though you can replace it if necessary). The standard battery is a 500 mAh Lithium Ion unit that provides up to five hours of talking time and 65 hours of standby time. An optional 1200 mAh battery adds another half-ounce to the weight, but considerably more to the talk and stanby time. A DialShuttle control makes it exceptionally easy to access the QCP-820's features, as well as scroll through the unit's phone directory.

Warranty: 1 year, parts and labor
Manufacturer's Suggested Retail Price: Varies with service provider and contract
Approximate Low Price: not available

Nokia 252

✔ BEST BUY

Because many consumers outside of major cities are still waiting for the digital networks that work with PCS digital cellular phones, this easy-to-carry, easy-to-use analog cellular phone from Nokia sets the pace. You'll get more than you might expect from this model. Caller ID support, voice-mail alert, and one-button speed-dialing are just a few of the features that make the 252 a Best Buy. With almost two hours of talk time from a single charge (30 hours of standby time) and a contoured design that fits comfortably in the hand, the 252 will go anywhere. Nokia offers the 252 in a variety of colors. If you're on the go, then go with a little style and take the 252 along for the ride.

Warranty: 1 year
Manufacturer's Suggested Retail Price: not available
Approximate Low Price: not available

Motorola StarTAC 7760

Recommended

The StarTAC 7760 is one of the smallest cellular phones available, and at 3.7 ounces, also one of the lightest to carry. The StarTAC 7760 is a dual-mode CDMA unit. It provides a headset jack, up to 170 minutes of talk time, and 100 hours of standby. It also offers a selection of ring tones and VibraCall silent alert. All CDMA phones use pretty much the same basic chipset, so the StarTAC 7760 offers features such as a 99-number phonebook.

It's not difficult to set up the unit's nine TurboDial keys, which provide one-touch dialing for the most frequently called numbers. We found the StarTAC's quality and fidelity excellent, though obviously this will depend on your carrier and the location and conditions under which you are calling to and from.

Warranty: 1 year, parts and labor (limited)
Manufacturer's Suggested Retail Price: Varies with service provider and contract terms
Approximate Low Price: not available

ANSWERING MACHINES

Answering machines come with many features developed for your convenience. With the addition of digital technology, answering machines can become a high-tech communications center right in your home. Phone company options such as caller ID and call waiting have also had an impact on telephones and answering machines; getting units that help these services can be an important part of the buyer's decision.

FEATURES AND TERMINOLOGY

Announce Only: You set the machine to deliver an outgoing message only. It does not allow recording of incoming messages. It's useful for a business wishing to announce hours of operation.

Autodisconnect: This lets you pick up the telephone and automatically stop the answering machine.

Remote Turn-on: This lets you turn on your machine when you are away from home.

Room Monitor: You can monitor sounds in a room while you are away via beeperless remote.

Time/Day Stamp: The machine shows the time and day a message was received.

Toll-saver: This is a money-saving feature. The machine rings four times before answering the first call but only rings once to answer

190

subsequent calls. Thus, you can call your number and know by the second ring that there are no messages, then hang up to avoid a toll charge.

VOX: This allows incoming calls of any length, up to the tape's capacity. The machine records as long as the person continues to speak, deactivating within a few seconds after the caller hangs up.

Casio Phonemate TI-355

✓**BEST BUY**

The new Casio Phonemate TI-355 phone has a terrific built-in digital answering machine that adds almost nothing to the size, or complexity, of the phone. The phone part of the TI-355 is pretty much standard, with a clear sounding hands-off speakerphone. Caller ID is supplied (if you subscribe to this service), and you can pop the stored caller ID information directly into the auto-dialer if you wish. The TI-355 has a voice guided "Data Dial" control to store numbers. As with many of Casio Phonemate's all-digital answering machines, the one built into the TI-355 has 14 minutes of message-recording capability. You can access messages remotely via a voice menu provided to make it easier to retrieve messages, and because the recording is digital, you can jump instantly through messages you want to skip. The TI-355 also provides selective erase, so you can keep some messages and delete others. The TI-355 does not have a backup battery, but unlike many digital answering machines, a power failure doesn't completely erase everything that's stored. The time display resets to 12:00 after 20 minutes without AC, but the greetings, stored messages, and stored caller IDs remain.

Warranty: 1 year (limited)
Manufacturer's Suggested Retail Price: $90
Approximate Low Price: $68

Casio Phonemate TA-119

✓**BEST BUY**

The Casio Phonemate TA-119 offers top-of-the-line features at an affordable price. The TA-119 uses digital memory to store up to 20 minutes of messages. You can also use the TA-119 to easily record memos for others in your home or office. A 9-volt battery prevents the loss of messages and greetings if the power goes out. You can record up to ten different greetings and switch between them easily. Since the TA-119 is digital, you can speed through messages and selectively save or delete messages you've listened to. The TA-119 retails for under $30, and with all the features it offers at that price, there's not much incentive to go cheaper.

Warranty: 1 year (limited)
Manufacturer's Suggested Retail Price: $29
Approximate Low Price: not available

Sony SPP-A967

Recommended

The Sony SPP-A967 consists of a 900MHz phone with a digital answering machine built into the base. Unlike some of the units we reviewed, the SPP-A967 is not usable as a phone from the base unit, since it contains neither a speakerphone nor a separate keypad. All calls also need to be placed from this handset. The SPP-A967's handset has an LCD display, which displays caller ID. There's also a 20-number caller ID memory and a 50-number autodial memory. The handset offers a jog dial control, so you can quickly page through the stored numbers. For even quicker access, you can also program three one-touch keypad buttons. The base contains an answering machine with three mailboxes, so a caller can direct their message to a specific recipient. Messages are stored in flash memory, so they won't be lost if you have a power failure. Compared with other units we've looked at, the Sony SPP-A967 is somewhat expensive. On the plus side, its spread-spectrum technology, which constantly changes the frequency being used between the handset and the base station, provides greater security against eavesdropping.

Warranty: 1 year, parts and labor
Manufacturer's Suggested Retail Price: $250
Approximate Low Price: $180

COMPUTERS

As much as computers seem to change every year, one fact remains constant: Prices drop as technology rises. For the past few years, an entry-level PC has run about $1,200. A good, midrange system brings the price up to about $1,700. A top-of-the-line system with all the bells and whistles is just over $2,700. And even when prices stabilize, as they do from time to time, the technology inside the box gets better. That means today's $1,500 PC often outperforms last year's $3,000 unit. We have to pay a price to keep up with the amazing progress we continue to see in the PC market, but it's a price that pays off in the long run. Technologies that looked like science fiction a decade ago beckon to us from catalogs and store windows.

PCs continue to grow more powerful and more loaded with standard features. So don't worry about what's looming over the horizon, because today's PCs already offer power and versatility.

HOW TO SHOP

All this progress can make a PC purchase an intimidating prospect, especially if it's your first computer. But with the design of today's PCs, obsolescence isn't nearly as great a concern as it used to be. Video cards, CD-ROM drives, and other components can be upgraded with better equipment as it comes on the market. Pentium processors can be replaced with faster chips from Intel and its competitors. Hot new technologies, such as DVD-ROM drives, are only a credit card and a screwdriver away.

Whether you're looking for a family computer, a business system, a portable companion, or a game machine that blows Nintendo 64 off the map, it's a great time to be buying a new PC. Even entry-level PCs now ship with fast Pentium processors, plenty of RAM, CD-ROM drives, and sound cards. Midrange machines with large monitors and 3D graphics that would have required a $20,000 workstation a few years ago are still under the magic $2,000 mark. And with the addition of a simple modem, millions of pieces of information on the Internet are only a mouse-click away—all for an insignificant monthly fee.

NOTEBOOK PCs

Notebook PCs are undergoing a similar revolution. CD-ROM drives and sound cards, options found only on the most expensive notebooks a year or two ago, are standard on all but the least expensive units today. Not only are powerful notebooks easier on the wallet, they're easier on your back as well. The latest trend is modular notebooks that put the CD-ROM drive and extra battery in a "slice" that clips on to the bottom of the unit. When you need access to your word processor, spreadsheet, and e-mail, detach the slice and just bring along a four-pound lightweight. When you need full multimedia capabilities, take the whole thing on the road.

FEATURES AND TERMINOLOGY

Although computers have become much easier to use over the years, a basic understanding of computer terms is useful.

Bytes: RAM and ROM are measured in bytes, which are made up of bits. A bit (binary digit) is the smallest unit of data. Its value is either one or zero. A byte is a group of bits, usually eight, that stands for one character (it could be a letter, number, or symbol) and is treated as a unit of data. A kilobyte (KB) is roughly 1,000 bytes, while a megabyte (MB) is about a million bytes. A gigabyte (GB) equals 1,000MB. With more RAM, a computer can run powerful programs faster. You can increase the amount of RAM by adding chips or expansion cards.

Central Processing Unit (CPU): Often referred to as a microprocessor, this is a computer's "brain." Like car engines, CPUs run at different speeds, usually measured in megahertz (MHz). The CPU and the computer's software-based operating system regulate the flow of data between the computer's internal components, as well as between the computer and its printer, monitor, or other peripherals.

Disk Drive: A disk drive transfers data and programs back and forth between a disk and RAM. There are different sizes of floppy drives and hard-disk drives. The disk drives differ in diameter (usually 5.25 or 3.5 inches) and height (there are full-height, ½-height, and even ⅓-height drives). Disk drives also differ in the average speed at which they randomly access data from the disk. This access time is measured in milliseconds (ms). A good hard drive should have an access speed of between 10ms and 15ms.

Motherboard: The CPU, RAM, ROM, connecting circuits, and other parts are found on the main circuit board, called the motherboard. This board often has slots for expansion cards, which are circuit boards that increase a computer's functions, speed, or memory.

Mouse/Trackball: The CPU usually receives data from an input device such as a disk drive or keyboard; sometimes data will come from a mouse or trackball. A mouse is a small device that you move around on a desktop or a pad to move the cursor or on-screen pointer. The buttons on a mouse allow you to access on-screen functions. Trackballs also have buttons, but instead of moving the mouse on a level surface, you merely spin the trackball in its socket to position the cursor.

Operating Systems: Today's IBM-compatible personal computers available in stores use the Windows 98 operating system. Some clearance or older models may sport Windows 95, which differs little from the 1998 version. Other operating systems include System 8.5 for Macintosh computers and OS/2, an operating system designed and sold by IBM, which, like Windows and System 8.5, uses icons and folders and other graphical elements to represent computer commands.

Peripherals: Besides the basic components of a CPU, RAM, and a disk drive, a personal computer uses other devices to display or relay information. The most essential of these external devices are a monitor, a printer, and a modem. Always figure in the cost of these components when shopping. Almost all computers come as a package, with these three devices and others included in the final price, but savvy buyers can mix and match these components to lower the price or to gain more power for their dollar.

RAM/ROM: The CPU manipulates data and software programs in random-access memory (RAM). When the computer is turned off, RAM loses its contents. Another type of memory, read-only memory

(ROM) retains its contents even when the power is off (a small lithium battery in the computer keeps ROM alive). ROM stores essential information about the PC that must be kept intact, such as the clock and the list of components inside the computer (the size of the hard disk, for example, or the amount of memory). ROM can be found in all kinds of devices, from computers to modems to microwave ovens. RAM, on the other hand, is confined to those devices that have to make quick and complicated calculations: your computer, your printer, the video card that sends signals to the computer monitor, and so on. Printers, for example, use internal RAM buffers to store data received from the computer. These buffers allow you to use the computer even when it's sending documents to the printer.

Storage: Programs and data can be saved to magnetic disks. As a rule, today's computers ship with a standard-size 3.5-inch floppy disk drive, which accommodates 1.44MB disks (referring to the amount of data a disk can store) that can be inserted and ejected as needed, and which are housed in a plastic casing. Hard disks, by comparison, are normally fixed in place and provide a much bigger storage area—literally thousands of times bigger than floppy disks. Hard disks work at high speeds, so they can load software into RAM more quickly and make programs run much faster than floppies can. This makes them suitable for storing your programs and working files, while disks are used for storing copies of your information or for files you don't need very often.

When shopping for disks, avoid the inexpensive, no-name variety. Considering the value of information that could be lost if a disk fails, buying poorly made disks save you nothing and could end up costing you in the long run.

THE RATINGS

At the end of each review, you'll find a rating based on a scale of 1 (worst) to 10 (best).

Documentation: This rating judges whether or not the manuals and on-line help are effective and well-organized.

Expandability: This rating (for computer systems) is determined by the availability of and capacity for add-ons or peripherals. Portable computers are given an expandability rating because most of them have provisions for adding more memory, a modem, or other peripherals.

Ease of Use: This rating (for peripherals) is based on the efficiency of setup and operation of the product.

Overall Value: This rating compares the product's price to its performance, ease of use, and features. Accordingly, an overpriced item will not have a high overall rating, even if it is an excellent product.

Performance: This rating tells how well the product performs its various functions. Keep in mind that the performance ratings of different items can't always be fully compared unless the products are similar.

BEST BUYS 2000

Our Best Buy and Recommended computer systems and peripherals are listed below. Products within each category are listed according to quality. The best of the Best Buys is listed first, followed by our second choice, and so on. A Best Buy or Recommended designation only applies to the model listed—it does not necessarily apply to other models made by the same manufacturer or to an entire product line.

We have tried to provide accurate prices in this chapter. However, the release of new products, the withdrawal of older products, and strong competition in certain markets cause prices to change constantly. To complicate matters further, the availability of dynamic RAM (DRAM) chips (the kind supplied with computers and peripherals) often varies, which can cause price fluctuations. This means that the retail and low prices in this chapter might differ from what you find at your local store. Be sure to contact several dealers and compare their prices.

HOME & SMALL OFFICE COMPUTERS

Quantex GX500

✓BEST BUY

Quantex touts the GX500 as the "Ultimate Game PC." To give the system the horsepower it needs for even the most processor-intensive games, the GX500 sports one of Intel's new Pentium III processors running at 500MHz. The Quantex uses a motherboard running a 100MHz system clock. Our review system had 128MB of fast SDRAM, which filled two of the motherboard's three DIMM sockets. With 128MB DIMMs used in all three sockets, the GX500 can be upgraded to 768MB of RAM. The large hard disk isn't the only storage the GX500 features. It also includes a 100MB Zip drive, which makes it easy to back up large game files and subdirectories or transport large files from one system to another. A large 19-inch Quantex monitor is included with this configuration. The XP 190DF uses a NEC Chromaclear CRT with a .25mm dot pitch and has digital on-screen controls to make it easy to precisely adjust the geometry, color purity and temperature, and convergence. Wavetable audio with 3-D positioning is provided by an Aureal PCI sound card, and the speaker system is a new three-piece ADA305 Digital PowerCube system from Altec Lansing. The standard-size mini-tower case is roomy and offers two open 5.25-inch bays should you want to add a tape backup or CD-R or CD-RW drive. Two more internal brackets give you the space to add additional hard disks. The motherboard offers a bit less room for expansion. However, this system is very nicely equipped, so future expansion should not be a major consideration for most purchasers. A 56K modem is included, so you can get onto the Internet right away. The keyboard is a Microsoft Natural Elite ergonomic model. While the software collection is largely game oriented, there's something for everyone in the bundle.

Specifications: operating system, Windows 98; RAM (std/max), 128MB SDRAM/384MB; CPU/MHz, Pentium III 500MHz; disk drives, 3.5-inch disk drive, 100MB Zip drive; hard disk, 13GB Ultra DMA; storage bays, two open 5.25-inch external bays, two

open hard disk mounting brackets; CD-ROM/DVD-ROM, 4.8×
DVD-ROM drive with software MPEG-2 decoding; expansion slots,
three open ISA slots (one shared with PCI slot); ports, two serial,
parallel, two USB, game/MIDI; monitor, 19-inch Quantex XP
190DF Natural Flat .25mm dot pitch; software included, Windows
98, Microsoft Office 97 Small Business Edition, Heavy Gear,
Battlezone, Interstate 76

Ratings: overall value, 8; performance, 10; expandability, 7;
documentation, 6
Warranty: 1 year, labor (first year is on-site); 3 years, parts
Manufacturer's Suggested Retail Price: $1,885
Approximate Low Price: $1,657

Apple iMac

Recommended

The newest iMacs come in five "flavors"—straw-
berry, tangerine, grape, lime, and blueberry. Regardless of the
color you select, the innards are the same: a 266MHz PowerPC
G3 processor, 512KB Level 2 cache, and 32MB of SDRAM. The
iMac can accommodate up to 256MB of RAM in two DIMM slots
(though you'll have to remove the 32MB of SDRAM currently in one
of the slots to upgrade this far), and the memory upgrade can be
accomplished by the user, though not as easily as most PCs can be
upgraded. The backup battery can also be replaced by the user.
These are the only internal upgrades you can make to an iMac.

The 6GB drive on the iMac, while smaller than the 12GB to
16GB drives now showing up on some of the new Pentium III systems, is about the same size as those found on similarly priced PCs.
Built-in speakers provide decent sound quality, and the SRS surround sound is very good. A built-in microphone, located at the top
of the screen, easily picks up speech even at normal volumes.
Apple's 15-inch monitor uses conventional shadow-mask technology and has a somewhat coarse .28mm dot pitch, but is driven by
an ATI Rage Pro Turbo video chip set with 6MB of VRAM and provides good quality images and excellent video performance. Apple

claims that its PowerPC G3 is as powerful as Intel's Pentium II processor. The Macintosh OS 8.5 operating system is still as intuitive as the original. And that ease-of-use flows through to the software that runs on the iMac. With its selection of cool colors and decent performance, the iMac provides a great experience.

Specifications: operating system, Mac OS 8.5; RAM (std/max), 32MB SDRAM/256MB; CPU/MHz, PowerPC G3 266MHz, 512KB of Level 2 cache; hard disk, 6GB IDE; CD-ROM/DVD-ROM, 24× CD-ROM drive; ports, printer, sound output, sound input, SCSI, 10/100BaseT Ethernet; monitor, integrated 15-inch color; modem, 56K; software included, AppleWorks, Microsoft Internet Explorer, Microsoft Outlook Express, Adobe PageMill, Quicken for Macintosh Deluxe 98, Kai's Photo Soap SE, World Book Macintosh Edition, Williams-Sonoma Guide to Good Cooking, Nanosaur.

Ratings: overall value, 7; performance, 8; expandability, 5; documentation, 8

Warranty: 1 year, parts and labor

Manufacturer's Suggested Retail Price: $1,199

Approximate Low Price: $1,119-$1,194

iDOT.com 400K6-2

Recommended

The AMD K6-2 processor used in this system runs at a fast 400MHz, but plugs into the same Socket 7 that older Pentium processors used. This particular motherboard uses the Via Technologies Apollo VP3 core-logic chip set and provides a somewhat larger than usual 1MB of Level 2 cache, which helps boost system performance. Our review system came with 64MB of SDRAM, which is fairly typical of mid-sized systems these days. If you need more RAM, the motherboard can accommodate up to 384MB. The 400K6-2 is pretty easy to upgrade and expand. The PC comes in a standard minitower case with easy-open side panels. The 400K6-2 has lots of room inside for additional drives and peripheral cards. Two open 5.25-inch bays provide space for a DVD-ROM drive or

CD-RW drive. The open 3.5-inch bay can accommodate a second hard disk, though with the very large 10.1GB hard disk the iDOT.com PC comes with, it might be a while before you need to add a second hard disk. And, if you want to install a SCSI or network adapter card, the 400K6-2 offers five open peripheral slots, three PCI and two ISA. As with most PCs, however, you lose the use of one of the slots because one ISA slot and one PCI slot share the same case opening on the rear panel. The 400K6-2 comes with a 40× CD-ROM drive. You can order a DVD-ROM drive as an option, however. Another upgrade from the standard 400K6-2 configuration is the Microsoft Natural Keyboard Elite. iDOT.com also offers a variety of software in addition to the Windows 98 operating system. Our review unit came with Corel's WordPerfect Suite 8, which provides word processing, a spreadsheet, and presentation graphics. You can also get Microsoft's Office 97 Small Business Edition for bit more money. The iDOT.com 400K6-2 holds its own with other similarly priced PCs. The FutureMark Multimedia-Mark benchmark we used for testing shows that the iDOT.com performs in the same ballpark as a similarly configured 400MHz Celeron-based system we also reviewed.

Specifications: operating system, Windows 98; RAM (std/max), 64MB/384MB; CPU/MHz, AMD K6-2 400MHz, 1MB Level 2 cache; disk drives, one 3.5-inch; hard disk, 10.1GB Ultra ATA IDE hard disk; CD-ROM/DVD-ROM, 40× CD-ROM drive; storage bays, two open 5.25-inch bays, one open 3.5-inch bay; expansion slots, three PCI, two ISA; ports, serial, parallel, PS/2, headphone, microphone, two USB; monitor, 17-inch iDOT; software included, Windows 98, Corel WordPerfect Suite 8

Ratings: overall value, 8; performance, 7; expandability, 8; documentation, 6

Warranty: 3 years, parts and labor (first year on-site); 5 years, parts and labor, processor and main board RAM

Manufacturer's Suggested Retail Price: $1,119

Approximate Low Price: not available

BUSINESS/HI-POWERED COMPUTERS

Compaq Prosignia 330 Desktop

✔**BEST BUY**

The Prosignia is aimed at the small to mid-size business that wants a high-quality system using industry-standard parts. This makes it easy to repair or upgrade a Prosignia over its lifetime. The Prosignia models are built to order. Unlike other model lines, Compaq does not sell the Prosignia directly—you must purchase it from a value-added reseller (VAR). You can configure the system either with the VAR or directly on Compaq's Web site, and Compaq will build the system you order and deliver it to you. The Prosignia is an entire package that comes with a host of online services and even a Compaq-sponsored leasing plan, should you desire it. The Prosignia is available with your choice of processors, ranging from an Intel Celeron up to the 500MHz Pentium III. To go along with that fast processor, the motherboard is topped off with 128MB of fast SDRAM, and can hold a maximum of 384MB. The hard disk in our review model was huge, 22.6GB, with lots of room on the drive for applications and files. The hard disk is also pre-loaded with your choice of software. The most common choice is the one our unit had, Microsoft Office 97 Small Business Edition, an antivirus utility, and a variety of training software from Que. The hard disk is not the only storage you get. In addition to a standard 3.5-inch disk, which can be replaced with an optional 120MB LS-120 drive, the Prosignia comes standard with a 100MB Iomega Zip drive. This drive is omitted if you choose the LS-120. The Prosignia 330 has one additional bay open, so it won't be difficult to add a second hard disk if needed, but that's about all the room you'll have for future drive expansion. The Prosignia has a total of four open peripheral slots—two PCI and two ISA. The other slots are filled with top-notch peripherals. Our review model contained an optional PCI modem, a 56K unit. This can be replaced with a 10/100BaseT Ethernet network card if you'd prefer. Audio is provided by a Sound Blaster Live wavetable card, and sounds very nice through the Altec Lansing ACS-44 three-piece speaker set provided. The monitor provided was a very nice S900 19-inch model. This is a value-priced display based on conventional shadow-mask technology, but still it provides some really nice features, such as a sharp .22mm dot pitch and extensive on-screen controls. Driving the display is an STB Velocity 4400 video card. Based on the Riva TNT chip set, and with 16MB of video RAM, this card resides in the Prosignia's 2× AGP slot and provides outstanding video performance on both business multimedia and games. The Prosignia 330 is far from being inexpensive, but you're not paying a lot for what you get, which includes proven Compaq quality and service.

Specifications: operating system, Windows 98; RAM (std/max), 64MB SDRAM/384MB; CPU/MHz, Intel Pentium III 500MHz, 512KB Level 2 cache; disk drives, one 3.5-inch, one Iomega 100MB Zip drive; hard disk, 22.6GB Ultra ATA hard disk; CD-ROM/DVD-ROM, 4× DVD-ROM drive; storage bays, one 5.25-inch bay; expansion slots, two ISA slots, two PCI slots (one slot is shared); ports, one serial, one parallel, joystick/MIDI/headphone, microphone, line-out, two USB; monitor, Compaq S900 19-inch; software included, Windows 98, Microsoft Office 97 Small Business Edition, Norton AntiVirus, Macmillan SAMS 10 Minute Guides, Compaq Internet Services

Ratings: overall value, 9; performance, 10; expandability, 8; documentation, 8

Warranty: 3 years, parts and labor

Manufacturer's Suggested Retail Price: $2,799

Approximate Low Price: $2,392

Hewlett-Packard Brio BAx

Recommended

Hewlett-Packard's latest Brio BAx displays a growing trend, especially in business-oriented systems. HP's Brio line is targeted for small to mid-sized businesses, and the newest Brio BAx comes housed in HP's micro-tower case. Measuring a scant 14.3×7.7×13.2 inches, the unit provides lots of functionality in a small box, but not much room for future upgrades. Even though the case is small, the HP Brio BAx is a typical 500MHz Pentium III-based system. The Brio BAx motherboard uses Intel's 440ZX core-logic chip set, which provides support for the 100MHz front-side bus. The motherboard will accommodate up to 512MB of SDRAM in a pair of DIMM sockets. Our review unit had a single 128MB DIMM. That's more than enough memory for most business users, even if you need to run multiple tasks or connect to a network. Because the Brio BAx is a system meant to appeal to business users, HP has included both a suite of manageability tools, including SMART II hard disk monitoring, and your choice of connectivity options. You can get either a 56K modem or a 10/100BaseT network interface card. The audio is provided by an integrated Cirrus Logic Crystal CS4280 chip set; however, HP does not provide speakers with the Brio BAx. Figure another $50 to $100 for speakers unless you intend to simply plug in a set of headphones. The video controller is built into the system's motherboard, making it almost impossible for most users to upgrade in the future. Fortunately, the chip set HP uses is the excellent Matrox MGA-G200. It provides both 8MB of SDRAM and 2× AGP bus performance, so future upgrades probably won't be necessary. The Brio BAx has no open drive bays, and comes with a 4× DVD-ROM drive and an HP Sure-Store CD-Writer Plus 8100, a CD-RW drive that can burn standard CD-Rs as well as CD-RWs. The 4× DVD-ROM drive, which uses software MPEG-2 decoding, provided very good performance. Compared to some of the other vendors' offerings, HP's Brio BAx is a bit expensive, but it has a lot going for it.

Specifications: operating system, Windows 98 (Windows 95 and Windows NT 4.0 are also offered); RAM (std/max), 128MB/512MB; CPU/MHz, Pentium III 500MHz, 512KB Level 2 cache; disk drives, one 3.5-inch; hard disk, 13GB Ultra ATA IDE; CD-ROM/DVD-ROM, 4× DVD-ROM drive, HP SureStore CD-Writer Plus 8100; storage bays, no open bays; expansion slots, two PCI slots, one ISA slot; ports, one serial, one parallel, PS/2, headphone, microphone, two USB; software included, Windows 98, Microsoft Office 2000 Small Business Edition, McAfee VirusScan

Ratings: overall value, 7; performance, 10; expandability, 4;
documentation, 8
Warranty: 1 year, parts and labor
Manufacturer's Suggested Retail Price: $1,449 (estimated street
price)
Approximate Low Price: $1,183-$1,399

PORTABLE COMPUTERS

Dell Inspiron 7000

✔**BEST BUY**

Dell's Inspiron 7000 packs all the power of a desktop PC into a portable package. This notebook has the power to take all your applications on the road, whether you're balancing the company books or playing Flight Simulator. The most noticeable aspect of the Inspiron 7000 is its TFT LCD screen. At 15 inches, it's the largest screen currently available on a notebook PC, with approximately the same viewable area as a 17-inch desktop monitor. The screen supports 1024×768 resolution and handles lower resolutions with aplomb. Powering the screen is an 8MB ATI Rage Pro 3D graphics chip set, the only notebook graphics adapter that can smoothly run 3-D games in addition to business applications. The Inspiron 7000 is available with processors ranging from 366MHz to a whopping 400MHz, fast enough to run the most demanding programs. The computer will support up to 384MB. Hard disks up to 25GB are available. The keyboard is large and comfortable for a laptop. The wrist rest surrounds a Synaptics touchpad, which includes special features to make tasks like scrolling in documents easier. Other built-in features include a 56K modem and USB, serial, parallel, PS/2, and monitor ports. If you opt for a DVD-ROM-equipped Inspiron (CD-ROM models are also available), Dell will include hardware DVD video acceleration inside the notebook, saving you from having to fill one of the PC card slots with a DVD card. The Inspiron's 2× DVD ROM drive module includes an integrated disk drive, avoiding the swapping necessary with some notebooks that support only one drive at a time. You can remove the drive to install a second battery, doubling the 2.5-hour battery life. The Inspiron comes bundled with either Microsoft Office or Microsoft Works, so it's ready to work right out of the box. Dell's support is top-notch, via both phone and a Web page so sophisticated that it can inform you of software updates for your individual PC's configuration. The only real downside to what's nearly the perfect notebook is its size—at ten pounds with AC adapter, the Inspiron will keep you shoulder muscles in shape.

Specifications: operating system, Windows 98; RAM (std/max), 32MB/384MB SDRAM; CPU/MHz, Pentium II 333MHz or 336MHz; disk drives, internal; hard disk, 4GB, 6.4GB, or 8GB; storage bays, none; PC card slots, two Type I, two Type II, or one Type III; ports, USB, serial, parallel, PS/2, monitor; screen, 14.1-inch or 15-inch XGA TFT; battery, lithium ion; weight, 10 pounds; sound, Soundblaster Pro-compatible SRS 3D sound; CD-ROM/DVD-ROM, 24× CD-ROM drive (2× or 4× DVD-ROM drive optional); modem, 56K; height, 2.1"; width, 12.5"; depth, 10"
Ratings: overall value, 10; performance, 10; ease of use, 8; documentation, 8
Warranty: 3 years
Manufacturer's Suggested Retail Price: $2,755
Approximate Low Price: not available

DATA STORAGE DEVICES

Imagine your computer's hard disk as a cabinet where you store your books and papers. Eventually, you're going to fill up that cabinet. Unless you throw away some of your books and papers, you're going to have to buy a larger cabinet or add a second one. And just like the cabinet shelves in your own home, it seems no matter how much extra capacity you start out with, stuff will come along to fill up all the available space.

STORAGE CAPACITY_____

Today's newest hard disks have capacity undreamed of only a few years ago. And prices have fallen so rapidly that consumers can readily buy all the storage space they need by purchasing a big hard disk at the initial sale or by adding a hard disk later. A more flexible option is a removable storage drive. These devices aren't as fast as hard disks, but they offer virtually unlimited storage capacity. When you fill a cartridge, you simply eject it and pop in a new one.

Removable storage has grown so popular and so inexpensive that many computer manufacturers are including Zip drives as standard equipment. Also, 100MB disk drives and 200MB disk drives, which use special high-capacity disks, have also appeared on the market. One advantage of these new drives is that they work with older 1.44MB disks, so you can buy one with your new PC and never have to worry about adding equipment to access older files stored on older disks. Removable storage cartridges have pushed aside tape drives as backup devices.

Castlewood Orb 2.2GB

✔ BEST BUY

The Orb drive, a new removable-media drive, stores 2.2GB per disk, nearly nine times as much data as even the new Zip 250 drives store per disk at about the same price. The Orb uses 3.5-inch disks that resemble the disks used on the Iomega Jaz and Syquest SparQ drives. The difference here is that the Orb disks use a new magnetoresistive (MR) technology that promises better reliability than competing drives, which are based on older, hard-disk technology. Another benefit to the Orb's technology is speed. With a transfer speed of 12.2MB per second, the Orb drive transfers data at the same rate as a hard disk. This means it's not only useful as extra storage, but also for speed-sensitive applications, such as recording video to disk. The Orb drive is available in versions for just about every possible drive connection. Be aware that the USB and parallel versions will be dramatically slower than the other technologies. Installing the internal EIDE version is easy—insert the drive in an open bay, connect the EIDE and power cables, and install the Orb software. The Orb Tools package includes disk maintenance software and a hard-disk backup program. The downsides to the Orb are related to its newness. Although rival drives can't compete on a price and performance basis, they have the advantage of time in the field. If you want to take a large file to a local print shop, chances are they have a Zip or Jaz drive, but the Orb's newness means it will be a while before it's useful for file exchange with others. But if speed, storage, and price are more important than the ability to share data with others, Castlewood's Orb drive is the logical choice for your storage needs.

Specifications: available for, IBM PCs and compatibles; minimum requirements, Windows 95, Windows 98, or Windows NT; Pentium 100MHz or faster processor; available 3½-inch bay; SCSI, parallel, EIDE, or USB connection.
Ratings: overall value, 9; performance, 10; ease of use, 7; documentation, 7
Warranty: 1 year
Manufacturer's Suggested Retail Price: $200
Approximate Low Price: $169-$189

Iomega Zip 250 SCSI

Recommended

Iomega offers both SCSI and parallel versions of the Zip 250 drive—you must have either a Macintosh or a SCSI-capable PC to use the SCSI version. Now, 250MB still doesn't seem like that much, especially with similarly priced drives, such as the Castlewood Orb, that are capable of holding nearly ten times as much. But many will appreciate the drive's benefits: You can still exchange data with owners of 100MB Zip drives and, in our experience, Zip disks are more reliable storage media than higher-density media. When used with the new Zip 250 disks, which sell for less than $20 at most retailers, the SCSI version of the Zip 250 shows a marked improvement in speed over previous models, especially when saving data. It's still not as fast as a hard disk, but it's fairly snappy. However, the parallel version of the Zip 250 is not noticeably faster, because the speed of the parallel port slows the drive down. The Zip 250 will also read from and write to older Zip 100 disks, although at a speed resembling the original drive. This is very handy if you need to exchange data with users who still use Zip 100 drives, or if you have old data stored on Zip 100 disks. The drive ships with Iomega Utilities software, which includes a fairly powerful hard disk backup program, 1-Step Backup/Restore. Other improvements include an on and off switch, a much smaller power supply that handles both American and European currents, and a restyled case. Documentation is still a bit skimpy, but is worlds more complete than the documentation for earlier Zip products. There are faster drives out there with more capacity, but since the Zip is the most successful removable drive yet, the Zip 250 is the clear choice if you plan to exchange files with others.

Specifications: available for, IBM PC and compatibles, Macintoshes.

Ratings: overall value, 8; performance, 8; ease of use, 9; documentation, 7

Warranty: 1 year

Manufacturer's Suggested Retail Price: $200

Approximate Low Price: $199

MONITORS

Many computer buyers don't give enough thought to the monitor when making a system purchase. Don't get distracted by processor speeds and CD-ROM specifications and forget the monitor. The display screen is equal to the CPU, RAM, and hard disk as one of the most important components in your computer system.

HOW TO SHOP

The right monitor can make the difference between a pleasant computing experience and one scattered with eyestrain and headaches. When choosing one, consider two factors before all others: size and resolution. You should consider 15 inches as an absolute minimum size. When viewing a monitor's size, make sure to check the viewable area specification. A 17-inch monitor may have a tube that gives 16 actual inches of viewable display, while a competing unit might have a tube with only a 15.3-inch diagonal measurement. That 0.7 inch can make a noticeable difference.

Resolution refers to the size of the items on the screen. For example, a resolution of 640×480 shows larger icons than a resolution of 800×600. As a rule, bigger monitors can display higher resolutions without sacrificing clarity, while smaller monitors work better at lower resolutions.

Another specification to consider is dot pitch, which measures a monitor's clarity. Screen pictures are composed of tiny dots. The dot pitch refers to the spaces between those dots. The smaller the number (the closer the dots), the crisper the display. A dot pitch of 0.28 should be considered an absolute maximum, with .26 or .25 optimal (but more costly).

Ask about the monitor's refresh rate, which measures how often the screen is updated each second. Most people don't detect any flickering of the screen at rates of 72Hz and higher. Monitor makers list the refresh rate as it relates to screen resolution.

The best test of a monitor is your own eyes. Try a few different models at the store. Ask the sales clerk to set the monitor at different resolutions to find the most comfortable viewing size for you, then make sure the monitor will support a comfortable refresh rate at that resolution.

Sony GDM-F400

✔ **BEST BUY**

The GDM-F400 is Sony's latest monitor, featuring a redesign of its already highly regarded Trinitron display tube. The Trinitron was the first CRT to use stripes of phosphors and an aperture grille mask rather than the more common shadow mask. This aperture grille design produces a much sharper and clearer image on the face of the display. The GDM-F400 improves on this design with an FD Trinitron display, which offers a flatter face. This new design produces much less distortion in the corners and edges than the previous Trinitrons displayed, and Sony intends to keep the FD Trinitron CRTs for only its own Sony-brand products. A 19-inch monitor might seem excessive for many users, but with prices falling, the larger monitor provides both the ability to work at the higher resolutions many video cards now offer and the ability to use the display for presentations and viewing DVD videos, if your PC is so equipped. The GDM-F400 is excellent for both purposes. All on-screen adjustments are made using a small joystick on the front panel, and the Sony has comprehensive adjustments for geometry, color temperature, and vertical and horizontal convergence. Inputs are provided for standard DB-15 and BNC connectors, and the base of the display holds a built-in USB hub. There are certainly decent 19-inch monitors priced below the GDM-F400's $1,000 tag, but the GDM-F400 is reasonably priced, and its excellent performance makes it the best.

Specifications: available for, IBM PCs and compatibles, Macintoshes (includes an adapter for Macintosh use).
Ratings: overall value, 8; performance, 10; ease of use, 10; documentation, 8
Warranty: 3 years, parts, labor, and CRT
Manufacturer's Suggested Retail Price: $1,000
Approximate Low Price: $950

Mitsubishi Diamond Pro 900u

✔**BEST BUY**

The Diamond Pro 900u uses a Diamondtron aperture grille CRT with a very fine .25mm grille pitch, supplemented by a new tube design that Mitsubishi calls Natural Flat, which eliminates the surface curvature found in most monitor designs. The result is a flat screen that provides an undistorted image and virtually eliminates reflected glare. We liked the comprehensive set of controls the Diamond Pro 900u offers. These include color temperature (a must for high-quality desktop publishing or graphics), screen geometry, and moiré. They can be controlled from a set of four buttons on the unit's front panel or by connecting a second cable between the PC's USB port and one of the two upstream USB connections on the display. A software utility then lets you make all the adjustments from a pop-up utility on the PC. Three downstream USB ports are available on the monitor, and the connectors are located underneath the monitor's front bezel, making it easy to connect a USB mouse or keyboard to your system through the Diamond Pro 900u's USB hub. Mitsubishi rates the Diamond Pro 900u as having a maximum resolution of 1600×1200 at 75Hz, but recommends that the monitor be used at 1280×1024 at 85Hz. At the recommended 1280×1024 settings, we could see single-pixel lines and focus was as sharp in the corners as it was at the center. The Mitsubishi Diamond Pro 900u would have been too expensive for the average consumer just a year or two ago. However, now that users change their PCs every couple of years but keep the monitor for longer, the Diamond Pro 900u is a good investment.

Specifications: available for, IBM PCs and compatibles, Macintoshes (adapter included for use with Macintoshes); width, 17.9"; height, 18.2"; depth, 18"
Ratings: overall value, 9; performance, 10; ease of use, 10; documentation, 5
Warranty: 3 years, parts and labor
Manufacturer's Suggested Retail Price: $699
Approximate Low Price: $559-$639

Optiquest L700

Recommended

The L700 is a 15.1-inch LCD monitor from Optiquest, which is well known for its reasonably priced, feature-packed CRT displays. It offers a viewable area that's not much less than a 17-inch CRT monitor, and resolution, preset at the factory, of 1024×768 at 60Hz. You can use the display at different refresh rates or drop the resolution down to 800×600 or less, but using the factory preset values gives the display its best images. Installing the monitor is easy, and the disk that comes with it has an install program that sets up Windows 95 or Windows 98 with the correct .inf file. There is no separate adjustment software utility, but the display itself features on-screen controls for screen geometry, moiré adjustment, and even color temperature, an adjustment usually found on only higher-end CRT monitors. Running the DisplayMate utility's monitor setup tests, we found that the Optiquest L700 had perfect screen geometry and no moiré right out of the box. The L700 had no streaking and no stuck pixels, and pixel tracking was dead-on, showing none of the timing problems that still sometimes plague desktop LCDs. Resolution at the factory preset of 1024×768 is excellent. Our single criticism of this unit is that the backlighting is slightly uneven. But on our tests of color purity we found excellent screen response and no trace of ghosting. The Optiquest does not contain built-in speakers or a microphone. For the money, the Optiquest L700 offers excellent performance.

Specifications: available for, IBM PCs and compatibles, Macintoshes (Macintosh use requires a Macintosh cable adapter, available from Optiquest free of charge); width, 16"; height, 14.2"; depth, 7.2"

Ratings: overall value, 9; performance, 9; ease of use, 10; documentation, 6

Warranty: 1 year, backlight; 3 years, parts and labor

Manufacturer's Suggested Retail Price: $1,036

Approximate Low Price: $999

MODEMS

It used to be that buying a modem was a confusing exercise, with technical terms like v.32bis and MNP5 to deal with. Much of the technical confusion is now gone, with features such as error correction and compression standard on practically all modems. Now the biggest concern is speed. You won't find anything slower than 28,800 bps, except at clearance sales. Today, that's the minimum speed of choice for most people.

HOW TO SHOP

The minimum speed on any modem you buy should be 28.8K. An inexpensive and smart compromise is the 33.6K modem. Be wary of modems that claim to double speeds by using two phone lines—such a setup normally requires two online accounts, an unjustified expense to most consumers. If you buy a brand-new computer with a modem built in, chances are you will get a 56K modem. Ask the sales clerk if the modem supports the V.90 standard or if it can be modified to support the highest standard. If the answer is no, ask that the modem be substituted for a newer model at the same cost, or have the modem removed and subtracted from the purchase price, then buy a newer model yourself and have it installed.

Now that the international communications standard has been set for high-speed modems (called the V.90 standard, in modem sales literature), a 56K modem (56,700 bps) is the fastest modem you can buy for a personal computer using ordinary telephone lines. Before buying a modem at that speed, check the maximum speeds supported by your Internet service provider.

3Com U.S. Robotics 56K Voice Faxmodem Pro ✓BEST BUY

U.S. Robotics was the first modem vendor to ship 56K modems, which were based on its x2 technology. And the 56K Voice Faxmodem Pro is compatible with the V.90 standard that now defines 56K operation and is backward compatible with its own x2 standard as well. The modem's extra features make it worth the extra cost. As with most high-end modems, the 56K Voice Faxmodem Pro can transmit and receive using fax frequencies. Coupled with the Symantec WinFax PRO 8.0 software, which is included, this lets you receive faxes when your PC is turned on and send files from your PC to other fax machines. Even when the PC is turned off, you can access the modem's speaker-phone capabilities by pressing a button on the top panel of the unit. Two additional buttons let you raise and lower the volume, and a fourth button mutes the speaker phone. The Connections CD-ROM, which is included with the 56K Voice Faxmodem Pro, has software that lets you set up voice-mail boxes, and a fax-on-demand application, which lets callers select a document stored on your PC and have it faxed to their fax machine. Setup is simply a matter of connecting the modem to your PC and installing the software. The 56K Voice Faxmodem Pro can be connected to a serial communications port or a USB port. Most PCs made in the last few years have one or two USB ports, making the connection even easier. If all you want to do is surf the Web, you can get by with a much less expensive modem than the 56K Voice Faxmodem Pro. But if you're a serious user and want a reliable modem that provides excellent response, great fax support, lots of extra software, and very responsive speaker-phone capabilities, the 3Com U.S. Robotics 56K Voice Faxmodem Pro fits the bill.

Specifications: available for, IBM PCs and compatibles, Macintoshes (software provided only for Windows 95 and Windows 98); width, 7"; depth, 6"; height, 2.5"
Ratings: overall value, 10; performance, 10; ease of use, 10; documentation, 10
Warranty: 5 years, parts and labor. Warranty is extended to free lifetime parts and labor, factory repair, or replacement when modem is registered within 90 days of purchase.
Manufacturer's Suggested Retail Price: $199
Approximate Low Price: $119-$185

Multi-Tech Systems MessageSaver

Along with the modem, this tiny package contains a digital answering machine that can play your message and record up to 30 minutes of calls, even when the PC is turned off. The MessageSaver automatically detects fax calls and can save up to 30 pages. When you boot up your PC, the MessageSaver lets you view or print any stored faxes. You can set up and operate the modem from the modem's front panel, but it's a lot easier to use the included software to manage the modem's functions.

Using the PhoneTools utility, you can save the voice messages and faxes stored in the MessageSaver onto your PC. If your PC is off, you can listen to and erase messages from the modem's front panel. The status light labeled EC blinks to let you know you have messages waiting. And you can retrieve messages from a remote telephone when you are traveling. This unit doesn't take much desk space, especially considering that it now replaces both a modem and an answering machine. However, the small icons on the front panel can be hard to decipher, and it is easy to lose the tiny box under a manual or piece of paper and not discover the blinking message light for hours. Still, the MessageSaver incorporates the right mix of features in an attractive and simple-to-use package.

Specifications: available for, IBM PCs and compatibles, Macintoshes. Software provided for only Windows 95 and Windows 98.
Ratings: overall value, 10; performance, 10; ease of use, 8; documentation, 10
Warranty: 10 years, parts and labor, if modem is registered within 90 days of purchase.
Manufacturer's Suggested Retail Price: $219
Approximate Low Price: $151-$177

PRINTERS

A couple of decades ago, futurists predicted that computers would usher in a paperless society. However, the overall effect of the computer revolution seems to be that a lot of us are using more paper than ever. Today's printers can create such amazing results that many computer users are printing everything from greeting cards to company newsletters. The best news for today's printer buyers is that even the least expensive, entry-level printers produce stunning results.

HOW TO SHOP

The printer market has segmented primarily into two types of printers: color inkjets and black-and-white laser printers. The quality of a printer is measured by how many dots per inch (dpi) it can place on a page. The higher the number, the better the print quality. Today's inkjets support 360 or 720 dpi, and lasers achieve 600, 1,200, or more dpi.

If speed or top-notch printed text is what you seek, a laser printer is the tool of choice. Essentially, a laser printer is a photocopier with a microprocessor and RAM added to make it smarter. It prints using the same technology as the Xerox machine at your local library. Black-and-white laser printers are no longer expensive to purchase and maintain. Even inexpensive, entry-level printers now sport resolutions of 600 dpi, which is good enough for all but professional publishing applications.

The primary differences among consumer laser printers relate to image quality and speed. The quality of printed graphics can vary dramatically between different brands, which is why you should always look at a print sample with both text and graphics before making a final purchase decision.

PRINTER SPEED

Printer speed is rated in pages per minute (ppm), with 4, 6, and 8 ppm being common speeds. Be aware, however, that the ppm rating refers to the speed of the printer's drum ability to put toner on paper. Much of the time spent in printing actually occurs before that point, when the printer is creating the page image; some printers do this dramatically faster than others that have the same ppm rating. Also watch the amount of RAM built into the printer—less than 1MB of RAM may result in lower speeds or the inability of the printer to print a full-page image because the printer's "brain" is too small to hold all the necessary information.

COLOR PRINTERS

If you want to add a splash of color to your documents, there's an inkjet in your future. Color laser printers exist, but they're still priced in the stratosphere. The good news is that today's color inkjets rival lasers in black-and-white print quality, if not speed, and can print near-photographic-quality color images.

One primary difference between color printers is the number of print cartridges they require. Traditionally, the most inexpensive color printers hold only one cartridge; you must swap black and three-color cartridges, depending on the type of document you're printing. Two-cartridge printers simultaneously hold color and black cartridges. These not only have better print quality, but you may eventually save the money in cartridge costs, since single-cartridge printers must mix all three colors to create black when doing mixed color/monochrome documents.

Like all technology, this setup is changing. Customers were so dissatisfied with the single-cartridge model that almost every color inkjet sold today uses the dual-cartridge system. Inkjet printers that specialize in photo printing can even use special "photo cartridges," which provide six colors instead of the basic four colors used in most color ink jets. Those four colors—cyan, magenta, yellow, black—are the basis for the CMYK label you see on many color printers. Photo printers work by letting users pop out the black cartridge and pop in the photo cartridge (which usually carries three inks—black, light cyan, and light magenta). The six color process is superior to the four-color process when printing photos because it captures flesh tones and other subtle shades more accurately.

Hewlett-Packard DeskJet 1120C ✓ BEST BUY

The 1120C prints more than just ordinary 8.5×11-inch documents with aplomb: It's designed to print oversize stock as large as 13×19 inches with images as large as 11×17 inches. Because it's designed to handle such large paper, this printer is big—it's 22.8 inches wide and 26.3 inches deep when fully extended. The main tray holds 150 sheets of paper and another ten sheets can be loaded into the secondary tray without disturbing the primary paper supply. Many printers today generate their lifelike color using six or even seven color cartridges. The 1120C uses just four. However, this doesn't negatively affect the quality of your printouts. HP claims that the 1120C's innovative color system is capable of generating 16 discrete dots of ink for each printed pixel, resulting in excellent color definition. In fact, images are virtually photo-quality when using photographic paper. A few unique features really capitalize on this printer's over-size print capability. The best of the lot is SmartZoom, which lets you print documents designed for standard 8.5×11-inch stock as poster-sized 11×17-inch graphics. A booklet mode lets you print multiple pages to a larger-size page, then fold and bind it like a booklet, and mirror mode is particularly handy for printing to T-shirt transfer paper. With the 1120C, you can mirror-image anything, even plain text. Looking for a way to print photos and other documents at sizes beyond the traditional 8.5×11-inches? Then you need the Hewlett-Packard DeskJet 1120C.

Specifications: available for, IBM PCs and compatibles.
Ratings: overall value, 10; performance, 9; ease of use, 9; documentation, 10
Warranty: 1 year with Express Exchange.
Manufacturer's Suggested Retail Price: $499
Approximate Low Price: $470

NEC SuperScript 870

The NEC SuperScript 870 prints 600 dots per inch ✓**BEST BUY** at a speedy eight pages per minute—and it does it for about $350. This model is fairly slim, measuring about 15 inches wide and 11 inches deep. Output from the 870 is sharp and clean, exactly what you'd expect from a 600 dpi printer. Graphics are a bit dark and lack contrast, but perfectly adequate for most applications. The printer is true to its claim of eight pages per minute, and the printer seems capable of handling almost any print job with its 2MB of memory. If a particularly complex graphic uses too much memory to print, the included Adobe Memory Booster compresses the image and prints it anyway, though the output might look a bit degraded. The multi-purpose tray holds 150 sheets of paper, and the manual feed tray holds ten transparencies or 20 envelopes. You can add a

500-sheet cassette if you expect to run a lot of paper through the printer. A network card is available so you can make the 870 a network device. The printer driver is packed with every feature you can imagine. It supports watermarks, two-sided printing (the printer tells you how to reinsert paper to print properly on the flip side), booklet printing, and n-up printing. In fact, you can print as many as 16 pages to a sheet of paper using NEC's highly versatile n-up controls. You can also enlarge pages and poster-print documents across multiple pages. To conserve power, you can set this Energy Star-compliant printer to automatically power-down after a short period of time, and we particularly liked the way the printer automatically reprinted sheets after a jam. If you have a small office and need a reliable, easy-to-use printer, look no further than the Super-Script 870.

Specifications: available for, IBM PCs and compatibles.
Ratings: overall value, 9; performance, 9; ease of use, 9; documentation, 10
Warranty: 2 years with ServiceXpress extended warranty options
Manufacturer's Suggested Retail Price: $349
Approximate Low Price: $336

HOME OFFICE PRODUCTS

The home office has become a fixture in many households as Americans continue to venture out on their own and more companies encourage flexible working arrangements. Performing the tasks normally done in the office, however, means that you'll have to add equipment with capabilities usually found at the workplace. In most cases, this means you'll need a fax machine, a photocopier, and perhaps a scanner.

HOW TO SHOP

Before purchasing any office equipment, you need to determine what you have to accomplish with it. Multifunction fax and printer combinations (often called MFPs), for example, can take the place of a fax machine, printer, and even a scanner. But they might not be the answer for everyone. Another consideration is your office layout and budget.

WHERE TO BUY

Products in this category are priced competitively and are widely available at many specialty stores and national chain stores. Many can even be ordered over the Internet. It's also a good idea to watch your weekly newspaper for special offers as manufacturers often offer rebates at certain times of the year.

BEST BUYS 2000

Our Best Buy and Recommended home office products follow. Products within each category are listed according to quality. The item we consider the best of the Best Buys is first, followed by our second choice, and so on. Remember that a Best Buy or Recommended designation only applies to the model listed—it does not necessarily apply to other models made by the same manufacturer or to an entire product line.

DESKTOP COPIERS

Desktop photocopy machines might not be necessities in many home offices, but they are an important piece of equipment for anyone who regularly makes numerous copies of multiple-page documents. New models take advantage of technological advances to provide excellent copy quality and features once found only on larger commercial machines. Prices are also coming down as these products face competition from multifunction fax machines and scanners.

TYPES OF COPIERS

Two types of desktop copiers are available: moving platen or fixed platen. Less expensive machines often use a moving platen, which literally moves the item being copied over the copier lens. Moving-platen machines might or might not offer reduction and enlargement. Copy time on these units is slower, and it's difficult to copy bulkier items such as books. Even though these machines are often smaller and lighter than fixed-platen copiers, they require more space due to their moving platen. They can also be more expensive to operate.

Although fixed-platen copiers offer more versatility and are slightly more expensive, they might also be a more economical choice in the long run. Many machines are now being offered with such features as automatic document feed, second paper trays, preset enlargement/reduction settings, and text/photo mode settings.

Sharp AL-1041

✔ **BEST BUY**

The AL-1041 offers a high-quality ten-pages-per-minute (ppm) office copier that can also function as an eight-ppm laser printer when necessary. Sharp's AL-1041 offers a Scan Once Print Many (SOPM) system that scans the document to be copied only once, then prints the copies without additional scans. This speeds up the print process when you are making multiple copies. Also, using a combination scanner/laser printer lets you precisely reduce and enlarge documents with ease. The Sharp AL-1041 has great quality 600 dpi output whether you're using it as a printer or copier. It comes with a parallel cable and Windows driver software. However, this unit easily fits the bill if you never plug it into a PC and use it solely as a fast office copier.

Specifications: pages per minute, 10; dpi, scan, 400; dpi, output, 600; height, 11.5"; width, 20.4"; depth, 17.5"; weight, 40 lbs.
Warranty: 3 years, with limited second-day exchange
Manufacturer's Suggested Retail Price: $549
Approximate Low Price: not available

Xerox WorkCentre XD100

✔ BEST BUY

Rather than just a copier, the WorkCentre XD100 actually scans the document on its platen and then routes this scan to a laser printer contained in the unit. Output quality is excellent. It's also fast. The WorkCentre XD100 churns out copies at up to ten ppm. It also offers all of the premium copier features including reduction and enlargement from 50 to 200 percent. Front panel controls are clearly marked with easy-to-understand icons, and the first copy pops out of the unit in under ten seconds. In addition to serving as a high-quality office copier, the WorkCentre XD100 is also a laser printer. It prints at eight ppm with 600 dpi resolution, includes drivers for Windows 3.x, 95, and NT, and also bundles a free parallel cable. In short, this is a copier for professionals who demand perfection.

Specifications: pages per minute, 10; height, 12"; width, 20"; depth, 17.5"; weight, 41 lbs.
Warranty: 3 years, parts and labor (on-site)
Manufacturer's Suggested Retail Price: $550
Approximate Low Price: not available

Canon PC420

Recommended

The PC420 uses a single cartridge that contains toner, developer, and the imaging drum. This makes maintenance a snap. Cartridges are available in five colors (black, brown, blue, red, and green). Colors other than black only yield about 1,000 copies per cartridge while black yields up to 1,600 copies. The PC420 uses a moving copyboard. If you use the "F" mode, the copier will just churn out copies until the 50-sheet input tray runs out. After about 22 seconds, copies start coming out at 4 copies per minute. An automatic shut-off kicks in after you haven't used the copier for about 5½ minutes. The Canon PC420 does have a downside, however. It's less expensive than the fancy digital laser copiers because it has fewer features and it is slower. Some of the more expensive models in the PC copier line offer reduction and enlargement, which you won't find on the PC420.

Specifications: pages per minute, 4; height, 4.1"; width, 14.1"; depth, 15.9"; weight, 18 lbs.
Warranty: 1 year, parts and labor
Manufacturer's Suggested Retail Price: $595
Approximate Low Price: $300

SCANNERS

Today's scanners pack versatility, quality, and performance into increasingly smaller machines. A scanner can substantially expand the capability of a computer system by allowing the direct transfer of graphics and printed text to the system.

TYPES OF SCANNERS

Most scanners on the market today are either flatbed or sheet-fed. Handheld scanners, the third type available, are becoming less popular as the others continue to come down in price. Flatbed scanners offer the most versatility and convenience. They can be used to scan thick objects, such as books; and portions of oversize objects, such as maps and charts. Sheet-fed scanners, which resemble portable printers, are convenient for scanning single sheets of paper and business cards but cannot be used with magazines or books unless the material to be scanned is torn out first.

FEATURES

Scanners generally come bundled with operating-system-specific software that controls the scans and adjusts scanned images. Many scanners now come with optical character recognition (OCR) software for scanning text. Communications software that allows faxing directly from the scanner is also included with many units. All use a light-sensitive charged-coupled device (CCD), which converts the scanned image to an electronic signal, which is then digitized and stored on the hard drive of your computer. Bits are used to describe the color and gray-scale images. The higher the number, the more colors or image depth of the machine.

Genius ColorPage Vivid Pro II Film

✔ **BEST BUY**

The Genius ColorPage Vivid Pro II Film has a transparency adapter built into its lid so that it can scan 35mm slides, film, and other transmissive media. It offers a letter-sized platen, CCD-based sensor design, 36-bit color depth, and a true optical resolution of 600×1,200. Another nice feature is the single "Scan" button that automatically launches the TWAIN driver. The software bundle includes PhotoImpact SE and iPhoto Express—both from U-Lead Software—and TextBridge OCR. To top it off, a parallel port interface is featured so the unit is easy to install. The ColorPage Vivid Pro II Film provided very good performance in all of our testing. Slides were scanned at 2,400 dpi, and when reset down to the printer's resolution, showed sharp detail and accurate color. The scanner also did a nice job on the photos we scanned.

Specifications: height, 4.4"; width, 6.8"; depth, 11.3"; ports, parallel port interface; minimum requirements (PC), Windows 95, 98, or NT
Warranty: 1 year, parts and labor
Manufacturer's Suggested Retail Price: $129
Approximate Low Price: not available

Canon CanoScan FB 620U

✓BEST BUY

The CanoScan FB 620U is a lightweight 4.4-pound CIS sensor-based scanner with a USB interface that's not much larger than the A4 document size it can accommodate on its platen. It offers 36-bits of color depth and an optical resolution of 600×600 dpi. A single "Scan" button on the scanner's front panel can be set to start the scan when pressed. Otherwise the scan can be launched from the TWAIN driver. Canon was one of the first vendors to offer software bundles with its equipment and the CanoScan FB 620U continues that tradition by bundling a Canon Creative Image CD-ROM that offers the ScanGear CS-U TWAIN driver for Windows 98, Adobe PhotoDeluxe 3.0, and TextBridge Plus. Also included is a Toolbox CS utility that provides copying, scanning, faxing (if your PC has a fax modem), or e-mailing when the front-panel button is programmed for it. This scanner is a great performer and is a pleasure to use.

Specifications: height, 2.5"; width, 10.1"; depth, 14.7"; weight, 4.4 lbs.; ports, USB (excludes add-on USB board); available for Windows 98
Warranty: 1 year, parts and labor (with limited instant exchange program)
Manufacturer's Suggested Retail Price: $130
Approximate Low Price: not available

Visioneer Strobe Pro for Windows

Recommended

The 30-bit color depth, 300×600 dpi optical resolution Strobe Pro is one of the few sheet-fed scanners to remain on the market. It is small enough to fit between the keyboard and monitor, and an adjustable paper path allows the document to be returned from the top of the Strobe Pro. Installation of this USB-interfaced scanner was simple and a serial port is available for users not running Windows 98 or who lack a USB port. The Strobe Pro's scan quality is very good and color quality is quite accurate. Scanning starts automatically when a sheet is fed into the unit. Optionally, the included TWAIN driver can be used to scan from within a Windows application. Visioneer includes the terrific PaperPort desktop interface, which lets you drag and drop the scanned document to the desired application. Also included in the software bundle is Visioneer OCR, PictureWorks PhotoEnhancer, and several Web publishing utilities.

Specifications: height, 2"; width, 11"; depth, 2.5"; weight, 1.34 lbs.; ports, USB or serial port interface; available for Windows NT and Macintosh
Warranty: 1 year, parts and labor
Manufacturer's Suggested Retail Price: $200
Approximate Low Price: $189

DESKTOP FAX MACHINES

Fax machines are becoming a necessity of business life. They are a combination of low-resolution image scanner and a printer. When sending a fax, the document is passed over a sensor that converts the image into digital format. That data is then transmitted over the phone lines to the receiving fax machine, which converts it back to an image and prints it out.

TYPES OF FAX MACHINES

Fax machines vary the most in the printing technology they use. Thermal fax machines, which use heat-sensitive paper, are pretty much disappearing from the market, with even inexpensive units using a ribbon that allows plain paper to be used. More upscale fax machines incorporate an inkjet or laser printer engine. Both of these provide excellent quality output. Laser-based fax machines are more expensive to buy initially, but less expensive to operate over the long run if you receive lots of faxes.

Brother IntelliFAX 3750
Brother's IntelliFAX 3750 is a lot larger than many ✓**BEST BUY**
other fax machines and operates very quickly. It has a Super G3

33.6Kbps modem, rather then the more common 14.4Kbps. However, when the IntelliFAX 3750 is talking to a standard fax machine, it operates at the slower speed. A Dual Access function makes you even more productive: You can start scanning your outgoing fax while you are still receiving an incoming fax. The IntelliFAX 3750 can serve double-duty as an extra printer for your PC. It's not really a multifunction device—and it's not marketed as such—but the IntelliFAX 3750 includes a parallel printer port, so you can use it as a laser printer. The IntelliFAX 3750 has a large paper capacity—200 sheets—and a document memory that can store up to 300 pages. Outgoing documents from the unit's 30 page automatic document feeder are scanned into memory very quickly. Stored documents that have been received by the 3750 can be retrieved remotely and forwarded to another fax machine if desired.

Specifications: modem, 33.6Kbps; height, 18″; width, 13.2″; depth, 9.9″; weight, 18.7 lbs.
Warranty: 90 days, replacement (limited)
Manufacturer's Suggested Retail Price: $899
Approximate Low Price: $736

Canon FAXPHONE B640

✔ **BEST BUY**

Canon's FAXPHONE B640 is initially somewhat more expensive than other fax machines, but its ink-jet engine is less expensive to operate in the long run. The FAXPHONE B640 uses a monochrome black ink cartridge similar to those used in Canon's printers. The input tray can hold 100 sheets of paper, and the ADF feed can accommodate 20 sheets of letter-sized documents or ten legal-sized pages. The unit does not come with a telephone handset. Also absent is the familiar output hopper for pages faxed or printed. The FAXPHONE simply outputs incoming faxes onto the table. One-button copying can provide up to 99 copies of a page, and there are ten one-touch and 20 speed memories. The B640 provides excellent 360×360 dpi resolution and the output from our tests looked excellent. Unfortunately, this machine's speed is not much faster than that of thermal film-based fax machines.

Specifications: engine, ink-jet-based printing engine; width, 14.5";
depth, 11.7"; height, 13.3"; weight, 11.9 lbs.
Warranty: 1 year, limited (instant exchange warranty program)
Manufacturer's Suggested Retail Price: $249
Approximate Low Price: $190-$220

Panasonic KX-FP121

Recommended

The Panasonic KX-FP121 is a thermal film, plain
paper fax machine. It's a bit expensive for a fax machine based on
thermal film technology. However, this unit does have a lot of excellent features, such as up to 28 pages of document memory, fax
broadcasting, and 106 number autodialer. The KX-FP121 will allow
you to place and receive calls using the included handset. Or, if
you so desire, you can use the internal, full-duplex speakerphone—
meaning that speaking and listening can occur at the same time.
But the KX-FP121 still has a few features up its sleeves. This unit also
acts as a digital answering machine. It has caller ID capability—if
you subscribe to that service—and automatically recognizes
whether an incoming call is standard or a fax. Like other thermal
film fax machines, print quality can only be called fair. But if you
want a fax machine that does a lot—but doesn't cost a lot—the
Panasonic KX-FP121 is definitely worth looking at.

Specifications: engine, thermal film print engine; height, 6"; width,
12.5"; depth, 11.5"
Warranty: 1 year, parts and labor (limited)
Manufacturer's Suggested Retail Price: $200
Approximate Low Price: $190

PERSONAL DIGITAL ASSISTANTS

Personal Digital Assistants (PDAs) have undergone dramatic evolu-
tion, gaining color, smarter programs, and better Internet connectivity. Despite these advances, though, PDAs still rely on desktop
computers for printing, permanent storage, and other necessities, so
you can't replace your desktop PC with a pocket computer.

3Com Palm IIIx

✔ **BEST BUY**

The Palm IIIx maintains the dark plastic case, flip cover, and form of the earlier Palm III. This offers real advantages, because it means the Palm IIIx is compatible with the wealth of add-on hardware available for the earlier units. The Palm IIIx's screen includes an improved backlighting feature for use in dark environs, as well as new support for 16 levels of grayscale graphics. The Palm IIIx also sports double the memory of its predecessor, a whopping 4MB. There are literally thousands of commercial, shareware, and freeware programs available for the Palm platform, the vast majority of which can be ordered online. Like all Palm PDAs, the Palm IIIx comes with built-in Calendar, To Do, Contact, and Memo applications, as well as a free full-fledged PIM, called Palm Desktop, for your desktop computer. New to the Palm IIIx is support for synchronizing data with Microsoft Outlook. Keeping your desktop PIM and your Palm synchronized couldn't be easier—just drop the Palm IIIx into the included cradle unit and press a button.

Specifications: available for IBM PCs and compatibles, Macintoshes; operating system, Palm OS 3.1; RAM, 4MB; screen, color 160×160 gray-scale; battery, two AAA batteries; expansion slots, one; weight, 6 oz.
Warranty: 1 year
Manufacturer's Suggested Retail Price: $369
Approximate Low Price: $276-$329

Vadem Clio

✔ **BEST BUY**

The Vadem Clio is the most ingeniously designed personal computing device since the first clamshell notebook. This keyboard-equipped PDA, billed as a "PC Companion," is thin and versatile, and has a brilliant screen design that makes the unit useful in a wide variety of situations. The screen sits on a swinging arm that lets you use it in three positions. The Clio's screen-only mode is more useful than those in typical Windows CE units, thanks to the inclusion of ParaGraph's CalliGrapher software. Not only does this utility do a great job of recognizing printed characters, but it even does a remarkable job of recognizing less-than-legible handwriting. Other software includes the typical Windows CE programs, such as Pocket Word, Excel, Access, and PowerPoint. In addition, Vadem includes ViewFinder, which makes it easy to track your Outlook organizer data, and BSQUARE's bFAX software. If you need a small machine for e-mail and Web browsing while on the road, the Clio is an excellent choice, with the biggest downside being its inclusion of only a 33.6Kbps modem. Battery life is superb. The rechargeable battery is rated at 12 hours.

Specifications: available for IBM PCs and compatibles; operating system, Windows CE; RAM, 16MB; screen, color 640×480; battery, rechargeable lithium ion; PC card slots, one; ports, one CompactFlash slot, modem, 33.6Kbps

Warranty: 1 year
Manufacturer's Suggested Retail Price: $999
Approximate Low Price: $794-$879

Philips Nino 510

The most obvious feature of the Nino 510 is its | Recommended | color screen, which supports 320×240 pixels at 256 colors. Like all palm-sized Windows CE units, input is through a series of buttons and through writing on the touchscreen with the unit's stylus. Philips has addressed one of Windows CE's biggest problems—awkward handwriting recognition—by bundling a copy of Paragraph's excellent CalliGrapher handwriting recognition software. The Nino sports a voice-recorder button for taking voice notes; these can even be attached to e-mail messages. Unfortunately, the Nino has no built-in modem, but an add-on 19.2Kbps modem is available for about $90. The Nino ships with 16MB of memory, expandable to 48MB using the unit's CompactFlash slot. Synchronization with your PC is done through an included docking station, or using the unit's infrared port. Along with the usual address, task list, and calendar software, the software bundle includes NinoVoice, NinoImage for viewing graphics, and AvantGo, which lets you view Web pages offline. Other included programs are CoolCalc, MobileSoft Expense Manager, and BSQUARE bFax faxing software. There's a rechargeable battery pack that gives up to eight hours of use, or you can use a set of AA alkaline batteries.

Specifications: screen, 320x240, 256 colors; RAM, 16MB; battery, rechargeable; weight, 8 oz.; operating system, Windows CE
Warranty: 1 year (limited)
Manufacturer's Suggested Retail Price: $499
Approximate Low Price: $328-$399

MULTIFUNCTION MACHINES

Multifunction machines, also often called MFPs, provide a fax, printer, and scanner in a single desktop unit. If you need all of these capabilities and don't have much room, an MFP might be the way to go. The latest crop of units have excellent quality printers incorporated into them, and scanner quality is improving. Keep in mind, though, that if you have the room and budget, separate components generally provide the highest quality.

Canon MultiPASS L6000

✓ **BEST BUY**

The muscle behind the Canon MultiPASS L6000 is a Canon laser printer engine with 600 dpi output quality. The paper tray holds 100 sheets and the automatic document feed has a 30 sheet capacity. The scanner portion of the unit is monochrome and provides software interpolated resolution of up to 600 dpi. Faxing and fax broadcasting can be performed through a PC using the modem incorporated in the MultiPASS L6000. Provided with the MultiPASS L6000 is a CD-ROM with Xerox TextBridge OCR and Canon's own WebRecord application. The CD-ROM also contains drivers that let Windows use the MultiPASS L6000 as a standard laser printer. You can use your PC to access the TWAIN drivers, and through applications that support TWAIN you can access the scanner.

Specifications: engine, laser-based printing engine; height, 9.5";
width, 14.4"; depth, 14.4"; weight, 19 lbs.
Warranty: 1 year (limited with InstantExchange program)
Manufacturer's Suggested Retail Price: $599
Approximate Low Price: $511-$587

Samsung MJ4500C

| Recommended |

The Samsung MJ4500C is fax machine, a high-
quality sheet-fed color scanner, and a color ink-jet printer. The included scanner offers 300-dpi resolution and 24-bit color depth.
Included in the software bundle is a TWAIN driver that allows the
scanner to be used with any TWAIN-compatible Windows software
package. Samsung includes NewSoft's Presto! PageManager (a
document management application), Presto! PhotoAlbum (for or-
ganizing your scanned images), MyScan (an entry-level image editor), and SmartFax and WinFax for scanning and faxing. The unit
functions as a fax machine and copier even when your PC is turned
off. Samsung incorporates a color printer into this "fax machine."
The printer engine that Samsung uses is a single printhead design
that can accommodate either a three-color cartridge or a standard
black cartridge. Printing a composite black—a combination of the
three colors—makes the Samsung one of the slowest units in our
testing, taking almost 15 minutes to complete our 11-page test document. Output quality, however, is excellent, and swapping cartridges is quick. The MJ4500C offers excellent 1,200×1,200 dpi
print resolution and good quality color scanning. The fax side of
this unit includes such premium features as an extensive 80-page
document memory, broadcasting, and one-touch speed keys. These
features make the Samsung MJ4500C a very good value.

Specifications: engine, three-color ink-jet engine; dpi, scan, 300;
height, 12.8"; width, 7.5"; depth, 14.2"; weight, 11.9 lbs.
Warranty: 1 year, parts and labor
Manufacturer's Suggested Retail Price: $449
Approximate Low Price: $349

HOME FITNESS

Americans are increasingly concerned with good health and fitness, and this is a trend that will continue into the next century. With the vast array of home fitness equipment available, many of us are now able to find a few hours a week to lose weight and become more physically fit.

GETTING FIT

Home exercise equipment has such great appeal because it is often difficult to find time in our busy schedules to visit a health club or gym. If you are serious about getting fit or losing weight, home exercise equipment might be the solution. The key is to buy the best aerobic exercise equipment you can afford and use it on a regular basis. Many experts suggest that you should purchase a machine that you enjoy using and one that gets your heart rate up. (An increased heart rate is crucial for effective burning of calories.)

To be effective, though, exercise must be combined with a well-balanced diet. There are easily hundreds of food products and drinks that have been designed for this purpose. It is important to remember that you can eat healthy and economically from the basic food groups. Nutritionists agree that we should all cut down on our intake of fat and increase our intake of fruits and vegetables.

HOW TO SHOP

It is important to shop wisely for home exercise equipment that you will use on a regular basis. Avoid trendy or cute equipment. Take the time to learn which machines will best help you accomplish your desired goals. Each of the following categories have additional buying tips to help you choose a product that suits your exercise needs.

All home exercise equipment carries some type of warranty against defects in workmanship. The time period covered usually ranges from 90 days to the lifetime of the original purchaser. As a rule, extended warranties are indications of quality in home exercise equipment.

BEST BUYS 2000

Our Best Buy, Recommended, and Budget Buy home fitness products follow. Products within each category are listed according to quality. The item we consider the best of the Best Buys is first, followed by our second choice, and so on. A Budget Buy describes a less-expensive product of respectable quality that perhaps sacrifices some of the performance and/or convenience features of a Best Buy or Recommended product. Remember that a Best Buy, Recommended, or Budget Buy designation only applies to the model listed—it does not necessarily apply to other models made by the same manufacturer or to an entire product line.

EXERCISE CYCLES

Exercise cycles continue to be popular for home use, and there are many on the market. Besides the standard upright models, several models offer upper-body workouts as well. The latest designs use recumbent seating, which supports your lower back with an upright lounge-chair seating style. Recumbent models also leave your hands and arms free to use weights for upper-body exercise while you pedal the cycle.

HOW TO SHOP

Try as many exercise cycles as possible before making your final purchasing decision. You should pick a unit that is comfortable to sit on and pedal. Choose an exercise cycle that other family members can easily use.

WHERE TO BUY

Exercise cycles come in such a wide range of prices that they can be found at all kinds of retail outlets, from department stores to specialty stores. If you're buying your first exercise cycle, you might want to seek out entry-level price points at mass merchants. But if you're upgrading from your current cycle, or just very serious about this workout, you might prefer units found at higher prices in the specialty stores.

FEATURES AND TERMINOLOGY_____

Belt Drive: Belt drives use tension on a belt to gauge resistance.

Recumbent: Recumbent cycles are ridden in a reclined seat.

Upright: Upright cycles are ridden in an upright position.

Lifecycle 5500HR Exercise Bike ✔BEST BUY

This is the new and improved model of last year's Consumer Guide™ Best Buy in exercise cycles. Life Fitness has truly taken the best and made it better. A new belt drive system really does make the cycle quieter and it also makes the pedal action smoother throughout the workout. Changing the Message Center Console to provide constant readouts lets you monitor your progress at any time and helps you keep on target. Plus, the 1999 model now has 20 levels of intensity for programmed workouts, with something for everyone from beginners to marathoners. Of course, all the Best Buy features of last year are still relevant, such as hands-free heart rate monitoring; a wide, springless seat; closed-cell urethane handle grips for a soft but solid feel; and front casters for easy storage. The Lifecylce 5500HR is top dollar—but top quality, too.

Specifications: height, 55"; width, 22.75"; length, 46"; weight, 87 lbs.
Warranty: 3 year, parts
Manufacturer's Suggested Retail Price: $1,699
Approximate Low Price: not available

Keys CardioMax Exercise Bike 550 Budget Buy

This is the newest of new exercise cycles, with only a prototype available at the time of review. But Keys Fitness is bringing a solid name to a strong contender at this entry-level price point. Unlike many models in this price range, the CardioMax has a fully electromagnetic resistance system and a surprisingly smooth and silent belt drive. Console readouts cover all the basics, including time, speed, calories, distance, and pulse. Heart rate is monitored with a hands-free and not altogether uncomfortable ear clip. Also surprising, even at $299, there are programming capabilities for the user. The CardioMax from Keys is solid, dependable, and with just enough special features to make it a very practical Budget Buy.

Specifications: height, 57"; width, 21.5"; length, 42"
Warranty: 1 year, parts
Manufacturer's Suggested Retail Price: $299
Approximate Low Price: not available

ROWING MACHINE

Rowing provides a zero-impact, fluid type of exercise. Although rowing machines have fallen in popularity as new and more advanced types of home exercise equipment become available, there are still several good rowing machines on the market. The better models accurately reproduce the catch-and-pull motion of rowing and provide a true total-body exercise.

HOW TO SHOP

When shopping for a rowing machine, look for a smooth gliding seat and sturdy guide rail that is long enough for your legs. The unit should be able to accommodate both tall and short rowers.

WHERE TO BUY

Fewer and fewer manufacturers are making rowing machines. Specialty shops will be the best place to find what selection there is in this product category.

FEATURES AND TERMINOLOGY

Air Resistance: Uses a fan for resistance.

Magnetic Resistance: Uses magnetic reaction to control resistance.

Concept II Model C

✔**BEST BUY**

The Concept II Model C is a well-made flywheel/ fan rowing machine that provides a lifetime of rowing exercise for the entire family. The wide, comfortable seat slides easily on a strong aluminum I-beam. The adjustable footrests are deep and flex naturally. The foot straps hold your feet firmly in place. A solid maple handle, covered with molded rubber grips, acts as the oar. The easy-to-read electronic monitor is centrally located and mounted on a movable arm. The monitor displays time for 500 meters, calories per hour, duration of workout, average stroke rate, heart rate (optional), total calories, on/off, and memory recall. In addition, there are three levels of operation: automatic, preset workout, recall (plus extra functions for advanced users). An optional computer interface for training, performance logging, and racing is available at an extra cost. The unit folds for storage and has built-in casters.

Specifications: height, 34"; width, 24"; length, 96"; weight, 70 lbs.
Warranty: 2 years, parts; 5 years, metal frame parts
Manufacturer's Suggested Retail Price: $765
Approximate Low Price: $725

TREADMILLS

Treadmills are popular because they provide an indoor means for walking or running. This is a type of exercise that is not only worthwhile but enjoyable for most people. Basically, a treadmill consists of a wide belt that is stretched over a bed and around two or more rollers. Most units are powered by a motor, but some are powered by the user. Motor choices include AC or DC powered. An AC motor commonly runs at one continuous speed and relies on a transmission to regulate speed. A DC-powered unit uses variable voltage to regulate the speed at which the belt spins.

HOW TO SHOP

Choose a model that has a wide belt and is long enough for your stride. If you plan on running more than walking, choose a treadmill with at least a 1 1/2-horsepower motor. Better units will also have some type of cushioning between the belt and bed, a feature that you will appreciate if you jog or run on the machine.

WHERE TO BUY

Treadmills come in such a wide range of prices that they can be found at all kinds of retail outlets. If you're buying your first treadmill, you might want to seek out entry-level price points at mass merchants. But if you're upgrading from your current model, or just very serious about this workout, you might prefer units found at higher prices in the specialty stores.

FEATURES AND TERMINOLOGY

Adjustable Incline: Lets you vary the steepness of hill walking.

Monitor: Indicates belt speed and other factors, such as heart rate, mph, distance, etc.

Workout Programs: Automatically adjust speed and incline to pre-set routines.

ProForm CD Coach Treadmill PFTL9858

✔ **BEST BUY**

This is truly breakthrough technology at an amazingly affordable price. ProForm has combined workout programming with the audio power of a CD player to create an "interactive" treadmill. The CD player in the control panel actually connects with the digital programming of the treadmill to operate speed, incline, and all aspects of treadmill operation in accordance with a pre-programmed workout. The CD Coach disc provides verbal encouragement from actual personal trainers who "walk you through" each workout. Although there are only two programs from which to choose, the excitement of the CD aspect of this product makes both entertaining adventures. Added bonuses to this unique treadmill are the oversized deck (18"×60"), the SpaceSaver folding design for easy storage, the built-in book rack, the water-bottle holder, and the 2-pound hand weights. You get a lot for your money with the CD Coach Treadmill from ProForm, making it an all-round Best Buy.

Specifications: height, 55"; width, 36.5"; length, 76"; motor, 2.5 hp
Warranty: 90 days, parts and labor
Manufacturer's Suggested Retail Price: $999
Approximate Low Price: not available

Life Fitness 4500HR

| Recommended |

The Life Fitness 4500HR treadmill doesn't come at an entry-level price, but then it's not meant for the entry-level exerciser. At a glance, you don't see the $2,599 difference in this treadmill. The 1.5-hp motor is standard power, the deck is no larger than most, and the control panel has an ordinary appearance. But with Life Fitness you're buying durability and sophistication. These units are solidly built, evidenced by the uncommon lifetime warranty on the shock absorbers that truly make jogging on this product a low-impact exercise. The sophistication comes in the programing features of the 4500HR. Patented Heart Rate Zone Training programs operate the treadmill to automatically adjust speed and incline to maintain the desired heart rate. The unit also comes with nine different workout programs pre-installed, allowing the user to choose from programs such as Hill, Fit Test, Fat Burn, 45-Minute Cross-Train, and more. If you're serious about exercise, Life Fitness has some serious advantages.

Specifications: width, 31.5"; length, 73"; height, 46"; motor, 1.5-hp; weight, 171 lbs.
Warranty: 1 year, labor; 3 year, parts; lifetime, shock absorbers
Manufacturer's Suggested Retail Price: $2,599
Approximate Low Price: $2,499

Keys 8500

The Keys 8500 is a near club-quality treadmill with a 2.0-horsepower motor that is strong enough to deliver constant performance at any workout speed level up to 10 mph. The deck is wide (20"×56") and cushioned to add a degree of comfort to the walk or run. The Keys 8500's best feature, however, is the control panel. Membrane switches and an easy-to-use Custom Speed Bar make controlling your workout especially easy. The large LED screen puts monitoring your status a glance away. On the rail, you'll find special toggle switches to adjust elevation or speed. Programming is limited to either four pre-set programs or two user programs, but this unit's quality makes it a value for the money.

Specifications: width, 20"; length, 56"; weight capacity, 400 lbs.; motor, 2.0 hp

Warranty: 1 year, labor; 3 years, parts; 5 years, motor

Manufacturer's Suggested Retail Price: $1,999

Approximate Low Price: not available

Weslo Cadence 1020 Treadmill WLTL 2808

The price is right for this entry-level treadmill. While it may not look or feel quite as "solid" as other models listed here, the Weslo Cadence 1020 is a very effective piece of machinery. A strong 2.25-hp motor takes the belt up to 10 mph, and the deck (16"×50") is larger than some. A simple thumb-press sensor provides quick heart rate information, and the control panel tracks the usual monitors of speed, time, distance, and calories. The SpaceSaver feature also makes it easy to store when not in use. If you're just starting out with an exercise program, the Cadence 1020 will serve you well without wearing out your wallet.

Specifications: motor, 2.5-hp

Warranty: 90 days, parts and labor

Manufacturer's Suggested Retail Price: $499

Approximate Low Price: not available

HOME GYMS

Home gyms have made enormous strides in recent years, and they are now more advanced than ever before. Many units offer a lot of exercise options, including rowing, leg curls, leg extensions, inner and outer thigh exercises, abdomen crunches, and pull-downs. Quality construction is easy to spot in home gyms: The tube frame should be at least two-inches square, pulleys should be easy to adjust (usually by setting a pin), benches and seats should be padded and covered with an easy-to-clean material, and the finish should be chrome or enamel.

HOW TO SHOP

Knowing what types of regular exercise you prefer will enable you to choose the best equipment. Keep in mind that home gyms take up space, however, so you will require a space that measures at least 10×10 feet. Write down the dimensions of the room in which you plan to set up the gym and carry that information with you while shopping.

WHERE TO BUY

Home gyms can be found in almost all retail outlets; however, you want a knowledgeable sales clerk to tell you how the features of one compare to features of another. This might mean going to a sporting goods store, if not a specialty fitness store.

FEATURES AND TERMINOLOGY

Aircraft-grade, Coated Cables: Cables that are used in aircraft and coated for smoother operation.

Multistation: Accommodates positions for more than one user at a time.

Weider Pro 9645 Gym WESY9645

✔**BEST BUY**

This home gym is all you could want for yourself and a couple of your friends—and all for less than $500. That's what makes the Weider Pro 9645 Gym a Best Buy. There are many products that may seem a little sturdier, or have some special materials or mechanisms, but Weider keeps it simple and complete with this unit. It has eight workout stations, including bench press, butterfly, leg developer, high pulley, low pulley, military press, leg press, and assisted dip/chin-up. Also, there are three stations, so the workout can be a group affair. Using a vinyl-encased, 235-pound dual stack, weight can be adjusted in 10-pound increments. Steel construction of the gym should hold up after years of use in the home.

Specifications: height, 71"; width, 48"; length, 72"
Warranty: 30 days, money back; 90 days, parts and labor; 2 years, frame
Manufacturer's Suggested Retail Price: $499
Approximate Low Price: not available

Parabody 375 Home Gym 375101

Recommended

There's a lot more that goes into the Parabody 375 Home Gym, but it costs a lot more, too. Still, the quality of construction and special features of this unit certainly make it a Recommended buy. While there's only one station, the efficiency of space in this design allows it to be placed against a wall if preferred. Specially designed real feel 1:1 pulley ratios give the user a smooth lift and lower motion. Meant to last a lifetime, the Parabody 375 uses materials that will never lose their performance, such as premium quality coated aircraft cables and sealed ball bearing fiberglass reinforced pulleys. The manufacturer has also considered subtle elements of design that enhance use. For instance, press arm handles are angled to reduce stress on the wrists during pressing. Leg press and calf raise bars are optional.

Specifications: height, 83"; width, 45"; length, 107"; weight, 420 lbs.
Warranty: lifetime (limited)
Manufacturer's Suggested Retail Price: $1,549
Approximate Low Price: $1,475

STAIR CLIMBERS

Stair climbers are excellent machines for burning up calories and exercising the major muscle groups of the lower body. Add-on accessories for the upper body can provide a total body workout. An all-out workout on a stair climber can consume as much energy as you are capable of producing.

HOW TO SHOP

When you shop for a stair climber, look for sturdy, padded handrails to aid balance, electronic programs to keep you interested, and easy-to-set resistance settings. A sturdy steel or aluminum frame is a must. The best stair climbers keep your feet on an even plane with the floor at all times, allowing natural foot articulation.

WHERE TO BUY

Quality stair climbers are almost exclusively a specialty store item. However, some of the larger sporting goods chains will have models from which to choose.

FEATURE AND TERMINOLOGY

Pre-programmed Course: Automatic programming that changes resistance at preset intervals.

Stairmaster FreeClimber 4400PT

✓ BEST BUY

To say the Stairmaster FreeClimber 4400PT is a standout from all the rest is actually a design statement. The most notable distinction about this stepper is its unique, rail-less design. It forces the users to have a more upright posture throughout the exercise and this, says Stairmaster, helps users burn more calories with a more effective lower-body workout. It also means this model will fit easily in limited space, with a footprint of only 2'×4' for the entire unit. The advanced circuitry of the electronic console provides motivating programs, quick-start workouts, and even a fitness test to gauge your best level of exercise. The braking system is also electronic, accurately controlling the rate of pedal descent. The

4400PT also includes Polar Heart Rate monitor capability. It has a top price, but it's a Best Buy.

Specifications: height, 69"; width, 22"; length, 41"; weight, 126 lbs.
Warranty: 45 days, labor; 3 years, parts
Manufacturer's Suggested Retail Price: $2,350
Approximate Low Price: not available

EverYoung Vertical Ascent Climber EY73500

Recommended

Not a stair climber per se, the Vertical Ascent Climber from EverYoung is still a strong Recommended buy for the climbing action this simple—but effective—equipment renders. The unique Adjustable Braking Resistance System uses heat resistant components and lube impregnated bearings for quick and easy resistance changes in the climb. Arm and hand motions are synchronized with the legs for a smooth, efficient transfer of power. The LCD Window Display offers push-button control to view time, steps, tempo, load, and calories per minute. The Vertical Ascent Climber is a step up from steppers and stair climbers, but at this price it's an easy step up to take.

Specifications: height, 88.2"; weight, 33.5"; length, 41"
Warranty: 1 year, labor; 2 years, parts; lifetime, frame
Manufacturer's Suggested Retail Price: $599
Approximate Low Price: not available

SKI MACHINE

Cross-country skiing provides total body fitness. The poling motion builds upper-body strength, the leg motion builds leg and lower-back strength, and combined motions add to a complete cardiovascular workout. Ski machines duplicate the total workout of cross-country skiing in a non-impact manner that does not require snow, thus enabling you to work out all year.

HOW TO SHOP

There are two basic types of ski machines: independent leg motion and dependent leg motion. The former is harder to master but offers a better workout and a closer simulation of real cross-country skiing. Dependent models commonly cost more. Most ski machines fold for storage and some have wheels for easy movement. Try several machines before making your final choice.

WHERE TO BUY

Ski machines are a special piece of exercise equipment usually requiring a specialty fitness store to find a selection to choose from.

FEATURES AND TEMINOLOGY

Preset Resistance Settings: Provides automatic programming of total workout.

Variable Incline: The ability to change the degree of slope.

NordicTrack Classic Pro Skier NT28601   ✔BEST BUY

This is an upgraded model of last year's Best Buy of the same name. The oak and steel construction are still part of this sharp-looking unit, but this Classic Pro features an adjustable hip pad that helps in steadying your body through the exercise motion. The seven levels of resistance set by the flywheel allow you to work your upper body as hard as you want to. There are also various settings for resistance in the leg exerciser. Elevation changes can be made manually. Optional accessories include a bookholder and heart-rate monitor.

Specifications: height, 96"; width, 36"; length, 88"; weight, 53 lbs.
Warranty: 1 year, parts and labor
Manufacturer's Suggested Retail Price: $599
Approximate Low Price: not available

TOTAL BODY MACHINES

Total body conditioning machines are a new concept in fitness. They can resemble ski simulators and striders, stair climbers, or even treadmills, but these units allow you to perform a number of exercises at the same time, hence the name "total body machines." Prices are high, but these machines offer no-impact, aerobic exercise and a terrific total body workout.

HOW TO SHOP

Try out display models of these units to make sure you are comfortable with the multiple action of the exercise. If you don't think you can coordinate it, there might be another type of combined-action total body machine more suited for you.

WHERE TO BUY

Go to specialty stores and be specific about the total body workout you want. These salespeople are experts and can suggest a number of options for you.

FEATURES AND TERMINOLOGY

Electromagnetic Brake: Uses magnetic currents for accurate braking control.

Elliptical Motion: The continuous striding of pedals moving in constant opposing motion.

Reebok Body Trec II

✔**BEST BUY**

The Reebok Body Trec II provides a total body workout for all family members, regardless of ability level. This unit resembles a walking or jogging machine. Your feet move in a natural elliptical motion, providing a no-impact workout for less stress on the joints. As you walk, your hands grasp poles that move in conjunction with your leg motion. This results in a smooth, fluid movement that tones arms, chest, back, hips, legs, and glutei. The unit can be operated in forward or in reverse. It is constructed of welded structural steel and requires no lubrication. Its eight preprogrammed exercise courses include Vail Pass, steady climb, and competition. The easy-to-read display registers calories burned, calories per hour, distance traveled, speed attained, and time remaining or elapsed. An optional heart rate monitor is also available.

Specifications: height, 62.5"; width, 28.5"; length, 62.5"; weight, 175 lbs.
Warranty: 1 year, labor; 2 years, parts
Manufacturer's Suggested Retail Price: $2,995
Approximate Low Price: $2,700

True Natural Trainer TNT 2000

| Recommended |

True Fitness has long been a leader in treadmills, but with the TNT 2000, they combine the benefits of the treadmill with the development of the upper body. The key to the total body workout of the TNT 2000 lies in the simplicity of the design. There is no drive motor for the treadmill, but rather precision rollers that move the treadmill according to the steps of the user, adding to development of calves, quads, and glutei. The long handles that extend to the user's chest are used for the push/pull motion that develops abdominal, back, chest, shoulder, and arm muscles. Push-button controls on the handles adjust the resistance as you go. An added benefit of the new TNT 2000 is its appearance. The sleek, modernistic design makes for an inviting piece of equipment and a great addition to any home gym.

Manufacturer's Suggested Retail Price: $3,995
Approximate Low Price: not available

ELLIPTICAL MACHINES

Elliptical machines are a relatively new product, resulting from the popularity of the commercial units found in health clubs. The term "elliptical" comes from the oblong pattern the pedals make when in motion. Elliptical machines, or cross-trainers as they are sometimes called, combine the exercise motions of some of the most popular pieces of equipment: treadmill, stair climber, exercise cycle, and ski machine. The end product is a low-impact machine that gives a great cardiovascular workout and works a wide range of lower body muscles. Because elliptical machines can be adjusted, you can glide (in an elliptical motion) as you would on a ski machine or, with a simple adjustment of the pedals, get more of a stair-stepping or bike action. Your feet remain flat at all times within the pedals so there is no strain on back, hips, or joints.

HOW TO SHOP

All elliptical machines are not created equal, and you should try out several models before purchase. Inspect the welded parts, flywheel, resistance belt, and materials used for construction. A quality machine will be obvious.

FEATURE AND TERMINOLOGY

Toggle Displays: Displays that can be switched between two options, such as pulse/calories burned, speed/distance, and time/resistance level.

Reebok Personal Trec

Here's another club-quality product now available ✔ **BEST BUY** to consumers, and it's that quality of construction and performance that makes it a Best Buy—even at its somewhat demanding price-tag. First of all, it is solidly made of heavy-gauge welded structural steel. Second, the natural elliptical motion is a perfect re-creation of your natural walking or running motion. In operation you'll appreciate the response of the computer-controlled magnetic brake system, the same one found on Reebok's club equipment. There are eight programmed courses for the user to choose from, and a control panel that displays time, speed, distance, calories, and heart rate. Originally built for club use, the Reebok Personal Trec is especially durable, ensuring trouble-free use for years in the home. Its textured finish is abrasion resistant, and special UHMW bearings require no lubrication. The Reebok Personal Trec makes getting the most out of elliptical exercise easy.

Specifications: height, 65.25"; width, 26.25"; length, 58"; weight, 175 lbs.
Warranty: 1 year, parts and labor
Manufacturer's Suggested Retail Price: $1,995
Approximate Low Price: $1,800

Healthrider Elliptical CrossTrainer HREL 0998

Recommended

A lot of extras make the Healthrider Elliptical CrossTrainer—while not a top-of-the-liner—certainly a Recommended buy. Construction is sturdy enough to make the Healthrider last a long time in the home. Other features make the CrossTrainer really fun and easy to use. Toggle displays reveal pulse/calories burned, speed/distance, and time/resistance level. A simple plus/minus button on the control provides instant regulation of resistance. Healthrider's patented EKG Grip Pulse Sensor is built into the rail—monitoring your pulse is as easy as gripping the durable, foam-covered arms. The CrossTrainer comes with four preprogrammed workouts, two for aerobics and two for fat burning. It also features the manufacturer's popular Power Incline system for easily changing the workout slope. The CrossTrainer is a lot of equipment for the price.

Specifications: height, 64"; width, 24"; length, 73"
Warranty: 90 days, parts and labor
Manufacturer's Suggested Retail Price: $899
Approximate Low Price: not available

HOME IMPROVEMENT

Maintaining a home—whether it be a house, condo, or apartment—can be a time-consuming and expensive task. If you want additional information on the safety and effectiveness of these or any other units you may consider purchasing, you can consult public safety organizations such as the National Safety Council.

BEST BUYS 2000

Our Best Buy, Recommended, and Budget Buy home improvement products follow. Products within each category are listed according to quality. The item we consider the best of the Best Buys is first, followed by our second choice, and so on. Remember that a Best Buy, Recommended, or Budget Buy designation only applies to the model listed—it does not necessarily apply to other models made by the same manufacturer or to an entire product line.

ELECTRIC DRILLS

Cordless drills are increasing in popularity and are now offered in 9.6-, 12-, 14.4-, and 18-volt models. Cordless circular and reciprocating saws are also available in 14.4- and 18-volt versions. Many units are offered in kit form, which typically contain a drill (and a saw), two batteries, a charger, and a carrying case. While cordless tools are quite capable, their price tag is commonly two or three times as much as a similar corded unit.

Black & Decker Firestorm FS144

✔ BEST BUY

The Firestorm 14.4V is probably the most versatile drill for use around the home and shop. It features a 24-position clutch; two-speed gear box (high and low); variable speed (0-900 rpm); electronic brake; and an ergonomically balanced, midhandle design with rubber comfort grip. The forward/reverse switch is conveniently located above the trigger. It has a one-handed keyless chuck with automatic spindle lock for quick changing of drill bits. This drill can reach up to 300 inch/pounds of torque so it is powerful enough for almost any drilling/fastening task. The unit comes with a high-capacity nickel cadmium battery and a three-hour charger.

Specifications: chuck size, 3/8" keyless; weight, NA
Warranty: 2 years
Manufacturer's Suggested Retail Price: $129
Approximate Low Price: not available

Black & Decker VersaPak
Cordless Pivot Driver 750

✔**BEST BUY**

This 3.6-volt cordless screwdriver is the latest addition to the popular VersaPak system of tools that use batteries that are interchangeable throughout the line. This unit differs from other cordless screwdrivers in that the handle can be locked in either the in-line position or in a pistol-grip position for use in hard-to-reach areas. This unit also features an automatic spindle lock system that offers greater control when starting and finishing screws. With the screwdriver in the off position, the system locks the screwdriver in a set position, allowing for manual use when needed. The forward, reverse, and power buttons are conveniently located.

Specifications: weight, 1 lb.
Warranty: 2 years
Manufacturer's Suggested Retail Price: $36
Approximate Low Price: not available

Skil Warrior Plus 14.4
Cordless Drill/Driver 2582-04

✔**BEST BUY**

If you are looking for a well-balanced cordless drill for the home or shop, the Skill Warrior Plus 14.4 is an excellent choice. This lightweight drill/driver features a midhandle design with two gear ranges (0-400 & 0-1200 rpm). It also features reversible and variable speed and a keyless chuck. The forward/reverse switch is located above the trigger. Four planetary gears deliver 175 inch/pounds of torque. This drill comes with two batteries, a one-hour charger, and a plastic carrying case.

Specifications: chuck size, ⅜" keyless; weight, 3 lbs., 8 oz.
Warranty: 2 years (limited)
Manufacturer's Suggested Retail Price: $194
Approximate Low Price: $77-$90

Ryobi 14.4 Volt
Cordless Drill/Driver R10520K2

✔ **BEST BUY**

The Ryobi 14.4 volt cordless drill/driver is an excellent choice for use around the home and shop. This lightweight drill/driver features a wraparound cushion with a center handle design with two gear ranges (0-375 & 0-1350 rpm). It also has reversible and variable speed features and a keyless chuck. The forward/reverse switch is located above the trigger. The metal planetary gear system provides durability at high torque. This well-balanced cordless drill comes with two batteries, a one-hour diagnostic battery charger, and a plastic carrying case.

Specifications: chuck size, ½" keyless; weight, 5 lbs., 12 oz.
Warranty: 2 years
Manufacturer's Suggested Retail Price: $159
Approximate Low Price: $124

Skil Classic Corded Drill 6250-44

Recommended

The Skil Classic Corded Drill is a good choice as a general-purpose household drill. This unit has a 4-amp motor that is double insulated and has a 6-foot power cord. It also has reversing and variable speed (up to 2500 rpm) features and a keyless chuck. This design is comfortable in smaller hands. A lock-on button is located on the bottom of the handle and the trigger is equipped with a speed-adjusting dial. A spirit level, an aid for drilling horizontal holes, is located on the top of this drill. The Skil Classic comes with a 24-piece bit set and a plastic carrying case.

Warranty: 2 years (limited)
Manufacturer's Suggested Retail Price: $96
Approximate Low Price: $60-$79

ELECTRIC SANDERS

Several companies now offer palm-sized finish sanders, and these are a good sanding tool for both homeowners and professionals. The Mouse Sander (Black & Decker), for example, has a number of attachments that are used for polishing and scrubbing. The Profile Sander (Porter-Cable) is a handy detail sander with a variety of special heads for sanding irregular shapes. This is an ideal sander for furniture and molding refinishing. A belt sander is also a handy tool for larger sanding and shaping projects.

Black & Decker The Mouse MS500K   ✔ BEST BUY

The Mouse sander/polisher is a versatile power tool for general sanding, polishing, and scrubbing. This palm-sized unit resembles a miniature iron (with V-shaped base). It includes Velcro-backed sanding, polishing, and scrubbing pads, which can be attached or can be removed quickly—simply stick or peel off. The Mouse runs at 11,000 orbits per minute and features soft rubber grips, a one-finger on/off button, and an ergonomic design for comfort and control. The Mouse is sold in a storage case with 23 assorted polishing, sanding, and scrubbing accessories.

Specifications: volts, 110
Warranty: 2 years
Manufacturer's Suggested Retail Price: $59
Approximate Low Price: $48-$52

Porter-Cable Variable
Speed Profile Sander Kit 9444vs   ✔ BEST BUY

The Porter-Cable 9444vs is an excellent choice for detail sanding of woodwork, moldings, and other odd shapes. This unit comes with 17 different sanding profiles, including those for use in difficult locations and tight corners. To use, just choose a suitable shaped profile, attach adhesive backed paper, insert the profile into the mounting plate, and begin sanding. The 1.8-amp motor runs from 2,100 to 6,000 orbits per minute and will remove old paint and smooth most shapes quickly. The 9444vs also includes a heavy-duty carrying case and a dust wand that can be attached to a shop vac. A single speed unit is also available.

Specifications: motor, 1.8 amps; weight, 3 lbs, 12 oz.
Warranty: 1 year
Manufacturer's Suggested Retail Price: not available
Approximate Low Price: $109-$116

Ryobi Variable Speed Belt Sander BE321
✓ **BEST BUY**

The Ryobi BE321 is a professional-grade belt sander that can easily accomplish the largest sanding project. This unit features a variable speed (755-1148 square feet per minute), 5.4-amp motor (its speed is adjusted with a thumb wheel located on the front handle). The BE321 also features a lock-on trigger, a ten-foot two-prong power cord, and a dust collection bag. Belt tracking is adjusted with an alignment knob on the left side of the unit. Sanding belts are installed or removed with a simple lever. This sander can use a variety of different grit sanding belts (1 supplied) measuring 3 inches wide by 21 inches long. Optional accessories include a sanding frame, a bench clamp, and a sharpening kit.

Specifications: motor, 5.4 amps; weight, 7.9 pounds; belt size, 3"×21"
Warranty: 2 years
Manufacturer's Suggested Retail Price: $185
Approximate Low Price: $99-$148

Ryobi 1/6 Sheet Finishing Sander S551
Recommended

The Ryobi S551 is a useful pad-type sander for finish sanding in the workshop. The 1.5-amp motor powers up to 1,200 orbits per minute. This unit can use cut pieces of sheet sandpaper, which are held in place with quick-action paper clamps. This sander also features a ten-foot two-prong, all-weather power cord. The on/off switch is located on the top front of the palm-sized grip.

Specifications: motor, 1.5 amps; weight, 2.1 lbs.; paper size, 3"x4½"
Warranty: 2 years
Manufacturer's Suggested Retail Price: $45
Approximate Low Price: not available

____CIRCULAR SAWS AND JIGSAWS____

Corded circular saws and jigsaws are handy for do-it-yourself projects. A wide selection is currently available. Improvements such as lightweight housings, no-mar bases, and quick-change blade mechanisms (on jigsaws) are now common features.

Skil Legend Circular Saw 5155K

✓**BEST BUY**

The Skil Legend 5155K features a 2.4-horsepower, double-insulated motor with burnout protection and a six-foot power cord. This two-handled saw has a lateral lock-off trigger for safety, and a blade guard-lifting mechanism conveniently located close to the rear sawdust discharge chute. The depth-of-cut adjustment lever is located on the rear of the blade guard, and a scale indicates depth of cut for various thicknesses of plywood. The table can be adjusted for bevel cuts up to 45 degrees. A line-of-cut indicator is pre-stamped on the front of the table and indicates 45 and 90 degrees. This saw comes with a 20-tooth chisel, 7¼-inch blade, and a plastic carrying case.

Specifications: blade speed, 4,600 rpm; weight, 9.6 lbs.
Warranty: 2 years (limited)
Manufacturer's Suggested Retail Price: $99
Approximate Low Price: $49-$53

Ryobi 7¼" Circular Saw CSB130

✓ **BEST BUY**

The Ryobi CSB130 is a well-made unit that will fill the needs of the advanced do-it-yourselfer. This unit features a 2¾-horsepower, double-insulated motor and a ten-foot power cord. This two-handled saw has a spindle lock for easy blade changes, and a blade guard-lifting mechanism conveniently located close to the adjustable rear sawdust discharge chute. The depth-of-cut adjustment knob is located to the rear and below the motor and a scale clearly indicates the depth of cut for various thicknesses of plywood. A unique cord clip on the left side of the handle keeps the power cord out of the cut area. A small, clear plastic window located between the blade guard housing and the handle deflects sawdust and enables the user to view the cut. The table can be adjusted for bevel cuts up to 51½ degrees. A line-of-cut indicator is notched in the front edge of the table and indicates 45 and 90 degrees. This saw comes with a 24-tooth carbide blade, onboard blade wrench, and plastic carrying case. This is a reasonably priced circular saw with a number of unique features that should provide years of dependable service.

Specifications: blade speed, 5,000 rpm; weight, 11 lbs., 8 oz.
Warranty: 2 years
Manufacturer's Suggested Retail Price: $90
Approximate Low Price: $79-$85

Black & Decker C2020K

✓ **BEST BUY**

The Black & Decker C2020K circular saw is probably the most innovative circular saw to be introduced in decades. It is designed for homeowner use and will easily cut plywood and dimensional lumber (2×4, 2×6, etc.). This saw is 1½ to 2½ pounds lighter and 40 percent quieter than the average circular saw on the market. It has a 6½-inch carbide blade for extended life and use. A unique feature is the patented Sightline Window, which allows you to view the cut line on the material from above. Standard features include a wraparound bail handle; adjustable dust chute (which can be attached to a shop vac); kerf indicator markings on the shoe;

and a wider, more stable adjustable base. The WoodHawk comes in a handy plastic carrying case with blade wrench.

Specifications: blade speed, 4,300 rpm; weight, NA
Warranty: 2 years
Manufacturer's Suggested Retail Price: $69
Approximate Low Price: not available

Skil Classic Jigsaw Kit 4470-44

✔ **BEST BUY**

The Skil Classic Jigsaw features dynamic vibration reduction, which greatly reduces most vibration normally produced by jigsaws. This saw also features a 4-amp, double-insulated motor with a six-foot power cord. Other features include five-position orbital cutting action, a four-position shaft lock for scroll cutting, a dial-type speed adjustment, and an anti-splinter position on the base. A clear plastic chip deflector slides up to permit blade changes. This saw also has a contoured trigger and lock-on feature. The base can be adjusted for bevel cutting, left or right. A dust chute on the rear of this saw can be connected to a shop-vac. This saw comes with a selection of blades and a plastic carrying case.

Specifications: blade speed, variable; weight, 4.1 lbs.
Warranty: 2 years (limited)
Manufacturer's Suggested Retail Price: $114
Approximate Low Price: $60

Ryobi Variable Speed Jigsaw JS048

✔ **BEST BUY**

The Ryobi JS048 is a good choice for general home and shop use. This saw comes with a number of unique features that make it a Best Buy, including three orbital settings and a non-orbital setting and a base plate that can be adjusted for bevel cuts at 45 degrees, left or right. A clear chip shield pivots upward to make blade changing easy. This saw also has a one part adjustable trigger with a lock-on feature. Blades are held in place with an allen-head screw and the unit is supplied with an allen wrench that is stored in the base plate. This unit comes with a ten-foot power cord, blade storage compartment, and one general purpose saw blade. An optional edge guide is also available.

Specifications: blade speed, 0-3000 rpm; weight, 3.4 lbs.
Warranty: 2 years
Manufacturer's Suggested Retail Price: $89
Approximate Low Price: $80

ROUTERS

A router is a handy power tool for a variety of home improvement projects. A wide selection of units is available. Generally speaking, there are three basic types: two-handed routers, plunge routers, and one-handed (or barrel) routers. The basic two-handed router can be used for all routing tasks and is usually the lowest priced router on the market. Two handed routers will have a horsepower rating of $7/8$ hp to $3\frac{1}{4}$ hp. Plunge routers have more advanced features and are more versatile for all types of wood working. Horsepower ratings for plunge routers are from $1\frac{1}{2}$ hp to $3\frac{1}{4}$ hp. One handed or barrel routers are primarily designed for trimming laminate material and have a power rating in amps (from 3.8 to 5.6) rather than horsepower. A router table will greatly increase the capabilities of both two handed and plunge routers. All manufacturers offer a good selection of routers for both do-it-yourself projects and commercial applications.

Ryobi Router Kit R165S

The Ryobi R165S is a rugged $1\frac{3}{4}$-horsepower ✓**BEST BUY** router for general use in the shop. A large spindle lock is located on top of the motor and makes bit changing simple with a supplied wrench. A work light and clear chip shield aid visibility. Depth of cut adjustments are easy with the depth adjusting ring and locking clamping lever. A carrying case is included and a wide variety of optional accessories is available.

Specifications: collet size, $\frac{1}{4}$"; weight, 7 lbs., 8 oz.
Warranty: 2 years

Manufacturer's Suggested Retail Price: $79-$89
Approximate Low Price: $50-$70

Skil Classic Plunge Router 1845-02

> Recommended

The Skil 1845-02 was recently introduced to complement the other fine tools in the Skil Classic Series. This two-horsepower plunge router has a number of worthwhile features that will appeal to a wide range of woodworkers. The soft-start, variable-speed motor is controlled with a thumbscrew located on the top of the motor housing. The trigger is located on the right handle and has a lock-on feature. The collet lock, the state-of-the-art Jacobs keyless locking mechanism, does not require the use of a tool to change router bits. A clear plastic chip deflection shield is located in the front base of the unit. This unit also features an adjustable depth-of-plunge gauge, fine-depth adjustment knob, and lever-lock to lock the router in any position. A plastic carrying case is included.

Specifications: weight, 7.3 lbs.
Warranty: 2 years (limited)
Manufacturer's Suggested Retail Price: $221
Approximate Low Price: $119-$157

Ryobi Plunge Router RE600

> Recommended

The Ryobi RE600 is a professional-grade tool that will easily handle any routing task. The powerful 3-horsepower variable-speed motor is double-insulated and has a soft-start feature. This tool features convenient handles with a plunge lock, toggle switch, and speed control dial on the right side; brushes that can be easily replaced; and an eight-foot power cord. Also included is a spindle lock button and a soft-start feature. This router will accept both ¼- and ½-inch router bits. A variety of optional accessories are available for the RE600.

Specifications: collet size, ¼" & ½"; weight, 13.6 lbs.
Warranty: 2 years

Manufacturer's Suggested Retail Price: $286
Approximate Low Price: not available

GARAGE DOOR OPENERS

Garage door openers offer both convenience and safety because they let you open and close your garage door while remaining in your vehicle. They are widely available in home centers and range in price from $130 to $350. Installation is usually not difficult but requires basic power and hand tools as well as do-it-yourself skills. Complete installation should take less than a day, and the work will be easier to accomplish with an extra pair of hands. Some units come complete with a guide rail, while others require that you purchase the appropriate size rail for your installation. This can add from $80 to $90 to the price.

SAFETY FEATURES

All new garage door openers are required to have several safety features to prevent injury. One feature automatically reverses door travel within two seconds after coming in contact with an obstruction. Another common safety feature is an electric eye that reverses door travel if anything gets in its path. The electric eye is mounted about 12 inches up from the floor on the door jamb.

REMOTE CONTROLS

Today, almost all garage door openers come with at least one remote control and a wall-mounted, doorbell-like button for operating the door from inside the garage. Advanced security features are standard on all high-end and many mid-priced units. Sears, for example, offers remote controls that select a new access code from billions of combinations each time the unit is used, and that number is never repeated. Many types of accessories are also available to make opening and closing your garage door more convenient. These include keychain-size remote controls, exterior keypads, and exterior security lighting systems.

Sears Craftsman 53662

✔**BEST BUY**

The Sears Craftsman 53662 garage door opener is a dependable ½-horsepower chain-driven unit. Standard safety features include an infrared safety reversing sensor (which stops the door and reverses door motion before the door makes contact with any objects in its path); safety reverse (which automatically reverses the door when it meets an obstruction); a 4½-minute light delay; a lock switch that locks out all hand-held radio signals to prevent access while you are away; and an emergency release, which allows manual door operation during power failures. A control console allows for operation of the door from inside the garage and has an independent light switch. The unit comes with two remote control units that feature a "rolling code" that automatically rolls to a new entry code from a base of 100 billion codes each time the door is opened. This unit can also be used with keypad wireless controls, which are available at additional cost.

Specifications: engine, ½ hp
Warranty: 1 year, parts; 5 years, motor
Manufacturer's Suggested Retail Price: $170
Approximate Low Price: not available

Sears Craftsman 53663

✔**BEST BUY**

The Sears Craftsman is a dependable ½-horsepower screw-drive unit. It features Sears' Motor Vibrations Isolation System™, which reduces motor vibration, resulting in quieter operation. Standard safety features include an infrared safety reversing sensor, which stops the door and reverses door travel before making contact; safety reverse, which automatically reverses when it meets an obstruction; a 4½-minute light delay; and an emergency release, which allows manual door operation during power failure. A standard control console allows for operation of the door from inside the garage. The unit comes with two remote control units that automatically choose a new entry code each time the door is opened.

Warranty: 1 year, parts; 5 years, motor
Manufacturer's Suggested Retail Price: $190
Approximate Low Price: not available

Sears Craftsman 53664

Recommended

The Sears Craftsman 53664 is a quiet and dependable ½-horsepower belt-drive unit. It features the Motor Vibrations Isolation System™, which reduces motor vibration, resulting in quieter operation. Standard safety features include an infrared safety sensor that stops and reverses door travel before making contact with an obstruction, a safety reverse that automatically reverses the door when it comes in contact with an object, a 4½-minute light delay, and an emergency release that allows manual door operation during power failure. A standard control console allows for operation of the door from inside the garage. The unit comes with a keyless entry system and two remote control units that feature a "rolling code" system that automatically chooses a new entry code each time the door is opened.

Warranty: 1 year, parts; 5 years, motor
Manufacturer's Suggested Retail Price: $219
Approximate Low Price: not available

SAFETY EQUIPMENT

Smoke detectors, carbon monoxide (CO) detectors, and fire extinguishers are important safety equipment that every home or apartment should be equipped with. Smoke detectors can warn you early that a fire has started in the home. CO detectors can warn you and your family if this deadly gas is present in your home. The proper use of a reliable fire extinguisher can save you thousands of dollars in damage by putting out a small fire quickly.

BEST BUYS 2000

Our Best Buy safety equipment follow. Products within each category are listed according to quality. The item we consider the best of the Best Buys is first, followed by our second choice, and so on. Remember that a Best Buy designation only applies to the model listed—it does not necessarily apply to other models made by the same manufacturer or to an entire product line.

SMOKE DETECTORS

Smoke detectors operate by one of two possible methods: ionization or photoelectricity. Some of the high-end units use both methods of smoke detection. Ionization involves the use of a small, harmless amount of radioactive material to make the air in an internal chamber conduct electricity. When smoke passes into this chamber, the flow of electricity is interrupted and the alarm is sounded. Ionization alarms are inexpensive (commonly under $20) and widely available. They pose no threat to your health or the environment. Photoelectric smoke detectors, like all photoelectric systems, shine a tiny beam of light toward a sensor. When smoke passes through this beam, it breaks the stream and the alarm is sounded.

First Alert Double Sensor
Smoke Alarm SA301B/C

✔ **BEST BUY**

The First Alert SA301B/C is a high-quality, dual ionization-and-photoelectric smoke and fire detector. The unit has two test buttons and an 85-decibel alarm horn. One of the test buttons is clear plastic and flashes about four times a minute to let you know the unit is working. The alarm will beep once a minute (for about 30 days) when the battery requires replacement. It comes with a 9-volt battery, metal mounting hardware (including bracket, screws, and anchors), and an informative booklet.

Specifications: diameter, 5¾"; depth, 2½"; weight, 11 oz.
Warranty: 10 years (limited)
Manufacturer's Suggested Retail Price: $31
Approximate Low Price: $20-$25

First Alert Escape Light
Smoke Alarm SA150B/C

The First Alert SA150B/C uses the ionization method of smoke detection and is a good choice for halls and stairways. This unit has a built-in "escape" light to illuminate the way in the dark. The light is activated at the same time as the alarm, and the bulb is replaceable. A gold-colored test button can be activated either by pressing or by shining a two-D-cell flashlight (up to 15 feet away). The alarm horn sounds at 85 decibels. The alarm will beep once a minute for about 30 days when the battery requires replacement. This unit requires two 9-volt batteries (which are included). Batteries are installed in the face of the unit after opening the hinged cover. The unit comes with complete mounting hardware and an informative booklet.

Specifications: diameter, 5¼"; depth, 1¹⁵⁄₁₆"; weight, 8 oz. (with battery)
Warranty: 10 years (limited)
Manufacturer's Suggested Retail Price: $22
Approximate Low Price: $12-$15

First Alert 10 Year Lithium Power SA10YRCL

This is a top-of-the-line ionization smoke detector ✔**BEST BUY** with an 85-decibel alarm horn. The unit has a clear plastic test button for testing the unit and a blue plastic button for silencing the unit for about 15 minutes if the unit sounds due to nuisance smoke (cooking smoke in the kitchen, for example). The unit must be activated by turning a screw on the back before use. Batteries are permanently installed and cannot be replaced, so you must buy a new unit when the 10-year battery dies. The alarm will beep once a minute (for about 28 days) when the detector requires replacement. It comes with a plastic mounting bracket, mounting screws, and screw anchors. An informative booklet is also included.

Specifications: diameter, 5½"; depth, 2¾"; weight, 9 oz.
Warranty: 10 years (limited)
Manufacturer's Suggested Retail Price: $27
Approximate Low Price: not available

CARBON MONOXIDE (CO) DETECTORS

The only way to detect this colorless, odorless, deadly gas is to install a CO detector in the home. The Consumer Product Safety Commission (CPSC) recommends installing at least one carbon monoxide detector with an audible alarm near the sleeping area of the home. Most CO detectors resemble smoke alarms in appearance. Some units plug into an electrical outlet and have a battery backup as well. Others are operated by a 9-volt battery. First Alert recently introduced a battery-powered combination smoke and CO detector.

First Alert FCD3

✔ **BEST BUY**

The First Alert FCD3 CO detector is a top-of-the-line, 9-volt-battery-operated unit that can be placed or mounted anywhere in the home. To activate this unit, simply pull the factory seal tab to expose the internal sensor, which lasts for approximately five years. This detector has a test button that can also be used to silence the alarm. The green battery button flashes twice a minute to indicate the unit is operational. The alarm horn sounds at 85 decibels. This unit is supplied with mounting hardware and an informative booklet.

Specifications: height, 5⅝"; width, 8⅝"; depth, 2⅛"; weight, 11 oz.
Warranty: 5 years (limited)
Manufacturer's Suggested Retail Price: $40
Approximate Low Price: $29-$39

First Alert Combination Smoke and CO Alarm SC01

✓ **BEST BUY**

The First Alert Combination Smoke and CO Alarm is the first unit in the industry to detect both smoke and elevated levels of CO. The smoke alarm uses the ionization method of smoke detection. When smoke is detected the alarm sounds three long beeps and a red-colored flame indicator flashes. When elevated levels of CO are detected, a single on-and-off tone sounds with a flashing red-dot pattern. A large test/silence button is located on the face of the unit. A green battery indicator light flashes several times a minute to let you know the unit is operational. The unit chirps when the battery requires replacement. A yellow service light flashes when the unit should be replaced. This unit can be mounted on a wall or ceiling. The unit is supplied with a 9-volt battery, mounting hardware (including screws and anchors), and informative booklet.

Specifications: height, 2⅛"; width, 5¼"; weight, 11 oz.
Warranty: 5 years (limited)
Manufacturer's Suggested Retail Price: $50
Approximate Low Price: $36-$44

Night Hawk Premium Plus KN-COPP-B

✓ **BEST BUY**

The Night Hawk KN-COPP-B (manufactured by Kidde Saftey) operates on 3 AA batteries and has an 85-decibel alarm. This unit continuously monitors and displays a digital reading of CO levels—normally zero—and the amount of life left in the batteries. Replace the batteries when the display shows LB (low battery). This detector is also equipped with a peak level button that will indicate the highest CO level since the unit was reset or powered-up. The unit has a test/reset button that tests and silences the alarm. A fold-out foot allows the unit to be placed on a table or shelf, or it can be wall mounted (hardware included). An informative booklet is also included.

Specifications: height, 2½"; diameter, 7"; weight, 1 lb.
Warranty: 5 years (limited)
Manufacturer's Suggested Retail Price: $43
Approximate Low Price: $37-$41

FIRE EXTINGUISHERS

Check the dial gauge on your fire extinguisher monthly. The needle on the gauge indicates whether the unit is operable or in need of recharging. When required, have the unit recharged by a qualified professional—you can usually find these professionals listed under Fire Extinguishers in your Yellow Pages. Recharging is required after every use, no matter how brief.

First Alert Multipurpose
Fire Extinguisher FE1A10GW

✔**BEST BUY**

The First Alert FE1A10GW fire extinguisher is a dependable, multipurpose, dry chemical unit for fighting all types of small fires around the home. It is also U.S. Coast Guard approved. This lightweight fire extinguisher is powerful enough to douse all classes of fires. The unit has an ergonomic plastic handle/trigger, a pull ring, and an easy-to-read dial-type gauge that tells at a glance the charge condition. This unit also has a quick release bracket for wall mounting and easy-to-read three-step instructions printed on the side. This extinguisher cannot be recharged.

Specifications: height, 15¹⁹⁄₃₂"; diameter, 3⁹⁄₁₆"; weight, 3.6 lbs.; Rating, 1-A, 10-B:C

Warranty: 5 years (limited)
Manufacturer's Suggested Retail Price: $20
Approximate Low Price: $11-$15

Kidde KHO-FA340

The Kidde KHO-FA340 is a multi-purpose, dry chemical unit. While the unit is rated for fighting all classes of fires, it is especially useful for B:C class fires. It has plastic handles, a plastic breakaway pull ring, a dial-type gauge for checking the charge condition, and a flexible hose. It is supplied with a plastic, U-shaped wall-mounting bracket that holds the unit just below the handles. Easy-to-read three-step instructions are printed on the side of the unit. This extinguisher can be recharged after use.

Specifications: height, 17"; width, 5.7"; depth, 4.8", weight, 9 lbs.; Rating, 2-A, 10-B:C
Warranty: 6 years (limited)
Manufacturer's Suggested Retail Price: $30
Approximate Low Price: $23-$29

Kidde Fire Out Foam 466620

The Kidde 466620 is the first of its kind designed for consumer use. It is an excellent choice for fighting all types of home fires, and foam is easier to clean up after than a conventional chemical fire extinguisher. This unit comes with an aerating nozzle designed specifically for use with foam, an easy-to-read gauge that indicates charge condition, and an ergonomic handle/lever. A wall-mounting bracket is also supplied. Quick, clear directions are printed on the aluminum container.

Specifications: height, 16¾"; width, 6⅛"; depth, 5⅛"; weight, 7 lbs. 8 oz.; Rating, 8-A, 70-B:C
Warranty: 5 years (limited)
Manufacturer's Suggested Retail Price: $45
Approximate Low Price: not available

SNOW REMOVAL

Because snow throwers are seasonal items, you can often save money by buying one off-season. And because they are pretty basic machines, and models are slow to be replaced, your choices remain fairly consistent from year to year. Worth noting, however, is the fact that during the last year some popular models have increased the engine horsepower. This might be in response to heavier-than-normal snow storms in recent seasons.

HOW TO SHOP

Nearly all snow throwers have Tecumseh Snow King engines or similar engines that are specially engineered for cold weather and wet conditions. Electric starters are either standard or optional on most units, and we recommend them. Look for handles, grips, and controls that are conveniently located and that can accommodate large mittens.

FEATURES AND TERMINOLOGY

Auger-propelled Snow Thrower: This type of unit has rotating rubber or rubber-edged blades on the auger that make contact with the ground surface, propelling the snow thrower forward as the blades dig into the snow. These machines are not very effective on gravel or on concrete or asphalt surfaces that are in poor condition.

Discharge Chute: This is a partially or fully enclosed tube that directs the snow up and out. The chute is usually rotated with a crank. For safety, the machine must be turned off before attempting to dislodge clogged snow or debris in the auger housing or discharge tube.

Impeller: This is a bladed wheel located behind the auger that propels the snow at high speed into the discharge tube.

Single-stage Thrower: This type of unit employs only an auger to collect and discharge snow.

Two-stage Thrower: This type of unit uses both an auger and an impeller to collect and discharge snow. It can handle a higher volume of snow than can single-stage models and can propel snow longer distances.

BEST BUYS 2000

Our Best Buy, Recommended, and Budget Buy snow throwers follow. Products within each category are listed according to quality. The Best Buy is listed first, followed by our second choice, and so on. A Best Buy, Recommended, or Budget Buy designation only applies to the model listed—it does not necessarily apply to other models made by the same manufacturer or to an entire product line.

___SINGLE-STAGE SNOW THROWERS___

Single-stage (meaning the auger shoots the snow directly out the discharge chute) snow throwers have 20- to 22-inch-wide clearing paths. Single-stage snow throwers are for homeowners with relatively small spaces to clear. Despite their small size, these snow throwers are capable of handling fairly heavy snows, but the going might be slow. The biting action of the auger blades propels the machine, so they occasionally need some pushing help from you. These are the simplest snow throwers to use and maintain, and easier to store because they are compact and relatively lightweight.

Toro CCR 2450 GTS
✔ **BEST BUY**

The already first-rate Toro CCR 2400 GTS just got even better. They changed the model number to CCR 2450 GTS and gave it a new, improved engine. The unique elliptic-shaped Power Curve auger made from two tough, reinforced rubber strips feeds and cleans extremely well and can take a lot of abuse in stride. The top handle folds down, so this trimmer takes up very little storage space. Electric start is optional. However, you shouldn't need it, considering GTS stands for "guaranteed to start"—this unit will kick to life on one or two pulls or Toro will fix it free of charge for up to five years.

Specifications: engine, 5-hp, 2-stroke; clearing path, 20"; auger diameter, 8"
Warranty: 2 years, full; 5 years, GTS
Manufacturer's Suggested Retail Price: $650
Approximate Low Price: $600-$630

John Deere TRS21

Recommended

Ruggedly constructed and enclosed in a smoothly designed housing, the TRS21 has a good reputation for dependable performance with a lot of power. The chute crank is nicely located and the large grip on the deflector mask is unusually easy to use. The upper handle folds for compact storage and easier transport. Electric start is optional.

Specifications: engine, 5-hp, 2-stroke; clearing path, 21"; auger diameter, 9"
Warranty: 2 years
Manufacturer's Suggested Retail Price: $669
Approximate Low Price: $600

Yard Machines 140

Budget Buy

The 140 from Yard Machines is a great buy for the price in the single-stage snow blower marketplace. It is well made and a reliable performer. The 11-inch opening height is ample and the auger design is very good. The rugged 5-inch polymer chute will not clog, rust, or freeze. An added bonus is the inclusion of a scraper blade. The handle folds, which makes this machine easy to store.

Specifications: engine, 3-hp, 2-stroke; clearing path, 21"; auger diameter, 8½"
Warranty: 90 days, no fault; 1 year
Manufacturer's Suggested Retail Price: $299
Approximate Low Price: not available

___TWO-STAGE SNOW THROWERS___

If you live in the snow belt and have an average-size walkway and driveway, a medium snow thrower (5 to 8 horsepower) should be adequate for just about any weather surprise. They're an excellent all-around choice—neither too big nor too expensive. They also provide wider clearing paths. Like their larger siblings (9 horsepower and above), they are two-stage machines, meaning they are self-propelled with the auger ingesting the snow and throwing it against a rotating impeller, which propels it out the chute. All but a few models are wheeled and use special high-traction tires. Those few that don't have wheels are propelled with wide, cleated rubber tracks. Large snow throwers are for heavy-duty use. They have more powerful engines and provide wider clearing paths. They're an excellent choice for homes with huge driveways, long lanes, or very long sidewalks and in areas with predictably very heavy snowfalls.

5 TO 8 HORSEPOWER

Ariens ST724

✔**BEST BUY**

In response to consumers wanting more power in 24-inch clearing path two-stage snow throwers, Ariens has reduced the price of their ST724, 7-hp model, making it a Best Buy. Ariens snow throwers have a reputation for strong construction and easy operation. This unit features their variable speed Disc-O-Matic drive that tailors power and speed to your needs. This a superior thrower at a great price. Electric start is optional.

Specifications: engine, 7-hp; clearing path, 24"; auger diameter, 11"
Warranty: 5 years (limited)
Manufacturer's Suggested Retail Price: $949
Approximate Low Price: $920

Snapper 17243

`Recommended`

The 17243 with electric start is a solid Snapper veteran. It does just about everything right. This mower has a big auger, great fuel capacity, a really high intake opening, and a great clog-free chute. The convenient 4-speed on-the-go shifting provides you with a variety of work speeds. You can operate this mower with one hand, and the nicely arranged controls are easy to manipulate. Drift cutters are standard and a snow cab is an available accessory.

Specifications: engine, 7-hp; clearing path, 24"; auger diameter, 12"
Warranty: 2 years, engine; 3 years, machine
Manufacturer's Suggested Retail Price: $1,100
Approximate Low Price: $920-$1,000

Yard Machines E640F

`Budget Buy`

Take one look at this machine's big engine, wide cutting path, and the 20-inch intake height and you'll see that this snow thrower is a real bargain for budget-conscious shoppers. The E640F features standard push-button electric start and Yard Machines's typically high-quality serrated edge auger blades. These blades make short work of clearing ice and hard-packed snow. This snow thrower has six forward and two reverse speeds. Controls allow for easy single-handed operation.

Specifications: engine, 8-hp; clearing path, 26"; auger diameter, 12"
Warranty: 90 days, no fault; 2 years, consumer guarantee
Manufacturer's Suggested Retail Price: $749
Approximate Low Price: not available

9 HORSEPOWER AND ABOVE

Craftsman 88626

✔**BEST BUY**

The 88626 can be considered both a Budget Buy and a Best Buy now that it has been given a powerful 9-hp engine and a compact frame to maximize maneuverability—at a fairly affordable price. The intake height of 17½ inches is impressive. The fuel tank and oil reservoir are both large. This snow blower comes with electric start and a headlight is optional. It features six forward and two reverse speeds. Controls are simple and conveniently located. (A promotional price of $749 should be available.)

Specifications: engine, 9-hp; clearing path, 26"; auger diameter, 10"
Warranty: 2 years, parts and labor
Manufacturer's Suggested Retail Price: $899
Approximate Low Price: $749

Toro Power Shift 1332

Recommended

This machine was already a very serious snow thrower before Toro made it more powerful. They bumped up the horsepower on their popular 1232 Power Shift from 12 to 13 and it now goes by the model number 1332. Power Shift means that a quick shift of a lever moves the wheels to the rear, doubling the weight on the front, to practically eliminate any chance of riding up or slipping in the heaviest snows. This unit's unique drum auger is very effective in deep snows. A differential provides independent traction to the wheels for easier turning. The heavy-duty gearbox has four forward and two reverse speeds. Electric start is standard. Chains, lights, cab, and drift breakers are options.

Specifications: engine, 13-hp; clearing path, 32" ; auger diameter, 12"
Warranty: 2 years, full
Manufacturer's Suggested Retail Price: $2,100
Approximate Low Price: $1,900

LAWN CARE

Lawn care needs can differ dramatically depending on where you live, how large your lawn is, what the terrain is like, and even how fast your grass grows. You can find lawn care equipment to accommodate just about every preference or physical limitation and how much time and effort you want to spend caring for your lawn. When shopping for lawn care equipment, keep in mind increasing concerns both federally and locally about air and noise pollution from lawn care products powered by small gas engines.

HOW TO SHOP

Because competition in the lawn care equipment business is very stiff, there tends to be not much price difference between stores. Watch for early spring and late fall sales for the best prices. Servicing dealers, who offer additional amenities such as repair, delivery, and on-the-shelf parts supply, might be a good option, but prices might be somewhat higher.

FEATURES AND TERMINOLOGY

Bump Feed: This feature lets you advance the string on a string trimmer during operation by bumping the cap on the cutter head against the ground. Some designs have automatic string feed.

Deck Leveling: This feature lets you adjust the cutting blade(s) to cut parallel with the ground surface. Some are much easier to use than others—a topic worth discussing with your salesperson.

Hydrostatic Drive: This feature can be found on many riding mowers and tractors, as well as a few self-propelled walk-behind lawn mowers. It provides smooth, shiftless propulsion using hydraulic power. A few new tractor models have quite satisfactory infinitely variable belt drives, which are somewhat less expensive.

Mulch Plug/Mulch Plate: Devices often used on convertible muching/discharge mower decks to plug or cover the discharge outlet in the shroud while in the mulch and collection modes.

Overhead Valve (OHV): This describes the design of engines with intake and exhaust valves located on top of the cylinder head. These engines are often considered to be more efficient than engines with side-located valves.

Power Takeoff (PTO): This is the power output shaft(s) found on tractors and riding mowers. It drives the mower blade(s) (and sometimes optional attachments). Mechanically engaged and disengaged clutches might be cheaper, but electric-clutch models are awfully nice.

Self-propelled: Describes walk-behind mowers propelled by either the front or rear wheels, which are driven by a combination of belts, gears/discs, or hydraulics.

Tool-free Adjustments: Refers to adjustments such as blade height, deck leveling, deck removal, or maintenance procedures that by product design do not require the use of tools.

Turning Radius: Turning radius is one-half the diameter of the uncut circle when mowing with the wheels turned the maximum amount. Zero-turning-radius riders can turn 180 degrees in their own length.

BEST BUYS 2000

Our Best Buy, Recommended, and Budget Buy lawn care products follow. Products within each category are listed according to quality. The item we consider the best of the Best Buys is first, followed by our second choice, and so on. Remember that a Best Buy, Recommended, or Budget Buy designation only applies to the model listed—it does not necessarily apply to other models made by the same manufacturer or to an entire product line.

LAWN MOWERS

Choosing the right mower for your yard depends on the terrain and the amount of trees, fences, and plantings you have. For small, flat lots less than 1/4 acre, corded electric mowers are good choices. For 1/4-acre lots, push-type gas mowers will frequently suffice. For lots up to 1/2 acre, self-propelled gas models are the best choices.

ELECTRIC MOWERS

Black & Decker MM850

This mower is attractively styled and features a tough, lightweight polymer deck. It's equipped with an extra strong motor and delivers the equivalent of a four-horsepower gas mower at full torque. A single-lever simultaneously adjusts all four wheels to any of seven cutting height positions. It comes ready to mulch or rear bag and a side discharge chute is optional. The fail-safe hand grip is quite comfortable to use. The handle folds for easy mower storage.

Specifications: width, 19" deck; weight, 50 lbs.
Warranty: 2 years, full; 5 years, deck
Manufacturer's Suggested Retail Price: $220
Approximate Low Price: $199

Black & Decker LM100

Although Black & Decker's LM100 mower is an economy model, it is a very satisfactory performer. It has a durable steel deck and side discharge; bags are sold separately. This mower has individual wheel height adjusters. It folds for storage and transport.

Specifications: width, 18" deck; weight, 42 lbs.
Warranty: 2 years, full
Manufacturer's Suggested Retail Price: $140
Approximate Low Price: $129-$139

Toro E 120

Recommended

This electric mower has a unique design. It features a belt drive that Toro claims delivers the cutting effort of a five-horsepower gas mower. It has acoustic foam baffling to make this machine a quiet runner. It is also very light, which is always important when you have to push a mower. An excellent cord lock and cord management system keeps your power source in check. Other features include a bumper to protect trees and shrubs; turf-friendly tires; and a folding, three-position handle for easy storage and transport.

Specifications: width, 18″ deck; weight, 38 lbs.
Warranty: 2 years, full
Manufacturer's Suggested Retail Price: $249
Approximate Low Price: $239

GASOLINE-POWERED PUSH-TYPE MOWERS

Yard Machines 518N
In spite of its low price, the high-wheel 518N of- **✓BEST BUY** fers a lot—including an excellent mulching system and rear bag. However, a side discharge deflector is optional. This mower's easy rolling performance is particularly nice on less than flat terrain or long grass. The engine has a larger than average recoil system that results in easy starting. The mowing height can be adjusted manually with your fingertips to nine positions.

Specifications: width, 21″ deck; weight, 90 lbs.
Warranty: 90 day (no fault); 2 years (limited)
Manufacturer's Suggested Retail Price: $249
Approximate Low Price: not available

John Deere JS60
This exceptionally well-made mower features a | Recommended | rolled-edge lip, an internally smooth dome-shaped deck to provide rigidity, and efficient grass cutting. The large, 9-inch diameter tires have rounded treads to minimize turf damage. Cutting height is adjustable in seven increments. This mower comes set up for efficient mulching. A side discharge chute is standard, and a rear bag is optional. The handle folds for storage.

Specifications: width, 21" deck; weight, 73 lbs.
Warranty: 2 years
Manufacturer's Suggested Retail Price: $359
Approximate Low Price: not available

Craftsman 38822

The 38822 is priced to sell. It comes with a decent mulch system installed within its domed deck. You can either mulch, discharge, or bag (using the optional catcher, model number 33076). The Eager 1 engine promises to start on one pull—and really does. Nine individual wheel cutting height adjustments are available.

Specifications: width, 22" deck; weight, 72 lbs.
Warranty: 2 years
Manufacturer's Suggested Retail Price: $170
Approximate Low Price: $159

GASOLINE-POWERED SELF-PROPELLED MOWERS

Toro Personal Pace SR21S

✔**BEST BUY**

The Personal Pace is a self-propelled mower that really does travel at your "personal pace," from 0 to 4 mph without levers or gears to change. The faster you walk the faster it mows. Slow your pace and the mower slows. When you stop, so does the machine. Toro's renowned recycler system is standard and a rear bagger is optional. Personal Pace is available in four different models with different engines, deck materials, mulching systems, and included features at prices ranging from $419 to $629.

Specifications: width, 21" deck; weight, 80 lbs.
Warranty: 5 years, full
Manufacturer's Suggested Retail Price: $469
Approximate Low Price: $429-$449

Craftsman Hi-Wheel 37756

Recommended

The 37756 features Craftsman's popular Eager 1 one-pull starting system. Also included is the EZ-3 mulching system, which lets you either mulch, bag, or discharge (with the optional 33303 clipping deflector). The excellent 2.4-bushel, rear-mounted bag has a lift top for easy handling. The 14-inch rear wheels are sturdy and have ball bearings; the front wheels are gear driven. Such a setup makes this mover very easy to maneuver.

Specifications: width, 22" deck; weight, 83 lbs.
Warranty: 2 years
Manufacturer's Suggested Retail Price: $360
Approximate Low Price: $349

Scotts High Wheel 22646X8

Recommended

This mower is priced right and features a lot of power. The rolled-edge steel deck enhances its ability to suspend clippings for multiple chopping and smooth cutting. Scotts' unique blades are sharp on both edges to achieve double life by simply reversing the blades when one side dulls. The mower converts from mulch to discharge without tools. The adjustable, rigid mount handle makes it very easy to steer and comfortably accommodates operators of different heights.

Specifications: width, 22" deck
Warranty: 2 years
Manufacturer's Suggested Retail Price: $289
Approximate Low Price: $279

RIDING MOWERS

Conventional rear-engine riding mowers are good choices when the lot is a little larger and reasonably flat, or when you simply want to do less walking or speed up the mowing task. Relatively more expensive and much more maneuverable, but not as well known, are zero-turning-radius riding mowers.

CONVENTIONAL RIDING MOWERS

Yard-Man Yard Bug 325

Cute as a bug, the Yard Bug drives like a car, with all controls at your fingertips. Press the foot pedal and you automatically go in variable-speed belt drive. A unique and very satisfactory integrated 2- to 5-bushel grass collector, accessed by lifting the seat, has a monitor that tells you when it is full. Mulching and side discharge kits are standard.

Specifications: width, 27.5″ single-blade deck
Warranty: 90 days (no fault); 2 years (limited)
Manufacturer's Suggested Retail Price: $1,049-$1,099
Approximate Low Price: $999-$1,049

Sears Craftsman Mulch-and-Ride 27011

The 27011 is attractively priced. However, it features higher priced features such as electric key start, mulching capability, and front and rear Turf Saver tires that are easy on the lawn. It has good leg room and provides excellent operating visibility. The shifter for the five-speed transmission is conveniently located, as is the cutting height control.

Specifications: width, 30″ single-blade deck
Warranty: 2 years (limited)
Manufacturer's Suggested Retail Price: $899
Approximate Low Price: $849

ZERO-TURNING-RADIUS RIDING MOWERS

Simplicity ZT1 438

The Simplicity ZT1 438, a twin hydrostatic transmission zero-turner, is particularly attractive because it is compact. In addition to fitting into snug spaces, this mower is easy to access and store. It is operated by short throw levers that are conveniently located next to the hand rest. The engine is a Kohler Command. A unique Simplicity suspension system and free floating design make this mower very stable and provides excellent cut quality. Twin catchers, turbo collectors, mulcher/leaf shredders, dump carts, headlight, and armrests are available as options.

Specifications: width, 38" 2-blade deck
Warranty: 2 years
Manufacturer's Suggested Retail Price: $3,599
Approximate Low Price: not available

Ariens E-Z Rider EZR1 540/915010

Recommended

This unit has a particularly rugged frame and heavy components. It features a Kohler Command engine and dual hydrostatic transmissions to provide travel and steering with dual wrap-around levers. Electric start and electric PTO are standard. Manual deck lift is functionally located and easy to use. For $250 less you can opt for a Briggs & Stratton Vanguard engine. Other options include headlights, grass collector, mulching system, and snow blade.

Warranty: 5 years, limited
Manufacturer's Suggested Retail Price: not available
Approximate Low Price: $3,600-$3,799

LAWN TRACTORS

Lawn tractors are smaller and usually have lighter frames and axles than garden tractors. Because of their lighter build, they are less likely to be able to handle serious engaging attachments and snow throwers. On average, they are less expensive than garden tractors.

Simplicity Express 15.5H

✔ BEST BUY

The Simplicity 15.5H, the new offering from the manufacturer known as The Express, is quite a good value. Powering this mower is a Briggs & Stratton Intek OHV engine with hydrostatic drive—all conveniently controlled with a single lever. There is also a less powerful 14½ horsepower model with a 5-speed gear drive available for $1,599. Mulching and bagging kits are optional on both models.

Specifications: width, 38″ 2-blade deck; 38″ 2-blade mower deck
Warranty: 2 years
Manufacturer's Suggested Retail Price: $1,899
Approximate Low Price: not available

Snapper LT18OH48DBV2

Recommended

This popular mower features a sturdy Briggs & Stratton Vanguard engine and hydrostatic drive. Some other nice touches are step-through boarding access, a cast-iron front axle, and electric PTO. All of the controls are easy to reach. It doesn't hurt that this mower is nicely styled and has a very comfortable, high-backed seat. Snapper's highly regarded Ninja mulching kit, a snow thrower, and blades are optional accessories.

Specifications: width, 48″ 3-blade deck; weight, 505 lbs.
Warranty: 2 years, engine; 3 years, Snapper parts
Manufacturer's Suggested Retail Price: $3,500
Approximate Low Price: not available

Murray 40504X92

Budget Buy

At this price, the Murray 40504X92 is a Budget Buy. However, this tractor has a lot of the quality features of higher-priced units. The quality Briggs & Stratton engine has a cast-iron cylinder sleeve. The deck has Murray's simple and accurate tool-free deck leveling system as well as their exclusive "Wide-Body" design, which provides a wider body and lower center of gravity for good stability. This mower steers and handles quite easily. It has a 5-speed fender-located shift transmission. Bagging and mulching kits are optional.

Specifications: width, 40" 2-blade deck
Warranty: 2 years
Manufacturer's Suggested Retail Price: $799
Approximate Low Price: not available

GARDEN TRACTORS

If you need a tractor for tasks beyond mowing, and if your property size is moderate, your best bet is a lawn tractor. If your property is quite large and you do a lot of garden work and towing, pushing, and snow throwing, consider opting for a garden tractor.

Craftsman 27322

✓**BEST BUY**

The Craftsman 27322 is a lot of heavy-duty tractor for the money. It features an excellent Kohler Pro engine, beefy automatic transmission, and a ready-to-mulch deck (which is convertible without blade change to side discharge and bag—with optional bagger kit). Any number of cutting height settings will be stored in this unit's memory. It has full instrumentation and electric PTO. Large 24-inch rear tires ride easy and protect turf. This mower accepts a wide variety of front and rear attachments.

Specifications: width, 50" 3-blade deck
Warranty: 2 years (limited)
Manufacturer's Suggested Retail Price: $3,399
Approximate Low Price: not available

Scotts S2554

Recommended

Made for Scotts by John Deere, this heavy-duty tractor is powered with a Kohler OHV engine and features quick, easy handling—both on- and off-deck. The automatic transmission is very easy to use. PTO engagement is electric. The cut height can be adjusted quickly via a rotary dial. A deluxe, high-back seat is standard. Options include a mulching kit, two-bag bagger, snow blade, tiller, 42-inch snow thrower, wheel weights, and chains.

Specifications: width, 54" 3-blade deck; weight, 606 lbs.
Warranty: 2 years (or 90 days, non-residential use)
Manufacturer's Suggested Retail Price: $3,998
Approximate Low Price: $3,700

Yard-Man U804H

Budget Buy

The U804H utilizes Yard-Man's new "AutoDrive" high-low range, foot-controlled, clutchless, "drives like a car," infinitely variable speed drive system. This highly descriptive system is a great—and much cheaper—alternative to hydrostatic drive. The engine is Briggs & Stratton's highly regarded Intek OHV. The nice, tight-turning steering is almost carlike. Deck height is easy to adjust and the mulching deck is standard. Optional "Fast Attach" accessories include a bagger, dozer blade, and snow thrower.

Specifications: width, 46" 3-blade deck
Warranty: 90 days (no fault); 2 years (limited)
Manufacturer's Suggested Retail Price: $2,199-$2,229
Approximate Low Price: $2,000-$2,198

STRING TRIMMERS

String trimmers use spinning nylon line to cut grass, weeds, and light brush. Some models swivel to do lawn edging, and a few accept a steel brush blade for trimming heavier brush. Some have detachable heads that can be quickly converted to drive other implements, such as edgers, mini-cultivators, blower/mulcher/vacuums, and even snow throwers.

ELECTRIC MODELS

Stihl FE55

✔ BEST BUY

The Stihl FE55 is the electric string trimmer the competition is compared to. The FE55 is light and extremely quiet. It features a curved shaft, an adjustable loop handle, and a built-in clamp to secure the extension cord from accidentally pulling out. Contributing to the low noise is a special "quiet line." Bump feed is used to advance the string.

Specifications: weight, 9.2 lbs.
Warranty: 2 years
Manufacturer's Suggested Retail Price: $90
Approximate Low Price: $79

Black & Decker Grass Hog GH400

This innovative string trimmer is ergonomically designed and attractively priced. In addition to standard string trimmer duty, this unit serves as a "Groom 'N Edge" lawn edger. With the touch of a button the head indexes 180 degrees and provides a reference point for precise line edging. A feed spool senses string length and automatically advances It when necessary. A cord lock prevents accidental disconnection.

Warranty: 2 years
Manufacturer's Suggested Retail Price: $59
Approximate Low Price: $54

GASOLINE MODELS

Stihl FS36

This heavy duty trimmer is well known for its power ✓**BEST BUY** and durability. The FS36 features a curved shaft and has comfortably padded top loop and throttle grips. The loop grip is adjustable. The air cleaner is large and easily serviced. String is advanced with bump feed. An optional "Polycut" head is available for thinning and working large areas quickly.

Specifications: weight, 10.8 lbs.
Warranty: 2 years
Manufacturer's Suggested Retail Price: $140
Approximate Low Price: $129

Ryobi TrimmerPlus 1079r

The TrimmerPlus is a small 4-cycle engine string trimmer with interchangeable attachments. Only slightly heavier than a 2-stroke product, this new trimmer should meet environmental rules well into the next century—and without the need to mix oil with the gas. The 1079r can also accommodate a brush blade. With an extra-long split shaft, other optional heads include a blower, a vac, an edge trimmer, a cultivator, a hedge trimmer, and a tree pruner; all of which can be exchanged instantly with snap connectors. The engine is professional duty.

Specifications: weight, 12.9 lbs.
Warranty: 2 years
Manufacturer's Suggested Retail Price: $239
Approximate Low Price: $199

CORDLESS MODELS

Ryobi 150r

The Ryobi 150r is light and well balanced, making it a favorite of lighter stature users. It has demonstrated its ability to nicely trim an average size lawn on a single charge for years. Just hang it in its wall-mounted charging bracket and this unit will be ready to go the next time it is needed. It has a simple and dependable bump feed. The top grip can be adjusted easily.

Warranty: 2 years
Manufacturer's Suggested Retail Price: $99
Approximate Low Price: $74-$79

Sears Craftsman 78354

Recommended

Nicely thought out, this string trimmer also doubles as an edge trimmer by pushing a button to swivel the head. It also has a guide to help make the cuts neat. The head functionally feeds out string as it is needed. The angle of the top loop handle can be adjusted to provide the most comfortable feel. This trimmer comes with a wall mount charger bracket.

Warranty: 1 year
Manufacturer's Suggested Retail Price: $90
Approximate Low Price: $89

BLOWER/VACS

Blower/mulcher/vacuums are important tools for keeping lawns and gardens tidy. All of the units we review automatically chop up, mulch, or shred debris as it is sucked up and ejected into the collection bag. The reduction is accomplished by the impeller blades and, in some models, is aided by flails directly in front of the blades. There is not a great deal of difference in performance between gas and electric models.

ELECTRIC MODELS

Ryobi Mulchinator Vacuum RESV1300

✔ **BEST BUY**

With the permanently mounted blower and vac tubes molded together, you can instantly switch from blower to vacuum mode "on the fly" with a simple flip of a lever. This eliminates the need to stop and exchange tubes. The collection bag mounts closely under the bottom tube for excellent balance and comfort. The motor, which has a two-speed switch, stays in the same orientation in both modes so there is no need for complicated grips. In the fall of 1999, a 31 cc gas engine version, RGBV3100, priced at about $129, became available with similar features and specs.

Specifications: mulching ratio, 10:1; weight, 9 lbs.
Warranty: 2 years
Manufacturer's Suggested Retail Price: $79
Approximate Low Price: not available

Toro QuieTech Super BlowerVac 51589

Recommended

This model is quiet without compromising power. The handle offers easy one- or two-handed operation. The significant noise reduction comes from "mufflers" in the blower intake and inside the blower tube. The bag is large and the zipper is easy to use. The motor has a two speed switch and an excellent power cord retainer.

Specifications: mulching ratio, 10:1
Warranty: 2 years, full
Manufacturer's Suggested Retail Price: $100
Approximate Low Price: not available

GASOLINE MODEL

Homelite Vac Attack

✓ BEST BUY

With a hefty "Zip Start" engine, which is indeed easy to pull and quick to start, this Homelite unit also has low vibration and a unique patented design that directs exhaust down the tube for quieter and cleaner operation. The size and position of the bag makes it comfortable to handle in the vac mode. The blower tube is a good length and the vac tube is tapered and contoured for good suction.

Specifications: mulching ratio, 12:1; weight, 10.9 lbs.
Warranty: 2 years
Manufacturer's Suggested Retail Price: $139
Approximate Low Price: $99-$129

FOOD PREPARATION

Today, the name of the game in cooking is speed. Few people can make a habit of spending hours in the kitchen turning out magnificent lunches and dinners. Still, no one wants to sacrifice quality and flavor in their daily meals. To respond to this need for efficient, quality food preparation, manufacturers have created a variety of appliances to handle every job, large and small.

BEST BUYS 2000

Our Best Buy, Recommended, and Budget Buy food preparation products follow. Products within each category are listed according to quality. The best of the Best Buys is first, followed by our second choice, and so on. Remember that a Best Buy, Recommended, or Budget Buy designation only applies to the model listed—it does not necessarily apply to other models made by the same manufacturer or to an entire product line.

FOOD PROCESSORS

Food processors now come in an assortment of sizes—from the larger and more versatile food preparation centers to the compact and handy mini-choppers. Selecting the appropriate unit (or units) to serve your needs is a matter of determining what you need in a food processor.

WHAT SIZE IS RIGHT?

Bigger, more powerful machines can knead enough dough for two to three loaves of bread, slice and shred produce for salads, blend together ingredients for a party-size batch of guacamole, or slice whole fruits or vegetables through an expanded feed tube. Fancier machines not only perform all the functions of a food processor, but also come with added attachments that enable them to function as stand mixers, blenders, or mini-choppers. Some models feature disc attachments for cutting julienne vegetables or French-fry potatoes. Smaller models save workspace and are perfect for lighter tasks, such as dicing a single onion or a handful of herbs, or blending a cup of mayonnaise. Mini-choppers specialize in chopping small items, such as garlic cloves, nuts, or bits of chocolate. These small units also are handy for making up single servings of baby food.

You may discover that one machine serves many purposes in the kitchen. The larger machines offer the most functions and versatility, while carrying a higher price tag. Smaller machines do an admirable job with basic tasks and smaller quantities. Compact models might be just right for one person or smaller families.

FEATURES AND TERMINOLOGY

Motor Base: Generally speaking, the bigger the machine, the more powerful the motor, but some of the compact models pack a surprising punch.

On/Off/Pulse: These are the common speeds for a processor: "on" for continuous action; "off"; and "pulse," which provides short, consecutive rotations of the blade for controlled chopping.

Stainless-steel All-purpose Blade: Also called an "S" blade, this is used for chopping, mixing, blending, pureeing, or kneading. Some machines have separate dough blades or hooks.

Work Bowl: This is usually transparent. Some machines include extra bowls as well as blender carafes for added features and convenience.

SAFETY TIPS

Once you've chosen a unit, read through the instructions to thoroughly familiarize yourself with the functions. Be sure to follow all the safety precautions; keeping the unit stable and the cord out of the way is essential. Remember that the blades are extremely sharp and should be handled with care. All manufacturers nowadays are taking precautions to make their units as safe and trouble-free as possible, so you will notice that virtually every unit is now equipped with a safety interlock system that will not allow the unit to operate if the bowl and cover are not properly in place.

LARGE FOOD PROCESSORS

Cuisinart Food Preparation Center DLC-7SFP   ✓ **BEST BUY**

From Cuisinart's Professional Series, the DLC-7SFP Food Preparation Center combines all the functions of a full-size food processor with those of a traditional mixer. This unit comes equipped with a stainless-steel chopping blade, a plastic dough blade, a medium slicing/shredding disc, a stainless-steel whisk attachment, a plastic spatula, and two covers. Use the compact cover for chopping and mixing tasks and the standard cover with both large and small feed tubes for slicing and shredding all sizes of produce. This unit's powerful motor and oversize work bowl simplify tasks such as chopping vegetables, shredding lettuce, and mixing pastry and bread dough. A whisk attachment converts the unit to a stand mixer for whipping cream, egg whites, or mashed potatoes. The 14-cup Lexan work bowl is made to withstand temperature shifts and can accommodate more than two pounds of ground beef, or enough dough for three one-pound loaves of bread in a single batch. You can even shred an entire head of cabbage without emptying the work bowl. Two fingertip switches operate the unit in "on" or "pulse" modes. This unit includes a dual-function feed tube assembly that takes a bit of practice to master, but it is well worth the effort for the convenience of processing whole potatoes, cucumbers, carrots, or other large produce items. The DLC-7SFP also comes with the Cuisinart how-to video filled with helpful tips and techniques. Optional attachments include fine and medium julienne discs, a fine shredding disc, and a French-fry disc. In addition, the Cuisinart DLC-7SFP includes ultra-thin, thin, medium, thick, and extra-thick slicing discs. All parts on this model, except the motor base, are dishwasher safe.

Warranty: 3 years (limited); 5 years, motor (full)
Manufacturer's Suggested Retail Price: $330
Approximate Low Price: $297-$299

KitchenAid 11-cup Ultra
Power Food Processor KFP600

✔ **BEST BUY**

KitchenAid's Ultra Power Food Processor expands its versatility by combining a mini chopping bowl with the popular 11-cup work bowl. In addition to the two work bowls and chopping blades, the KFP600 comes with a reversible thin slicing/shredding disc, a medium slicing disc, a medium shredding disc, a dough blade, and a plastic spatula. The full-size chopping blade and mini chopping blade are made by Sabatier, the renowned knife manufacturer. You can process up to six cups of chopped beef or produce, or enough dough for two medium loaves of bread. You can also utilize this model's mini chopper for preparing smaller batches of diced nuts, herbs, or spices. The mini chopper bowl can handle up to one cup of semi-liquid ingredients or one-half cup of solids. For storage convenience, this unit adds an accessory box, which houses all the blades/discs when not in use. Bowls and blades are dishwasher safe. Other features include Clean Touch control pads for on, off, and pulse modes; and smooth rounded surfaces that easily wipe clean. Available in cobalt blue, empire green, and onyx black, as well as white, the KFP600 is sure to blend with any decor.

Warranty: 1 year (total replacement)
Manufacturer's Suggested Retail Price: $250
Approximate Low Price: $199-$235

MID-SIZE FOOD PROCESSORS

KitchenAid Ultra
Power 7 Food Processor KFP450

✔ **BEST BUY**

The Ultra Power 7 KFP450 is KitchenAid's newest and most versatile model. It comes equipped with a seven-cup clear work bowl, a mini work bowl, and a citrus juice press. Powerful yet compact, the KFP450 speeds through everyday food prep chores, from blending and kneading dough to chopping nuts or pureeing steamed vegetables. A pressure-operated juicing attachment dispenses juice directly into the bowl. A multipurpose chopping blade and a mini chopping blade are made by the well-known Sabatier knife manufacturer. Other accessories include a cover with feed tube and food pusher, thin slicing/shredding and medium shredding discs, and a spatula/cleaning tool. The smooth, rounded base sits firmly on a countertop. Touchpad controls for on, off, and pulse modes are easy to use and maintain. All parts, except the base, are dishwasher safe for easy cleaning.

Warranty: 1 year (total replacement)
Manufacturer's Suggested Retail Price: $160
Approximate Low Price: $139-$150

Cuisinart Pro Classic DLC 10S

✔ BEST BUY

The Cuisinart Pro Classic DLC-10S chops, slices, and shreds carrots and cabbage for coleslaw in a fraction of the time it would take to do by hand. The unit's reduced size and price tag make it perfect for smaller families or those who cook or entertain less frequently. The Pro Classic comes with a seven-cup clear work bowl, a clear cover with both large and small feed tubes, and a flat cover for use during kneading, mixing, or pureeing. Other attachments include a stainless-steel medium slicing disc, a medium shredding disc, a stainless-steel chopping/mixing blade, a plastic dough blade, and a spatula. The three-position lever switches from "off" to "on" to "pulse" in seconds. The multi-function feed tube assembly is challenging at first; however, the versatility it offers for processing both large and small produce items is well worth the extra effort. A how-to video is also included, which shows step-by-step assembly and helpful tips for maximizing the machine's potential. Optional attachments include an assortment of thick and thin slicing and shredding discs. All parts, except the motor base, are dishwasher safe.

Warranty: 3 years (limited); 5 years, motor (full)
Manufacturer's Suggested Retail Price: $159
Approximate Low Price: $139-$149

Krups OptiPro Food Processor 705

Recommended

The Krups OptiPro Food Processor features contemporary styling with smooth, tapered sides. The low profile saves counter space and provides for easier cleaning. The eight-cup work bowl is slightly larger than other mid-sized machines and can accommodate up to 1.6 pounds of bread or pizza dough, a family-size batch of soup or pureed vegetables, and 15 ounces of whipping cream—thanks to a unique whipping disc. Standard equipment includes a clear work bowl with lid, a stainless-steel chopping blade, slicing and shredding discs, a plastic dough blade, a whipping disc, and a plastic spatula. Dial control has two speeds, plus pulse for achieving uniform results. The work bowl doubles as a storage center, holding blades and discs when not in use. Other features include a watertight bowl base (which eliminates leaks when working with liquid ingredients), plastic edging along sharp blades and discs for safer handling, and a domed lid design that facilitates slicing and shredding tasks so food doesn't lodge between blade and cover. All parts, except base, are dishwasher safe.

Warranty: 1 year
Manufacturer's Suggested Retail Price: $160
Approximate Low Price: not available

COMPACT FOOD PROCESSORS

KitchenAid Little Ultra Power KFP350

✓ **BEST BUY**

For a compact unit the KitchenAid Little Ultra Power Food Processor packs a surprising punch. Its powerful motor goes to work on tough jobs like bread dough or ground beef. The Little Ultra Power also includes two work bowls for added convenience. Use the five-cup work bowl for grinding up to one-half pound of meat, chopping up to one and one-half cups of raw vegetables, or blending up to two cups of herb butter or mayonnaise. Use the mini chopper bowl for smaller jobs, like chopping a handful of herbs or mincing garlic cloves. Clean Touch control pads simplify operation for hassle-free operation, with no crevices to trap dirt and food particles. An effortless touch of your finger controls the machine in on, off, or pulse modes. Automatic braking stops the action of the blade instantly when the off button is pushed. Standard equipment for the Little Ultra Food Processor includes the clear, five-cup work bowl, a cover with feed tube and pusher, a reversible slicing/shredding disc, a multipurpose stainless-steel chopping blade, a mini chopping blade, a mini work bowl, a cover, and a spatula. Both the multipurpose chopping blade and mini chopping blade are made by Sabatier, the manufacturer of quality knives. The smooth base is easy to wipe clean; all other parts are dishwasher safe.

Warranty: 1 year (total replacement)
Manufacturer's Suggested Retail Price: $130
Approximate Low Price: $89-$99

Salton Maxi Mix FP25

Budget Buy

A straightforward design and affordable price tag make the Salton Maxi Mix an exceptional value. The Maxi Mix FP25 comes with a compact motor base, a clear three-cup work bowl, a continuous feed chute, a stainless-steel chopping blade, a reversible slicing/shredding disc, and a plastic spatula. The compact design saves counter space and lets you store the unit out of sight in a cabinet or pantry cupboard. Both the base and the work bowl are equipped with easy-grip handles for worry-free processing. A handy feature included with this model is the continuous feed chute, which lets you slice or shred unlimited quantities directly into a waiting bowl. You can process up to one cup of meat cubes in a single batch. Rubber feet add stability.

Warranty: 1 year (limited)
Manufacturer's Suggested Retail Price: $35
Approximate Low Price: not available

MINI-MINCERS

Cuisinart Mini-Prep Processor DLC-1

✔**BEST BUY**

Modeled after its larger counterparts, the Cuisinart Mini-Prep Processor lives up to its maker's reputation. A sturdy base, powerful motor, and oversize 21-ounce capacity work bowl handle the toughest mincing tasks. The patented reversible stainless-steel chopping blade does an excellent job chopping onions or nuts, blending individual servings of sauce or dressing, grinding coffee beans and spices, and grating chocolate and cheeses. One of the few mincers to offer dual speeds, this unit features two press-and-release levers that operate the unit in low or high speed with pulse control. Use the high speed with the blade's blunt edge for grinding and grating hard foods. Use the low speed and sharp edge for soft or watery foods. The Mini-Prep is small enough to tuck away in a drawer or cabinet, while it also features hidden wrap-around cord storage to minimize counter clutter. The work bowl and lid disassemble easily and are dishwasher safe.

Warranty: 18 months (limited)
Manufacturer's Suggested Retail Price: $40
Approximate Low Price: $29

Krups Speedy Pro Mini-Chopper 720

✔**BEST BUY**

With a larger-than-average work bowl and taller-than-average base, the Krups Speedy Pro Mini-Chopper stands apart from other mini choppers. A powerful motor is designed to tackle chopped beef, nuts, or hard cheeses, such as Parmesan. This unit comes with a clear three-cup capacity work bowl, a stainless-steel multipurpose chopping blade, a clear cover with two openings for adding last-minute ingredients during processing, and a power base. A thumb-operated control button features pulse/on/off action for achieving even results. For slightly liquid ingredients, such as sauces or baby food, the Speedy Pro's capacity is reduced to about 11 ounces.

Warranty: 1 year
Manufacturer's Suggested Retail Price: $45
Approximate Low Price: $29

Black & Decker 2-Speed Super Chopper SC400 `Budget Buy`

Compact yet versatile, the Black & Decker 2-Speed Super Chopper features an oversize work bowl that can handle up to two medium onions, three hard-cooked eggs, or about one and one-half cups of mushrooms in a single batch. This unit comes with a chopping blade and a two-cup clear work bowl with cover. The contoured base provides a firm grip. High/low pulse-operated speed control affords precision results. Low speed is for coarse chopping, while high speed works best for fine mincing. Hold either button down for continuous processing. Bowl, lid, and blade are dishwasher safe for easy cleanup.

Warranty: 1 year
Manufacturer's Suggested Retail Price: $30
Approximate Low Price: $19-$24

ELECTRIC MIXERS

For mixing batters, whipping cream, or mashing potatoes, there is no substitute for the familiar and reliable mixer. With its unique beater design, the mixer is able to mix, whip, mash, or blend a variety of consistencies, from thin cake batters to thick cookie dough. And many mixers now come with added attachments, such as dough hooks (for kneading bread or pizza dough), whisks (for whipping extra volume into cream or egg whites), and immersion blender rods (for blending frothy beverages). No other machine can surpass the mixer when it comes to aerating (increasing the volume by incorporating air into light batters, such as whipping cream or egg whites).

TYPES OF MIXERS

Traditional stand mixers, with their supplied work bowl(s), offer the most power, with the added advantage of hands-free mixing.

These powerful machines make short work of everyday jobs such as blending cookie dough or creaming butter with sugar. Portable or hand mixers are less expensive and have the advantage of storing easily when not in use. A relatively new option is the stand/hand combination unit, which offers the convenience of both types of mixes and usually costs considerably less than a traditional stand mixer. If versatility is what you're looking for, the combination unit is a sensible choice.

PORTABLE MIXERS

Cuisinart Smart Power CountUp Hand Mixer HTM-9LT

✔ **BEST BUY**

The Cuisinart CountUp HTM-9LT offers the ultimate in convenience with its digital touchpad speed controls and electronic "CountUp" timer that tracks mixing time automatically. Forget setting the timer; simply depress the power button to activate the machine on its lowest setting. The digital display shows mixer speed (1–9) and time elapsed in minutes and seconds. Electronic touchpad controls let you switch between speeds with a gentle touch on the increase speed (+) or decrease speed (-) buttons. The lower speeds are well suited for folding or start-up mixing. Higher speeds are extremely fast for quick whipping and aerating. Sturdy wire beaters have no center posts for dough to climb and clog mixing action. Made of stainless steel, these beaters cut cleanly, even through heavy cookie dough. The unit also comes with an oversize stainless-steel whisk for use with whipping cream and egg whites. Other features include a rotating cord that is designed to stay out of the way during mixing and a plastic spatula for scraping bowl sides. Beaters and whisk are dishwasher safe for easy cleanup.

Warranty: 3 years (limited)
Manufacturer's Suggested Retail Price: $80
Approximate Low Price: $60-$69

KitchenAid Ultra Power Plus Mixer KHM7TWH

✔ **BEST BUY**

KitchenAid's line of hand mixers features the same quality and performance one would expect from a leading manufacturer of kitchen products. The Ultra Power Plus comes with stainless-steel Turbo Beaters—wire beaters that cut through heavy batters and also act as efficient whisks with light batters. Because the beaters have no center posts, dough cannot climb and clog mixing action. Clean Touch control pads let you move between speeds with an effortless touch of your thumb. Press the up arrow to increase speed or the down arrow to decrease speed. Other features include "soft start," "extra fast," and "slow" speeds for precision beating, whipping, mashing, and blending. An electronic sensor automatically adjusts when more power is needed to maintain a consistent speed. Touch the stop button to halt mixing at any time. Optional attachments include a liquid blender rod and stainless-steel dough hooks.

Warranty: 1 year (total replacement)
Manufacturer's Suggested Retail Price: $80
Approximate Low Price: $69-$70

Braun MultiMix 4-in-1 M880

Recommended

The Braun MultiMix 4-in-1 Handheld Food Preparation System is a versatile appliance that handles all the functions of a hand mixer, immersion blender, and mini chopper, plus tackles tough bread dough. Standard equipment includes two heavy wire beaters, two sturdy dough hooks, an immersion blender rod and beaker, and a chopper attachment with ten-ounce clear work bowl and cover. The beaters are angled for efficient blending of ingredients. Three speeds and a plus option provide an adequate range for various mixing and blending chores. This unit is a bit more complicated than others in its class, but its expanded functions are worth the extra effort.

Warranty: 1 year (limited)
Manufacturer's Suggested Retail Price: $50
Approximate Low Price: $39

STAND MIXERS

KitchenAid Ultra Power Stand Mixer KSM90

✔ BEST BUY

The KitchenAid KSM90 Ultra Power's superior performance has set the standard for quality mixers for three generations. An extra powerful ten-speed motor tackles the most strenuous chores effortlessly and can also be ready in a minute for all your light mixing. Standard equipment for the KSM90 includes a 4½-quart stainless-steel mixing bowl, a handle, a flat beater, a dough hook, a stainless-steel wire whisk, and a non-sealing bowl cover. Unique "planetary" mixing action spins the beater and rotates it around the stationary bowl for maximum bowl coverage. The bowl locks into the base of the mixer for hands-free mixing and added stability. Rubber feet keep the mixer in position while protecting your counter. The unit's own weight (more than 20 pounds) also acts to keep this mixer firmly in place. A rainbow of colors and numerous attachments offer a virtually limitless assortment of consumer choices. Accessories include a food grinder, a pasta maker, a fruit/vegetable strainer, a rotor slicer/shredder, a grain mill, a citrus juicer, a can opener, an extra three-quart mixing bowl, extra bowl covers, a fabric cover, a food tray, a two-piece pouring shield, and a temperature-retaining water jacket. The newest attachment is a pasta roller/cutter that converts the KSM90 into a powerful pasta machine.

Warranty: 1 year (total replacement)
Manufacturer's Suggested Retail Price: $270
Approximate Low Price: $199-$250

Toastmaster Global Design Standmixer 1770U

Recommended

The toastmaster 1770U Heavy Duty Stand Mixer is designed for frequent use. Part of Toastmaster's new "Global Design," this mixer is similar in design to the KitchenAid stand mixer, featuring the same planetary motion for mixing—the stand mixer and bowl remain stationary as the beater, whisk, or dough hook rotates in and around the bowl. The unit features a powerful motor, a mixing bowl with splatter guard, a dough hook with pastry deflector, a beater, and a whisk. The unique swivel arm can be moved into five positions by pressing the arm's release button. Positions one, two, and three are used with the mixing attachments while four and five are designed for use with optional accessories, such as a food processor, meat grinder, ice-cream maker, blender, and citrus juicer. Select from four speeds along the dial control or choose "park," a setting that aligns the drive mechanisms so that mixing attachments may be raised and removed. Other features include dishwasher-safe attachments, wrap-around cord storage, and rubber feet for stability.

Warranty: 1 year
Manufacturer's Suggested Retail Price: $180
Approximate Low Price: $169

BLENDERS

For crushing hard food items or for thoroughly combining liquids with solids (for example, when making soup), the traditional blender cannot be surpassed. The carafe and its added power not only crush the ice but also protect the user from flying ice particles and splashes. Carafe blenders vary by model, giving consumers a choice between glass, plastic, and stainless-steel carafes, push-button, dial, and touchpad controls, and specialty features, such as separate ice-crushing and pulse switches.

IMMERSION BLENDERS

The newest addition to the blender market is the immersion or hand blender. These long, thin blending rods excel at jobs involving soft food items, such as pureeing cooked vegetables, or blending fruit smoothies or milk shakes. These tools are also terrific for use with hot foods, such as soups or sauces that require extra care in handling. The immersion blender also offers the added convenience of being able to go directly into a drink cup, saucepan, or other container for quick blending without having to transfer contents to separate blender carafe. For added versatility, many immersion blenders also come with chopping or whipping attachments to help them function as mini choppers or hand mixers.

TRADITIONAL BLENDERS

Cuisinart SmartPower
7-Speed Electronic Blender SPB-7

✔ BEST BUY

The Cuisinart SmartPower SPB-7 Blender is sleek and sophisticated. Its touchpad control buttons operate in either continuous or pulse modes. Choose from six settings, such as stir, chop, liquefy, and puree. Or you can opt for maximum power with "ice crush." The ice-crush setting is strong enough to crush ice cubes in seconds. The 40-ounce glass jar and stainless-steel blade assembly create a whirling "tornado-like" motion for fast, efficient blending with either hot or cold liquids. Internal ribs keep the action focused down at the blade so solids do not go unprocessed. The two piece plastic cover has a removable two-ounce cap so extra ingredients can be measured and easily added. Slip-proof feet add stability, and a cord storage compartment prevents counter clutter. All parts—except the motor base—are safe for the dishwasher.

Warranty: 3 years (limited)
Manufacturer's Suggested Retail Price: $90
Approximate Low Price: $69-$79

Krups Power X Plus Combination 243

✔ BEST BUY

The Krups Power X Plus is a combination blender/food processor. This model features a dial control that lets you select from 14 variable speed settings without stopping the motor. Separate buttons control "power burst" and "ice-crush" features. The powerful motor speeds through everyday blending chores from mixing up a batch of salsa to crushing ice for frozen beverages. This unit comes equipped with a large 48-ounce, easy-pour glass carafe and lid with removable two-ounce measuring cup. The ice crusher and power burst buttons are touch-and-release to afford a pulse-like control. The carafe locks into position on the base to provide maximum control and stability. The food processor attachment includes a three-cup work bowl and stainless steel chopping blade. Other features include a stable base with rubber feet and hidden cord storage.

Warranty: 1 year
Manufacturer's Suggested Retail Price: $80
Approximate Low Price: $59-$60

Black & Decker PartyMate Drinkmaker DM100 | Recommended

The Black & Decker PartyMate Drinkmaker is both sporty and practical. This unit's unique feature is a VersaPak rechargeable battery system that powers the unit—whether it's in the kitchen, out on the deck or patio, or even at the beach or park. This durable blender has a water-resistant base and a shatterproof 32-ounce carafe, making it well suited for blending frozen drinks or fruit smoothies out in the yard or by the pool. This unit's two battery sticks and rechargeable base can handle up to three gallons of crushed ice drinks on a single charge. Other features include a detachable jar, lid with a built-in mesuring cup, easy-to-use pulse control button, and stainless-steel blades. VersaPak batteries are interchangeable with other VersaPak-powered Black & Decker products. After normal use, batteries recharge in about four hours. This blender's compact design allows for easy storage. The jar, lid, and cap are all dishwasher safe. This unit is sold exclusively through Infomercial, 1-800-BDFLAVOR.

Warranty: 1 year (limited)
Manufacturer's Suggested Retail Price: not available
Approximate Low Price: $60

KitchenAid Ultra Power 5-speed Blender KSB5 | Recommended

The KitchenAid Ultra Power KSB5 is an extremely powerful blender. This unit features state-of-the-art touchpad controls and an electronic mixing sensor that adjusts the power to match the task at hand. Five speed settings—from stir to liquefy—and pulse can handle all your blending needs, from routine iced drink to a gourmet cheese dip. The thick-walled glass carafe is sturdy yet heavy—especially when filled to its 40-ounce capacity. Internal ribs and a sensible blade design combine for efficient blending action. Other features include a dishwasher-safe jar, a quick-lock lid, and cord storage. The KSB5 is available in a rainbow of colors to match any decor. A chrome model is also available at a slightly higher cost.

Warranty: 1 year (total replacement)
Manufacturer's Suggested Retail Price: $130
Approximate Low Price: $90-$120

IMMERSION BLENDERS

Cuisinart SmartStick CSB-55

✔ BEST BUY

The Cuisinart SmartStick features an exclusive extendable shaft that allows you to customize the length (up to two inches) of the blender according to the depth of the container with which you are currently working. To operate the unit, simply depress the thumb-control switch. Press and release for pulse, or hold for continuous action. A powerful, but surprisingly quiet, motor speeds through tasks such as pureeing cooked vegetables for soup or blending light batters. A four-speed control lever lets you select the desired speed—one or two for whipping or light blending, and three or four for mixing or chopping. This unit also comes with a Mini-Prep Chopper Grinder attachment and reversible metal chopping blade that can be used to chop hard foods such as coffee beans or nuts, as well as softer items such as herbs, boiled eggs, or mushrooms. Other features include a whipping attachment for cream or egg whites, a clear mixing/measuring beaker, and a counter or wall-mount storage bracket. Beaker and blender shaft with blade are dishwasher safe.

Warranty: 3 years (limited)
Manufacturer's Suggested Retail Price: $80
Approximate Low Price: $59

Braun Multiquick Hand Blender + Chopper MR430HC

✔ **BEST BUY**

A compact and versatile appliance, the Braun Multiquick Hand Blender MR430HC consists of a slim blending rod with detachable shaft, a stainless-steel blade, a whisk attachment, a clear resealable one-pint mixing/measuring beaker, and a mini-chopper attachment. This unit is perfect for chores that involve stirring, mixing, or blending soft food items, or combining solids with liquids, such as when making soups. The slim design is perfect for blending a milk shake right in the glass or pureeing cooked tomatoes directly in the saucepot. To use, simply assemble the unit by twist-locking the blade stem onto the shaft. Then press the control switch on the hand grip to activate the motor. An up and down pulsing motion provides the best results. The whipping attachment can be used for making whipped cream or mashed potatoes. To clean the blender, simply rinse all parts, except motor base, in hot, soapy water. Shaft, chopper bowl, and mixing/measuring beaker are also dishwasher safe.

Warranty: 1 year (limited)
Manufacturer's Suggested Retail Price: $30
Approximate Low Price: not available

TOASTERS

Today's toasters have come a long way. Enhancements such as electronic sensors and cool-touch exteriors have vastly improved both performance and safety. Many manufacturers now produce toasters, and it is not difficult to find inexpensive models at any department store—if toasting bread is all you want to do. The models listed here are top-of-the-line toasters that offer a number of convenient options, such as defrosting and light pastry settings, as well as the ability to handle thicker food items, such as bagels.

KitchenAid Ultra Power
Plus Electronic Toaster KTT261

✓ BEST BUY

The KitchenAid Ultra Power Plus KTT261 is sleek and sophisticated with touchpad controls and a digital display. This unit features a single, extra-long, wide slot for toasting bread slices up to one-inch thick, frozen waffles, and bagels. An electronic Accu-sense heat sensor delivers even browning, and an Even-Heat system helps retain moisture so that breads are not dried out. To use, position bread in slot, select toast setting (from one to nine) by pressing the up or down arrow touchpads, and press the carriage lever down. The centering rack adjusts automatically to keep food upright. An indicator light signals that the unit is operating. When toasting is complete, the carriage lever raises the toast and the unit shuts off. Other settings include "frozen," which first defrosts, then toasts the bread; "reheat," which warms previously toasted foods; and "bagel," which is specially designed for even toasting of bagels. To facilitate removal of bread, the carriage lever has an extra-lift feature that raises bread up higher. To interrupt toasting at any time, simply press the stop/reset button and the carriage lever will raise immediately. Other features include a slide-out crumb tray, a sturdy cool-touch housing, and wrap-around cord storage.

Warranty: 1 year (total replacement)
Manufacturer's Suggested Retail Price: not available
Approximate Low Price: $100

Rival SensorToast TT9442C

Recommended

The Rival SensorToast TT9442C is an affordable machine that toasts up to four slices of bread, pastries, or other convenience foods at a time. Built-in sensors measure temperature and moisture levels within the toaster and automatically adjust browning for even results. Each side features separate browning controls that let you select the preferred setting(s) for each set of toasting slots. Other convenience features include a cool-touch exterior, self-centering guides that adjust to the thickness of the food to hold bread upright for even toasting, and a snap-open crumb tray.

Warranty: 1 year (limited)
Manufacturer's Suggested Retail Price: $30
Approximate Low Price: not available

Black & Decker
Toast-It-All Deluxe Toaster T2400

Budget Buy

The Black & Decker Toast-It-All Deluxe Toaster is a simple and economical machine that can handle all your toasting needs, from toasting thick slices of homemade bread to preparing frozen pastries, waffles, and bagels. This unit has two extra-wide toasting slots with bread guides that adjust automatically to hold bread upright and centered in the slot. A dial control lets you select your darkness setting (from one to five). An extra-large carriage lever is easy to use and will automatically remain half-lowered to keep items warm without overtoasting. Electronic controls include a heat sensor that monitors temperature and moisture levels and adjusts to maintain consistent performance batch after batch. Other convenience features include a bagel setting that toasts the inside of the bagel without overbrowning the outside, a cool-touch exterior, and a removable crumb tray.

Warranty: 1 year, parts and labor
Manufacturer's Suggested Retail Price: $30
Approximate Low Price: not available

TOASTER OVENS

Toaster ovens not only toast but also perform the additional functions of baking and broiling. They come in handy for making open-faced sandwiches or other items that cannot be accommodated by the vertical slots of toasters. Toaster ovens come in a variety of styles, from smaller models that can handle up to four slices of bread to larger models that can roast an entire chicken. Of course, the larger the capacity, the more room the unit will occupy on your counter, so be sure you choose the right capacity to suit your needs.

DeLonghi Air Stream
Convection Toaster Oven AS670
✔ **BEST BUY**

The DeLonghi AS670, with its turbo convection system, cooks foods up to 30 percent faster than traditional ovens. The exclusive turbo fan distributes heat within the oven for fast, even results. This unit's other unique feature is its multilevel cooking capability, with two racks for accommodating extra batches or two different items simultaneously. Three control dials let you select function (broil, toast, bake, fan bake), oven on/toast color (from light to dark), and temperature (from keep-warm/200°F to broil/450°F). An indicator light signals when the oven has reached the desired temperature. Remove one of the trays and you've got an extra-large capacity oven that can handle oversize roasts, pies, and casseroles. This unit comes with a DuraStone enameled porcelain bake pan, a broil rack, and two cookie sheets. Other features include a full-view glass door, a continuous-cleaning interior with an interior light that lets you monitor cooking progress, a removable crumb tray, and cord storage. A pizza stone is available separately.

Warranty: 1 year
Manufacturer's Suggested Retail Price: $180
Approximate Low Price: $130-$160

Black & Decker Convection
Countertop Oven/Broiler CTO9000
✔ **BEST BUY**

The newest in Black & Decker's line of quality toaster ovens, the CTO9000 features a convection fan that circulates air throughout the oven for fast, efficient cooking. An extra-large interior can accommodate a standard 9-by-13-inch baking pan or casserole dish. Three dial controls let you set the oven temperature, select toast color, and/or start the unit using the automatic oven timer. The timer can be set up to 90 minutes for baking or broiling functions. A bell signals when the designated time has elapsed, and the oven shuts itself off. Other features include an oven pan with broil rack, an easy-clean coated interior, cool-touch ThermaGuard top and sides, and a slide-out crumb tray.

FOOD PREPARATION

Warranty: 1 year, parts and labor
Manufacturer's Suggested Retail Price: $160
Approximate Low Price: not available

Farberware Deluxe Electronic Toaster Oven/Broiler FT0800

Recommended

Part of Farberware's Millennium line, the Deluxe Electronic Toaster Oven/Broiler features three control dials that let you select a cooking program (broil, bake, warm, or toast), set oven temp (250°F–450°F), or toast color (light, medium, dark). The unit also includes an automatic timer (up to 60 minutes). At the end of cooking time, a bell sounds, and the toaster shuts itself off. Separate toast buttons allow you to manually start or stop the toaster oven. Conveniences of this unit include a wipe-clean, brushed stainless-steel exterior; a multi-position slide-out oven rack; a full-view glass window; a slide-out crumb tray; an on light; and an oven pan with broiling rack. This unit can accommodate up to six slices of bread, one standard-size frozen dinner, a standard casserole dish, or a whole chicken.

Warranty: 1 year
Manufacturer's Suggested Retail Price: $125
Approximate Low Price: $100

Black & Decker Toast-R-Oven Plus TRO 6100CT

Budget Buy

For quick and convenient countertop cooking, the Black & Decker Toast-R-Oven Plus is an affordable unit with lots of extras. This unit features an electronic heat sensor that monitors internal temperature and adjusts automatically for consistent results. An enlarged capacity handles a six-cup muffin pan, a 1½-pound meatloaf, or a whole chicken. Other features include a non-stick interior, a cool touch ThermaGuard exterior, an oven pan with broiler rack, a pull-out crumb tray, a bell signal, an on light, and a timer with automatic shut-off. Three large dials control temperature, toast color, and timer. A separate start/stop toast button activates the unit in toast mode.

Warranty: 1 year, parts and labor
Manufacturer's Suggested Retail Price: $110
Approximate Low Price: $100

JUICERS/JUICE EXTRACTORS

Krups Optifruit Juice Extractor 291

✓**BEST BUY**

The Krups Optifruit Juice Extractor is a space-saving unit that offers the healthful benefit of fruit or vegetable juice with the touch of a button. This unit consists of a clear juice pitcher with handle and pouring spout, a clear pulp collector with handle and cover, and an extractor assembly with pusher and lid. A single on/off switch activates the motor. Feed prepared fruit and vegetable pieces through the tube. Applying gentle pressure with pusher ensures even results. Pulp is automatically ejected into its own 34-ounce container, which removes for easy emptying. Juice pitcher (30 ounces) has both ounce and liter measurements. Clear containers let you easily monitor juice and pulp levels. Other features include an automatic pause when juice pitcher is removed, a fruit tray for loading smaller fruits (such as cherries), and cord storage. All parts, except motor base, are dishwasher safe.

Warranty: 1 year (limited)
Manufacturer's Suggested Retail Price: $95
Approximate Low Price: $50-$60

Toastmaster Citrus Juicer 1107

Budget Buy

The Toastmaster Citrus Juicer is an economical and practical machine. This unit consists of a large (40-ounce) transparent pitcher with ounce and liter measurements, a pouring handle and spout, two juicing cones (large for oranges and grapefruit, and small for lemons and limes), and a dust cover. Other features include an adjustable pulp control, a sturdy base, and cord storage. The low price tag on this product makes it an exceptional value.

Warranty: 3 years
Manufacturer's Suggested Retail Price: $15
Approximate Low Price: $10-$13

STEAMERS

Krups OptiSteam Plus 652

✔**BEST BUY**

The OptiSteam Plus lets you prepare family-size batches of healthy steamed vegetables and rice, without the added calories of butter or cooking oil. Model 652 comes with two separate transparent steaming trays (14 cup and 10 cup) that stack, allowing you to prepare two different items or a double batch of your favorite foods at once. The larger tray also divides into two compartments for cooking several different foods simultaneously. Trays can be used together or separately. Simply fill water reservoir, assemble unit, and place prepared foods into tray(s), then set the automatic timer. Steam begins flowing after 30 seconds. Oblong trays are designed to accommodate longer foods, such as asparagus or crab legs. A separate six-cup rice bowl converts the unit to a rice cooker. An exclusive external spout lets you add more water without removing the steaming basket, and a thermal safety feature protects the unit from overheating if the water tray becomes empty. Other features include a water-level indicator, a 60-minute timer with automatic shut-off, and hidden cord storage. Trays and bowls are dishwasher safe.

Warranty: 1 year
Manufacturer's Suggested Retail Price: $65
Approximate Low Price: $50

Salton Vitamin Bar VP3

Budget Buy

The Salton Vitamin Bar features double-stacking steaming baskets that let you prepare large batches or multi-course meals simultaneously. This unit consists of a base, a water reservoir, a heating element, an on light, a timer, a removable drip tray, two steaming baskets, a rice bowl, and a lid. To use, arrange vegetables or other foods in steaming basket(s), fill water reservoir to desired level (depending on length of steaming), position baskets, and set timer for necessary cooking time. When the set time elapses, a timer bell signals, and the unit shuts itself off. The Salton Vitamin Bar can also be used to heat pureed vegetables or mashed potatoes, or to cook/steam frozen or canned vegetables, fresh or frozen seafood, poultry, meat, and most grains.

Warranty: 1 year (limited)
Manufacturer's Suggested Retail Price: $30
Approximate Low Price: not available

ICE-CREAM MAKERS

Krups La Glacier 358

✔ **BEST BUY**

The Krups La Glacier Ice Cream Maker features a quick-freezing double-insulated cylinder that provides ample chilling power without the hassle of ice and salt. The double insulation helps this unit retain a frozen state longer for better results. The unit consists of a freezer bowl, a lid, a mixing paddle, and a power mixing arm for fully automatic mixing. The see-through lid with feeder hole lets you watch the progress of the ice cream while also adding fruit, nuts, or chips without interrupting mixing. Before using, it is necessary to freeze the cylinder for a minimum of eight hours. Continual storage of the cylinder bowl in the freezer is recommended so that the unit is ready at a moment's notice. The Krups La Glacier makes up to 1½ quarts of basic ice cream, sorbet, or other frozen dessert. An automatic mixing feature stirs and scrapes the walls of the cylinder, blending air into the mixture for a creamy texture. It takes 20 to 30 minutes for ice cream to reach a desired consistency. As the mixture thickens and the paddle senses resistance, it will automatically change direction. Paddle and lid are dishwasher safe.

Warranty: 1 year (limited)
Manufacturer's Suggested Retail Price: $80
Approximate Low Price: $60-$70

Salton Big Chill ICM21

Budget Buy

The Salton Big Chill features a rotating bowl and a separate freezer disc that mixes the ice cream into a creamy soft-serve texture. Standard equipment includes the mixing bowl, a paddle, a freezer disc, a see-through cover with hole for adding mix-ins during freezing, and a motor base. To use, first freeze the disc (preferably in the coldest part of the freezer at zero degrees) for 6-12 hours. Insert frozen disc into plastic mixing bowl and place the bowl atop motor base. Attach paddle and cover and turn unit on. Immediately pour ingredients through hole in lid. A separate cup is provided that lets you seal the lid during the mixing process. Freezing takes anywhere from 20 to 30 minutes, depending on mixture being processed (note: alcohol slows down the freezing process). Unit makes up to 1½ quarts of ice cream, sorbet, or other frozen dessert.

Warranty: 1 year (limited)
Manufacturer's Suggested Retail Price: $50
Approximate Low Price: $40

BREAD MAKERS

Salton Breadman Plus TR800

✔**BEST BUY**

The Salton Breadman Plus is an easy-to-use machine that boasts 54 bread settings, including basic white bread, French, whole wheat, fruit or nut bread, batter breads and cakes, bake only, dough only, and jam. Choose from three horizontal loaf sizes, three crust colors, and "normal" or "rapid" bake cycles. Specialty features include a digital display window with touchpad controls for crust color, loaf size, bread cycle, time, and start/stop. A separate row of indicator lights shows which function is being performed: knead, rise, bake, complete, or time delay, which lets you preset completion of baking up to 15 hours ahead of time. This unit also has a power-failure backup, which stores the active program in memory and lets you return to bread-making within an hour of the elapsed time. Start-to-finish bread baking takes as little as 3½ hours in basic cycle or just over 2½ hours in rapid-bake cycle.

Warranty: 1 year (limited)
Manufacturer's Suggested Retail Price: $180
Approximate Low Price: $100-$120

West Bend Automatic
Bread & Dough Maker 41053

✔**BEST BUY**

The West Bend Automatic Bread & Dough Maker offers the option of baking either a one and ½ pound or 2 pound loaf of bakery-style bread. One speedy feature of this machine is its ability to produce a loaf of basic white bread in an hour, called "Bread Express." Other features include a viewing window that lets you check the progress of your bread, and a digital display panel that lets you select basic, whole wheat, sweet, quick bread, one-hour, or dough only settings, as well as light, medium, or dark crust. Simply add ingredients to the pan (liquids first, followed by dry, and then yeast), press the "bread select" button to choose your setting, then press the start/stop button. Breadmaking times for traditional loaves vary between three hours (for basic, light crust) and three hours and 50 minutes (for whole wheat, dark crust). Quick breads are ready in about two hours. Additional features include a 13-hour time delay, a keep-warm function that operates for three hours after bread is finished baking, and an alert signal that tells you when to add additional ingredients, such as nuts or raisins.

Warranty: 90 days
Manufacturer's Suggested Retail Price: $130
Approximate Low Price: not available

Toastmaster Fast Bake Bread Box Plus 1145 `Recommended`

The Toastmaster Bread Box Plus 1145 offers a number of specialty options at a very affordable price. Its most attractive feature is a Fast Bake option that produces a loaf of bread in just under one hour. Other features include an automatic timer that lets you have fresh bread first thing in the morning, after work, or whenever you desire. This unit boasts 84 programs including standard, whole wheat, French, and sweet bread programs, as well as cake dough, pizza dough, and jam settings. You also select loaf size (1-, 1.5-, or 2-pound), and crust color (light, medium, or dark). An indicator panel displays the stage of bread making (preheat, knead, rise, bake, or warm) and time remaining in cycle. This unit produces a traditional loaf of bread in approximately three hours on basic, two hours on rapid, and just under one hour on Fast Bake. Other features include a nonstick bread pan, viewing window, and easy-to-use touchpad control.

Warranty: 3 years (limited)
Manufacturer's Suggested Retail Price: $120
Approximate Low Price: $100

COFFEE MAKERS

With the multitude of different coffee makers on the market, selecting the right model to suit your particular needs may seem an overwhelming task. You can narrow the choices considerably, however, if you first select the type and size of coffee maker you need.

TYPES OF COFFEE MAKERS

Automatic-drip Coffee Makers: These units consist of a power base (with water reservoir), a filter holder, a carafe, and a built-in warming plate or a carafe stand. Optional features include permanent gold-tone or screen filters, which replace the standard disposable paper filters; digital clocks with timers to preset the start of coffee making; automatic shut-off; and a pause-to-serve function, which lets you halt brewing long enough to pour a cup of coffee. The newest and most attractive offerings in this category include water filtration systems that remove chlorine, bacteria, and other contaminants from drinking water before brewing; flavor systems that can adjust the strength of the coffee—from mild to robust—to suit your taste; and a combination machine that can grind coffee beans just prior to brewing for the freshest possible taste. Larger machines can make up to 12 cups but can usually be set for smaller servings. Personal-size machines make up to four cups at a time and save counter space. Single-cup machines are available, which, in many cases, brew directly into a travel mug for convenient on-the-road coffee consumption. All automatic-drip coffee makers require periodic cleaning or decalcifying to remove mineral deposits. This is accomplished by brewing a cycle with a special cleaning solution or a mixture of vinegar and water.

Electric Percolators: These are self-contained carafes with built-in brewing mechanisms, permanent filter baskets, and lids. Many have detachable cord sets. These units brew coffee by pumping hot water over and through coarse grounds at an incredibly fast (cup-a-minute) speed. A new introduction in this category is the programmable percolator, which, unlike its predecessors, can be set to brew automatically. Sizes range from four to 12 cups for standard percolators and anywhere from 12 to 30 cups and up to 100 cups for the largest percolator urns.

Espresso/Cappuccino Makers: These machines operate by heating water and using steam or pump pressure to force the water through fine grounds quickly for maximum flavor extraction. Steam can then be diverted through a nozzle to foam milk for cappuccino. Of the two types, pump machines are the more powerful, heating water to the optimal temperature (190–197°F as recommended by the Specialty Coffee Association of America) then propelling it through fine-ground beans in about 20 to 30 seconds. The fast rate of expulsion produces a rich layer of foam, known as crema, which is the mark of great espresso. Though steam machines do not possess the power of pump machines, they do produce a good strong cup of espresso and are generally smaller and less expensive than pump models. Combination units are also available, which make regular brewed coffee as well as espresso and cappuccino.

Coffee Mills: Because a good cup of coffee starts with quality ingredients, always be sure to use fresh coffee. Grinding your own from freshly roasted beans is simple with a coffee mill or grinder. The mills, also called burr grinders, use wheels to produce a variety of grinds from very fine espresso grinds to coarser grinds for use in percolators. These units are larger and more expensive than standard blade grinders; however, the increased capacity and ability to select from a number of different grinds make them ideal choices for the most discerning coffee drinker. No matter which type you decide to buy, be sure to store your beans in an airtight container in your freezer and grind only the amount needed immediately before brewing.

AUTOMATIC DRIP COFFEE MAKERS

Krups CompacTherm Deluxe 209

The Krups CompacTherm Deluxe is a programmable unit that features an attractive ten-cup double-insulated thermal carafe. Available in white or black, the CompacTherm Deluxe sports an array of specialty features, including electronic brewing cycles, 24-hour clock timer, deep-brew filtering system, and automatic shut-off at the end of the brewing cycle. Thanks to its closed design, the carafe retains heat and flavor for up to four hours. Push-button controls let you select one to three cups for a small pot or four to ten for a full pot. Other features include an easy-to-read water level indicator, lighted on-switch, and hidden cord storage. A reusable goldtone filter is available separately.

Warranty: 1 year (limited)
Manufacturer's Suggested Retail Price: $140
Approximate Low Price: $60-$119

Cuisinart Automatic Brew & Serve DTC-800

✔ BEST BUY

The Cuisinart Automatic Brew & Serve is designed for convenience. The thermal carafe, which you brew right into, retains heat and flavor for hours. The pour-through lid lets you pour coffee without removing the lid. Specialty features include pause & serve, which allows you to interrupt brewing long enough to sneak a cup; automatic shut-off upon completion of brewing cycle; and an audible beep to signal completion of brewing. The 8-cup carafe can be removed from its base for fast, easy serving at your kitchen table, desk, or sitting room. Other features include a swing-out filter basket, water-level indicator, and lighted on-switch.

Warranty: 3 years (limited)
Manufacturer's Suggested Retail Price: $112
Approximate Low Price: $80

Toastmaster Coffee Maker 576U

`Recommended`

The Toastmaster 576U is a state-of-the-art unit that brews up to 10 cups of coffee of varying strengths. A charcoal water filter is designed to remove chlorine and other impurities from tap water in order to provide a fresh taste. Filters should be replaced after 60 uses or 6 weeks. A brew strength selector regulates the brewing based on the amount of coffee being prepared. Other features include auto shut-off, which turns the coffee maker off after 2 hours; pause & serve, which lets you interrupt the flow of coffee to pour a quick cup; a nonstick warming plate; and touch-control buttons. The programmable clock/timer lets you set the time to make a pot of coffee up to 24 hours in advance. The unit has a swing-out cone filter basket, lighted on/off switch, hinged water tank, water-level indicator, and cord storage.

Warranty: 3 years
Manufacturer's Suggested Retail Price: $80
Approximate Low Price: not available

Black & Decker VersaBrew Plus DCM1250

`Recommended`

The Black & Decker VersaBrew Plus features attractive styling and a number of convenience features. The DCM1250 brews 12 cups of traditional automatic-drip coffee. A programmable clock/timer lets you preselect brewing time up to 24 hours in advance. This function can also be canceled at any time to brew coffee immediately. An easy-to-clean warming plate keeps brewed coffee hot for up to two hours, then shuts itself off automatically. Other functions include a brew-interrupt feature that lets you sneak a cup, water-level indicator, swing-out filter basket, and easy-to-use touchpad control panel. Carafe, lid, and filter basket are dishwasher safe. A replacement carafe is also available separately.

Warranty: 1 year, parts and labor
Manufacturer's Suggested Retail Price: $80
Approximate Low Price: $30

PERCOLATORS

Cuisinart Classic Cordless Percolator PER-12   ✓BEST BUY

The Cuisinart Classic Cordless Percolator is a sleek unit, with a stainless-steel body that sits atop a power base for brewing, then detaches for serving. The stay-cool bottom lets you transport and serve coffee virtually anywhere the mood strikes. This unit prepares 4 to 12 cups of piping hot coffee in about ten minutes. The gleaming stainless-steel body is attractive and functional. A clear knob on the lid allows you to monitor percolating but must be allowed to cool down before the lid can be removed. The permanent coffee basket filter has convenient measurements etched on the side, and the inside of the percolator has water-level markings to take the guesswork out of coffee making. Other features include a tapered no-drip spout, a cool-touch percolator handle, a ready light, and cord storage.

Warranty: 3 years (limited)
Manufacturer's Suggested Retail Price: $98
Approximate Low Price: $69-$85

Farberware Millennium
Programmable Percolator FCP512S

✔**BEST BUY**

The Farberware Millennium Programmable Perco-
lator features durable stainless-steel construction from the pump well
to the body and cover. This unit's unique feature is a programmable
clock/timer that allows you to program the unit to brew at a prede-
termined time. To begin brewing immediately, simply press the
on/off button. Other features include a see-through knob that lets
you monitor brewing, a permanent coffee filter basket and lid, and
a stay-cool handle and base to protect hands and surfaces. This unit
brews between 2 to 12 cups of coffee at a cup-a-minute speed.
When brewing is completed, the unit switches to a keep-warm mode
to maintain the ideal drinking temperature for up to two hours. After
two hours, the percolator shuts itself off automatically. For cordless
convenience, the percolator lifts off its power base for serving. All
parts except percolator and power base are dishwasher safe.

Warranty: 1 year (limited)
Manufacturer's Suggested Retail Price: $100
Approximate Low Price: $55-$75

COFFEE URNS

Farberware Percolator Urn FSU236

✔**BEST BUY**

The Farberware Percolator Urn is constructed of
heavy-gauge stainless steel to provide many years of use. Suitable
for household or commercial gatherings, this unit can brew from
12 to 36 cups of fresh, hot coffee at a rate of less than one minute
per cup. Once brewing is completed, the urn switches to keep
warm, maintaining an ideal drinking temperature. A hard plastic
base protects surfaces. Elegant design makes this unit suitable for
display in the dining room, patio, or wherever coffee is to be
served. Stay-cool handles and lid knobs also provide safe, easy
handling. Other features include a no-drip spout for clean dispensing of coffee, a break-resistant dishwasher-safe plastic brewing basket, and an indicator light that signals when coffee is ready.

Warranty: 1 year
Manufacturer's Suggested Retail Price: $175
Approximate Low Price: $120-$175

Farberware Hot Water Urn FKE500

| Recommended |

The Farberware Hot Water Urn is designed for quick, easy dispensing of hot water for tea or other instant beverages. This unit features a 3.2-quart water reservoir, an easy-to-read water-level indicator, a removable lid, and a ready light. Constructed of durable stainless steel, this unit is a welcome complement to the coffee urns used at large gatherings.

Warranty: 1 year
Manufacturer's Suggested Retail Price: $100
Approximate Low Price: $70

ESPRESSO/CAPPUCCINO MAKER

Salton Spresso Machine PE 1,2,3

✔ **BEST BUY**

The Salton Spresso 1,2,3 takes the guesswork out of making espresso at home. Just fill the removable water reservoir with fresh, cold water, and switch the machine on. Select "coffee" on the temperature switch and, when the green light indicates, drop in a ready-to-use "pod" or pouch pre-filled with European roasted Arabica coffee, then turn the function selector to dispense coffee. Coffee brews in approximately 10 to15 seconds. For additional cups, simply wait for the green light again, drop in another pod, and go. When brewing is complete, the used coffee pod falls into its own container for quick, easy removal. The pre-filled pods eliminate the need to fuss with exact measuring of fine coffee grounds. Enough pods are included to brew 50 cups. This unit features a universal water-filter holder, which uses any cylinder-type filter (not included). An additional steam function can be used to heat and froth milk for cappuccino or cafe latte. A step-by-step instructional video is included.

Warranty: 1 year (limited)
Manufacturer's Suggested Retail Price: $250
Approximate Low Price: $200-$229

COMBINATION COFFEE/ESPRESSO MAKER

DeLonghi Coffee Cappuccino CC-100

✔ **BEST BUY**

The DeLonghi Coffee Cappuccino is a state-of-the-art machine with touch-control buttons, a 24-hour programmable clock/timer, and a patented easy-froth dispenser, which dispenses frothed milk right into your cup. It can brew up to ten cups of your favorite drip coffee, then top it off with frothy milk to make cappuccino, latte, hot cocoa, or mocha java. A replaceable water filter eliminates chlorine taste. Other features include an easy-to-read water-level indicator, a permanent gold-tone filter basket, an automatic shut-off, a non-stick warming plate, a ready buzzer, and indicator lights. The drip tray and milk reservoir remove easily for cleaning in the dishwasher.

Warranty: 1 year
Manufacturer's Suggested Retail Price: $160
Approximate Low Price: $100-$149

COFFEE MILLS AND GRINDERS

Salton Automatic Coffee Mill CM4

✔ **BEST BUY**

The Salton Automatic Coffee Mill CM4 is a compact, efficient unit that produces uniformly ground coffee in varying degrees of fineness. Select anything from extra fine for espresso makers to coarse ground for percolators or urns. The bean chamber holds up to 4 ounces, or enough for up to 18 cups of coffee. Depress the unit's "on" button to activate the motor. Hold for continuous grinding or press and release for pulse grinding. Beans are processed in seconds and grounds are dispensed into a separate storage container. A safety interlock feature prevents the grinder from operating if the grounds container is not in the proper position. The grounds receptacle removes for easy dispensing and cleaning. A wrap-around cord is featured for easy storage.

Warranty: 1 year (limited)
Manufacturer's Suggested Retail Price: $30
Approximate Low Price: $20

Krups Chrome Touch Grinder 408

The Krups Chrome Touch Grinder features a powerful, yet exceptionally quiet, motor with a uniquely shaped stainless-steel blade to achieve fast, even results. The grinding chamber can accommodate up to 3 ounces of coffee beans or enough for approximately 15 cups of coffee. To use, simply pour the beans into the chamber, lock the clear lid in place, and press the power button. For a coarse grind, process the beans for five to seven seconds. For a fine grind, or for larger quantities of beans, hold the button for up to 12 seconds or longer. Alternately, you can use the Chrome Touch to automatically grind beans for either percolator, automatic-drip, or boiler espresso machines. This grinder is not recommended for pump espresso machines, which require an ultra-fine grind. Clean with a soft brush and damp cloth.

Warranty: 1 year (limited)
Manufacturer's Suggested Retail Price: $45
Approximate Low Price: $30-$35

Braun Coffee & Espresso Mill KMM30

The Braun Coffee & Espresso Mill KMM30 features a unique precision milling system that uses grinding wheels instead of blades to produce the proper grind for all types of coffee makers. Available in white or black, this unit has an adjustable control dial with 24 grind settings from coarse (for percolators) to extra fine (for espresso). It also has an automatic quantity selector with timer, which determines the grinding time based on the number of cups of coffee desired. To shorten or stop the grinding process, simply return the timer to the off position. The conical bean container holds up to 8 ounces of coffee beans or enough for up to 60 cups of coffee. Ground coffee is dispensed into a separate container that has a rounded bottom to allow easy removal. The grinding container, lid, and ground coffee container all remove for easy cleaning in warm, soapy water or in the upper rack of a dishwasher.

Warranty: 1 year (limited)
Manufacturer's Suggested Retail Price: $60
Approximate Low Price: $40-$50

DeLonghi Electronic Coffee Grinder DCG-1   ✔BEST BUY

The DeLonghi Electronic Coffee Grinder features state-of-the-art programming that automatically calculates the optimal grinding duration to achieve coarse, medium, or finely ground coffee. This sophisticated grinder effectively takes the guesswork out of delivering the perfect grind every time. Just measure the beans, pour them into the chamber, and set the portion control switch for the desired amount (4 to 12 cups) of brewed coffee. Press the thumb-operated button to activate the unit. Hold the button for continuous grinding or press and release for pulse. Then just watch the indicator to know when to stop grinding. Lights indicate the state of the grind: red for coarse, amber for medium, and green for fine. The inner bowl is stainless steel. This unit can also be used to grind herbs, nuts, or spices. It is available in white or black.

Warranty: 1 year
Manufacturer's Suggested Retail Price: not available
Approximate Low Price: $25-$40

TEA KETTLES

Cuisinart Cordless Automatic Kettle KUA17   ✔BEST BUY

The Kettle KUA17 is as attractive as it is functional. A sleek yet durable stainless-steel body has a rounded, classic design, with a stay-cool black handle. The unit sits atop a shallow base that supplies power to the kettle. To use, fill kettle with fresh, cold water—up to 1¾ quarts. A maximum fill mark is located inside the kettle. Position kettle on power base and plug into power supply. Depress on/off button to activate. An indicator light glows to signal operation. Water heats in minutes and the kettle shuts itself off automatically after reaching the boiling point. Once the water is heated, the kettle can be removed from the base for convenient cordless serving. Other specialty features include a dripless pouring spout with splash guard, a concealed heating element that will not rust or corrode, and a cord storage. Base, handle, and easy-grip lid are all made of hard plastic for safe, comfortable handling.

Warranty: 3 years (limited)
Manufacturer's Suggested Retail Price: $140
Approximate Low Price: $120-$130

Salton Electric Kettle KE2 ✔**BEST BUY**

The Salton Electric Kettle is a self-contained unit that boils up to eight cups of water in a matter of minutes. Shell, handle, and spout are constructed of white plastic, with a black, heat-resistant base to protect countertops. Other features include a built-in whistle that alerts you when water has reached the boiling point, and boil-dry protection, which guards against overheating.

Warranty: 1 year
Manufacturer's Suggested Retail Price: $25
Approximate Low Price: not available

Black & Decker Kettle with Whistle KE1610W ✔**BEST BUY**

The Black & Decker Kettle looks a lot like a stove-top kettle with its dome design, rounded handle, and pouring spout. The difference is that this unit has its own fast-heating element that heats water in less than half the time of a stove-top kettle. A built-in whistle sounds when water has reached the boiling point. Other features include a safety thermostat that shuts the unit off if the kettle is empty. A maximum water-level marking is located inside the spout. This unit has an easy-care cool-touch plastic exterior. The kettle holds about eight cups of water.

Warranty: 2 years (full)
Manufacturer's Suggested Retail Price: $25
Approximate Low Price: not available

West Bend Tea Kettle 6400

Recommended

The West Bend Tea Kettle is a compact unit that holds four cups (one quart) of water. This unit comes equipped with a steam guard, which directs heat away from your hand when pouring; a whistle, which sounds when water begins boiling; a boil-dry thermostat to prevent overheating if kettle boils dry; and a maximum fill line to prevent overfilling. The unit is constructed of white plastic, which remains relatively cool to the touch. The handle and base are heat-resistant for safe handling.

Warranty: 90 days
Manufacturer's Suggested Retail Price: $27
Approximate Low Price: not available

Oster Cordless Electric Kettle 3207

Recommended

The Oster Cordless Electric Kettle is a no-nonsense unit with some surprising plusses. This unit consists of a solid plastic shell (enclosed, except for the pouring spout) and a compact power base. Extras include an easy-view water-level indicator, cup and quart measurements, cord storage, and a tapered, comfort handle. To use, simply fill kettle to desired level (maximum of ten cups), set unit on base, and flip on/off switch to "on" position. The kettle begins heating and automatically shuts itself off after boiling.

Warranty: 1 year
Manufacturer's Suggested Retail Price: $50
Approximate Low Price: $35

MICROWAVE OVENS

The microwave oven has become a staple in today's homes. Many purchasers are in the position of buying their second or even third oven, and as a result know exactly what features they are looking for. The demand today is for easy-to-operate units that take up a minimum of space, yet provide ample interior cooking capacity. Consumers are looking for fast cooking, pleasant styles to complement their kitchens, and quality for the price. In answer to these demands, microwave oven manufacturers are competing to offer smaller, lighter-weight units, with larger oven cavities, higher wattages, sleeker styling, and more convenience features at lower and lower prices.

Inverter technology has become more widely available in microwave ovens in the past year. These ovens use an inverter instead of a transformer. The result is increased interior space, larger turntables, and a lighter-weight unit. These units also generate more wattage (cooking power) and therefore can cook faster and in a more energy efficient manner. Typically more expensive microwaves, these units are being offered in limited quantities at introductory prices comparable to the prices of conventional units. They are, however, still somewhat new to the U.S. marketplace and their degree of acceptance remains to be seen.

HOW TO SHOP

Before you shop, answer the following simple questions. Your answers will help ensure that you purchase the best microwave oven for your use.

Where will this microwave oven go? The choices include on the countertop or on a cart, over the range, or built into the wall or cabinets. Select the type of unit that complements your lifestyle and measure carefully to ensure the unit you select will fit into your available space. If you plan to build it into your kitchen, make sure a trim kit is available. Not all manufacturers provide them.

How large a unit do you need? Generally speaking, the larger your family, the larger the oven you should choose. Ovens typically come in four sizes: full size, family size, medium size, and compact. Full-size models measure from 1.5 cubic feet to 2.1 cubic feet, and are best for larger families, built-in applications, and those who truly enjoy cooking. Family-size models measure from 1.2 cubic feet to 1.4 cubic feet and are a good choice for smaller families and those on a budget. A medium-size unit measures from .9 cubic feet to 1.1 cubic feet and is a good choice for small kitchens, apartments, and offices. Compact units are those measuring .7 cubic feet or less and are appropriate for places where there is very little space, such as small boats, campers, or dorm rooms.

What wattage oven do you require? The larger the unit, the higher the wattage is likely to be. The higher the wattage, the faster the food will cook. Compact units are usually rated at 700 watts or less. Medium, family-size, and full-size units typically offer from 825 to 1,100 watts. It is probably wise to give more weight to features than wattage, providing wattage falls within this range.

What special features do you want? Recommended features include digital display and touchpads. A dial is not recommended, as it is very imprecise and can lead to overcooking. Automatic features for cooking, reheating, and defrosting are also important and will add little, if any, cost to the microwave. Of the automatic features, the ones operated by a sensor are the best performing.

WHERE TO BUY

Many stores offer microwave ovens. Stores that specialize in appliances tend to have more knowledgeable salespeople. As a result, if you are building the product into your kitchen or need specialized assistance, these types of stores will be your best choice. These stores also tend to service the products they sell. Discount stores, national chain stores, and home centers are also common places to find microwave ovens. These stores usually offer a nice selection of compact, mid-size, family-size, and full-size ovens at attractive prices. It is advisable to select carefully, as the advertised products do not always include the best selection of features.

Many manufacturers also have Web sites that can provide information about available products. Check model numbers carefully to ensure you get the exact features and color you desire.

FEATURES AND TERMINOLOGY_____

Automatic Defrost: This feature allows the food's weight and type to be keyed into the microwave's panel. A built-in mechanism then determines the amount of defrost time required to thaw the food.

Automatic Sensors: The newest of microwave technologies, this feature determines when food is cooked by measuring vapors in the oven. The majority of manufacturers are now installing sensors in their microwaves. Once a sensor has sounded, the oven automatically shuts off. Food should still be checked if it has been thouroughly cooked. Sensors are also used by some manufacturers to determine defrost times.

Browning Dishes and Trays: Browning dishes and trays are sometimes included with the microwave to create a more oven-cooked look for the food. Browning dishes have a metal content on the bottom that helps foods get crispier. Browning trays work in the same way, though neither provides the amount of crispness provided by a conventional oven.

Combination Sensor: This feature is available on only convection/microwave ovens. The sensor cooks the foods using both microwave energy and conventional heat. It is very convenient, as it serves to take some of the guesswork out of combination cooking.

Dual-mode Timer: Dual-mode timers provide a timer that times the food being prepared and can simultaneously be used as a kitchen timer. It is, in effect, two timers.

Instant-action Keys/Easy-touch Buttons: These features are on keypads that have preset times installed by the manufacturer to determine how long a dish should take to cook. Common instant-action keys are for potatoes, popcorn, pizza, and hot beverages. Some full-size and countertop microwaves have as many as 15 keys.

Interactive Displays: These are word prompts that high-end microwaves use to guide you through the cooking process. Some interactive displays can make the cooking process more complicated, especially if you have a lot of keys available at your fingertips.

331

Inverter Microwave Ovens: Relatively new to the U.S. market, these units have more cooking space and are lighter in weight. Performance is generally considered to be better than that of the conventional microwave. Microwave popcorn results might not be as satisfactory. They are also more energy efficient. The success and longevity of these units on the market remains to be seen, as does their service record.

Language/Weight Option: Language/weight option allows some models to show you cooking directions in other languages, generally Spanish and French. Weights of foods can also be translated by these models between pounds and kilograms.

Microwave/Convection Ovens: Microwave/convection ovens provide a more complete cooking environment than a microwave alone. Convection technology uses an electric element to provide heat, which is circulated through the oven. The combination microwave/convection oven allows for baking and other cooking of recipes that cannot be done in a microwave alone. These ovens work best when the two technologies are combined to quickly produce meats and other foods that are browned nearly as well as when prepared in a conventional oven. Some convection ovens have metal interiors that are hotter to touch when cooking is finished.

Turntables: Turntables are revolving plates, usually glass, inside a microwave that automatically turns food as it cooks. Turntables eliminate the need to open the microwave and turn the food by hand. Nearly all full-size and tabletop microwaves have turntables, and many compact and over-the-range models are now adding them. Some microwaves have turntables that automatically place the dish at the front of the oven when the cook time is finished.

BEST BUYS 2000

Our Best Buy, Recommended, and Budget Buy microwave ovens follow. Products within each category are listed according to quality. The item we consider the best of the Best Buys is first, followed by our second choice, and so on. A Budget Buy describes a less-expensive product of respectable quality that perhaps sacrifices some of the performance and/or convenience features of a Best Buy or Recommended product. Remember that a Best Buy, Recommended, or Budget Buy designation only applies to the model listed—it does not necessarily apply to other models made by the same manufacturer or to an entire product line.

_____FULL-SIZE MICROWAVE OVENS_____

Sharp R-530
A top choice for the third year in a row, the R-530 ✔**BEST BUY** excels in performance and value. This unit has a roomy 2.0 cubic feet of cooking space and 1,100 watts of power. It offers a 16-inch turntable, which is large enough to rotate a 9×13-inch dish. The sensor feature allows for effortless food preparation. A variety of automated cooking and defrosting programs add to the convenience. The help feature provides instructions in English, French, or Spanish. An optional kit makes this model an excellent choice for built-in use. The R-530 is available in black or white. Stainless steel is available at additional cost.

Specifications: height, 13⅜"; width, 24"; depth, 19⅛"; capacity, 2.0 cubic feet; cooking power, 1,100 watts; interior height, 10½"; interior width, 17⅜"; interior depth, 18⅝"
Warranty: 1 year, parts and labor; 5 years, magnetron tube
Manufacturer's Suggested Retail Price: $180
Approximate Low Price: $159-$179

General Electric JE1860
A new model from General Electric, the JE1860 in- ✔**BEST BUY** corporates all the features you could want in a microwave oven. This unit offers a turntable with an on/off switch, useful for accommodating large dishes. It boasts 1.8-cubic-feet capacity, 1,100 watts of cooking power, an easy-to-use sensor, and automatic de-

frost selections. It is an excellent choice for built-in use, as the General Electric company typically offers readily available trim kits (at additional cost). This model is available in today's most popular kitchen colors: black, white, and stainless steel.

Specifications: height, 13⁹⁄₁₆"; width, 23⁷⁄₈"; depth, 18¹³⁄₁₆"; capacity, 1.8 cubic feet; cooking power, 1,100 watts; interior height, 9¾"; interior width, 17¹⁄₁₆"; interior depth, 18⁵⁄₁₆"
Warranty: 1 year, parts and labor; 10 years, magnetron tube (limited)
Manufacturer's Suggested Retail Price: not available
Approximate Low Price: $220-$239

Panasonic NN-S969BA/WA

✔**BEST BUY**

This Panasonic microwave oven utilizes the relatively new inverter technology, and the result is more usable cooking space. This model boasts one of the largest interiors on the market: 2.1 cubic feet. Cooking times do not need to be calculated, thanks to the easy-to-use sensor feature. Other handy features include a turntable, a preprogrammed defrost, a popcorn key, a more/less control, and a one-minute touch pad. A trilingual display provides assistance in English, Spanish, or French. If you are planning built-in installation, check with your retailer regarding the availability of a trim kit. Panasonic offers this unit in black or white.

Specifications: height, 14"; width, 23⁷⁄₈"; depth, 18⁷⁄₈"; capacity, 2.1 cubic feet; cooking power, 1,100 watts; interior height, 10¹¹⁄₁₆"; interior width, 18⁷⁄₁₆"; interior depth, 18½"
Warranty: 1 year, parts and labor
Manufacturer's Suggested Retail Price: $190
Approximate Low Price: $159-$179

___FAMILY-SIZE MICROWAVE OVENS___

Sharp R-420

✔**BEST BUY**

Also a Best Buy in 1999, this Sharp microwave oven continues to be an outstanding value for the money. The cavity size is slightly larger than last year's model, standing at 1.4 cubic feet. Sensor keys eliminate the guesswork of microwaving foods. A 14⅛-inch turntable distributes the microwave energy and cooks food evenly. An automated defrost program and an interactive help system guide the user throughout the cooking process. A built-in kit is available from the manufacturer at additional cost. Sharp offers this unit in black or white.

Specifications: height, 12⅜"; width, 21¹¹⁄₁₆"; depth, 17⅜"; capacity, 1.4 cubic feet; cooking power, 1,100 watts; interior height, 9⁷⁄₁₆"; interior width, 15"; interior depth, 16¾"
Warranty: 1 year, parts and labor; 5 years, magnetron tube
Manufacturer's Suggested Retail Price: $160
Approximate Low Price: $129-$149

Quasar MQS-1395E/H

Budget Buy

This Quasar model can be found in stores at attractive prices. It offers an ample 1.3 feet of cooking space and a respectable 1,000 watts of cooking power. Although the MQS-1395E/H lacks the preferred sensor feature, it comes equipped with preprogrammed reheating, defrosting, and cooking modes. It also includes a popcorn key and a one-minute touch pad for easy cooking. Quasar offers this model in black or white.

Specifications: height, 12"; width, 21⅞"; depth, 16¾"; capacity, 1.3 cubic feet; cooking power, 1,000 watts; interior height, 9⅛"; interior width, 14¹⁵⁄₁₆"; interior depth, 15¹³⁄₁₆"
Warranty: 1 year, parts and labor
Manufacturer's Suggested Retail Price: not available
Approximate Low Price: not available

—MEDIUM-SIZE MICROWAVE OVENS—

Panasonic NN-S569BA/WA

The NN-S569BA/WA is a superb microwave oven for singles, couples, or small kitchens. This unit occupies very little space and still provides all the easy-to-use features needed in a microwave oven. The NN-S569BA/WA offers sensor cooking, sensor reheating, a turntable, and an automatic defrost program. The LED display is easy to read. For a late-night snack, a popcorn key is included. Other features include a one-minute selection and a more/less adjustment for individual tastes. Panasonic offers this unit in black or white.

Specifications: height, 20"; width, 12"; depth, 14³/₁₆"; capacity, 1.0 cubic foot; cooking power, 1,100 watts; interior height, 9"; interior width, 13⅞"; interior depth, 13¹⁵/₁₆"
Warranty: 1 year, parts and labor
Manufacturer's Suggested Retail Price: $150
Approximate Low Price: $129-$139

Sanyo EM-P495

Budget Buy

An excellent buy for the budget shopper, the EM-P495 can be found at attractive prices around the country. This unit features a recessed boomerang turntable—a unique solution to making room for oversize dishes. It offers 1.1 cubic feet of cooking space and 1,100 watts of power. Sensor and defrost programs are included. A dual-mode kitchen timer conveniently allows timer use while the oven is in operation. Word prompts are available for help, and a "favorites" key makes it easy to prepare your preferred selections time and again. A child lockout prevents operation by young children.

Specifications: height, 11⅜"; width, 20¹¹/₁₆"; depth, 16¹¹/₁₆"; capacity, 1.1 cubic feet; cooking power, 1,100 watts; interior height, 9¹/₁₆"; interior width, 13¹³/₁₆"; interior depth, 14⅝"

Warranty: 1 year, parts and labor; 5 years, magnetron tube (limited)
Manufacturer's Suggested Retail Price: $149
Approximate Low Price: $99-$129

___COMPACT MICROWAVE OVENS___

Sharp R-230

✔**BEST BUY**

A compact-size oven, this unit provides the basics for those who have neither the space nor need for a larger unit. This model has easy-to-use touch controls, an LCD display, and pre-programmed cooking and defrost modes. Small enough for space-deprived consumers, the R-230 offers 700 watts of cooking power and a turntable. Food preparation times for popular items such as popcorn, vegetables, and muffins have been preset into the model. This microwave oven does not feature the preferred sensor, but in this size and price range that feature is rarely offered. Sharp offers this compact microwave oven in black or white.

Specifications: height, 11⅝"; width, 18⅛"; depth, 14⅝"; capacity, 0.7 cubic foot; cooking power, 700 watts; interior height, 7⅞"; interior width, 12⅜"; interior depth, 12⅝"
Warranty: 1 year, parts and labor; 5 years, magnetron tube
Manufacturer's Suggested Retail Price: $100
Approximate Low Price: $89

Sanyo EM-N107W/B

Budget Buy

A solid performer, this Sanyo model offers all the basic features you'll need in a compact microwave oven. The model boasts 0.7-cubic-foot capacity and 600 watts of cooking power. Preprogrammed keys enable cooking for frequently microwaved foods. An automatic defrost feature makes defrosting easier and helps prevent premature cooking. One nice feature is the boomerang turntable, which brings the dish back to its original position. A dual mode kitchen timer and a popcorn key complete the unit. No sensor is provided, as is the rule at this low price. This model is available in white or black.

Specifications: height, 9³⁄₁₆"; width, 18³⁄₁₆"; depth, 13¹³⁄₁₆"; capacity, 0.7 cubic foot; cooking power, 600 watts; interior height, 7⁷⁄₈"; interior width, 11⁷⁄₁₆"; interior depth, 12¼"

Warranty: 1 year, parts and labor (limited); 5 years, magnetron tube

Manufacturer's Suggested Retail Price: $99
Approximate Low Price: $89

__MICROWAVE/CONVECTION OVENS__

Sharp R-930

✔**BEST BUY**

Also our top selection in 1999, this full-size microwave/convection oven boasts the ability to brown, bake, broil, crisp, and microwave. The oven operates in microwave, convection, or a combination of both modes. As a result, this oven can combine the speed of microwaving with the crisp brown results of traditional baking and roasting. The display panel is interactive, and, to aid the user, a help key is supplied. A sensor provides effortless cooking for commonly microwaved foods. A preprogrammed feature automatically computes the times for baking, roasting, and broiling. Juicy roasts and evenly browned cakes are just two of the many benefits that can be derived from this unit. A turntable is used to evenly circulate the microwave energy. Two removable convection oven racks are also included. The unit's size and versatility make it an outstanding choice for built-in use. The trim kit is offered separately at additional cost. Color selections come in charcoal or white.

Specifications: height, 14⁷⁄₈"; width, 24⁵⁄₈"; depth, 18¾"; capacity, 1.5 cubic feet; cooking power, 900 watts; interior height, 9⁵⁄₈"; interior width, 16⅛"; interior depth, 16⅛"

Warranty: 1 year, parts and labor; 5 years, magnetron tube
Manufacturer's Suggested Retail Price: $450
Approximate Low Price: $429-$440

General Electric JE1390
✔**BEST BUY**

This full-size unit offers the choice of microwave cooking, convection cooking, or the combination of the two. With an oven like the JE1390, you can achieve golden brown exteriors and moist interiors on roasts, turkeys, and baked goods. A sensor is featured for easy cooking and reheating of common foods. The model includes two racks for baking and roasting, a turntable, and an automatic defrost feature. The JE1390 makes an excellent choice for built-in use, thanks to its ample size. Built-in accessory trim kits, available separately at additional cost, allow for installation in a wall or cabinet, either alone or over a wall oven. General Electric offers this unit in black or white.

Specifications: height, 14⅞"; width, 22¼"; depth, 19⅞"; capacity, 1.3 cubic feet; cooking power, 850 watts; interior height, 10⅛"; interior width, 14½"; interior depth, 14½"
Warranty: 1 year, parts and labor; 10 years, magnetron tube (parts only)
Manufacturer's Suggested Retail Price: $439
Approximate Low Price: $399-$429

OVER-THE-RANGE
MICROWAVE OVENS

General Electric JVM1660
✔**BEST BUY**

General Electric has added plenty of convenience features to its newest sensor-equipped, over-the-range microwave oven. The JVM1660 includes a turntable on/off switch and an interactive display that offers helpful tips for efficient operation. A temperature probe is included for roasting, and an automatic defrost feature takes the guesswork out of cooking. Full cooktop lighting is provided, as well as a programmable night-light. An audio message center and an appointment scheduler serve as added convenience features for today's busy families. A 300 CFM, two-speed exhaust fan ventilates your cooking surface. The JVM1660 offers 1.6 cubic feet of cooking space, 1,000 watts of power, and eight categories of sensor controls. A handy cookbook is also provided. GE offers this unit in black, white, almond, and stainless steel.

Specifications: height, $16^{15}/_{32}$"; width, $29^7/_8$"; depth, $15^1/_{16}$"; capacity, 1.6 cubic feet; cooking power, 1,000 watts; interior height, $9^9/_{32}$"; interior width, $20^1/_4$"; interior depth, $14^{13}/_{32}$"
Warranty: 1 year, full; 10 years, magnetron tube
Manufacturer's Suggested Retail Price: not available
Approximate Low Price: $459-$469

Sharp R-1610

✔**BEST BUY**

An excellent choice for over-the-range microwave use is Sharp's new R-1610. It offers 1,000 watts of cooking power and 1.6 cubic feet of capacity. A removable rack increases the capacity of the unit. The R-1610 offers a sensor and 44 automatic menu selections. A memory feature recalls stored cooking instructions, and two automated defrost programs provide quick, accurate defrosting. The turntable offers an on/off switch, which is useful for oblong dishes up to 10×15 inches. Surface ventilation is provided by a two-speed, 300 CFM fan. Also included is a filter for non-vented installations. This model has a convenient work light and a night-light. Sharp offers this model in black, and comparable models come in white and almond.

Specifications: height, $16^3/_8$"; width, $29^{15}/_{16}$"; depth, $17^1/_{16}$"; capacity, 1.6 cubic feet; cooking power, 1,000 watts; interior height, $8^7/_8$"; interior width, 21"; interior depth, $14^7/_{16}$"
Warranty: 1 year, parts and labor; 7 years, magnetron tube
Manufacturer's Suggested Retail Price: $399
Approximate Low Price: $379

Whirlpool GH7145XF

Recommended

Slightly smaller than our other two choices, this model offers 1.4 cubic feet of space and 1,000 watts of power. The sensored cooking system provides automated cooking for eight food categories. Four automatic reheat functions and an automatic defrosting feature make this attractive model easy to use. The turntable is recessed and may be shut off to accommodate large dishes. The ventilation hood converts for vented or non-vented use and has a 4-speed touch control and an automatic off feature. Surface lighting is also provided. This model is available in white, black, or almond.

Specifications: height, 16¼"; width, 29¹⁵⁄₁₆"; depth, 15⅜"; capacity, 1.4 cubic feet; cooking power, 1,000 watts; interior height, 8¼", interior width, 20⅞", interior width, 13⅝"
Warranty: 1 year, parts and labor; 5 years, magnetron tube
Manufacturer's Suggested Retail Price: $475
Approximate Low Price: $429-$450

OVER-THE-RANGE
__MICROWAVE/CONVECTION OVENS__

General Electric JVM1190

✔ BEST BUY

Consistently a top performer, General Electric's over-the-range convection/microwave oven is an asset to any kitchen. This oven features sensor cooking controls for four food categories. The combination sensor is an incredibly useful feature that automatically computes combination cooking times. It allows the use of convection and microwave cooking to be used together, achieving the speed of microwaves and the crisp, browned surface of convection. A probe is included for cooking by temperature with either microwave or combination settings, and an automatic defrost setting takes the guesswork out of this job. Other features include a two-speed ventilation fan, a surface light, and a programmable night-light. The GE JVM1190 has 1.1 cubic feet of cooking space

341

and 825 watts of power. This model is available in white, black, almond, or stainless steel.

Specifications: height, 15½"; width, 29¹⁵⁄₁₆"; depth, 14¼"; capacity, 1.1 cubic feet; cooking power, 825 watts; interior height, 8¹⁄₁₆"; interior width, 18"; interior depth, 12½"

Warranty: 1 year, parts and labor; 10 years, magnetron tube (parts only)

Manufacturer's Suggested Retail Price: $689
Approximate Low Price: $649

Sharp R-1850 ✔ BEST BUY

The Sharp R-1850 has been a popular model for a number of years and for good reason. The oven combines the speed of microwaving with the baking, browning, and roasting performance of convection. An interactive display spells out programming steps, making the oven easy to use. And right at your fingertips is a custom help key that offers cooking hints and instructions for operation. Two racks are included (one for two-level baking and one for roasting, baking, or broiling). The 1.1-cubic-feet unit offers 850 watts of cooking power and features a sensor that automatically determines microwave cooking or reheating times for eight popular food categories. Additional automatic features compute broiling, roasting, and baking times. The 13-inch turntable enhances even cooking and can be switched off to accommodate oversized dishes. Also included are a hood light and a ventilation fan, appropriate for ducted or non-ducted installations. Non-ducted installations require an additional filter, which is sold separately. This model comes in black, white, or almond.

Specifications: height, 16¹¹⁄₃₂"; width, 29¹⁵⁄₁₆"; depth, 15⁹⁄₃₂"; capacity, 1.1 cubic feet; cooking power, 850 watts; interior height, 8¹⁄₁₆"; interior width, 17⅛"; interior depth, 13³⁄₁₆"

Warranty: 2 years, parts and labor; 7 years, magnetron tube
Manufacturer's Suggested Retail Price: $600
Approximate Low Price: $579-$599

RANGES

Although many tasks previously done by the range are now performed by the microwave oven, the range remains a staple in today's kitchen. Its importance lies in its versatility and long history of use in the American kitchen. The range is certainly the best tool for many jobs. For example, no other appliance can offer the control of a sauté or sauce like the range. And an oven's ability to turn out crisp, browned surfaces on meats and baked goods is unsurpassed by any other appliance.

HOW TO SHOP

The basic choices that have to be made are determined by the kitchen the appliances are to be installed in. Usually appliances are purchased either to replace an existing unit or to be installed into a new or renovated kitchen. In a replacement situation, the amount of space and the available fuel will often dictate the choice. In a new or renovated kitchen, there is often a bit more room for flexibility.

Fuel choices today include electric, gas, or dual-fuel. Gas ranges tend to be more popular among home chefs because of their instant response time, easy control, and visible flame. Also, in many regions of the country, gas tends to offer a lower operating cost than electric appliances.

Historically, coil elements were the choice for electric ranges and cooktops. Today an increasing number of electric units are sold with smooth-top cooking surfaces. The ease of cleaning is the primary reason for this tremendous growth in popularity. Look for radiant ribbons encased in glass-ceramic surfaces, but be prepared to use only flat-bottom cooking vessels. Halogen elements are also available. They heat quickly, but cost a bit more and are not as common as the radiant ribbons.

In gas ranges and cooktops, ease of cleaning and smoothness of surface are the most popular features. For the most effortless cleaning, select sealed gas burners. Flush grates offering a smooth surface for moving pans are a nice feature, but one that still commands a fairly high price.

Dual-fuel kitchens usually have gas for the cooking surface and electricity for the oven operation. This can be accomplished in one unit or by using a cooktop and wall oven. Often dual-fuel is the choice of gourmet cooks and bakers. They enjoy the precision of gas surface units and prefer the evenness of electric baking, usually with a convection oven. Choosing dual-fuel, however, can significantly add to the cost of new appliances.

In addition to fuel, space and cabinets in the kitchen will determine selections. Not all manufacturers make built-ins to fit every space. The choices may be limited by the space occupied by the former appliance or by the design of the kitchen itself.

WHERE TO BUY

Typically, ranges, cooktops, and wall ovens are purchased in a local appliance store or a national chain store. Local appliance stores often have the best selection of models on display and they tend to have a more knowledgeable sales staff. They often have products in stock and their own service departments. Because of this advantage, however, prices may be slightly higher.

Many national chains do not have an extensive display of products, especially built-in ones. Usually, they will order these products for you. On the other hand, items such as freestanding ranges are usually stocked and readily available. The selection usually includes the most common and less expensive choices. Ask about service, as it varies from store to store.

In addition to stores, knowledge regarding appliances is available to the public on the Internet. Most manufacturers have Web sites, which describe their products and provide specifications as well as dealer services. A lot of time can be saved by doing comparative shopping with a computer and a modem, instead of going store to store.

It is also important to note that many manufacturers offer the same basic body of an appliance in different models. Each model number will vary slightly to indicate a change in features or colors. Check with your dealer to ensure you receive the exact features and color you desire.

RANGES

Ranges contain a cooktop and an oven in a one-piece unit. The most typical unit is 30 inches wide, although other sizes are available. For today's busy families, the range with a self-cleaning oven has become the standard.

The three styles of ranges are known as freestanding, drop-in, and slide-in. A freestanding unit is designed to sit on the floor by itself and has finished sides. The drop-in and slide-in units are made to fit between two cabinets and do not have finished sides. A drop-in typically hangs from the countertop and may require cabinetry at the bottom. A disadvantage of this may be the loss of the storage drawer. A slide-in literally slides between the cabinets and sits on the floor. Generally, slide-in and drop-in ranges are less expensive than freestanding units and offer a continuous countertop-to-range surface.

COOKTOPS

An alternative to the range is the cooktop. Cooktops fit into the top surface of a cabinet. They may be placed against a wall in an island. Units may range in size from 18 to 48 inches, containing two, four, six, or more burners. The average cooktop is 30 to 36 inches wide and fits in a cabinet 24 inches deep.

Modular style cooktops have bays, which accept various interchangeable elements and accessories. Accessories include griddles, grills, woks, rotisseries, roasters, and steamers. The griddle and grill are considered the most useful. Catalogs from the manufacturer will outline all the choices, as stores often do not have the space to display them all.

Ventilation is needed for every cooktop. Either downdraft or updraft ventilation must be selected. Updraft uses an overhead hood, while downdraft uses a powerful fan, which is located at the cooktop's surface and vented to the outside. Many modular cooktops require downdraft ventilation. Proper ventilation is imperative and should be described in detail by the dealer.

WALL OVENS_____

When a cooktop is selected, the next choice is the wall oven. Wall ovens today are usually built into a large cabinet. Convection, a feature where hot air circulates in the oven, is a useful feature for more even cooking and baking. It does, however add significantly to the cost of the oven. Ovens are available single, double, or in combination with a microwave. Gas ovens are sized for 24-, 27-, and 30-inch cabinets. Electric ovens are usually sized at 27- and 30-inch cabinets. In kitchens with limited space, 30-inch wall ovens are a nice choice and fit directly under many cooktops. Check with your dealer for compatibility.

COMMERCIAL-STYLE RANGES_____

We've included commercial-style ranges in this chapter for users who desire restaurant-quality kitchen equipment in their homes. Commercial-style ranges generally produce more heat than standard ranges. As a result, they require a high-powered ventilation system. The don't require special clearance or gas connections, though many manufacturers do recommend stainless-steel backsplashes between the cooktop and the hood because of the added power of the burners.

RANGE HOODS_____

A vital—and often overlooked—element to a successful kitchen is a proper ventilation system. Range hoods absorb, filter, and redistribute air in the kitchen. Usually positioned above the cooktop, they not only filter cooking odors and smoke, but also absorb residual fumes left behind by gas cooktops, making your kitchen safer, cleaner, and more comfortable.

Standard horizontal or vertical range hoods typically run a vented line through a hole in a wall or through a ceiling. Many modular cooktops have a downdraft ventilation system included with the unit. These systems come built into the range-hood system and must be used for the cooktop to operate properly.

When purchasing a ventilation system, it's important to make sure the hood is powerful enough to match the range and cooking applications. For example, a user who owns a powerful commercial-style range and plans on regularly deep-frying foods will require a much more powerful ventilation system than a user who owns a standard gas oven. Hoods are rated in cubic feet of air (cfm) moved per minute. A minimal recommendation is a hood that is rated at 180 cfm or more. Cooktops and commercial-style units will require additional cfm. Check with the range manufacturer for specific details and recommendations when choosing an appropriate range hood.

BEST BUYS 2000

Our Best Buy, Recommended, and Budget Buy ranges, ovens, and range hoods follow. Products within each category are listed according to quality. The item we consider the best of the Best Buys is first, followed by our second choice, and so on. A Budget Buy describes a less-expensive product of respectable quality that perhaps sacrifices some of the performance and/or convenience features of a Best Buy or Recommended product. Remember that a Best Buy, Recommended, or Budget Buy designation only applies to the model listed—it does not necessarily apply to other models made by the same manufacturer or to an entire product line.

GAS RANGES

FREESTANDING GAS RANGES

Amana ARG7600

A pilotless, 30-inch model, the ARG7600 offers the **✔ BEST BUY** versatility of three sizes of gas burners. Each burner is equipped with durable cast-iron grates and porcelain burner bowls. The small burner is rated at 5,000 Btu, for delicate, low-heat tasks. The medium burner offers 9,100 Btu, for basic daily cooking; while the two large, high-powered burners offer 12,500 Btu, for times when more heat is required. Front-mounted controls are easy to reach, but might be a concern around small children. The spacious, self-cleaning oven features a large viewing window, two racks, and an interior light. Broiling is done in the oven with a fast, high-powered broiling element. A convenient storage drawer is included. This unit is available in white-on-white or almond-on-almond.

Specifications: height, 46½"; width, 30"; depth, 28¼"; interior height, 16"; interior width, 23"; interior depth, 17½"
Warranty: 1 year, full; 2 years, parts and labor; 5 years, gas surface burners (limited)
Manufacturer's Suggested Retail Price: $749
Approximate Low Price: $699

Whirlpool GS395LEG   ✔ **BEST BUY**

This 30-inch self-cleaning range features an easy-clean cooking surface and sealed gas burners with cast-iron burner grates. The surface burners offer a variety of Btu ratings to meet the needs of individual cooks. One is rated at 6,500 Btu, one at 7,500 Btu, one at 9,500 Btu, and one at 12,500 Btu. The unit is convertible for natural gas or propane gas use. Waist-high broiling and electronic ignition add to the convenience of this range. The oven offers a color-coordinated glass door, which is removable for easier cleanup of spills. An automatic oven light and a storage drawer are also included. Color selections for this model include white-on-white, almond-on-almond, and black-on-black.

Specifications: height, 46¹³⁄₁₆"; width, 29⅞"; depth, 25"
Warranty: 1 year, parts and labor (full); 5 years, parts and labor (limited)
Manufacturer's Suggested Retail Price: $799
Approximate Low Price: not available

KitchenAid KGRT500F | Recommended |

This model, though somewhat higher in price than similar models, delivers outstanding features, quality, and performance. A pilotless ignition unit, it features easy-access, front-top mounted controls. The four sealed gas burners are set in a contained cooktop, with no drip bowls to wash or burner boxes to clean. Two of the burners are rated at 6,000 Btu and two are rated at 10,000 Btu. Convenience features, not often offered on competitive models, include a fluorescent cooktop light and a nightlight. The self-cleaning oven offers variable temperature broiling, with a large surface area element for fast, even broiling results. Included are two oven racks and a removable storage drawer. The viewing window on this unit, however, is only standard size. Color selection is either white or almond.

Specifications: height, 44⅜"; width, 30"; depth, 25½"; interior height, 15¾"; interior width, 23¹⁄₁₆"; interior depth, 18¼"
Warranty: 1 year, parts and labor; 5 years, parts (limited); 10 years, parts (limited)
Manufacturer's Suggested Retail Price: $1,299
Approximate Low Price: $1,050

DROP-IN/SLIDE-IN GAS RANGES

General Electric JGSP44

This 30-inch slide-in model features electronic controls, cast-iron grates, and sealed burners. A maximum output burner and a simmer burner offer cooking flexibility. The grates and drip pans are removable for easier cleaning. The oven offers a self-cleaning feature with delay option and variable cleaning times. Broiling is done in the oven. The viewing window is standard size. A storage drawer is included. The unit requires a filler strip, which is included, or an optional backguard. This range comes in white, almond, or black.

Specifications: height, 36¼"; width, 30"; depth, 29½"; interior height, 15³⁄₁₆"; interior width, 22¹¹⁄₁₆"; interior depth, 17¹⁄₁₆"
Warranty: 1 year, full, parts and labor
Manufacturer's Suggested Retail Price: $959
Approximate Low Price: not available

KitchenAid KGST300T

Recommended

This KitchenAid slide-in model offers quality and reliability at a somewhat higher price than competitive models. It features a tempered glass cook-top with four sealed gas burners. Two of the burners are rated at 6,000 Btu and two are rated at 10,000 Btu. The electronic controls are mounted on the top front of the unit. The self-cleaning oven offers variable-temperature broiling and an oven light. The viewing window is standard size. A filler plate is included with the unit for installation against the back wall. A convection oven is available on a similar chassis at additional cost. This unit is available in almond or white.

Specifications: height, 38"; width, 30⅞"; depth, 25½"; interior height, 15¾"; interior width, 23¹⁄₁₆"; interior depth, 18¼"

Warranty: 1 year, full; 5 years, parts (limited); 10 years, parts (limited)

Manufacturer's Suggested Retail Price: $1,379

Approximate Low Price: $1,157

GAS COOKTOPS AND MODULAR GAS COOKTOPS

Jenn-Air CCG2423

✔ BEST BUY

One of the best cooktop values on the market, the Jenn-Air CCG2423 30-inch cooktop offers four sealed burners and porcelain-on-cast-iron burner grates. This unit is convertible to LP gas and features infinite control settings. Both a simmer burner (6,500 Btu) and a maximum output burner (12,000 Btu) are included and serve to provide flexibility for the cook. The model provides electronic ignition/re-ignition and accepts the Jenn-Air wok accessory. It can be installed alone or over one of a number of 30-inch wall ovens. It is available in black or white.

Specifications: height, NA; width, 30"; depth, 21"

Warranty: 1 year, labor; 2 years, parts; 5 years, parts (limited)

Manufacturer's Suggested Retail Price: $609

Approximate Low Price: $590

Thermador SGCS365RB

A 36-inch black cooktop with a five-burner config-
uration, this model offers plenty of useful features for those who truly
enjoy cooking. It features electronic ignition/re-ignition and can be
converted for LP gas use with an optional conversion kit. The sealed
burners provide for easy clean-up, while the porcelain-on-cast-iron
burner grates provide durability. The burners offer a high degree
of temperature control and accuracy with an incredible range of
210 Btu to 12,500 Btu distributed among the 5 burners. The continuous surface grates enable the user to smoothly move large cooking vessels from burner to burner. The configuration also allows for
the cookware to span two burners. This unit can be paired with either an updraft or downdraft ventilation system and accepts wok or
griddle accessories. White porcelain or stainless steel finish are
available at an additional cost.

Specifications: height, 4"; width, 36"; depth, 21"
Warranty: 1 year, parts and labor
Manufacturer's Suggested Retail Price: $1,199
Approximate Low Price: $1,150

Jenn-Air CVDX4180

Among the most versatile modular cooktops on the
market, this model accepts more accessories than many other comparable models. Available accessories include a wok, a big pot element, a big pot grate, a griddle, and a rotiss-kebab. The design
combines two gas burners and an electric grill. This unit truly strives
to offer maximum flexibility and is convertible to a four-burner cooktop using coil, halogen, or radiant cartridges. The sealed gas burners offer electronic ignition/re-ignition and are appropriate for LP
use. This unit requires downdraft ventilation and is not designed to
be used with a ventilation hood. It is an excellent choice for installation in an island or peninsula. This model is wider than others in
its class and might require space beyond the standard cutout. A
similar model fueled totally by gas, with limited accessory options,
is available. Color selections include black or white.

Specifications: height, NA; width, 32⅜"; depth, 21⅛"
Warranty: 1 year, parts and labor; 2 years, parts
Manufacturer's Suggested Retail Price: $949
Approximate Low Price: $919

BUILT-IN GAS OVENS

Whirlpool SB160PEE
✔**BEST BUY**

This basic, 24-inch, self-cleaning unit makes a fine choice for replacing an existing wall oven. The 2.9-cubic-foot unit includes an electronic clock with oven controls and a minute timer. Broiling is done in-oven. The unit also features a glass door, an automatic oven light, two racks, and a porcelain broiler pan with grid. This model comes in black-on-black or white-on-white.

Specifications: height, 40"; width, 23⅞"; depth, 25⅜"; interior height, 16"; interior width, 17"; interior depth, 18½"
Warranty: 1 year, parts and labor
Manufacturer's Suggested Retail Price: not available
Approximate Low Price: $799-$829

Amana AOGD2750
✔**BEST BUY**

The Amana AOGD2750 is a 27-inch, double, wall oven. Features include a variable-time self-clean cycle, electronic oven controls, and a 12-hour automatic shut-off. Each cavity offers 3.3 cubic feet of cooking space and includes two racks. Broiling can be done at variable temperatures. Interior oven lights, removable glass doors, and viewing windows are included on both ovens. The unit comes in white-on-white and black-on-black.

Specifications: height, 54⅝"; width, 26⅝"; depth, 27½"; interior height, 16"; interior width, 19¼"; interior depth, 18⅝"
Warranty: 1 year, full; 2 years, parts
Manufacturer's Suggested Retail Price: $2,099
Approximate Low Price: $1,965

COMMERCIAL-STYLE GAS RANGES AND COOKTOPS

Thermador PCS366US

✔**BEST BUY**

This 36-inch range-top offers six commercial-style burners, sealed for easier cleanup. Configurations offering a grill or griddle are also available in this size. The surface units offer a 15,000 Btu capacity, with two extra-low burners for simmering. The durable cast-iron, porcelain-coated burner grates interlock to create a continuous surface for easily moving pans from burner to burner. Automatic electric ignition and re-ignition eliminates the need for a pilot light. One nice safety feature is the light, which indicates when a gas burner is on. This can be a real advantage when using a very low flame. Also available is a conversion kit for LP gas use. One of the various back guards must be selected for proper installation, and a high-powered ventilation system is recommended. The unit comes in stainless steel, with a brass trim option.

Specifications: height, 9½"; width, 35⅞"; depth, 26½"
Warranty: 1 year, parts and labor
Manufacturer's Suggested Retail Price: $2,349
Approximate Low Price: $2,105

Viking VGSU161

✔**BEST BUY**

The Viking VGSU161 is a six-burner cooktop designed to fit into a 36-inch cutout. The sealed burners provide from 950 to 14,000 Btu and have brass flame ports and porcelain/cast-iron burner caps. An automatic electric ignition and re-ignition feature is included. Large, cast-iron burner grates provide a durable and continuous surface for moving large pots from burner to burner. The knobs, which are of commercial design, are easy to read and employ push-to-turn as a safety feature for homes with young children. Separate spill collection areas surround each burner and hold 1¼ quarts of liquid each. Conversion to LP gas is an option. This model comes in black, white, or stainless steel finishes.

Specifications: height, 4³/₁₆"; width, 36³/₄"; depth, 21"
Warranty: 1 year, parts and labor; 5 years, surface burner (limited)
Manufacturer's Suggested Retail Price: $1,400
Approximate Low Price: $1,375-$1,399

ELECTRIC RANGES

FREESTANDING ELECTRIC RANGES

Amana ART6511

✔**BEST BUY**

This smooth-top Amana electric range measures 30 inches wide and provides quality, durability, value, and performance. The cooking surface provides four radiant heating elements: one 6-inch, one 7-inch, one 8-inch, and one dual 6-inch/9-inch. The flat cooktop offers a lip to help contain spillovers. The range features an on indicator light, an important safety feature for smooth-tops. A self-cleaning unit, this range has electronic touch control. Also included are an oven light, a storage drawer, and an extra-large viewing window. This unit comes in white-on-white, black-on-black, and almond-on-almond. Amana also offers an upgraded version (with a different model number) that includes a convection oven at additional cost.

Specifications: height, 46½"; width, 30"; depth, 28¼"; interior height, 16"; interior width, 23"; interior depth, 17½"
Warranty: 1 year, full; 2 years, parts (limited); 5 years, glass-ceramic top and electric surface elements (limited)
Manufacturer's Suggested Retail Price: $699
Approximate Low Price: not available

KitchenAid KERC607G

✔**BEST BUY**

A superb unit, this range sells for a somewhat higher price than our other selections because it includes a convection oven. For serious cooks, the additional expense might be well worth it. The cooktop on this 30-inch model provides four powerful radiant elements, one of which is expandable to accommodate various pan sizes. Infinite heat controls are included, as are hot-surface indicators. The oven offers variable-time self-cleaning and variable-temperature broiling. A convenient storage drawer and an automatic light with manual switch are included. The smaller depth of this unit makes it a popular selection for those who do not wish to have the range protrude from the cabinetry. The wide selection of colors include white, biscuit, almond, black, and stainless.

Specifications: height, 44⅜"; width, 29¹⁵/₁₆"; depth, 24½"; interior height, 15¾"; interior width, 23¹/₁₆"; interior depth, 16⁵/₁₆"
Warranty: 1 year (full); 5 years, parts (limited); 10 years, parts (limited)
Manufacturer's Suggested Retail Price: $1,349
Approximate Low Price: not available

Maytag MER5730   ✔ BEST BUY

Also a Best Buy in 1999, this 30-inch range offers a sleek, easy-to-clean flat surface. Convenience features include removable knobs and a self-cleaning oven. The four surface elements are of the radiant ribbon type and are imbedded in the flat cooktop surface. A durable porcelain back panel is provided. Surface indicator lights let the user know when the elements are hot. The oven is electronically controlled and features a light, a clock, a delay start function, and a storage drawer. An optional half-rack is available to increase the flexibility of the oven. The included oven viewing window is smaller in size than the windows many comparable models offer. The unit comes in white, almond, monochromatic white, or monochromatic almond.

Specifications: height, 46¾"; width, 29⅞"; depth, 26⅛"; interior height, 16½"; interior width, 23"; interior depth, 18⅛"
Warranty: 1 year, parts and labor; 2 years, parts; 5 years, parts (limited)

Manufacturer's Suggested Retail Price: $729
Approximate Low Price: $659-$699

DROP-IN/SLIDE-IN ELECTRIC RANGES

KitchenAid KESC300B

| Recommended |

The KitchenAid 30-inch KESC300B slide-in range provides a sleek built-in look. The smooth-top unit features four radiant elements with a dual-circuit expandable element. The controls are conveniently front-mounted. Hot-surface indicator lights are provided as a safety feature. The thermal oven offers variable-time self-cleaning and variable-temperature broiling. An automatic timer and a removable storage drawer are handy additional offerings. The viewing window is standard size. An upgraded unit with a convection oven and a larger viewing window is available at additional cost. The KitchenAid KESC300B is available in white, almond, or black.

Specifications: height, 38"; width, 30⅞"; depth, 25¾"; interior height, 15¾"; interior width, 23⅟16"; interior depth, 18¼"
Warranty: 1 year, full; 5 years, parts (limited); 10 years, parts (limited)
Manufacturer's Suggested Retail Price: $1,149
Approximate Low Price: not available

General Electric JDP39

| Budget Buy |

General Electric provides one of the widest selections of drop-in ranges. They produce units in a number of colors and two sizes. This 30-inch drop-in unit offers electronic controls and a lift-up porcelain-enameled cooktop. The elements are plug-in coils with removable drip pans. The unit features a self-cleaning oven and a removable frameless, glass door. As is typical with drop-in units, this range does not have a storage drawer. This unit comes in white or black.

Specifications: height, 30½"; width, 30"; depth, 26"; interior height, 15¾"; interior width, 22¾"; interior depth, 17"
Warranty: 1 year, full
Manufacturer's Suggested Retail Price: $749
Approximate Low Price: not available

ELECTRIC COOKTOPS

General Electric JP350

✔**BEST BUY**

Also a Best Buy in 1999, GE's frameless, 30-inch electric cooktop offers an easy-clean patterned surface. This model boasts four radiant ribbon heating elements, one with a dual 6-inch/9-inch feature. Two of the other elements are 8 inches and one is 6 inches. Four hot-surface indicator lights are provided for safe operation. The controls are mounted along the right side. This unit has flush-mount capability and comes in white-on-white, black-on-black, or almond-on-almond.

Specifications: height, 3⅜"; width, 29⅜"; depth, 20½"
Warranty: 1 year, parts and labor; 4 years (limited)
Manufacturer's Suggested Retail Price: $549
Approximate Low Price: not available

Jenn-Air CVEX4270

✔**BEST BUY**

One of Jenn-Air's newer designs, this modular cooktop comes with an electric grill and one open bay, ready to accept your choice of optional cartridges. Cartridges vary in price and are in addition to the cost of the cooktop. Typically, this unit is purchased with one or two surface element cartridges, providing two or four heating elements. Cartridges can be selected in coil, halogen, or radiant formats. Grilling can be done in either bay. Optional accessories include a wok, a big pot element, a griddle, a grill cover, an energy saver grill, and a rotiss-kebob. Ideal for placement in an island or peninsula, this unit must be installed with a downdraft ventilation system. It is offered in black or white.

Specifications: height, NA; width, 30¹⁵⁄₁₆″; depth, 21⅛″
Warranty: 1 year, parts and labor; 2 years, parts; 5 years, parts (limited)
Manufacturer's Suggested Retail Price: not available
Approximate Low Price: $570-$690

BUILT-IN ELECTRIC OVENS

Jenn-Air JJW8527

✓**BEST BUY**

A single, 27-inch electric oven, the JJW8527 offers plenty of value for the money. The unit is self-cleaning, with electronic controls and variable-temperature broiling. It can be installed under a counter or in a wall. The large viewing window makes it easy to watch foods as they bake. Known for versatility, Jenn-Air also offers this unit in a 30-inch version or with a convection feature at a higher price. A top-quality double-oven version is also an option. This model is offered in black or white.

Specifications: height, 27¾″; width, 26¾″; depth, 24⁷⁄₁₆″
Warranty: 1 year, parts and labor; 2 years, parts; 5 years, parts (limited)
Manufacturer's Suggested Retail Price: $839
Approximate Low Price: $810

KitchenAid KEBI171D

Recommended

The KEBI171D is a conventional single oven that can be installed in the wall or under the counter. The elements are hidden for easier cleaning. The unit is fully electronic and offers variable-time self-cleaning and variable-time broiling. Two halogen oven lights, a large viewing window, and a control lock complete the unit. This model is offered in white or black.

Specifications: overall height, 28¹⁵⁄₁₆″; overall width, 26¾″; overall depth, 23⅞″; interior height, 16″; interior width, 22″; interior depth, 18½″

Warranty: 1 year, parts and labor; 5 years, parts (limited); 10 years, parts (limited)
Manufacturer's Suggested Retail Price: $899
Approximate Low Price: $780-$799

RANGE HOODS

Broan 41000 Series

✓ **BEST BUY**

One of Broan's many quality selections, this economy-priced hood is non-vented and duct-free. It has two speeds and operates with rocker-type fan and light switches. The unit accepts up to a 75-watt lightbulb and includes a filter. It has an RHP (range hood performance) rating of 8.70. This model is available in 24-, 30-, and 36-inch sizes at additional cost. Color choices include white, almond, or stainless steel.

Specifications: height, 6"; width, 24", 30", or 36"; depth, 17½"
Warranty: 1 year, parts
Manufacturer's Suggested Retail Price: $93
Approximate Low Price: $40-$60

Rangeaire Chef H520-300

Budget Buy

Rangeaire Chef's hood features hemmed edges and an enclosed light. It offers four-way convertible design and a rating of 200 CFM to meet your venting needs. The two-speed motor has rocker-controls. A light enclosure protects your lightbulb for extended life. This hood is available in 24-, 36-, and 42-inch sizes at additional cost. It is available in white, almond, black, or stainless steel. Comparable models are available for vertical and non-vented applications.

Specifications: height, 5"; width, 24", 36", or 42"; depth, 17⅝"
Warranty: 1 year, parts
Manufacturer's Suggested Retail Price: $68
Approximate Low Price: $49

REFRIGERATORS
AND FREEZERS

Refrigerators and freezers are among the most expensive major appliances in the home—both in terms of purchase price and operating costs. A poor choice can be an expensive mistake; a wise choice, however, can provide real value in terms of cost and convenience.

BEST BUYS 2000

Our Best Buy, Recommended, and Budget Buy refrigerators and freezers follow. Products within each category are listed according to quality. The item we consider the best of the Best Buys is first, followed by our second choice, and so on. A Budget Buy describes a less-expensive product of respectable quality that perhaps sacrifices some of the performance and/or convenience features of a Best Buy or Recommended product. Remember that a Best Buy, Recommended, or Budget Buy designation only applies to the model listed—it does not necessarily apply to other models made by the same manufacturer or to an entire product line.

REFRIGERATORS

When choosing a refrigerator, your selection comes down to two basic considerations—your budget and your family's needs. You can spend several thousands of dollars on a refrigerator/freezer with all the bells and whistles, or several hundreds of dollars on a basic version that might be smaller and have few features—but still holds and chills food sufficiently. Manufacturers have concentrated their efforts on improving styling, performance, and convenience features, and the selection of refrigerators is broader and better today than ever.

HOW TO SHOP

Selecting a refrigerator that's right for your family's lifestyle and home requires a great deal of thought—and a measuring tape. You need to consider how your current model suits your needs as far as capacity and configuration, and whether you need more or less food storage area. You also need to look at the physical space in the kitchen; you might want a huge new fridge, but you might not be able to fit it into your kitchen without doing a major renovation.

WHICH MODEL?

Side-by-side Refrigerators: These models, with their large freezer capacity and convenient configuration, are the most popular refrigerator models. They are also the least energy efficient models. Most manufacturers offer a through-the-door ice maker/water dispenser as an option on all side-by-sides and while this is a popular feature, it is also the most frequent cause of repair for these models.

Top-freezer Refrigerators: These are the second most popular models. These tend to offer smaller freezer compartments than side-by-sides, and the freezer is at eye level, placing the refrigerator at a lower and less convenient place. Top-freezer models are less expensive than comparable side-by-side refrigerators. One benefit of the top-freezer models is that they can hold very large horizontal items like pizza boxes and birthday cakes while the fridge compartment in a side-by-side unit might be too narrow.

Bottom-freezer Refrigerators: These models are catching on in popularity, although manufacturers generally offer only one or two models of the freezer-on-the-bottom units. These refrigerator freezers are the most energy-efficient, and place frequently used refrigerator space directly at eye level. In general, most freezer doors swing open like the refrigerator doors, instead of sliding out like a big drawer as they once did. And as an added bonus, the freezer compartments on these models are larger than top-freezer models. Manufacturers add lift-out baskets and sliding shelves to make it easier for homeowners to reach their frozen foods in these models.

Built-in Refrigerators: These models are still specialty-type refrigerators. Many manufacturers offer built-ins as shallower versions of their other models to fit in flush with cabinetry, but they tend to be wider than other refrigerators to make up for the space they lose in depth. Homeowners can customize their built-in refrigerator to co-ordinate with their cabinets by adding custom-made panels that can be added to the refrigerator's facade. Most built-in models tend to have unfinished sides and tops, since they generally are not exposed to the kitchen.

Compact Refrigerators: These refrigerators are small models that are made to fit into a dorm room, bar area, or undersink location. Generally, compact units can hold a few day's worth of groceries. Once, these units were limited to small cube configurations, but today's compacts are very diverse in styling. These days, a compact refrigerator might include stainless steel exterior, sophisticated styling, and interior storage options. Compact refrigerators that fit under a kitchen counter might also suit the needs of those with disabilities.

WHERE TO BUY

Shop around at different types of stores to get an idea of what you're looking for. Larger department stores and chains can offer a wide selection and good prices. The downside is that their sales staff might not have background in this appliance category and might not be able to answer all of your questions.

A specialty appliance store can be a better bet. These are not necessarily more expensive than department stores, because they deal in volume purchases and can usually offer an attractive price on specific models. The salespeople at specialty appliance stores are usually very knowledgeable about the different models and features and can guide you in your search and selection. An added benefit is that appliance stores usually have a large selection of refrigerators and freezers in all styles and price ranges.

SIDE-BY-SIDE REFRIGERATORS

Whirlpool ED27PQXF

✓**BEST BUY**

Whirlpool's roomy 26.6-cubic-foot ED27PQXF is a great refrigerator/freezer. The refrigerator has a standard through-the-door crushed and cubed ice and water dispenser, sturdy handles, and three shelves that have a rim to contain spills. The shelves can be moved up or down within the refrigerator or removed to accommodate large items. The full-width crisper, meat pan, and snack bin all have see-through fronts. The door has four deep, gallon-size bins that can be adjusted to different heights. It also has a clear egg bin. The freezer has adequate space for a large family's frozen foods. There are four shelves on the door and four more shelves and a pull-out basket in the main compartment. The ED27PQXF is available in either white or almond.

Specifications: height, 69⅝"; width, 35½"; depth, 34⅝"
Warranty: 1 year, parts and labor; 5 years, sealed system
Manufacturer's Suggested Retail Price: $1,199
Approximate Low Price: not available

Amana SXD26V

Recommended

Amana's SXD26V offers many improved features and a solid, quality design. Some of the convenience and performance features include a through-the-door water and ice dispenser (a built-in water filter ensures that the water and ice are clear) and a beverage chilling area with adjustable temperature control. This model offers 25.8 cubic feet of food storage space with 16.2 cubic feet in the fresh food area alone—the space offered is truly cavernous. There is 26.1 square feet of shelf area in both the refrigerator and the freezer—enough to hold just about anything that might come along. There are three adjustable and one fixed spillsaver glass shelves and clear deli and crisper drawers in the main compartment. The refrigerator door has gallon container storage and a total of six shelves. The freezer has a slide-out wire basket and four shelves, plus adjustable height door baskets. The SXD26V is offered in a choice of white, almond, or black.

Specifications: height, 68½"; width, 35¾"; depth, 35⅛"
Warranty: 1 year, parts, labor, and travel; 5 years, sealed system (components and interior liners)

Manufacturer's Suggested Retail Price: $1,299
Approximate Low Price: $1,200

Maytag MSD2756

Recommended

An enormous side-by-side model, Maytag's MSD2756 has 26.5 cubic feet of space. This model is chock-full of every feature imaginable and features Maytag's Dual Cool design, with two thermostats that independently control the refrigerator and freezer. One unique feature is an elevator shelf that rolls up and down to accommodate items of varying sizes. The MSD2756 boasts two additional adjusting glass shelves, all with rims to contain spills. Standard on this model is a built-in water filter for the through-the-door ice and water dispenser. There's also two crispers with humidity control, a meat drawer, five gallon-size door bins, a tilt-out door bin, a tall bottle retainer, an egg cradle, can racks, and a dairy locker. The freezer has three slide-out wire baskets, two easy-tilt door baskets, and three fixed door bins plus automatic moisture control. This model is offered in white, almond, or black.

Specifications: height, 69¾"; width, 35¾"; depth, 33⅝"
Warranty: 1 year, parts and labor; 2 years, parts; 5 years, parts and labor, entire sealed refrigeration system and cabinet liner, exclusive of door liner
Manufacturer's Suggested Retail Price: $1,649
Approximate Low Price: $1,599

Frigidaire Gallery FRS26ZSH

Recommended

The FRS26ZSH has enough refrigerator and freezer space for a large family, plus a variety of storage features that make it easy to reach food items. The refrigerator has a "Smart Fit" shelf for tall items and easy access to foods located in the back of each shelf. There are two sliding glass shelves that have a rim to contain spills. The deli drawer and adjustable temperature meat keeper both have a see-through front for easy viewing of the contents. The adjustable temperature crisper has interior lighting. Additional features include four adjustable gallon door bins and an egg bucket. The freezer has four fixed door bins, three sliding wire baskets, and two shelves. This side-by-side unit has an ice and water filter system for its through-the-door water and ice system. The FRS26ZSH comes in polished stainless steel or black.

Specifications: height, 67″; width, 35¼″; depth, 35½″
Warranty: 1 year (full); 2 years, through-the-door ice and water dispenser (full); 5 years, cabinet liner and refrigeration system (limited)
Manufacturer's Suggested Retail Price: $1,699
Approximate Low Price: $1,500-$1,600

General Electric Profile TPX24PB

| Recommended |

This GE Profile model is a high-end refrigerator that includes all the bells and whistles. With 23.5 cubic feet total capacity—14.48 cubic feet of fresh food storage and 9.05 cubic feet of frozen food storage—the TPX24PB is roomy enough for most families. Like many of the higher-end refrigerators, this unit has a through-the-door dispenser for chilled water and cubed and crushed ice. In the fresh food compartment, the refrigerator has one adjustable humidity crisper, a convertible meat keeper with cold control, and one adjustable humidity snack pan suited to hold deli items and cheeses. Two of the three adjustable glass cabinet shelves have a rim to retain spills, and two of shelves slide out. The door has four door shelves—including two gallon bins and a beverage rack—plus a dairy compartment and an egg bin. There is a wire slide-out freezer basket and three cantilevered freezer shelves (two are adjustable). The freezer door includes two adjustable and two fixed shelves. The TPX24PB is available in white, black, or almond.

Specifications: height, 69¾″; width, 35¾″; depth, 28³⁄₁₀″
Warranty: 1 year, in-home parts and labor; 5 years, sealed refrigeration system and in-home parts and labor; lifetime, parts for see-through vegetable and fruit pans (limited)

Manufacturer's Suggested Retail Price: $2,299
Approximate Low Price: $2,000

Roper RS22AQXGW

Budget Buy

Roper's RS22AQXGW is an economical side-by-side refrigerator. It has smart styling and features that are normally found on more expensive models. The RS22AQXGW—part of Roper's Value Smart Series line—has 21.6 cubic feet of combined refrigerator and freezer space. A through-the-door automatic ice maker—including crushed—and water dispenser is standard with this model. The refrigerator compartment has a see-through crisper, a temperature-controlled meat pan, and adjustable glass shelves. The refrigerator door offers a see-through snack drawer for small items and five gallon-size storage bins. The freezer has three shelves, a bottom bin, and five door storage shelves. The RS22AQXGW comes in either white or almond.

Specifications: height, 65⅞"; width, 32½"; depth, 33½"
Warranty: 1 year, parts and labor; 5 years, sealed refrigeration system
Manufacturer's Suggested Retail Price: $899
Approximate Low Price: $599-$700

Hotpoint CSX25GPC

Budget Buy

Hotpoint's 25.2-cubic-foot side-by-side refrigerator has a variety of convenience features normally found in more expensive models, making the CSX25GPC a solid value. With 15.92 cubic feet of fresh food space, this refrigerator can accommodate the needs of a large and growing family. A through-the-door ice and water dispenser is standard, as is a built-in water filer. The interior has two adjustable humidity fruit and vegetable crisper drawers and a meat pan. Three full-width glass shelves are height adjustable. The door has a dairy compartment and utility bin, plus four shelves; two are gallon-sized for large containers, and can be adjusted for height. The freezer has 9.3 cubic feet of storage space.

Five door shelves and three adjustable wire freezer compartment shelves, plus a sliding freezer storage bin, hold plenty of frozen foods. The CSX25GPC is available in white or almond, with color-matched door handles.

Specifications: height, 69¾"; width, 35¾"; depth, 32½"
Warranty: 1 year, in-home, parts and labor (full); 5 years, parts and labor, in-home, sealed system (limited); lifetime, part only, see-through crispers (limited)
Manufacturer's Suggested Retail Price: $1,049
Approximate Low Price: $880-$1,000

TOP-FREEZER REFRIGERATORS

Maytag MTB2456A

✔ **BEST BUY**

Maytag's MTB2456A has retained its high rating for the second year. It's jam-packed with details in a no-nonsense design. This model provides 23.7 cubic feet of storage, including 16.1 cubic feet for fresh food and 7.6 cubic feet for frozen foods. The fresh food compartment has four half-width glass shelves, two crispers with humidity control, and a sealed glass crisper shelf, plus a can rack that holds two six-packs and a unique locking compartment. The door features three gallon-plus storage bins, two additional shelves, a tilt-out bin, and a dairy compartment. The MTB2456A's freezer has expandable wire shelves, a slide-out wire drawer, tilt-out door basket, and a light. The exterior has Maytag's sound-silencing system for quiet operation. This model comes in white, almond, or black.

Specifications: height, 68⅛"; width, 32¾"; depth, 33½"
Warranty: 1 year, parts and labor; 2 years, parts; 5 years, parts and labor, entire sealed refrigeration system and cabinet liner, exclusive of door liner
Manufacturer's Suggested Retail Price: $1,049
Approximate Low Price: $920-$950

Whirlpool ET18PKXGW

✔ **BEST BUY**

The Whirlpool ET18PKXGW is packed with convenience features while still providing an outstanding value. This top-mounted refrigerator features large handles that are easy to grip and a large 18.2-cubic-foot capacity. The refrigerator door has three adjustable, half-width gallon-size shelves to hold milk jugs or soda bottles, as well as an egg bin and a dairy compartment. Also featured are two see-through crispers and a meat pan. One full-width and two half-width adjustable shelves have rims to prevent spills from leaking out. The freezer has one full-width adjustable shelf and two door shelves. An automatic ice maker is optional. The ET18PKXGW is available in white or almond.

Specifications: height, 66¼"; width, 29½"; depth, 31⅛"
Warranty: 1 year, parts and labor; 5 years, sealed system
Manufacturer's Suggested Retail Price: $599
Approximate Low Price: not available

KitchenAid Superba KTRS22KH

✔ **BEST BUY**

KitchenAid's KTRS22KH is a full-featured top-mount refrigerator with a lot of storage capacity and several handy features. The refrigerator compartment has 15.2 cubic feet of space, while the freezer has 6.4 cubic feet of space. The KTRS22KH has four half-width adjustable glass shelves and one fixed shelf, all with a rim to contain leaks and spills. KitchenAid has included two humidity-controlled crispers and a meat locker, all with see-through fronts, plus an egg container. The door has a variety of storage options, including three height-adjustable gallon-sized bins, a fixed bottom condiment or bottle shelf with a divider, a dairy compartment, and a five-can beverage rack. Within the freezer are a full-width shelf and two door shelves, plus ice trays. An automatic icemaker is optional. Color choices are white, almond, or black.

Specifications: height, 66¼"; width, 32½"; depth, 32¾"
Warranty: 1 year, parts and labor (full); 5 years, parts and labor, sealed refrigeration system, refrigerator/freezer compartment, and

door liners; 10 years, parts only, sealed refrigeration system; lifetime, parts only, can racks and door bins
Manufacturer's Suggested Retail Price: $949
Approximate Low Price: $850-$900

Roper RT21AKXGW

Budget Buy

The Roper RT21AKXGW is a fairly large refrigerator with an array of features. This top-mount model provides a terrific value for the average family. With 20.9 cubic feet of space for fresh and frozen food, the RT21AKXGW has two clear crispers and a meat pan—both with a glass cover—as well as adjustable glass shelves. The door has storage bins for gallon-size containers and a dairy compartment. The freezer has an adjustable full width shelf and two door shelves. An automatic ice maker is optional. The RT21AKXGW comes in white or almond.

Specifications: height, 66⅛"; width, 32½"; depth, 31⅛"
Warranty: 1 year, parts and labor; 5 years, sealed refrigeration system
Manufacturer's Suggested Retail Price: $599
Approximate Low Price: $429-$500

Amana TM18V2

Budget Buy

Amana's TM18V2 is a top-mount refrigerator with plenty of storage space and a basic design. There is a total of 21.7 square feet of shelf area in the entire appliance—13 cubic feet in the fresh food compartment and 4.8 cubic feet in the freezer. The refrigerator compartment has two full-width, adjustable wire shelves and two crisper drawers. There are two gallon-container storage bins in the door and adjustable fresh food door buckets. The freezer has a full-width wire shelf and two door shelves. This 17.8-cubic-foot refrigerator fits into a 30-inch-wide kitchen cabinet opening. An ice maker and external water filter kits are optional. For a small- to medium-sized family on a budget, the Amana TM18V2 is a great buy. It is available in white or almond.

Specifications: height, 65⅜"; width, 29⅝"; depth, 33⅛"
Warranty: 1 year, parts, labor, and travel; 5 years, sealed system (components and interior liners)
Manufacturer's Suggested Retail Price: $549
Approximate Low Price: $520-$530

BOTTOM-FREEZER REFRIGERATORS

Amana BG21V

✓**BEST BUY**

The Amana BG21V is certainly worthy of its "Easy Reach" name. The refrigerator keeps all fresh food at eye level and the bottom freezer permits easy access. This model has a 20.5-cubic-foot capacity. There are three adjustable glass shelves and two clear humidity controlled crisper drawers. There's also a deli drawer and gallon-size adjustable door baskets. The freezer features a shelf, a pull-out basket, and a light that allows you to easily recognize and retrieve your frozen storage. An ice maker kit is optional. The available color choices are white or almond.

Specifications: height, 68⅜"; width, 32⅝"; depth, 33½"
Warranty: 1 year, parts, labor, and travel; 5 years, sealed system (components and interior liners)
Manufacturer's Suggested Retail Price: $869
Approximate Low Price: $820-$850

Whirlpool GB22DKXGW

Recommended

The GB22DKXGW from Whirlpool features a 21.8-cubic-foot refrigerator with the freezer on the bottom. It is a very substantial, deluxe model with some great features. For starters, this refrigerator has four half-width shelves, all with a spill guard feature. There are two translucent vegetable crispers with humidity control, a meat pan, and an egg bin. The door has two adjustable gallon bins with clear fronts, a handy feature when trying to find small condiment jars or other objects that may be in the back. There are also four additional door shelves and a dairy compartment. The freezer features a sliding basket that is handy for accessing frozen goods in the back, a full-width shelf, and two door shelves. An automatic ice maker is optional. Whirlpool offers this model in white, almond, or black.

Specifications: height, 67⅝"; width, 32⅝"; depth, 34⅝"
Warranty: 1 year, parts and labor; 5 years, sealed system
Manufacturer's Suggested Retail Price: $1,049
Approximate Low Price: $1,000

BUILT-IN REFRIGERATORS

KitchenAid KBRC36MHS

✓ BEST BUY

Although this model has a relatively shallow depth (23½"), KitchenAid's KBRC36MHS has a large capacity. In all, this refrigerator holds 20.8 cubic feet of food (15.4 cubic feet of fresh food and 5.4 cubic feet of frozen goods)—space ample enough for a good-sized family. This model is a bottom-mount, keeping fresh food at eye level. The main compartment has four half-width, height-adjustable shelves to accommodate tall or odd-sized items, as well as two clear humidity-controlled crisper drawers. A deli locker drawer runs the full width of the refrigerator and is underneath the crispers. This unique drawer will let you store large hors d'oeuvre trays, for example. The door has two adjustable door bins and a fixed bin that can hold gallon-sized items, plus two dairy compartments. The freezer has an extra-large lower basket that can easily hold layer cakes or a turkey, and an upper basket deep enough for small pizza boxes. In addition, the freezer includes an automatic icemaker. This model comes in stainless steel.

Specifications: height, 83⅝"; width, 36"; depth, 23½"
Warranty: 2 years, parts and labor; 6 years, parts and labor, sealed refrigeration system; 12 years, parts only, sealed refrigeration system
Manufacturer's Suggested Retail Price: $4,999
Approximate Low Price: $4,300-$4,500

Frigidaire FRS24BGG

Recommended

The Frigidaire FRS24BGG is a smartly styled, high-end refrigerator that has been sized in order to blend in or sit flush with most kitchen cabinets. The refrigerator and freezer sit side-by-side and feature a total of 23.5 cubic feet of space—14.5 cubic feet in the fresh food area and 9 cubic feet devoted to the freezer. That is quite a lot of room for even a large family's refrigeration needs. This model has all the bells and whistles, including a standard through-the-door ice and water dispenser. Within the fresh food area are three sliding, adjustable, spill-safe shelves. The see-through vegetable crisper is well-lit, and the unit includes a clear meat keeper and a deli drawer. The refrigerator door has two adjustable gallon bins, two shelves, and a dairy compartment. The freezer has two adjustable door bins, two fixed door shelves, a frozen food basket, and an interior light. This model comes in black or stainless steel doors with black handles and trim.

Specifications: height, 69¾"; width, 35¾"; depth, 27⅞"
Warranty: 1 year (full); 2 years, ice and water dispenser (full); 5 years, cabinet liner and refrigeration system (limited)
Manufacturer's Suggested Retail Price: $1,999
Approximate Low Price: not available

COMPACT REFRIGERATORS

General Electric Spacemaker TAX6SNX

✔ **BEST BUY**

The GE Spacemaker TAX6SNX is perfect for installing in a bottom cabinet or for use as a small, stand-alone refrigerator. It has 6.0 cubic feet of fresh food and freezer space. It is designed for folks who are short on space. The main refrigerator compartment has two adjustable cabinet shelves, three full-width door shelves, and a dairy compartment. The 0.49-cubic-foot freezer comes with two miniature ice trays. This Spacemaker model has the ability to be coordinated with cabinets with a special trim kit and is available in white or woodgrain.

Specifications: height, 34¼"; width, 23⅝"; depth, 25⅞"
Warranty: 1 year, carry-in parts and labor (limited); 5 years, carry-in parts for compressor (limited)
Manufacturer's Suggested Retail Price: $299
Approximate Low Price: $290

Whirlpool EL05CCXFW

Recommended

If space is at a premium, the 4.3-cubic-foot EL05CCXFW from Whirlpool may be a perfect solution. This compact refrigerator/freezer stands just 34 inches high. It has a removable meat/defrost tray; two full-width, removable slide-out wire shelves; and an adjustable temperature control. The door has three shelves, one of which is twice as high in order to accommodate two-liter bottles. The freezer is large enough to hold ice trays and some frozen foods. The EL05CCXFW is available in white.

Specifications: height, 34"; width, 18¾"; depth, 20⅞"
Warranty: 1 year, parts and labor; 5 years, compressor
Manufacturer's Suggested Retail Price: $190
Approximate Low Price: not available

FREEZERS

While most refrigerators have a freezer section, it's often not large enough to handle the needs of people who shop infrequently, cook in large quantities, or grow their own produce and wish to store it. A home freezer provides this extra storage space. Like refrigerators, freezers can be expensive appliances to run. But a freezer pays for itself over the years with the money you save by purchasing bulk meat and produce (or buying food that's on sale or priced seasonably low).

HOW TO SHOP

When evaluating freezers for purchase, you must consider two major factors: space and purpose. If you are planning to use the freezer to store items for several months at a time, and don't need quick access to all of your frozen foods, then a large chest freezer would be appropriate for you—if you have the space. Upright freezers take up as much square footage as a refrigerator would, and they generally afford easy access to all materials. Upright freezers generally cost more than chest freezers and they are less energy efficient. Some upright freezers offer an automatic defrost feature; all chest freezers require manual defrost.

Clearly, a freezer with an automatic defrost is more convenient. Some manual models have a power defrost cycle to speed the defrosting process. But there is one clear benefit to a manual freezer: avoidance of freezer burn. Automatic defrost freezers take the humidity out of the air, and the moisture out of frozen foods. A manual freezer won't leave your ice cream with that "skin" that it gets with time in an auto defrost model, for example. Helpful freezer options include an alarm that sounds whenever the freezer's internal temperature drops below a safe freezing level, and a food spoilage warranty wherein the manufacturer will cover the cost of any food that is ruined if the freezer breaks down.

UPRIGHT FREEZERS

Amana AUF150K

✔BEST BUY

With 15 cubic feet of storage space, this smart, compact freezer holds a deceptively large amount of frozen food. The AUF150K is a frost-free model with adjustable cold control and an audible alarm that signals when the interior temperature rises above freezing. The freezer's interior light makes quick work of finding items hidden in the back of the unit. Four door shelves and three removable interior shelves, a wire retaining gate, and a lock and key round out the freezer's feature list. This upright freezer is available in white.

Specifications: height, 60½"; width, 30"; depth, 28⁵⁄₁₆"
Warranty: 1 year, parts, labor, and travel; 10 years, sealed system parts, labor, and travel; 10 years, food loss (if spoilage is due to defects covered by the warranty)

Manufacturer's Suggested Retail Price: $589
Approximate Low Price: $499-$549

White-Westinghouse MFU17M3GW

Recommended

If you have the need to store a substantial amount of frozen food, White-Westinghouse's MFU17M3GW should be right up your aisle. This freezer features an enormous 17.1 cubic feet of storage space. The three interior shelves and five door shelves are all designed for maximum air flow. The door's shelves can hold a massive amount. One shelf holds juice and another has a swing down gate. Other features include adjustable temperature control, magnetic door seal, and a defrost drain. This unit is defrosted manually and is available in white.

Specifications: height, 64½"; width, 32"; depth, 26½"
Warranty: 1 year, parts and labor; 3 years, food spoilage (limited); 5 years, sealed system (limited); 10 years, compressor (limited);
Manufacturer's Suggested Retail Price: $399
Approximate Low Price: $379

Frigidaire MFU14M2GW

Recommended

The Frigidaire MFU14M2GW is a manual defrost freezer with 14.1 cubic feet of storage space. Its sturdy design features three fixed zinc interior shelves and a defrost drain. The door has five shelves, including a juice shelf. All of the shelves have silver shelf retainers. This is a no-nonsense freezer with enough space to serve the needs of any average family. It comes in white.

Specifications: height, 59"; width, 28"; depth, 28½"
Warranty: 1 year, parts and labor; 3 years, food spoilage plan (limited); 5 years, sealed system (limited); 10 years, compressor (limited)
Manufacturer's Suggested Retail Price: $349
Approximate Low Price: not available

CHEST FREEZERS

General Electric FCM9DAWH

GE's FCM9DAWH is a solid chest freezer with 8.8 cubic feet of freezer space. It is compact enough to be unobtrusive in a garage or basement. This manual defrost model has a removable sliding bulk storage basket so that foods placed on the bottom don't get overlooked or lost. The unit has an adjustable temperature control and a temperature monitor with an audible alarm to alert you if the temperature rises above freezing level—a very handy feature since expensive food spoilage could occur otherwise. Other features include a lock with self-ejecting key, an interior light, and a defrost water drain. GE offers this model in white.

Specifications: height, 34¼"; width, 41"; depth, 23¼"
Warranty: 1 year, in-home parts and labor; 5 years, sealed refrigeration system and in-home parts and labor (limited); food spoilage (limited)
Manufacturer's Suggested Retail Price: $329
Approximate Low Price: $299

Whirlpool EH070FXGW

Recommended

All of the Whirlpool chest freezers are sturdy and made of quality materials. This 7.0-cubic-foot model is compact enough to be unobtrusive in a corner of the garage or basement, yet it holds plenty of frozen food. It features a sliding storage basket that either lifts out or slides to one side and an adjustable temperature control. This unit defrosts manually through the drain. A power cord lock is also featured. The cabinet and lid are made of textured steel. The EH070FXGW is available in white.

Specifications: height, 35"; width, 31½"; depth, 24¼"
Warranty: 1 year, parts and labor
Manufacturer's Suggested Retail Price: $289
Approximate Low Price: $249-$269

DISHWASHERS

Over the years, dishwashers have changed their domestic status from luxury items to virtual necessities. They are still not universally accepted as major appliances in the sense that ranges and refrigerators are; however, they don't fit into the small appliance category in that you can't simply carry one home and plug it in. Like a washer, a dishwasher must be connected to a hot-water supply, electricity, and a drain. Dishwasher installation is further complicated by the necessity of locating it in the kitchen, where space is at a premium.

Despite all this, it's difficult for most people today to get along without a dishwasher. Modern dishwashers significantly reduce cleanup time and effort: they can do a good job of cleaning most dishes and pots without the need of pre-rinsing. They reduce sink and countertop space requirements for dealing with dirty dishes, and provide a place to store soiled dinnerware until you have time to wash them. And a dishwasher's resource consumption compares favorably to hand washing: The nine gallons or so that a dishwasher uses per load is less than what many people use in hand washing the same number of items.

HOW TO SHOP

Dishwasher prices range from less than $300 to more than $1,000, plus installation. Models selling for more than $600 have features such as electronic controls, stainless-steel interiors, extra dispensers and indicator lights, and better sound insulation and vibration damping. The least expensive models might have too few spray arms to do a good job on full loads; there are many models in the $400 to $600 range that will satisfy almost any requirement. You might get more bells and whistles on a higher-priced model, but they won't do a better job of washing dishes.

WHERE TO BUY

If you're replacing a dishwasher that failed, your choice of suppliers might well be limited by what's immediately available in your area. If you have some time to shop, though, you can take advantage of frequent sale pricing from catalog stores, department stores, and appliance dealers. It's a good idea to purchase a dishwasher from a source who can provide installation and service: Dishwashers are reliable appliances, but any appliance can break down.

FEATURES AND TERMINOLOGY

Controls: Push-button or dial controls are economical and reliable. Electronic touch controls can add up to $150 to the cost of the machine, but they offer a contemporary, high-tech look. Electronic controls may also include features such as indicator lights that tell you when a drain is clogged, when the wash arms are stuck, or how much time is remaining in the cycle. A child lock-out feature, which prevents children from activating the dishwasher, may also prove convenient for many households.

Dishwasher Cycles: Three basic cycles—normal wash, light wash (or water saver), and pots and pans—handle most loads. Quick rinse (or rinse-and-hold) allows you to rinse a partial load and wait until you load more dirty dishes before adding detergent and washing a full load.

Rinse-aid Dispenser: Many units have a feature that dispenses a special conditioner during the final rinse cycle. This aids in eliminating water spots and speeds up drying.

Sound Insulation: Today's dishwashers tend to be much quieter than those sold years ago. Manufacturers use various approaches, from wrapping interiors with fiberglass blankets to using quieter-running motors.

Time Delay: Time delay is a worthwhile feature that delays operation up to 12 hours. This allows you to take advantage of off-peak electric rates and to use hot water at a time when it is not being used by other household members.

Tub and Inner Door Materials: Stainless steel is a durable and expensive tub and inner door material. Polypropylene is durable and less expensive.

Washing Action: The best cleaning results are obtained with a three-level wash, though good results can be obtained with two-level action.

Water Heating: Many dishwashers have an automatic water-temperature booster system that ensures consistently hot water (140° Fahrenheit) during the wash and rinse cycles. This feature reduces the cost of operating your household hot water heater by letting you lower the thermostat to as low as 120°F. Some dishwashers also have a hot rinse option that heats water to about 160°F. Water at this temperature may be effective at killing germs.

BEST BUYS 2000

Our Best Buy and Budget Buy dishwashers follow. Products within each category are listed according to quality. The item we consider the best of the Best Buys is first, followed by our second choice, and so on. A Budget Buy describes a less-expensive product of respectable quality that perhaps sacrifices some of the performance and/or convenience features of a Best Buy product. Remember that a Best Buy, Recommended, or Budget Buy designation only applies to the model listed—it does not necessarily apply to other models made by the same manufacturer or to an entire product line.

BUILT-IN DISHWASHERS

Most dishwashers are 24 inches wide and are installed beneath a kitchen counter. They are wired into the electrical system of your home and connected to a hot-water supply and a drain, often shared with the kitchen sink. General Electric offers a model that will fit under the sink; most other dishwashers are installed adjacent to it. Replacing an old dishwasher involves minimal installation costs. More complex installations can cost up to several hundred dollars, depending upon location.

Amana DWA63A

✔**BEST BUY**

The DWA63A manages to control five cycles and 38 options with a single rotary dial and six touchpad buttons. Cycles include pots and pans, light wash, and plate warmer cycles in addition to normal wash and rinse and hold. The dishwasher includes a hard-food disposer and three selectable water levels. Amana has managed to make loading easier by eliminating the lower wash tower, relying instead on strategically located spray nozzles. Water is continuously filtered, to make sure that soil isn't redeposited on the dishes; the polypropylene filter is self-cleaning. Sound insulation is Amana's premium installation. There's a 140°F water temperature booster and an adjustable rinse aid dispenser with an indicator. Other indicators are for water heating, clean load, and delay start (six hours). It's available in white, black, or almond.

Specifications: height, 33¾"; width, 23⅞"; depth, 24¼"; water use, normal cycle, 6 gallons
Warranty: 1 year, parts and labor; 2 years, parts only, water distribution system; 20 years, parts and labor, tub and door
Manufacturer's Suggested Retail Price: $469
Approximate Low Price: not available

General Electric Profile GSD4630Z

✔**BEST BUY**

This is one of GE's full-featured models. It features GE's CleanSensor II technology, which senses soil in the water and adjusts cleaning cycles accordingly. The GSD4630Z includes triple filtration and a "Piranha" anti-jamming hard-food disposer, which not only prevents dirty water from re-soiling the dishes but also eliminates the need for pre-rinsing. There's a special cycle for glasses, one for china and crystal, a pots-and-pans cycle, a heavy-duty pot-scrubber cycle, a light-wash cycle, a rinse-only cycle, and a power pre-soak option—all controlled by a 10-element electric touchpad. Options include a child lock, an 8-hour delay start, and a power pre-soak for food-encrusted pots and pans. There's a dispenser for rinse aid and an indicator to tell you when it needs refilling. Durable nylon racks resist chipping, and this model has a lower rack with two rows of fold-down tines for flexibility in handling different size loads. Two baskets for cutlery and other small items are provided. GE claims that their dishwashers are the quietest of all the major brands. This model is available in white, black, or almond.

Specifications: height, 34"; width, 24"; depth, 25⅛"; water use, normal cycle, 8.4 gallons

Warranty: 1 year, parts and labor; 2 years, parts only, any part; 5 years, parts only, racks and electronic control; 20 years, parts and labor, tub and door liner

Manufacturer's Suggested Retail Price: $579

Approximate Low Price: $539-$550

Whirlpool DU910PFG

✔**BEST BUY**

This is the least expensive model that employs Whirlpool's 5-level tower wash system. Its five cycles are controlled by a rotary knob and five touchpad controls. An electronic sensor adjusts the wash cycle as needed to ensure a clean load. There's an adjustable 2- to 4-hour delay, an automatic high-temperature rinse, and an extra-high-temperature rinse. The DU910PFG has an oversize lower rack and an oversize cutlery basket. The sound insulation package is very good, although not up to the standard of Whirlpool's top-of-the-line models. It carries a 30-day warranty that lets you return the dishwasher if it's not quieter than your previous unit. This model is available in white, black, or almond.

Specifications: height, 33⅞"; width, 23⅞"; depth, 24"; water use, normal cycle, 6 gallons

Warranty: 1 years, parts and labor; 2 years, parts only, filter; 20 years, parts and labor, tub and door liner

Manufacturer's Suggested Retail Price: $349-$419

Approximate Low Price: not available

Frigidaire FDB834RFR/S/T

✔ **BEST BUY**

This 5-cycle model features eight electronic touch-pad controls that enable you to select from heat/no heat drying, high-temperature wash, high-temperature rinse, and an up to 4-hour delay start. A built-in heater assures proper water temperature for effective washing. It has a self-cleaning polypropylene filter with a glass trap, and a stainless-steel macerator for grinding hard-food particles. There's a rinse aid dispenser (with indicator) and a child lock. This model has Frigidaire's ultra-quiet insulation package. The silverware basket has a small item cover to keep things in place. This model is available in black, white, or almond.

Specifications: height, 34¼"; width, 23⅞"; depth, 24¼"; water use, normal cycle, 6 gallons
Warranty: 1 year, parts and labor; 2 years, parts only, water distribution system; 5 years, parts only, electronic control; 10 years, parts only, tub and door liner
Manufacturer's Suggested Retail Price: not available
Approximate Low Price: $369-$399

Amana DWA22A

Budget Buy

The Amana DW22A is a dishwasher that will fully satisfy most homes' needs. A rotary knob and a rocker switch control its basic four cycles (pots and pans, normal wash, light wash, and rinse/hold). It has a macerator to handle hard-food particles, a rinse aid dispenser, and a self-cleaning polypropylene filter. You can select between two water levels. This model lacks an internal heater, so it's not recommended for locations that don't have a reliable source of 140°F water.

Specifications: height, 33¾"; width, 23¼"; auger diameter, 24⅞"; water use, normal cycle, 6 gallons
Warranty: 1 year, parts and labor; 2 years, parts only, water distribution system; 20 years, parts and labor, tub and door liner
Manufacturer's Suggested Retail Price: $289
Approximate Low Price: not available

UNDERSINK DISHWASHER

General Electric GSM2100Z

This space-saving model can solve the problem of where to put a dishwasher in a kitchen with limited counter space. It's designed to be installed under a sink, rather than next to one. The unit can be installed directly under the sink or offset under a double sink to leave room for a waste disposer. The door of this dishwasher is sized normally, but the top of the washer is contoured to accommodate a sink and the associated drain plumbing. The combination of a single rotary dial and four push buttons allows you to select from five cycles (pot scrubber, normal, short wash, rinse and hold, and plate warmer) as well as two wash levels and a heated dry option. The dishwasher has a rinse aid dispenser. This model is available in white or almond; both colors have a black control panel. This model was also rated a Best Buy in 1999.

Specifications: height, 34" at front, 24" at rear; width, 24"; depth, 26¼"; water use, normal cycle, 8.2 gallons

Warranty: 1 year, parts and labor; 2 years, parts only, water distribution system; 10 years, parts and labor, tub and door liner

Manufacturer's Suggested Retail Price: $379-$409

Approximate Low Price: $359-$369

PORTABLE DISHWASHERS

If space is a premium, if you're renting, or if you just want to avoid installation expense, a portable dishwasher is a worthwhile alternative. Many manufacturers offer models with casters for easy mobility. When operating, simply plug the unit into an electrical outlet, connect it to the faucet, and put the drain hose in the sink. A portable model is generally similar to the same manufacturer's mid- to low-end built-in dishwasher. Most portables can later be built in.

General Electric GSC3400ZBL ✔ BEST BUY

This model uses the same economical three-level wash system as the manufacturer's built-in dishwashers. The wash water is 100% filtered, with a self-cleaning polypropylene filter (with a glass trap). The single rotary dial and seven push buttons control the cycles, pots and pans, heavy wash, normal wash, light wash, and rinse hold, as well as the 1- to 6-hour delay start feature. Buttons let you select high-temperature wash, high-temperature rinse, and heated dry. The unit moves easily on four casters, and can be converted to a built-in model. The cabinet is white with a gray laminate top; the front has a reversible color panel in black or white.

Specifications: height, 36⅛"; width, 24¾"; depth, 27"; water use, normal cycle, 8 gallons
Warranty: 1 year, parts and labor; 2 years, parts only, water distribution system; 10 years, parts and labor, tub and door liner
Manufacturer's Suggested Retail Price: $479
Approximate Low Price: $439-$450

Whirlpool DP840DWG ✔ BEST BUY

This model features five automatic cycles, plus enough options to bring the total of cycle and option combinations up to nine. A rotary knob controls all of these. Inside, there's a three-level wash system. The racks are PVC-coated to provide a durable surface. There's a in-rack silverware basket, which adds to loading flexibility. A splash-free disconnect valve allows you to use the sink faucet while the dishwasher is operating. The unit moves easily on four casters and is also suitable for permanent installation. The cabinet is white and the front comes in black or white.

Specifications: height, 36⅛"; width, 24"; depth, 26⅜"; water use, normal cycle, 7.2 gallons
Warranty: 1 year, parts and labor; 20 years, parts and labor, tub and door liner
Manufacturer's Suggested Retail Price: $499
Approximate Low Price: $399-$429

FLOOR CARE

The era of the one vacuum-cleaner household is fast becoming a thing of the past. The reason? Over the years, the vacuum cleaner has been refined and improved, giving rise to a new generation of specialized vacuums.

However, purchasing multiple cleaners doesn't simplify the shopping process. If you have several machines that aren't tailored to your home and habits, you will not get housework done as efficiently as you would with one cleaner that really suits your needs. So before you make any purchases, answer a few questions that will help you choose the right model (or combination of models).

HOW TO SHOP

The best shopping tip of all is to be educated about the advantages and disadvantages of the various categories of cleaners. Before you get started, keep in mind the following facts about vacs:

Look for features that suit your needs, such as a HEPA (high efficiency particular air) system if you have allergies; good tools if you have a lot of furniture, molding, and drapes to clean; longer cords and hoses if you have a large space; and lighter-weight machines if you need to transport the unit between floors. Try out a vac and make sure the attachments are easy to use, the dirtbag is easy to empty, and the unit is easy to maneuver.

More and more vacs include a HEPA system, which refers to a sealed filtration system that retains almost all (estimates range from 99.97 to 99.99 percent) of the dirt, dust, pollens, and mites In the air. It supposedly filters better than any other system and it is used in hospitals. Don't be fooled by such special features. Even though a vacuum may have a HEPA suction system, that doesn't mean it is a perfect performer. For example, a vacuum's ability to pick up all the dust, dirt, and pollen possible depends just as much on the design of the whole vacuum as on its filter system. The same applies for recently introduced dirt sensors. They only let you know when the vacuum has stopped picking up dirt, not necessarily whether there is still dirt left in the rug.

Don't be misled by the amount of amps. More amps do not necessarily mean more power. Amps refer to the amount of current the unit draws when its power is on; it doesn't have anything to do with cleaning power.

BEST BUYS 2000

Our Best Buy and Budget Buy floor-care appliances follow. Products within each category are listed according to quality. The Best Buys is listed first, followed by our second choice, and so on. A Best Buy or Budget Buy designation only applies to the model listed—it does not necessarily apply to other models made by the same manufacturer or to an entire product line.

__ALL-PURPOSE CLEANING MACHINES__

Sometimes an ordinary vacuum cleaner just won't do the job, and you need a specialized cleaning machine. There are plenty of options on the market, some of which incorporate features that were once found only on industrial-strength vacuums.

Steam cleaners are now a significant presence at retail outlets. Typically, these vacs are bigger-ticket items than their conventional counterparts, but they offer a lot of added cleaning capability. Also known as spray extraction machines, these units dispense a cleaning solution into the carpet; then a brush connected to the head of the nozzle agitates the carpet pile to loosen dirt before the dirt and water are sucked back into the machine.

Wet/Dry vacuum cleaners handle messy chores, indoors and out, that conventional vacuums can't. They can clean a muddy garage, suck up soapy washing-machine overflow, and gobble up whole chunks of dirt. These units, however, are noisy and lack many of the convenient features of standard vacuums. For ease of use, you'll want an easy-to-maneuver machine with widely spaced wheels (for stability) and one that changes from wet to dry pickup with the flip of a switch. Also check to see how difficult it is to remove the tank lid and look for a long power cord, detachable blowers, and an extra-wide hose.

Hoover SteamVac Ultra F5883-900

✔ BEST BUY

Deep steam cleaners have traditionally resembled canister vacuums. But with this model, Hoover has brought the ease and convenience of upright floor vacuuming to deep steam cleaning for carpets and upholstery. It looks much like a regular vacuum, complete with a hose, on-board tools (such as a bare floor attachment and two hand tools), and the ability to convert from floor cleaning to upholstery cleaning. This unit has an agitator comprised of five rotating and interlocking brushes, which really go to work on embedded dirt, and a powered hand tool with rotating brushes, which looks much like a shower-head and can be used virtually anywhere it can reach. A two-tank design (with the upper tank for cleaning solution and the bottom tank for dirty water recovery) eliminates the need for faucet hook-ups, while a handle with a fingertip solution control trigger allows you to regulate how much hot cleaning solution is sprayed into the carpet. The unit is lightweight enough to be transported between floors. Easy-to-use features include large, simple latches to empty the recovery tank; large easy-roll trundle wheels for increased maneuverability; an eight-foot hose; and a nozzle attachment that quickly converts the unit for cleaning carpeted stairs and upholstery. It also has see-through tanks, a built-in measuring cup for solution, a toe-pedal handle release, and a brush speed selector. Given the cost to rent steam cleaners, this unit can be an economical addition to a home that has lots of carpeting and upholstered pieces. It is made of high-impact polypropylene and is taupe and deep forest green.

Specifications: height, 45"; width, 12"; length, 20"; weight, 23.8 lbs.
Warranty: 1 year
Manufacturer's Suggested Retail Price: $329
Approximate Low Price: $209

Bissell Powersteamer Deluxe 1695

✔ BEST BUY

Bissell, like Hoover, has recognized that many of us want and need deep steam cleaners that are uprights to save wear and tear on our backs. The Powersteamer 1695 looks much like a regular vacuum and can be used to deep steam clean carpets and upholstery. It has onboard tools that include an attached ten-foot hose, and upholstery and crevice tools so it is possible to attack furniture and stairs. The Powersteamer features a "SmartClean" system that includes a powerful, three-motor setup; a "DirtLifter Power-brush" that attacks dirt on carpets and has a floating suspension to self-adjust to all various height adjustments; a "SmartMix" regulating system that adjusts the amount of cleaning formula used for specific tasks (gentle, normal, or high traffic); and a pump that automatically pretreats difficult stains. It also has an easy-to-fill tank that uses tap water, an extra-wide cleaning nozzle, and it can clean in forward and reverse motion. For clean-ups, the tank removes easily. Thanks to large wheels and a comfortable grip, the unit is extremely maneuverable. The 1695 is another economical addition to a home with lots of carpeting and upholstery.

Specifications: height, 26¾"; width, 20"; length, 14¾"
Warranty: 1 year
Manufacturer's Suggested Retail Price: $170
Approximate Low Price: not available

Eureka Enviro Steamer 300A

Budget Buy

Anyone who has gotten down on their hands and knees to scrub a ceramic tile or linoleum floor, or used a relatively messy mop, will truly appreciate this ingenious new steam cleaner from Eureka. The Enviro Steamer makes it possible to clean and sanitize hard surface floors (including treated hardwoods) quickly, easily, and with no wear and tear on the user's back. Configured like a stick vacuum, the unit features a steamer where a nozzle would be, which measures about one foot wide, six inches deep, and four inches tall. Fill it with just plain tap water (it uses no chemicals) and watch it go to work. The steam it creates is 220 degrees, and it lodges in a washable, reusable waffle weave "Magic Pad" attached to the bottom of the steamer. It also has a 25-foot cord, an adjustable handle, and it comes with an accessory pack that includes two pads and a tray to rest the unit on when warming or cooling it. It is made of high impact polypropylene.

Specifications: height, 30"; width, 12"; length, 7"; weight, 6 lbs.
Warranty: 1 year (limited)
Manufacturer's Suggested Retail Price: $100
Approximate Low Price: $99

____UPRIGHT VACUUM CLEANERS____

These are best for rug and carpet cleaning. They are equipped with an agitator—essentially a beater bar outfitted with bristles—that digs up embedded dirt and grit even from high-pile carpeting. The newer uprights are more lightweight than earlier models, so they're easier to handle on stairs but still not as maneuverable as canisters. The upright is also usually less efficient than the canister in above-the-floor cleaning (upholstery, windowsills, and draperies, for example) because the attachments needed to tackle these jobs are often less accessible, and the upright doesn't roll along as easily as the canister. A new generation of upright cleaners, however, stores cleaning tools on the unit, and some come with a permanently attached hose for greater convenience on those above-the-floor jobs.

Hoover Ultra Self-Propelled WindTunnel U6425-900

✔**BEST BUY**

Hoover touts the patented suction system of its WindTunnels as the best there is, and it very well may be for an upright. This model, which is one notch down from their top-of-the-line, offers a huge bang for your buck. Its improved features, sturdier construction, and superior performance rival all other luxury brands in its class. The unit's superior cleaning capacity does a remarkable job of picking up dust and dirt, thanks to the WindTunnel technology. This model includes a high efficiency filter, a brush roll that can be raised for hard floors, and edge groomers on both sides to clean baseboards. Despite its size, it is exceptionally maneuverable, thanks to its self-propelled feature. The design is sensible, with uncomplicated slide-button controls on the unit's base; an on/off switch in the "action-grip" handle; a durable snap-open easy-change bag compartment; and a powerful "dirt-finding" headlight. A carpet slide adjustment feature and a brush roll on/off switch are also included. A six-piece tool kit (including a stretch hose, a crevice tool, a dusting brush, extension wands, and upholstery nozzle) is conveniently placed at the top of the unit in a clear-plastic-covered storage box. It also has a built-in handle so it can be carried between floors, an extra-long power cord (31 feet) for added flexibility, and a bag check indicator. It is made of high-impact ABS thermoplastic and comes in an attractive forest green and gray color scheme.

Specifications: height, 43"; width, 15"; length, 14"; weight, 20.7 lbs.
Warranty: 1 year
Manufacturer's Suggested Retail Price: $350
Approximate Low Price: $280

Panasonic MC-V7399

✔**BEST BUY**

This sleek, elegantly designed vacuum from Panasonic is loaded with features that contribute to its superior performance. The unit employs HEPA filter technology, a seven-stage system that traps more than 99 percent of dust, dirt, and pollen. Its innovative energy-saving "smart handle" allows you turn the unit on or off by gripping the handle. Other critical features include a motor bypass that channels dirt directly into the bag, thus eliminating the chance of hard objects breaking fan blades or the belt; an electronic dirt sensor that remains red when an area is dirty and turns green when it is clean; and a "QuickDraw" system that automatically switches suction to the attached cleaning wand when it is removed and used. This unit also includes standard features found other top-of-the-line vacuums such as an automatic carpet height adjustment (including a setting for bare floors), dual-edge cleaning, a built-in headlight, and an easy-change bag. Also included is a wraparound rubber bumper that protects furniture, a 14-inch cleaning width, a 28-foot power cord with an automatic release, and a handle on the back to transport the unit between floors. Lastly, a five-piece onboard tool set (featuring a stretch hose that swivels 210 degrees, a dusting brush, an upholstery tool, a crevice tool, and a wand) allows for effortless cleaning. The MC-V7399 is an exceptionally quiet, efficient performer.

Specifications: height, 42"; weight, 18 lbs.
Warranty: 1 year, parts and labor
Manufacturer's Suggested Retail Price: $350
Approximate Low Price: $249

Bissell Lift-Off 3554

✔ **BEST BUY**

The name of this 12-amp twin motor upright alludes to a rocker, and for good reason: Its body lifts-off the frame in seconds to become a full-power canister. Thanks to a fat, easy-grip handle at the top of the can, the Lift-Off is easy to cart from floor to floor or lift to use on upholstery and walls. The vacuum itself is a new product for Bissell, which teamed up with 3M to develop the Filtrete filtration system, touted as the best performing, highest quality filtration system a vacuum can have. While the system is good, it's a bit noisy. But thanks to the unit's novel design and double-duty capabilities, it is a sound investment. It also sports six onboard tools: two extension wands, a dust brush, an upholstery tool, a crevice tool, and a stretch hose. Other features include a 35-foot electrical cord (with a quick release wrap), a furniture protection guard, and a wide beam headlight. It's easy to operate thanks to simple, straightforward controls and an easy-change bag.

Specifications: height, 44½"; width, 17⅕"; length, 14"; weight, 18 lbs.
Warranty: 1 year
Manufacturer's Suggested Retail Price: $180
Approximate Low Price: $126

Royal Dirt Devil Swivel Glide Vision 086910

Budget Buy

The newest and most advanced member of the Dirt Devil line, the Vision is elegantly colorful (in an intense burgundy) and is loaded with patented "Ultra-features" that increase its flexibility and performance. This unit features a snap-out dirt container (which is transparent), a rear wheel caster design (that makes pushing and maneuvering exceptionally easy), a power edger tool for baseboards and edges, a Hide-A-Hose system (which has a reach of 16 feet), and an edge wedge tool for stairs and corners. Other features include a HEPA filtration system (which claims to trap over 99 percent of dust and allergen particles in the air), a Motorguard System (which guards the 12-amp motor), a set of five onboard cleaning tools, a headlight, a 32-foot quick-release cord, and a carrying handle. The sensible price and stylish design, coupled with all the extras, make this unit a good all-around vacuum.

Warranty: 4 years; 6 years, motor
Manufacturer's Suggested Retail Price: $200
Approximate Low Price: $185

POWERHEAD CANISTER VACUUM CLEANERS

A strong canister vacuum cleaner with a powerhead offers the best features of the upright and the standard canister. It has a canister's rolling tank (usually equipped with a tool caddy), hose, and nozzle, combined with a powerhead outfitted with an agitator similar to an upright's. When you shop for a powerhead canister, carefully examine its brush roll. Some units have independent motors that let them dig deeper into thick-pile carpet. Others have turbo- or suction-driven brush tools, which have less strength but might still be adequate for your needs. Remember, try it out before you buy it.

Eureka Smart Vac 6865

✓ **BEST BUY**

Don't be fooled by the sleek chic silver lines of this powerhead vacuum: It's not just for show. This vacuum actually delivers a superior performance and is loaded with special features. It supplies optimum suction strength for cleaning both carpets and bare floors, and has an excellent (though not HEPA) Micron Filter System, which supposedly retains 100 percent of the dirt, dust, and pollen it picks up. Another new feature on the unit is a Quick Release Wand system that makes a quick change to above-floor cleaning extremely speedy and easy. The motorized carpet nozzle, complete with a headlight for working under furniture, has a double-sweep bristle brush roll that provides dual-edge cleaning. This unit is easy-to-maneuver, thanks to a swivel joint at the base of its hose. It has large easy-glide wheels, a seven-foot crush-resistant hose, a 25-foot power cord with an automatic rewind, and a comprehensive tool set (including two chrome steel wands, an upholstery nozzle, dusting and bare floor brushes, and crevice tool) conveniently stored in a Tool-Puk on top of the unit. Touches like a bag-full indicator, an automatic carpet height adjustment, and a nice carrying handle, make this a premium unit. Plus, given its chic good looks, this is one vacuum you may not want to put away.

Specifications: height, 8¼"; width, 13"; length, 20"; weight, 12 lbs.
Warranty: 1 year (limited)
Manufacturer's Suggested Retail Price: $320
Approximate Low Price: not available

Hoover WindTunnel S3630

✔ BEST BUY

The sleek styling of this powerhead canister, which sports molded storage compartments for easy access to onboard tools, gives it an aerodynamic look. The controls are coupled with a contoured "comfort" hand grip attached to the powerhead nozzle. This model has a motorized nozzle, a two-brush agitator (with brushed-edge cleaning on both sides), and a powerful headlight. The powerful motor does a superior job picking up dust and dirt, thanks to Hoover's Allergen Filtration System, which is designed to trap over 99 percent of all dust, dirt, and pollen, feeding them into an extra-large capacity, five quart plus bag. Other features include a six-foot swivel hose, a full-bag indicator, an onboard tool set (including two chrome extension wands, a crevice tool, dusting brush, furniture nozzle, and hard floor tool), a 25-foot retractable cord (with a foot-pedal rewind), and a large carrying handle for effortless transportation between floors. The WindTunnel is made of high-impact ABS thermoplastic and comes in deep forest green.

Specifications: height, 54½"; width, 14"; length, 16"; weight, 21.9 lbs.
Warranty: 1 year
Manufacturer's Suggested Retail Price: $370
Approximate Low Price: $279

____COMPACT CANISTER VACUUMS____

These units eliminate some of the shortcomings of uprights. They are usually quieter than uprights and do a fine job of cleaning bare floors and low-pile carpets. The canister nozzle's low profile permits better access under furniture, in tight spaces, and on stair treads. Easy-to-change attachments remove dust from walls, curtains, and lampshades. Because it lacks the upright's agitator, the canister is less effective than the upright at removing dirt that has sifted down into the carpet pile. Most new canister models are extremely lightweight and maneuverable, but their suction is generally less powerful than the uprights.

Eureka Smart Vac Mighty Mite 3685 ✔BEST BUY

The name Mighty Mite truly fits this unit, which looks like a sturdy little creature ready to pounce on dirt. Thanks to its light weight (just over 10 pounds) and clever design (oversized wheels and a large handle on its back), this vacuum is remarkably user-friendly. The unit is compact and easy to lift, so it can be used right where it's needed. Best of all, it features a true HEPA (high efficiency particulate air) sealed filtration system, which claims to filter 100 percent of pollens, dirt, and dust, making this unit a real bargain for its price and performance. It has relatively good suction for its size, though it works much better on bare floors. Eureka ingeniously conceals onboard attachments (including a carpet nozzle, a crevice tool, a dusting brush, an upholstery tool, a crush-resistant hose, and two wands) that are designed to work on a variety of household surfaces (such as sofas and drapes). Other nice touches include dual-edge cleaning on the carpet nozzle, oversized wheels, a 20-foot power cord, and an extra-long seven-foot hose. The Mighty Mite is a great multi-purpose vacuum that can complement an upright for carpets or suffice on its own in a residence that has mostly bare floors. It's made of sturdy ABS plastic in an alluring metallic silver.

Specifications: height, 11"; width, 8"; length, 15"; weight, 11 lbs.
Warranty: 1 year (limited)
Manufacturer's Suggested Retail Price: $160
Approximate Low Price: $99

Sharp EC-7311

✓BEST BUY

No compact canister will perform as well as a full-sized one, but the Sharp EC-7311 is a sleek, futuristic gray-blue compact canister and a surprisingly effective performer. It is quiet and has an efficient motor for a canister vacuum, which features a triple filter system that the company claims traps over 99 percent of all fine dust and pollen. It is small (ten inches wide and 14 inches long), lightweight (just over 10 pounds), and has built-in tools (a crevice tool, and built-in combination upholstery tool with a detachable brush). With extra-large wheels and a low center of gravity, it also proves to be smooth moving and extremely stable. Best of all, it's easy to change the bag (it has a simple, one-touch release), and it has an automatic rewind for its 16-foot cord.

Specifications: height, 8¾"; width, 9¾"; length, 14"; weight, 10.6 lbs.
Warranty: 1 year, parts and labor (limited)
Manufacturer's Suggested Retail Price: $129
Approximate Low Price: $95

Sanyo SC-24L

If cost is an issue and you're willing to sacrifice a bit of convenience, this little translucent ocean blue canister vacuum is the model for you. At eight pounds it's very lightweight, and thanks to chunky wheels and a handle smack on the back, it's easy to maneuver or tote from place to place. This unit has very good suction for a canister vacuum, and it's also bagless. It does have some drawbacks, however. The dirt bin has a healthy 2.6-quart capacity, but is a little messy to empty due to its design. The six-piece tool set offers all the tools (including floor and crevice tools, a round brush, two extension wands, and a flexible hose) you need to tackle myriad cleaning jobs, but the tools are not stowed onboard. Also, the 15-foot cord is not retractable.

Specifications: height, 10″; width, 8½″; length, 13″; weight, 6 lbs.
Warranty: 1 year, parts and labor
Manufacturer's Suggested Retail Price: $80
Approximate Low Price: $75

____STICK AND BROOM VACUUMS____

Compact vacuum cleaners and broom-vacs are available in many shapes and sizes. Designed for quick spot cleanups or dry spills, these scaled-down units can be a great convenience as long as you remember that they are intended for smaller jobs. The motors on minis have less power, and the dust bags or cups must be emptied often. Cordless minis are supremely portable and ideal for room-to-room touch-ups and for car care. Corded models are more powerful and won't run out of juice, but they have the same outlet limitations as regular vacuum cleaners.

Sanyo Transformax SC-15

✓ BEST BUY

Gimmicky products can backfire, but this little green "transformer" (which is actually three-vacuums-in-one) is a great success. It cleverly, quickly, and easily changes into three different types of vacuums: a stick, a portable canister, or a hand-held vacuum—

and it does a good job in every incarnation. Thanks to its four-stage filtration system, it has very good suction and is relatively quiet. As a stick vacuum, it has edge cleaning capabilities and is easy to maneuver, thanks to its large wheels. As a portable canister, it can be used with onboard tools such as a hose, two interlocking extension wands, and a crevice tool. And as a hand vacuum, it still retains its wide mouth. It can be stored upright without tipping over, or hung from the stick handle, which is designed for wall-mounted storage.

Specifications: height, 44"; width, 10"; length, 7½"; weight, 7.5 lbs.
Warranty: 1 year, parts and labor
Manufacturer's Suggested Retail Price: $100
Approximate Low Price: $85

Eureka Stick Vac 297

✓ **BEST BUY**

While electric brooms are not very powerful, the Superbroom bagless cleaning system is better and quieter than most. It has an efficient six-amp motor that is good for light tasks (spills or quick cleanups), and electronic speed control dials to adjust and regulate the power for specific cleaning tasks. A floor nozzle with four rubberized wheels (so it won't damage wood floors), a squeegee strip, and a Dual Edge Kleener are other nice features, especially since they make it easy to use on low carpets or bare floors. The unit's light weight (about seven pounds) and built-in carrying handle make it a breeze on stairs, but a transparent 1.8-quart dust cup is the best aspect of this electric broom since it eliminates the necessity for bag changes (although you do have to empty the cup frequently). It also has a 20-foot cord and comes in a fresh, school-bus yellow with black trim.

Specifications: height, 48"; width, 10"; length, 6½"; weight, 6.5 lbs.
Warranty: 1 year (limited)
Manufacturer's Suggested Retail Price: $80
Approximate Low Price: not available

HAND VACUUMS

Black & Decker DustBuster Plus 450

The Black & Decker Plus 450 does a superior job cleaning up small jobs. Like its predecessors, it continuously charges while it is stored in a wall-mounted base so it's always ready to use; during use the switch stays locked in the "on" position to reduce hand fatigue; and it uses recyclable batteries. This model also has a crevice tool for narrow spaces, an extension wand to reach high and low places, a furniture brush, a redesigned closed loop handle, and extra bowl capacity.

Specifications: height, 4"; width, 3½"; length, 16"; weight, 2.7 lbs.
Warranty: 2 years
Manufacturer's Suggested Retail Price: $40
Approximate Low Price: $36

Hoover Dubl-Duty Supreme S1117-900

Items such as cereal or pet food are sucked right into this model's extra-wide opening, and liquids are lifted out of carpets and off bare floors with a powerful rechargeable battery. The E-Z Empty cup has an eight-ounce capacity and can be cleaned simply by releasing a latch and pouring out the contents, while the reusable filter can be washed repeatedly for peak filtration and efficiency. The unit also features a comfortable hand grip and a wall rack for storage while recharging. It has a push-button power switch, which some may consider a deficit, and two tools instead of one (a crevice tool and squeegee), which may be more advantageous for some.

Specifications: height, 7"; width, 12½"; length, 5½"; weight, 3.7 lbs.
Warranty: 1 year
Manufacturer's Suggested Retail Price: $55
Approximate Low Price: $45

LAUNDRY CARE

Although there's been a great deal of speculation about future Department of Energy standards for energy use of laundry-care products, there has been little industry response. While some new machines designed to improve efficiency have already been introduced, the majority of washers and dryers available are essentially the same as what's been available for the past 40 years or so; improvements have been in details and convenience features.

HOW TO SHOP

Picking the machine that's right for you is an exercise in deciding just what features fit your lifestyle. Convenience features can add to the price of a machine, and extra features you don't use simply waste money. On the other hand, a machine that lacks features that are important to you is no bargain at any price.

BEST BUYS 2000

Our Best Buy, Recommended, and Budget Buy wahsers and dryers follow. Products within each category are listed according to quality. The item we consider the best of the Best Buys is first, followed by our second choice, and so on. A Budget Buy describes a less-expensive product of respectable quality that perhaps sacrifices some of the performance and/or convenience features of a Best Buy or Recommended product. Remember that a Best Buy, Recommended, or Budget Buy designation only applies to the model listed—it does not necessarily apply to other models made by the same manufacturer or to an entire product line.

WASHERS

The front-loading washers that were popular in the 1940s were replaced by less-efficient top-loaders when energy was cheap and plentiful; the top-loaders offered greater load capacities, no-stoop operation, faster cycles, and lower cost. But in the interest of conserving energy, the industry is now considering taking a giant step back to the future: The horizontal, front-loading washer is making a comeback in a considerably updated form. The front-loading washer offers significant energy savings, but its disadvantages—notably its considerably higher price—have prevented it from gaining wide acceptance. Although they use less water (hot and cold) than do their top-loading counterparts and have a more effective spin-dry cycle (reducing dryer operating costs), they have smaller load capacities, longer cycles, and are not as easy to load. Most washers available on the market today are top-loaders.

FEATURES AND TERMINOLOGY

Bleach and Fabric-softener Dispenser: If you use liquid bleach and/or fabric softener, these dispensers can be a convenience. They automatically add the liquids at the optimum time in the wash cycle.

Capacity: A washer's tub size is rated in volume—ranging from "large" (roughly 2 to 2½ cubic feet) to "extra large" (about 2½ to 3 cubic feet) up to "super large" (3 to 3½ cubic feet). Unless you're washing bulky items like comforters and ski parkas, figure on about a 10- to 12-pound maximum load for large-capacity machines and 14 pounds or less for extra large and super large ones. Front-loaders typically can handle 7 to 8 pounds.

Controls: Push-button electronic controls look high-tech, but they don't really offer any advantage over the older rotary ones. They break down more often, as well.

Speeds: Most washers have two speeds—one for regular and one for gentle wash.

Tub Material: Washing machine tubs are made of porcelain-covered steel, plastic, or stainless steel. All are durable, though porcelain tubs are more apt to chip.

Water levels: Some lower-priced machines have only one water level; as you go up in price, more levels are available.

TOP-LOADING WASHERS

General Electric WPSF4170W

GE's WPSF4170W is a super-capacity (3.2 cubic ✔**BEST BUY**
feet) washer that features no fewer than 17 wash cycles. It uses two
rotary knobs, a push button, and nine touchpad controls to provide
continuously variable water levels, five automatic fabric care selections, and an extensive collection of options, including extra
rinse and extended spin. There's a seven-second spot soak spray,
and a warm rinse is an available option. This washer features GE's
SensorWash temperature control, which adjusts incoming water
temperature to match the selected cycle's requirements. The unit includes both bleach and fabric softener dispensers. This model is
available in white or almond.

Specifications: height, 42"; width, 27"; depth, 25½"; volts/amps,
115/10
Warranty: 1 year, parts and labor; 5 years, parts only, lid, suspension system, and transmission; 10 years, parts only, outer tub; 20
years, parts only, basket
Manufacturer's Suggested Retail Price: $499
Approximate Low Price: $491

Kenmore 26902

This extra-large-capacity washer (3-cubic-foot tub) ✔**BEST BUY**
has several unusual features. It has a 3-speed motor, instead of the
usual 2, which permits an extra-low-speed agitation cycle for extremely delicate loads. The water level is continuously variable. The
unit has a total of 19 available cycles, including pre-wash, soak,
and special cycles for delicates and hand washables. An automatic
temperature control monitors the temperature of the water entering
the washer, and automatically heats or cools it to provide optimum
performance. There are dispensers for liquid bleach and fabric softener and a self-cleaning lint filter. This unit comes in white or almond.

Specifications: height, 42⅛"; width, 26⅞"; depth, 25½"; volts/amps, 115/10

Warranty: 1 year, parts and labor; 5 years, parts only, transmission; 10 years, parts only, transmission, outer tub; lifetime, parts only, basket

Manufacturer's Suggested Retail Price: $480

Approximate Low Price: not available

Frigidaire FWS747RFS

✔**BEST BUY**

Frigidaire's FWS747RFS is a super-size (3.0 cubic feet) top-loading washer that features a heavy-duty two-speed ¾-horsepower motor. Its five rotary knobs control 12 wash cycles, including a pre-wash soak, a power scrub cycle for heavily soiled loads, and an extra rinse cycle. The water level is continuously variable. A liquid bleach dispenser and liquid fabric softener are provided. This model is available only in white.

Specifications: height, 43⅝"; width, 27"; depth, 27"; volts/amps, 120/15

Warranty: 1 year, parts and labor; 5 years, parts only, transmission; 25 years, parts and labor, tub

Manufacturer's Suggested Retail Price: not available

Approximate Low Price: $359-$400

Maytag MAV8000

Recommended

This washer has enough features to satisfy almost anybody. Its rotary dial, 12 touchpad buttons, and two manual switches provide 14 cycles to choose from. The washer offers infinite temperature variability and an "autotemp" feature that maintains the preset water temperature even if the input water temperature varies. It has a tub that measures a full 3.2 cubic feet. The unit includes bleach and fabric softener dispensers, as well as a 30-day detergent dispenser that holds 100 ounces of detergent. A flexible load-sensor agitator varies the agitator action to match the load. A warm rinse is an option, as are an "ultracare" low-temperature cycle for hand washables and a "press care" cycle. The filter is self-cleaning. This model is available in white or almond.

Specifications: height, 43⅜"; width, 27"; depth, 28¼"; volts/amps, 120/15

Warranty: 1 year, parts and labor; 2 years, parts; 5 years, parts only, transmission and solid-state controls; 10 years, parts only, transmission, cabinet; lifetime, parts only, basket

Manufacturer's Suggested Retail Price: $749
Approximate Low Price: $719-$736

Amana LWA10A

Budget Buy

This economical Amana is an extra-large-capacity washer that can handle the washing needs of a large family. It features a stainless-steel wash tub and a three-rotary-knob control panel. One rotary dial selects one of three water levels, another selects water temperatures from three options (there's no warm rinse), and a third selects one of six available cycles (essentially timing variations on regular, delicate, and permanent-press). This model also features a helpful self-cleaning filter.

Specifications: height, 43"; weight capacity, 25⅝"; depth, 26"; volts/amps, 120/10

Warranty: 1 year, parts and labor; 5 years, parts and labor, transmission cabinet rust-through; 10 years, parts only, transmission; 20 years, parts only, stainless steel tub

Manufacturer's Suggested Retail Price: $419
Approximate Low Price: $399

FRONT-LOADING WASHERS

Maytag Neptune MAH4000

✔**BEST BUY**

The Maytag Neptune MAH4000 is Maytag's top-of-the-line front-loading washer. Its 2.9-cubic-foot tub has a larger load capacity than other front-loaders; Maytag doesn't specify, but the MAH4000 should be able to handle 12- to 13-pound loads, and be exceptionally tolerant of bulky loads such as sleeping bags and comforters. The Neptune, while not as stingy with hot water as some other front-loaders, nevertheless provides a 40 percent savings in terms of water and up to 65 percent total energy savings compared to a top-loader. An important energy-saving feature of the Neptune is its automatic water level control; this matches water level with varying load requirements. The combination of a rotary knob and 15 push-button controls provides virtually any conceivable combination of speeds, water temperatures, extra rinses, and high-speed spin-dry options. The Neptune has a stain cycle option to deal with stains and an 8-hour delay-start feature to let you pick the time that you want the cycle to start. The drum is stainless steel; the door can be set up to open from either direction. There are also dispensers for detergent, bleach, and fabric softener. The Neptune is available in white or bisque.

Specifications: height, 43¼"; width, 27"; depth, 28¼"; volts/amps, 120/15

Warranty: 1 year, parts and labor; 2 years, parts only, 10 years, parts only, replacements related to motor and cabinet rust-through; lifetime, parts only, stainless steel drum

Manufacturer's Suggested Retail Price: $1,099

Approximate Low Price: not available

ASKO 11505

Recommended

The ASKO 11505 is a high-quality—and high-priced—Swedish-built front-loading washer. While this design has several major advantages, including compactness, quiet operation, and extremely effective spin drying, the unit's major claim to fame is its economy. The ASKO uses only about 11 gallons of water per load (compared to the 40-plus gallons required by a typical top-loader). It also reduces the load on your home's water heater: The ASKO is connected only to your home's cold water supply, and heats its own water as required. This means that your laundry will not interfere with your other hot-water needs. The washer's 1.7-cubic-foot stainless-steel drum can be misleading, in part because there's no agitator to take up space. You can fill the drum only up to the bottom of the door opening. The ASKO's load size is roughly 9 pounds, instead of a top-loader's 12 to 14 pounds. Controls consist of a combination of three push buttons and two rotary knobs, which permit you to select water temperature (extra hot, hot, warm, or cold), basic cycle (regular, permanent press, or delicate), and cycle duration, as well as pre-wash and soak options. Water level is automatically set to match your load; there are two rinse speeds available, as well as an extra rinse program. Both inner and outer tubs are stainless steel, and there's a fabric softener dispenser. The 11505 is available in white only, although the washer face can accept designer panels. This model was also a Recommended buy in 1999.

Specifications: height, 32¼"; width, 23½"; depth, 24¾"; volts/amps, 220/30
Warranty: 1 year, parts and labor; 5 years, parts only, pump and motor; 25 years, parts only, tank
Manufacturer's Suggested Retail Price: $950
Approximate Low Price: not available

COMPACT WASHER

General Electric WSKS2060

✔ BEST BUY

This little unit is ideal for situations in which space is at a premium and washing requirements aren't excessive. It's a top loader with a 2.0-cubic-foot capacity, and a trio of rotary controls that let you select from two wash and spin speeds, three temperatures, and four water levels. The six cycles include a spin-only cycle. The WSKS2060 has dispensers for bleach and fabric softener and an easy-to-clean lint filter. It's available either as a portable or as a stationary unit, and you can purchase an optional rack that lets you mount a compact dryer over the washer to further reduce floor space requirements. This model is available in white or almond—both with a black control panel. This washer was also a Best Buy in 1999.

Specifications: height, 34¼"; width, 22¼"; depth, 24"; volts/amps, 120/15
Warranty: 1 year, parts and labor; 5 years, parts only, transmission
Manufacturer's Suggested Retail Price: $499
Approximate Low Price: $479-$490

DRYERS

Dryers are relatively simple appliances. They consist of a rotating perforated basket that holds damp clothes, a fan to blow air through the load, and a heater to keep the airstream at the desired temperature. The heater can be either gas or electric.

ELECTRIC OR GAS UNITS

For most people, there's really little choice between a gas and an electric dryer. If your home doesn't have natural gas, you'll buy an electric one. If you have an option, gas dryers are considerably less expensive to operate than electric ones in virtually all locations; they're also faster. A gas dryer, however, will cost $50 more than an electric one, and it will cost more to install, as it requires an outside vent and a piped-in gas connection.

FEATURES AND TERMINOLOGY

Cycles: Dryers typically offer a choice between a timed cycle, which lets you select how long you want the dryer to run, and automatic cycles, which can be set for how dry you want the clothes to be. The two basic automatic cycles are regular and permanent press. The permanent-press cycle introduces a cool-down period of about five minutes, during which the clothes are tumbled with no heat to minimize wrinkling. To these cycles a delicate cycle is often added; this cycle runs on reduced heat.

Drying Sensors: There are two ways of controlling an automatic-dry cycle: Either the machine can measure the temperature of the air leaving the clothes, or a humidistat (a device that directly measures the moisture in the clothes) can be used. Both methods work, but humidistats give more precise control.

Efficiency: The efficiency of a dryer depends on how good the washer's spin-dry cycle is and how fully the dryer is loaded. If you normally dry small loads, you're better off with a smaller-capacity dryer. Using automatic instead of timed-dry cycles also helps.

Temperature: In some dryers, the temperature setting is preset for each cycle; in others, it can be adjusted independently. We prefer to adjust the temperature independently.

Wrinkle Protection: Clothes left in a dryer after the dry cycle is finished can wrinkle, especially if they're warm. Many machines have an automatic cycle that will tumble the clothes intermittently, circulating unheated air through them, for up to 2½ hours.

Kenmore 68932/4

✓**BEST BUY**

This dryer has a capacity of seven cubic feet and a choice of five different drying temperatures, featuring an extra-low (140°F) temperature setting for delicates. It has an easy-loading hamper-style door, and a heated dry rack for items that you don't want to tumble. This dryer has a humidistat-controlled automatic cycle and several additional cycles. The anti-wrinkle cool-down time is adjustable. Controls are mechanical. Features include a drum light and a convenient front-mounted lint filter. This dryer has four-way rear venting and is available in white or almond.

Specifications: height, 43⅛"; width, 27"; depth, 27¾"; volts/amps, 120/6 (gas model); watts/volts/amps, 5400/240/27 (electric); gas heating element, 22,000 Btu
Warranty: 1 year, parts and labor
Manufacturer's Suggested Retail Price: $500
Approximate Low Price: $499

General Electric DPSR473EW/GE   ✔ **BEST BUY**

This is a super-capacity dryer with a 7.0-cubic-foot capacity. It uses three rotary knobs to provide four drying temperatures plus an air-fluff or no-heat setting. Features include an extra-care anti-wrinkling cycle option and an off/medium/loud alarm volume control. Another rotary knob is reserved for a manual start switch, while a fifth knob selects from timed dry, automatic permanent press, or automatic regular dry. This model includes an interior drum light and is available in white or almond. This model was also a Best Buy in 1999.

Specifications: height, 42"; width, 27"; depth, 25½"; volts/amps, 120/6 (gas model); watts/volts/amps, 5600/220/24; gas heating element, 22,000 Btu
Warranty: 1 year, parts and labor; 5 years, parts only, dryer drum
Manufacturer's Suggested Retail Price: $349
Approximate Low Price: $339

Frigidaire FDE/G647RFS   ✔ **BEST BUY**

The Frigidaire FDE/G647RFS is a 5.7-cubic-foot capacity dryer that features Frigidaire's two-way tumble dry system: The drum rotates clockwise for a period of time (4½ minutes for electric dryers and 7½ minutes for gas ones), and then reverses its rotation for 25 seconds to help untangle the load. Rotary-knob panels let you select from four temperatures and four basic cycles: timed, automatic regular, automatic delicate, and automatic permanent press. A humidistat is used to control the automatic cycles. Features include an interior drum light and an adjustable warning alarm volume control. This model comes in white only.

Specifications: height, 43⅝"; width, 27"; depth, 27"; volts/amps, 120/15 (gas model); watts/volts/amps, 4500/240/20; gas heating element, 20,000 Btu
Warranty: 1 year, parts and labor
Manufacturer's Suggested Retail Price: not available
Approximate Low Price: not available

ASKO 7705

`Recommended`

ASKO's 7705 dryer is a high-quality standard-capacity dryer that's unique in not requiring an outside vent; it has an internal condenser that removes water from the drying air. This not only eliminates the need for venting, but provides a significant energy saving by avoiding the discharge of hot, moist air from the dryer. This well-made machine offers drying cycles that are controlled by humidistats. There are four drying cycles: extra dry, normal, damp dry, and iron dry. In addition, anti-crease, low heat, and timed drying (5 to 90 minutes) are available. Other noteworthy features on the 7705 include a large door-mounted lint screen, air-fluff drying, and a delay start (up to 12 hours). The 7705 features a stainless-steel drum and easy-to-clean touchpad controls. It's designed to stack with an ASKO washer, making an ideal (if pricey) installation for limited spaces or areas without access to an outside wall. The ASKO's door opening is reversible. The hefty price makes this unit a Recommended selection rather than a Best Buy. This dryer is available only in white, and only in an electric version. Vented units are available at a lower cost.

Specifications: height, 32¼"; width, 23½"; depth, 23¾"; watts/volts/amps, 3150/220/30
Warranty: 1 year, parts and labor; 5 years, parts only, controls, pumps and motors; 25 years, parts only, stainless steel tank from rust
Manufacturer's Suggested Retail Price: $1,100
Approximate Low Price: not available

Amana LEA80/LGA80

`Recommended`

Amana's LEA80/LGA80 is close to being a top-of-the-line unit, differing from the top-of-the-line primarily in having rotary knob controls instead of electronic touchpads. It's a super-capacity dryer, with a 7.2-cubic-foot capacity. It features a stainless steel drum and an extra-wide reversible door for easy loading and unloading. There are eight cycles available, including a no-heat fluff cycle, and a continuously variable temperature control. Automatic drying cycles are humidistat controlled, and the timed dry cycle has a cool down provision at the end of the cycle. The low-temperature dry cycle works at only 129°F for delicate garments. A drum light and a front-located lint filter are convenience items; a stationary rack for items like sneakers can be a help. The end-of-cycle chime's volume is adjustable. An extended tumble is selectable from a panel-mounted toggle switch. This model is available in white or almond.

Specifications: height, 43"; width, 26⅞"; depth, 28"; volts/amps, 120/15 (gas model); watts/volts/amps, 5350/240/30; gas heating element, 22,500 Btu
Warranty: 2 years, parts and labor; 5 years, parts only, rust on cabinet; 20 years, parts only, stainless steel tank from rust
Manufacturer's Suggested Retail Price: $499
Approximate Low Price: $450

Maytag PYE2200

Budget Buy

Maytag's PYE2200 isn't loaded with bells and whistles, but it is a super-capacity (7.0 cubic feet) dryer that is a remarkably capable performer. It has two rotary knobs that control three temperature settings, a timed cycle, and an automatic regular cycle. The dryer doesn't include a drum light or extended wrinkle-out option, and it lacks a volume control for the end-of-cycle alarm. But there is solid value in this basic dryer. It's available in white only.

Specifications: height, 43¼"; width, 24½"; depth, 27½"; volts/amps, 115/15 (gas); watts/volts/amps, 4750/220/30
Warranty: 1 year, parts and labor
Manufacturer's Suggested Retail Price: $339
Approximate Low Price: $330

___COMBINATION WASHER/DRYER___

General Electric WSM 2420T/2480T ✔**BEST BUY**

If you're cramped for floor space, GE's unitized washer/dryer unit might be just what you need. The WSM 2420T (with an electric dryer) and WSM 2480T (with a gas dryer) are stacked combination units with the dryer permanently mounted over the washer so that they require a meager two feet of width in the laundry area. The washer features three cycles (regular, permanent press, and delicate), with three water levels and three temperature combinations controllable through rotary knobs. The dryer section has, in addition to a timed dry cycle, automatic regular, automatic permanent press, and air fluff cycles. The WSM 2420T requires a 208-240-volt power supply. Both the gas and electric models are available in white; the electric model is also available in almond.

Specifications: height, 71¾"; width, 23⅞"; depth, 27¼"; volts/amps, 120/15 (gas); watts/volts/amps, 3300/220/30; gas heating element, 10,500 Btu
Warranty: 1 year, parts and labor; 5 years, parts only, washer transmission
Manufacturer's Suggested Retail Price: $899
Approximate Low Price: not available

SEWING MACHINES

Basic machine-stitch formation hasn't changed in the 150 years since Elias Howe patented the sewing machine. What has changed are the machine's capabilities beyond the straight stitch and the ease with which it can accomplish an ever-increasing variety of sewing techniques on a wide range of fabrics. Some new models also feature an endless variety of embroidery stitches. These machines are on the pricey side but are well worth the cost for consumers interested in both craft and utility sewing.

FEATURES

Even if you'll never use half the stitches available on today's sewing machines, you will appreciate their time- and effort-saving features: electronic control, stronger motors, improved feeding systems, jam-free hooks, and more consistent thread tension. Easier operation often expands the fabric choices and techniques you're able to try. If you've avoided sewing silky fabric, for example, or garments with buttonholes because your machine can't handle them, it's time for an upgrade. At the upper price range, hobbyists are discovering new pleasure in elaborate hooped embroidery, previously possible only on professional equipment but now standard on several top-of-the-line home models.

HOW TO SHOP

Before you buy, spend time at various machines sewing with your preferred fabrics. How does each machine feel and sound? Does it sew balanced stitches without skipping or jamming, even on hard-to-sew fabrics? How easily and efficiently does it stitch a buttonhole? Examine the owner's manual for readability. Compare any problems and suggested solutions of the various machines you test. Perform the same tests on all machines for a fair comparison.

WHERE TO BUY

As you shop, assess dealers' knowledge, services, and reputation as well. After all, few appliances involve as many variables for proper operation—thread, fabric, needle, technique—as sewing machines. What kind of lessons do dealers offer? Will they be able to help you with sewing problems? Do they have on-site parts and repair services? Will they keep you up to date on new accessories and techniques? Will they stand behind the product if you're not satisfied? Ask about their trade-in policy should you decide to upgrade.

BEST BUYS 2000

Our Best Buy and Recommended sewing machines follow. Products within each category are listed according to quality. The item we consider the best of the Best Buys is first, followed by our second choice, and so on. Remember that a Best Buy or Recommended designation only applies to the model listed—it does not necessarily apply to other models made by the same manufacturer or to an entire product line.

__COMPUTERIZED SEWING MACHINES__

Computerized machines feature electronic operation plus a "memory." Select a stitch and the machine automatically adjusts for the ideal settings (you can change those settings if you wish). Most models include memory buttonholes, so you can repeat as many identical buttonholes as desired. Increased computer memory is responsible for the tremendous expansion of the sewing machine's creative capabilities. It became possible to combine, or "program," stitches into elaborate borders or patterns and to "write" with a built-in alphabet and numerals. The latest technology enables machines to interface with a personal computer for customizing designs.

Husqvarna/Viking #1+

✔**BEST BUY**

This is a sewing machine designed to do it all, from everyday jobs to intricate needlework. And thanks to its sturdy construction and smart engineering, which Viking is renowned for, it fits the bill. This machine is characterized by ease-of-use due to its Sewing Advisor, which is designed to automatically set the correct stitch, length, width, tension, and sewing speed of the machine when you enter the weight and type of fabric being sewn. It also features one-touch stitch selection, which includes a wide selection of utility stitches, including ten buttonholes, letters, numbers, and decorative stitches. They are stored on five interchangeable touch-button cassettes (three more are optional with more decorative stitches) that fit into the front of the unit and slide in or out at will. All these stitches are displayed on a large LCD screen, which details both stitch information and a diagram of the stitch pattern in use. Thanks to its optional software (the Husqvarna Embroidery Customizing System 5 for Windows 95 or Digitizing for Windows 95), when the embroidery unit and the electronically guided hoop are attached, this machine can produce a virtually limitless spectrum of decorative stitches, patterns, and motifs. It allows you to create your own designs or scan in designs from other media to create original embroidery. It also has a four-by-four-inch embroidery field (an optional four-by-eight-inch field is also available).

Specifications: height, 11"; width, 16"; depth, 7¼"; weight, 31 lbs.
Warranty: 1 year, parts and labor; 5 years, electrical components; 20 years, manufacturer's defective parts
Manufacturer's Suggested Retail Price: $4,299
Approximate Low Price: $4,000

Pfaff Creatives 7570

✓**BEST BUY**

Pfaff originally made commercial embroidery machines, which may explain why their models for home sewers combine strength and durability with an extremely straightforward control system and an unusually creative oeuvre of stitches. The 7570 offers 500-plus built-in stitch programs and can be used with Pfaff's PC-Designer Software for Windows to modify built-in stitches or create customized designs. It has a large LCD screen that lets you see stitches as they will look, including modifications you make to them in the planning stages. It also features an embroidery unit and an electronically guided hoop attachment with a large field that measures about 4.5 inches by 5 inches (a field that is approximately 3.5 inches by 9 inches is optional). Besides this, it has innovative Pfaff features that reflect state-of-the-art engineering and versatility. Pfaff's respected integrated dual-feed system, which is ideal for embroidery and quilting functions, feeds the fabric from above and below at the same time, thus exerting more control over fabric so it will not slip. Other features include a built-in electronic instruction book, twin or triple needle sewing, full needle-piercing power at half-speed, automatic needle threading, a jam-proof rotary hook, and a high presser foot lift for sewing thick fabrics or multiple layers. This unit sports a wide variety of utility stitches, such as ten buttonholes, overlock stitches, darning, hemstitching, and bar tacks and quilt stitches. The 7570 includes one design cassette and about 30 are available overall.

Warranty: 1 year, parts and labor; 2 years, electrical components; 25 years, manufacturer's defects in material and workmanship
Manufacturer's Suggested Retail Price: $3,599
Approximate Low Price: not available

NONCOMPUTERIZED
SEWING MACHINES

Because noncomputerized machines have no memory, their stitches are usually less complex than computerized machines'. You also must adjust the stitch length and width manually. But some of these models do have electronic circuitry. The most common electronic element is speed control, which allows full needle penetration power for any fabric weight even at the slowest speed. Electronic control also allows more precise reaction during the start and stop of motion, enabling the machine to make one stitch at a time for precise accuracy.

Bernina 1008
✔BEST BUY

The reputable Bernina is so straightforward and easy to use, directions are practically unnecessary. It is a sturdy machine that is often used in school home economics programs to teach sewing. Tension is self-gauged by the machine (via the CB-hook system), making it adjustment free. Simple operating controls are logically arranged and clearly marked for quick and easy adjustments, making it simple to alter stitch width and length. There are 16 practical and decorative stitches, including straight, zigzag, blind, and buttonhole, as well as special stitches for stretch fabrics.

Warranty: 1 year, labor; 2 years, electrical; 20 years, defects in material and workmanship
Manufacturer's Suggested Retail Price: $899
Approximate Low Price: $599-$699

Husqvarna/Viking Sew Easy 330

Recommended

The Sew Easy 330 (part of Viking's 300 series) fits its name perfectly. It offers astonishing utility, extremely user-friendly controls, and loads of features that make it a superb selection for any home sewer. Its 44 built-in stitches cover a wide variety of stitch types (including buttonholes). Other important features include an easy and efficient control system; a feed system that feeds all weights of fabrics evenly; a free-arm design for sewing cuffs, sleeves, and hems; an accessory tray and flatbed extension for sewing large items; drop-in jam-proof bobbins; adjustable stitch widths and lengths; an up-front horizontal spool system; twin needle sewing; a built-in bobbin winder; and electronic speed control. This sewing machine offers plenty of features and operational ease for the price.

Warranty: 1 year, labor; 5 years, electrical components; 20 years, defective parts
Manufacturer's Suggested Retail Price: $799
Approximate Low Price: $630-$700

ENVIRONMENTAL APPLIANCES

Making our home environments comfortable and healthy has become a priority in this modern era of air pollutants, heat indexes, and high pollen counts. These environmental control appliances can help ensure that your house is a clean, comfortable place for you and your family.

BEST BUYS 2000

Our Best Buy and Recommended environmental appliances follow. Products within each category are listed according to quality. The item we consider the best of the Best Buys is first, followed by our second choice, and so on. Remember that a Best Buy or Recommended designation only applies to the model listed—it does not necessarily apply to other models made by the same manufacturer or to an entire product line.

CEILING FANS

Ceiling fans can move large amounts of air in the home and can reduce cooling costs by providing air circulation throughout the house. Ceiling fans range in price from $30 to $1,000. Generally speaking, the more expensive the unit, the better it will perform and the more attractive the design. Unless you are looking for a ceiling fan that is a focal point in a room, however, a good low- to medium-priced fan will offer excellent air circulation and last for years.

QUALITY

Lower-priced fans are usually noisy. This is commonly caused by a poorly balanced motor and blades, poor bearing tolerance, or loose motor windings. For medium- to high-priced units expect a sealed, well-balanced motor and blades; heavy-duty castings; attractive design features (such as brass fittings and center-mounted blades); and sealed bearings. An important concern with ceiling fans is how low they hang in a room. Most ceiling fans are designed to be installed in a room with standard eight-foot ceilings. If you have low ceilings but would like a ceiling fan, look for a unit that mounts flush to the ceiling or has blades that extend from the sides of the motor rather than below it. However, if you have high ceilings, consider an extension tube for the fan to lower its height to the ideal eight-foot level.

FEATURES

The majority of ceiling fans have five blades, although four bladed models are also available in the smaller sizes. Blade sizes range from 29 to 62 inches across; 52 inches is the most popular size. Most fans use a pull chain to turn the unit on/off as well as for setting one of two or three speeds, and a switch for reversing the direction of the spin. In theory, a ceiling fan pushes air down to cool the room during the warm months, and pulls cool air up, which forces warm air down, during the heating season. Most fans have a light fixture or offer an optional lighting package.

Design House Rio Outdoor 1250

✔ **BEST BUY**

The Design House Rio Outdoor is designed and UL-rated for use outdoors, which makes it an excellent choice for an outdoor porch or covered deck. The motor is sealed, and the blades are made of acrylic for long life in humid conditions. This unit contains a low-wattage light fixture, which surrounds the motor housing and provides a soft, gentle light. It has a three-speed, reversible motor, and four 52-inch, acrylic white blades. Installation is simple and the fan can be flush mounted, standard mounted, or sloped (up to 35 degrees). Accessory items include wall-mounted controls, an acrylic light kit, and extension rods (12, 18, 24, 36, 48, 60, and 72 inches) for high ceilings. Also available as options are a dual fan speed and light dimmer control and a light fixture.

Warranty: lifetime (limited)
Manufacturer's Suggested Retail Price: $179
Approximate Low Price: not available

Hunter Sojourn II 25877

✔ BEST BUY

The Hunter Sojourn II is a top-of-the-line ceiling fan that features mid-body blade mounting. This configuration allows more headroom than conventional, below-the-motor blade mounting. Like all Hunter ceiling fans, the Sojourn offers excellent air movement and a quiet, reversible motor. There are three fan speeds: high, medium, and low. This fan will quietly move 9,400 cubic feet of air per minute (CFM) on high speed. There are two different models of the Sojourn II (model 25877 is white while model 25872 is brushed chrome), both with five 52-inch blades and different choices of blade colors, including white, black, cherry, and light oak. This unit is designed for a flush mount to the ceiling. Hunter also offers a variety of wall-mounted controls, light fixtures, and extension tubes for installation on high ceilings.

Warranty: 1 year, parts and labor (limited); lifetime, motor parts (limited)
Manufacturer's Suggested Retail Price: $315
Approximate Low Price: not available

Hunter Whisper Wind 78044

Recommended

The Hunter Whisper Wind 78044 ceiling fan is available with five reversible rosewood/medium oak 52-inch blades. The patented AirMax three-speed motor is quiet and reversible. This fan will quietly move 9,500 cubic feet of air per minute (CFM) on high speed. Installation is simple and includes three position options: flush to the ceiling, standard height, and extra long or angled (optional extension tubes are required for ceilings higher than eight feet). Accessory items include wall-mounted switch, remote control, optional light kits, and extension tubes. This is a dependable, medium-priced ceiling fan that should provide years of service.

Warranty: 1 year, parts and labor; lifetime, motor
Manufacturer's Suggested Retail Price: $215
Approximate Low Price: $118-$200

AIR CONDITIONERS

When shopping for a room air conditioner, it is important to choose a unit with enough cooling capacity for your space without getting one that is too large for your needs. A too-small unit won't cool the room enough. A too-large unit will waste energy and won't dehumidify the room properly. As a rule, it is better to buy several small units than to use one large air conditioner to cool several rooms.

Area to be cooled (in square feet)	Cooling capacity needed (in Btu)
up to 150	4,000-5,000
150-250	5,000-6,000
250-450	6,000-8,500
450-600	8,500-11,000
600-900	11,000-14,000
900-1,200	15,000-19,000

HOW TO SHOP

The majority of air conditioners are designed to be installed in conventional single- and double-hung windows (which open up from the bottom). Some models can also be installed in sliding windows as well. Air conditioners cannot be installed in casement or louvered windows. Measure your window before you go shopping for an air conditioner. All units have accordion-like wings that pull out sideways to seal the space between the air conditioner and the window frame. Most units can also be installed through a wall. Through-the-wall installation means cutting a suitable size hole in the wall and exterior siding, then adding a frame to support the unit. You'll have less air leakage in a through-the-wall installation, making your unit more effective in the summer and keeping the warm air in during the winter.

Air conditioners are not maintenance free. Clean the foam filter in the front of the unit at the beginning of the season and at least once a month. Simply remove the filter, rinse it under running water, let it dry, and reinstall. The exterior fins perform the actual heat exchange and should be kept as clean as possible. These fins are thin metal and bend easily so work carefully when dusting. If any of the fins become bent, carefully straighten them out with a piece of rigid plastic, such as a credit card. Rinse the fins on the exterior as well.

When shopping for air conditioners, pay close attention to the large yellow Energy Efficiency Ratio (EER) stickers on the front of the units. Since January 1, 1990, the federal government has required all room (window) air conditioners to have an EER of at least 8.0. The EER is computed by dividing cooling capacity, measured in British Thermal Units (Btu) per hour, by the watts of electricity used. The higher the EER, the more efficient the unit, and the less it will cost to operate.

5,000-12,000 BTU

Carrier TCA081P

✔BEST BUY

The Carrier TCA081P is the top model in the Siesta II series of window air conditioners. This model has three fan speeds, six-way air-flow control, exhaust control, and an energy-saver switch. It is a quiet and reliable unit suitable for bedrooms and living areas up to 400 square feet. It has a cooling capacity of 8,600 Btu/hour, and an EER of 10.0. This unit will fit into larger windows, from 26 to 36 inches in width, and requires a minimum opening height of 14½ inches. Also included in this model is a high-efficiency rotary compressor, easy-to-remove filter, automatic thermostat, built-in carry handle, and factory-installed expandable wing panels. As with all Carrier window-mount air conditioners, this model includes special locking screws to prevent removal of the unit and entry by intruders.

Specifications: length, 22"; height, 15½; depth, 14½"; weight, 63 lbs.; volts, 115; watts, 860
Warranty: 1 year, parts and labor; 5 years, sealed refrigeration system
Manufacturer's Suggested Retail Price: not available
Approximate Low Price: $339-$380

Panasonic CW-806TU 3-in-1

✔ **BEST BUY**

The Panasonic CW-806TU is a high-efficiency (EER rating of 10.0) window-mount air conditioner. It has a Btu/hour rating of 7,800. This unit can be installed in a double-hung window or sliding window (optional installation kit ME-68S required), or through a wall. It features a slide-out chassis for easy installation. A double-layered top panel adds strength and reduces vibration. Extra sound-absorbing insulation in the cabinet and the compressor's location in the rear of the unit make for quiet operation. Other features include a one-touch air filter, two cooling speeds, a separate thermostat, ventilation control, two fan speeds, left- or right-side power cord, and an economy operation mode.

Specifications: length, 17^{32}/$_{23}$"; height, 13^5/$_8$"; depth, 20^7/$_8$"; weight, 66 lbs.; volts, 115; watts, 780
Warranty: 1 year, parts and labor (in-home service); 5 years, sealed refrigeration system (in-home service)
Manufacturer's Suggested Retail Price: $480
Approximate Low Price: $349-$391

Sharp AF-M808X

Recommended

The Sharp AF-M808X is a window-mount air conditioner with a Btu/hour rating of 8,000. This unit is part of new line of window-mount air conditioners from Sharp that run about 25% quieter than competing units. The AF-M808X employs two independent motors—indoor fan and outdoor fan—letting you control the speed of the fans separately. This lets the indoor fan run at an optimal lower speed, reducing operational noise. Dial type controls adjust coolness and fan speeds (this unit has three fan speeds and a fan-only mode). It is compact and will fit into a small window frame (27^5/$_{32}$-inch minimum) or windows up to 38^{19}/$_{32}$ inches wide. Other features include an adjustable thermostat, one-touch filter, four-way air direction control, exhaust lever, slide-out chassis, and easy installation mounting kit. This unit is gray in color and controls are located on the top right face. It has an EER rating of 9.0.

Specifications: length, 22¹⁄₁₆″; height, 14¾″; depth, 24⁵⁄₁₆″; weight, 84 lbs.; volts, 115; watts, 880
Warranty: 1 year, parts and labor (in-home service); 5 years, sealed cooling system (limited)
Manufacturer's Suggested Retail Price: $400
Approximate Low Price: $380

Carrier TCB051B

The TCB051B is also part of the Siesta series of [Recommended] lightweight air conditioners from Carrier. This model is a good choice for a bedroom or other small living area up to 250 square feet. It has a Btu/hour rating of 5,100. The unit weighs only 46 pounds and the built-in carrying handle makes moving it easy. The filter is located in the front and it is easy to remove and clean. It has two fan speeds and an automatic thermostat. Built-in sound reducers that isolate moving parts, a rust-proof fan and blower wheels, and a high-efficiency fan motor contribute to this model's quiet operation. This unit has factory-installed expandable wing panels and special locking screws to prevent removal of the unit and entry by intruders. It has an EER of 9.0.

Specifications: length, 19″; height, 14″; depth, 11″; weight, 46 lbs.; volts, 115; watts, 570
Warranty: 1 year, parts and labor; 5 years, parts and labor on sealed system (limited)
Manufacturer's Suggested Retail Price: $245
Approximate Low Price: not available

12,000-18,000 BTU

Panasonic CW-1805SU

The Panasonic CW-1805SU is a large-capacity ✔ **BEST BUY** room air conditioner with a Btu/hour rating of 18,000. This unit can be installed in a double-hung window or through a wall. It has an air swing feature, which spreads cool air side to side during operation. Air flow can also be directed. It has two cooling speeds and two fan-only speeds. Other worthwhile features include a 4-way air deflection system, left or right hand power cord, ventilation control, one-touch air filter, economy operation mode, and slide-out chassis. It has an EER of 8.8. This unit requires a 230-volt electrical outlet.

Specifications: length, 26"; height, 16⅞"; depth, 28-25/32"; weight, 139 lbs.; volts, 230; watts, 2,050
Warranty: 1 year, parts and labor, (in-home service); 5 years, sealed refrigeration system (in-home service)
Manufacturer's Suggested Retail Price: $700
Approximate Low Price: $569-$589

AIR CARE APPLIANCES

The air in our homes is important for good health, and a number of factors can determine overall quality. During the heating season, for example, household air tends to be dry, the end result being a dry throat. Conversely, during the warmer months, air in the home tends to be laden with moisture, thus feeling warmer. Internal air can also contain a variety of airborne particles—from pets, carpeting, furnishings, and smoke—and breathing this air can cause respiratory problems. There are a variety of appliances designed to improve the quality of household air.

TYPES OF AIR CARE APPLIANCES

Humidifiers: If, during the heating season, you walk across a carpeted room and get a static electricity shock when you touch a doorknob or light switch you should consider increasing the humidity of your home. The two humidifiers we review are table-top units that are portable and simple to use. Either unit can be used in one room during the day and in a bedroom at night. Both units have replaceable filters to trap airborne particles and odors.

Dehumidifiers: These units are not just for keeping a basement dry year-round. In the summer, they can help keep your house cool by reducing the amount of moisture in the air. The unit we cover is a stand-alone unit that runs quietly and can be centrally located in the home.

Air Filters: These units come in a variety of sizes, capacities, and styles. The three models we cover have HEPA (High Efficiency Particulate Air) filters that remove the smallest of pollutants and pollen from the air. HEPA filters remove more 99% of all small particles in the air. If you have asthma, allergies, or respiratory problems, a unit equipped with a HEPA filter might help you to breathe easier. Because they filter large amounts or air, all air filters tend to be noisy, especially on a high setting. For this reason, you might want to locate your air filter in a corner of a room, rather than in the center. All units reviewed here are portable.

HUMIDIFIERS

Hunter Humidifier 33350

✔ BEST BUY

The Hunter Humidifier 33350 is a quiet, dependable unit. It features a PermaWick filter that never needs replacement. This unit offers a patented anti-bacterial system that provides 100-percent protection against bacteria, mold, and spores. Special polymers are molded into the plastic parts of the unit to prevent the growth of bacteria and other microorganisms. A regulated release system eliminates stagnant water around the filter to further prevent bacteria and germs. This unit has a refill light that indicates when the unit is low on water, and an auto shut-off feature in case the unit runs out of water. It has an adjustable humidistat, a two-speed motor, and an automatic moisture-regulation system. A specially designed clear plastic water tank makes for easy refilling with 3½ gallons of water. This unit covers 1,600 square feet of floor space.

Specifications: length, 20⅝"; height, 14⅛"; depth, 15⅝"; weight, 12 lbs. (empty)
Warranty: 1 year, parts and labor; 5 years, motor

Manufacturer's Suggested Retail Price: $105
Approximate Low Price: $69-$89

Bemis Humidifier 338 000

The Bemis Humidifier 338 000 is a quiet, table-top unit that can put up to 4½ gallons of moisture into your home per day. It can cover up to 1,020 square feet of floor space in a twenty-four hour period. This unit features a replaceable two-wick system and two replaceable air filters. It has three fan speeds, a special night setting, and an automatic humidistat for maintaining a desired humidity level. This unit has two tinted plastic water containers (1.6 gallons each), which are easy to remove and fill.

Specifications: length, 19½"; height, 12"; depth, 13¼"; weight, 10.5 lbs. (empty)
Warranty: 1 year (limited)
Manufacturer's Suggested Retail Price: $80
Approximate Low Price: $62-$70

DEHUMIDIFIER

Sears Kenmore Dehumidifier 5751

Recommended

The Sears Kenmore Dehumidifier 5751 is a large capacity unit. It features a two-speed fan, 24-pint collection pan, and drain hose connection. It also has a water-level control and auto shut-off when the collection pan is full. Other features include an automatic de-icer control, humidistat, and four swivel caster-type wheels for easy movement.

Specifications: length, 12⅗"; height, 22³⁄₁₀"; depth, 17"; weight, 61 lbs.
Warranty: 1 year, parts; 5 years, labor, sealed system
Manufacturer's Suggested Retail Price: $220
Approximate Low Price: not available

AIR FILTERS

Hunter HEPAtech 30375

The Hunter HEPAtech 30375 is a quiet, highly efficient air filter that can clean the air six times per hour in a 20×22-foot room. This unit features HEPA filtration with an additional sub-micron filter. The unit is portable and can be operated on a floor, table, or shelf, against a wall, or in a corner. It has electronic touch pad controls, a three-speed fan, a power indicator light, and an auto shut-off feature. A filter check light reminds you to replace the filter when required. This air filter was the quietest unit we tested.

Specifications: length, 18¼"; height, 22⅜"; depth, 11⅜"; weight, 19 lbs.
Warranty: 1 year, parts and labor; 5 years, motor
Manufacturer's Suggested Retail Price: $209
Approximate Low Price: $189-$210

Bemis Air Purification System 200-001

The Bemis 200-001 is a highly efficient system in a triangular design package. This is a portable unit that can be placed against a wall or on a table or shelf. It features true HEPA air filtration and has a pre-filter to extend the life of the HEPA filter. A sensor monitors the air flow in this unit and signals when the filter needs replacement. This unit will clean the air in a 17×20-foot room five times an hour. Electronic controls are located on the top of this model.

Specifications: length, 20¼"; height, 19"; depth, 14³⁄₁₆"; weight, 24 lbs.
Warranty: 5 years (limited)
Manufacturer's Suggested Retail Price: $209
Approximate Low Price: $171-$189

Honeywell Enviracaire Air Cleaner 12520 ✔**BEST BUY**

The Honeywell Enviracaire Air Cleaner 12520 is a large-capacity model that features true HEPA air filtration. It is cylindrical in shape and therefore takes in, filters, and discharges clean air in a 360-degree circle. On high speed, it can re-circulate the air in a 16×20-foot room six times an hour. The HEPA filter will remove 99.97 percent of all the particles in the air, including the most common allergens and pollutants. A wrap-around pre-filter extends the life of the HEPA filter and should be replaced every three months. Life of the HEPA filter is from three to five years depending on the type of air being filtered. This unit is lightweight and has a convenient top-mounted carrying handle for moving it from room to room.

Specifications: height, 12¾"; depth, 17¾"; weight, 17 lbs.
Warranty: 5 years (limited)
Manufacturer's Suggested Retail Price: $200
Approximate Low Price: $179-$189

PORTABLE HEATERS

While portable heaters come in a variety of sizes and fuel types, the units we review are both powered by electricity. Operate a portable heater on a sound, flat surface only. Keep any heater away from flammable materials, especially curtains, blankets, and other fabrics. Extension cords should not be used with portable electric heaters. Plug the unit directly into a wall outlet with a 20-amp rating.

Lakewood 7096 ✔**BEST BUY**

The Lakewood 7096 is an efficient, clean source of heat suitable for any room in the home. It resembles a miniature old-fashioned hot-water radiator with seven steel fins to disperse the heat. It is filled with diathermic oil, which is heated by internal elements and disperses heat quickly and evenly. The unit is sealed at the factory and never needs refilling. It has three heat settings: 600, 900, and 1,500 watts. The seven-foot-long power cord can be plugged into any 20-amp, grounded household outlet. A thermal fuse shuts off the unit to prevent internal overheating. This unit has a separate thermostat for constant temperature and automatic on/off cycling. The controls are located on the right side of the unit and are easy to read. It has two wheels and a heat-resistant handle, which makes moving the unit convenient.

Specifications: length, 16"; height, 25½"; depth, 6½"; weight, 28 lbs.
Warranty: 1 year, limited
Manufacturer's Suggested Retail Price: $50
Approximate Low Price: not available

Duracraft Oscillating Ceramic Heater CZ-320 ✔BEST BUY

The Duracraft Oscillating Ceramic Heater CZ-320 is a compact, efficient electric heater for home use. It features a ceramic heating element, two heat settings (750 and 1,500 watts), and has an adjustable thermostat to help maintain a desired temperature. When the oscillating button is pressed, the CZ-320 can disperse heat in a 90-degree left-to-right pattern or, with the switch off, in one direction only. The unit includes a fan-only setting. This unit has an internal high temperature circuit breaker to prevent overheating. Other safety features include a patented child-resistant Safeguard switch and a power indicator light. It has an six-foot-long power cord and a tip-over switch that turns the unit off if it is knocked over.

Specifications: length, 9"; height, 9½"; depth, 7⅞"; weight, 4 lbs.
Warranty: 3 years (limited)
Manufacturer's Suggested Retail Price: $35
Approximate Low Price: not available

BABY EQUIPMENT

Choosing the best baby products can be overwhelming for new parents. These days, the baby equipment industry is more innovative than ever, with companies racing to develop the most advanced products at the most competitive prices. That's great news, but it means the market can be confusing for the inexperienced shopper.

HOW TO SHOP

When buying baby equipment, keep in mind that your first considerations are safety, comfort, ease of use, and convenience; looks are a fringe benefit. However, given the demands of the market today, most of the following products have come a long way and are quite stylish. Gone are the days when babyish pastels or prints dominated design; most products today sport tailored or classic motifs and sleeker lines.

Baby products are available in many different types of stores. Although mass retailers almost always beat department stores when it comes to price, they don't offer the same services. For instance, the latter will often deliver and set up large pieces of equipment (such as cribs) or have repair departments. Ask about the services a store provides when making purchases.

SAFETY TIPS

Several organizations monitor juvenile products. The Juvenile Products Manufacturers Association (JPMA) rigorously tests and certifies products in categories not covered by government regulations. Products that pass the JPMA test may state this on their labels, so look for the JPMA seal of approval.

Make sure all hinges and rough parts are covered so that they cannot pinch or scratch your baby's fingers or toes. Look for baby-safe materials such as plastic and rubber; avoid metals because they can heat up from the sun. Also look for soft, comfortable fabrics, such as cotton.

Make sure that small parts are firmly secured. Small objects that could come loose represent a choking hazard for your baby.

Products meant to hold your baby should have a sturdy frame that won't tip over. Look for a high chair with a wide base, and for a stroller with large wheels and a substantial body that won't tip when you hang your bag on the handlebars. Check straps on car seats and high chairs to see that these will hold your baby securely.

Once you've made your purchase, it's important to stay on top of recall information in case the product turns out to be faulty. The U.S. Consumer Product Safety Commission keeps track of most children's products that have been recalled. The National Highway Traffic Safety Administration tracks recalled car seats. Also local newspapers routinely publish information about baby equipment recalls if a large manufacturer is involved.

BEST BUYS 2000

Our Best Buy, Recommended, and Budget Buy baby equipment follow. Products within each category are listed according to quality. The item we consider the best of the Best Buys is first, followed by our second choice, and so on. A Best Buy, Recommended, or Budget Buy designation applies only to the model listed—it does not necessarily apply to other models made by the same manufacturer or to an entire product line.

PORTABLE CRIBS AND PLAY YARDS

Play yards (or playpens) are the portable cribs that sport bassinet attachments. Even though classic playpens and portable cribs can be used interchangeably, it's better to use each of these products exactly as specified by the manufacturer. A piece of equipment intended only for use as a portable crib should not be used as a play yard, and vice versa. It's also important to stop using these units when your baby outgrows them; for the most part, they are intended for children less than 34 inches tall or weighing less than 30 pounds.

FEATURES

A portable crib is a handy piece of equipment for travel or for overnight visits to friends and relatives, but it should not be used on a permanent basis in place of a full-size crib. Most portable cribs are rectangular and have sturdy metal or plastic frames, hard bottoms covered with padding, and fabric sides with mesh panels. Generally, these cribs fold down into a compact package that fits inside the carrying case.

Some play yards closely resemble portable cribs, while others are a bit roomier and have mesh sides that allow parents a full view of the child inside. Some also have drop-down sides that make it easier to fold the unit away. These sides, however, should always be raised when the play yard is in use.

QUALITY

When purchasing either a portable crib or a play yard, first make sure that it's sturdy. Give it a shake to see whether it will tip over or accidentally collapse. Look for tightly woven mesh, so small fingers or buttons on baby clothing can't get caught. Also be sure that the mesh is securely attached to the top rail and floor of the unit and that any vinyl on the unit is sufficiently thick. Otherwise, when a baby sucks on it—or chews it when he or she is teething— small pieces can get stuck in the child's throat. For this same reason, make sure no foam is exposed for tiny fingers to pick at. Watch for sharp points or edges and exposed seams or hardware.

PORTABLE BASSINET/PLAY YARD

**Kolcraft Corner Suite Travel
Play Yard with Deluxe Bassinet 18184**

✓BEST BUY

Thanks to a unique triangular shape and profusion of extra features, this is one of the more innovative combination bassinet/play yards on the market. The disarmingly elementary configuration offers an advantage over the usual rectangular models, since it can fit in a corner to save floor space and actually provides the baby with more interior play space (its width and depth are both 42 inches). The removable bassinet attachment, which self-suspends about nine inches down from the top rail of the unit, is relatively sturdy (but never leave baby unattended when using this feature, or leave a young child in the room who can play with it and loosen it). It also features a built-in support pad that provides extra firmness for infants and a zippered compartment that can be used to safely store baby paraphernalia. All the standard features of a good travel play yard and portable bassinet are also included on this model. Its construction is sturdy but lightweight, and it incorporates padded railings so all corners are smooth. Strong nylon mesh on all sides allows parents to better see babies that are in the unit. This unit can be assembled and collapsed quickly and easily (even with the bassinet attached) into its own travel bag. An attractive tailored navy-and-white plaid fabric covers the unit. The only feature the unit lacks is wheels to easily move the unit from room to room.

Warranty: 1 year
Manufacturer's Suggested Retail Price: $130
Approximate Low Price: $90-$120

PLAY YARDS

Kolcraft Octagon Playard 18503   ✔ **BEST BUY**

At roughly 40 inches square, this may very well be the roomiest play yard on the market. Despite its large size, it is still relatively easy to set up and take down, thanks to double-drop sides with sturdy Stay-Loc hinges. Once collapsed, the unit is a manageable size for storage or travel, has a built-in carrying handle, and weighs only 20 pounds. While the strong steel frame and floorboard are covered with padded nylon casings and mats, the sides of the unit are a strong mesh that is easy to see through. Coupled with the unusual design of the frame, which features center support legs that extend diagonally to the unit's outside edges (instead of posts at each corner), this unit allows parents to view a child from every angle. The floor pad also comes in two different fabrics (vinyl or cloth) and is securely fastened to the bottom of the unit so a baby cannot roll under it and suffocate.

Warranty: 1 year
Manufacturer's Suggested Retail Price: $70
Approximate Low Price: $60

Cosco Padded Play Yard 05-388

`Budget Buy`

This fold-up play yard sports all the important features for anyone on a budget. Fabricated with a sturdy, powder-coat steel frame, this play yard has fully padded top rails and rail caps and legs. The floor boards feature padded vinyl mats (in a variety of patterns and colors) that can be removed for cleaning and are securely attached to the unit so a baby can't roll under the pad and suffocate. The sides of the unit are made of strong nylon mesh that is easy to see through, and the frame has support legs that extend diagonally to the unit's outside edges (instead of posts at each corner) to allow parents to view baby from every angle. Best of all, it measures a roomy 36 inches square. To collapse, it has double-drop sides with sturdy lockable hinges, which brings the sides down to a manageable size for storage, travel, or merely moving the unit from room to room. The only drawback is that the unit does not include a carrying handle, which would make it easier to transport.

Warranty: 1 year, parts and labor
Manufacturer's Suggested Retail Price: $44
Approximate Low Price: not available

SWINGS

When you shop for a swing for your baby, stability should be the most important concern. After that, you want to consider the ease of setting up and taking down, the padding and comfort of the seat, the winding mechanism or motor, and possibly the portability or adaptability of the swing. Some swings double as car seats and/or car beds. This may be the deciding factor for you, or you may decide not to pay for features you don't need.

Cosco Dream Ride Plus 08-980

This classic wind-up swing from Cosco is the perfect example of an exceptional product with remarkable upgrades. The swing seat is also a combination (rear-facing) car seat or (side-facing) car bed that can be used in a sideways cradle position in either the swing or car. It can also be switched from a sideways (cradle-style) position once on the swing to a conventional forward-facing position with a rotating motion without removing the whole seat. Unlike most of the deluxe models on the market, it operates on a winding mechanism instead of batteries—but the crank is unusually quiet to operate and much quieter than most battery-powered models. The swing runs for a full 30 minutes, and the unit features a Minute-Minder to time the mechanism as it winds down. This is the only infant restraint that, when used as a car bed, can be used in an air-bag seating position. It also has a stable, sturdy steel frame that can be easily folded for storage and travel.

Warranty: 1 year, parts and labor
Manufacturer's Suggested Retail Price: $119
Approximate Low Price: $100-$110

Fisher-Price Cradle Swing 79454

Versatility and special features makes this swing, which offers two different motions and is exceptionally easy to fold for storage, an excellent choice for anyone short on floor space. The A-shaped frame, which is sturdy but lightweight and requires only one movement to fold so it can be transported or moved, accommodates the seat with either a side-to-side swing that emulates a cradle, or a back-and-forth swing in the traditional mode. The seat also has a two-position recline; an easy-entry flip-open tray; a thick, machine-washable seat pad; and an activity bar with four spinning beads. The battery-operated swinging function has three speeds and is fueled by three D-size alkaline batteries. Overall, this unit is an effective performer thanks to all the functions it performs, but one word of caution: Keep extra batteries on hand.

Warranty: 1 year (limited)
Manufacturer's Suggested Retail Price: $80
Approximate Low Price: not available

Graco Open-Top Swing 1464

Recommended

Graco has been making open-top swings for several years now that don't have a bar across the top. This makes the unit easy to set up and allows easy access to the seat, making it much simpler and smoother to get the baby into and out of the seat and giving the unit a streamlined appearance. This particular model is the top-of-the-line and is loaded with extra features that make it well worth the price. Although the seat can't be used for other functions (such as a car seat or carrier), it can be set in four positions that range from sitting to reclining. The unit also has an advanced electronic drive, offers a choice of 15 electronic tunes with volume control, has a thickly padded removable and washable cloth seat cover that comes in a variety of patterns, and sports a tray-style toy bar outfitted with interchangeable toys. The simple, push-button control panel is located on the side, and this unit offers one of the few motors to feature six speed variations and a low battery indicator. The motor should run for up to 200 hours on four D-size alkaline batteries.

Specifications: height, 37½"; weight, 17.5 lbs.
Warranty: 1 year
Manufacturer's Suggested Retail Price: $100
Approximate Low Price: $90

Cosco Quiet Time Elite 08-989

Budget Buy

There's nothing more frustrating than running out of batteries when a baby is cranky and wants to swing, which might account for the popularity of the good old-fashioned wind-up model. This unit is a great choice if you opt for a classic, because it is well-designed, quiet (with its whisper-quiet winding and running operations), and most importantly, swings for a full 30 minutes after being fully wound. There's even a Minute-Minder gauge to show running time remaining. It also folds easily for storage or travel, and sports soft padded covers that come off for machine washing, a wide-stance sturdy steel frame, and over-wind protection to guard the winding mechanism. It also has an ergonomically designed seat, a T-bar with a push-button release for security, and a three-position reclining seat. This is a solid workhorse, thanks to its solid design and fabrication.

Warranty: 1 year, parts and labor
Manufacturer's Suggested Retail Price: $50
Approximate Low Price: $48

NURSERY MONITORS

Nursery monitors can help put your mind at ease when you're not in the same room as your baby. Keep in mind, however, that monitor systems are sensitive to interference from other environmental sources (such as physical obstructions or cordless phones), and they are no substitute for periodic in-person checks on your baby.

FEATURES

The monitor's transmitter stays in the baby's room and relays noise—from soft cooing to loud crying—to your receiver. Most transmitters pick up sounds within a 6- to 10-foot radius and can relay them as far as 150-200 feet, depending on the environment. Modern monitors come with extra features: Some come with nightlights, others are cordless for greater mobility, and some very expensive models feature video display units. One highly desirable feature is a range finder that beeps when the transmitter is too far from the monitor (so there's no more guessing about whether you'll be able to hear your baby if you're in the backyard).

Evenflo Monitor & Intercom 613000 ✔ BEST BUY

Since Evenflo's purchase of Gerry last year, they have redesigned their monitor line and this is their newest and most innovative offering. Not only is the sleek design of this monitor, which consists of two identical units that look like transistor radios, reminiscent of a walkie-talkie, it also works on the same principle. Parents can talk to their baby, and anyone else who is within listening range of the monitor. This makes it easy to verbally calm fussy babies without actually being present, or have a two-way conversation with older children. It also has all the benchmark features that make a good monitor, such as easy-to-use controls on the front of the unit, sound lights to alert parents to a baby's sounds over background noises, a low-battery indicator, adapters for outlet use, and a belt clip for hands-free operation. Folding antennas are another plus, especially for mobility and ease of use.

Warranty: 1 year, parts and labor
Manufacturer's Suggested Retail Price: $50
Approximate Low Price: $40-$45

Fisher-Price Infant-to-Toddler Monitor 71577 ✓BEST BUY

Essentially a cordless phone and child locator in one, this nursery monitor is a breakthrough "grow-with-me" product that combines the capabilities of a telephone and an alarm. It employs 900MHz telephone technology, which offers more clarity and a wider listening range than channel systems and enhances the unit's capabilities as a monitor for an infant. A detachable transmitter that clips to a toddler's clothing and sounds an alarm when he or she is out of range makes it ideal for use with an older child. It also features a compact, durable, water-resistant design; two channel selections to minimize interference; power and low battery indicator lights on both the parent's and child's units; and sound lights to alert parents to sound that they might not hear in a noisy setting. The child's unit can be used with an AC adapter and automatically converts to battery power when removed from the base, and it can also be attached to other products (such as a playpen). The design and reception capabilities of this monitor make it one of the best available. It requires three AAA batteries and one 9-volt battery.

Warranty: 1 year (limited)
Manufacturer's Suggested Retail Price: $50
Approximate Low Price: $40

Graco UltraClear Monitor 2700

Budget Buy

The old classic sound monitors are still very effective tools for listening in on your child, and this version from Graco is a good option. Thanks to an advanced telephone technology adapted to this unit, which compresses the signal and narrows it for better transmission, this unit has excellent reception. It also features a variable light display so parents can distinguish between a yawn and a cry, a rotary volume control, flexible antennas on both the transmitter and receiver, and AC adapters so the receivers can be used with 9-volt batteries or electric current. Controls are on the front of the unit and are easy to use. The only drawbacks are the lack of an out-of-range indicator and low-battery indicator.

Warranty: 1 year from date of manufacture
Manufacturer's Suggested Retail Price: $30
Approximate Low Price: not available

CAR SEATS

Car seats for infants and young children are mandatory in all states, and newborns may not be released from hospitals unless a parent has an appropriate restraint system to use on the trip home. All car seats are required to conform to Federal Motor Vehicle Safety Standards, but this does not mean that all seats are suitable for all children. It is important to be aware of the many varieties on the market so you can choose the appropriate car seat for your child. Options include infant-only, convertible, and booster car seats.

INFANT CAR SEATS

Infant car seats are intended for newborn babies up to about 20 pounds (a weight usually reached between nine months and one year of age). These car seats are used only in a rear-facing position in the car and must not be used in the front seat if the car is equipped with an air bag. If an air bag is deployed, it would strike the back of the infant's car seat at over 200 miles an hour, and the impact of this violent blow to the baby's head could cause brain damage or death.

Outside the car, however, these seats can double as carriers, feeding seats, or even rockers. This type of seat is also the best choice for low-birth-weight babies, because the convertible car seats that also accommodate older infants or toddlers are likely to be too large—even in the infant position—for smaller newborns. Remember, if the child does not fit correctly in the seat, the seat cannot provide optimum protection.

CONVERTIBLE INFANT CAR SEAT/STROLLERS

These products can come in handy as car seats, strollers, and infant carriers. Many parents enjoy the convenience of being able to take the baby from the car to the stroller without undoing and refastening complicated harnesses. If you're shopping for a convertible infant car seat/stroller, first read the introductions for car seats and for strollers to make sure the model you're considering has all the safety and comfort features recommended for a car seat or a stroller. In addition, check the fasteners that hold the car seat to the stroller—they should be sturdy and secure—and try it out to see whether conversion from car seat to stroller and back is quick and easy enough to suit your needs.

INFANT CAR SEAT

Fisher-Price Safe Embrace
Infant Car Seat 79725

✔**BEST BUY**

This one-piece car seat does not snap into a base that is left in the car, which makes it very simple to use. It offers a combination of safety features that make it an exceptional performer. To begin with, the seat base is contoured and has a position indicator that makes it easy to see if the seat is installed properly. It also has a five-point harness system (which has two shoulder belts, two lap belts, and a center belt) that is actually exceptionally easy and fast to adjust thanks to a sliding track system in the back of the seat that eliminates the slack in the belt with one movement. The locking clips that might be necessary to tighten or hold the seat in some cars are built right in to the frame of the car seat (most car seats feature separate clips that tend to vanish when you really need them), as is a special Secure-Lock Attachment that keeps the car seat from falling off shopping carts and locks or unlocks with one hand. It also features a thick, washable, removable pad and a retractable canopy to shield the baby from the sun. Like most other models in this category, it must be used in the rear-facing position only (and never in an air-bag-equipped position in the car). This particular model accommodates children up to 22 pounds (instead of the standard 20 pounds for most models in this category).

Warranty: 2 years
Manufacturer's Suggested Retail Price: $70
Approximate Low Price: $50-$65

CONVERTIBLE CAR SEAT

Fisher-Price Safe Embrace
Convertible Car Seat 79700

✔**BEST BUY**

Fisher-Price revolutionized the car seat market three years ago with its Safe Embrace convertible and booster car seats, which were the first car seats on the market to feature built-in tether straps that attach to the top of the car seat for use in its forward-facing position (they anchor the top of the car seat directly to the vehicle's frame). In a crash, the tether strap reduces the forward motion of the car seat and the child, significantly reducing the risk of injury. In fact, National Highway Traffic Safety Administration regulations proposed to take effect in the future might require these tethers on all car seats. This car seat also features a five-point harness system, built-in locking clips for easy installation of the car seat with the seat belt of a car, color-coded belt paths to make it easier to position and buckle children in correctly (blue for rear-facing infants, burgundy for forward-facing toddlers), and virtually universal vehicle compatibility thanks to the careful design of the unit. For those who plan to buy only one car seat, this is a superb option.

Warranty: 2 years
Manufacturer's Suggested Retail Price: not available
Approximate Low Price: $130-$140

CONVERTIBLE CAR SEAT/STROLLERS

Evenflo Trendsetter
Advantage Travel System 4981

The Evenflo car seat, which has a foam-grip Carry Right handle, thickly padded seat cover that removes for washing, and a canopy, is an exceptional car seat that can be used with its stay-in-the-car base or in a second car sans the base. Here it is coupled with the sturdy Trendsetter stroller, which features a five-position reclining seat, a pad for head support that can be used in the stroller or car seat, shock-absorbing all-round suspension, front pivot locks on the wheels for rough terrain, a large viewing port and sun visor on the canopy, one-hand steering, and a convenience console and snack tray on the handle. It also sports a large storage bin below the stroller. Both parts of this product are easy to use, although the snack tray can pose a problem if it is used for a hot beverage because a sudden stop or jolt can cause it to spill on the baby.

Warranty: 1 year, parts and labor
Manufacturer's Suggested Retail Price: $190
Approximate Low Price: $155-$180

Graco Ultimate Travel System 7497
✔**BEST BUY**

The 7497 combines an excellent car seat, which is highly rated in independent crash tests, with a good stroller, all at a very fair price. All these units function in four ways (as an infant carrier, infant car seat, infant stroller, and full-size stroller), and also make it possible to move a sleeping baby from a car to a stroller. This particular system uses a car seat that features a base that stays buckled inside the car, and a seat that audibly clicks into position on that base and sports a level indicator to demonstrate the correct angle. A rotating canopy on the seat freely adjusts to any position, and the seat has a comfortable, easily adjusted handle. The Lite-Rider stroller is loaded with features that make it a good performer, such as a sturdy, lightweight design with an ergonomic, padded handle; lockable, oversized dual swivel wheels; a large viewing port in the stroller canopy; a roomy, extra-large under-the-seat storage bin; a reclining seat; a washable fabric seat pad with an infant head support; and a removable snack tray. The large wheels give the unit an exceptionally smooth ride.

Specifications: height, 41¾"; weight, 22 lbs.
Warranty: 1 year
Manufacturer's Suggested Retail Price: $160
Approximate Low Price: $135-$150

BOOSTER CAR SEATS

Fisher-Price Safe Embrace 79751

✔**BEST BUY**

This booster seat consists of a thick, seat-shaped pad with a high back that surrounds the child's body and lifts him or her several inches off the seat of the car, thus making them the perfect height for the car's own three-point harness system. It features a lap belt positioner that keeps the belt across the child's hips, instead of abdomen, to better withstand the force of a crash. The high back with padded support for the child's head and neck helps keep the child upright and comfortable, even while sleeping, so the vehicle's belts remain safely positioned in case an accident should occur. It also sports minimum and maximum shoulder-height indicators imprinted right on the seat to check whether a growing child is the right size for the seat.

Warranty: 2 years
Manufacturer's Suggested Retail Price: $60
Approximate Low Price: $45-$50

Kolcraft Prodigy 53000

Like the Fisher-Price booster seat, this seat consists of a thick pad shaped like a bucket seat that surrounds the child's body and lifts him or her several inches off the seat of the car to make them the perfect height for the car's own three-point harness system. It also has belt positioners and shoulder-height indicators. While the high contoured seat back provides head and side support, it is a bit less enveloping than the Fisher-Price unit, which might make it more comfortable for larger framed children.

Warranty: 1 year
Manufacturer's Suggested Retail Price: $50
Approximate Low Price: $40-$45

TODDLER-TO-BOOSTER CAR SEAT

Century NextStep Stage II Car Seat 4920

This remarkable car seat redefines the booster category, changing it into a stage that extends from about a year, when an infant reaches 20 pounds, to age five or six, when that child reaches 65 pounds. It is used with its own shielded five-point harness system for children from 20 to 40 pounds, then with the car's own seat harness and belt when the child ranges from 30 to 65 pounds. For smaller children, it has a removable height-adjustable head support pad. The two-piece harness system is fast and convenient to use. For older children, a belt routing system makes it easy to use the car's own seat belt and chest harness; a Comfort Clip with three adjustable positions keeps the chest harness in the proper position (and off little necks), and adjustable side supports pivot down so it is easy for the child to get into the seat. The seat also features two seating positions (slightly reclining or

444

fully upright) for comfort at any age. This ingenious seat eliminates the need for two products (convertible and booster seats), because an infant can go straight to this and stay there until ready to forgo a car seat altogether.

Warranty: 1 year
Manufacturer's Suggested Retail Price: $100
Approximate Low Price: $85

STROLLERS

Many parents tend to buy infant carriages or standard strollers in addition to the umbrella strollers that can be carried around easily in the car. Today, however, the best strollers grow with your baby, combining the luxury of a carriage and the practicality of an umbrella stroller. Look for a lightweight, easy-to-fold stroller with removable padded seats, reversible handles, and large, durable wheels.

COMBI Savvy Z 2400

✔ BEST BUY

This is the most exceptional stroller on the market, thanks to its low weight (just 7.7 pounds) and superb design. It is loaded with advantages for both parents and the baby, and is so versatile and well-engineered it can even do for those who want to purchase only one stroller. The low weight is due to the use of aircraft aluminum for the frame, which also makes it exceptionally sturdy. Its outstanding engineering makes it easy to close, and it folds down to just ten inches in depth. It also has a seat that reclines to 140 degrees, an adjustable and removable canopy, a roomy storage bin under the unit, a footrest, and a cushion that is easy to remove for washing. Steering this lightweight stroller is smooth, easy, and even fun. It comes in five different chic motifs, ranging from a sedate classic pinprick dot to a wild leopard print.

Warranty: 1 year (limited)
Manufacturer's Suggested Retail Price: $199
Approximate Low Price: $170-$190

Cosco Deluxe Rock N Roller Stroller 01-634

This stroller is a solid performer loaded with extras that makes it an excellent choice for anyone who might want to buy only one unit (and the motion capabilities can be quite attractive for fussy babies). It also features a removable, reversible seat that can be used facing either direction or be completely removed and used as a bassinet. It has four reclining positions. There is also a one-step squeeze lever for fast collapsing, an adjustable, removable quilted canopy with a window, an oversized market basket, and dual brakes on the rear wheels. Finally, it has a wider frame, a shock-absorption system on all wheels, dual swivel front wheels, a removable full boot for cold weather warmth, an extra deluxe machine-washable pad, and an ergonomically shaped handle. Coupled with a sensible price, this stroller is a superb choice.

Warranty: 1 year, parts and labor
Manufacturer's Suggested Retail Price: $120
Approximate Low Price: $113

COMBI Spirit 456

Despite a hefty price, this extraordinarily sturdy, full-featured stroller is reasonable given the state-of-the-art engineering and high-quality materials that went into it. The Spirit 456 is extremely stable, durable, and lightweight (at just 16 pounds) due to the use of aircraft aluminum for the frame. The stroller is loaded with features for both the baby and parents, starting with the reversible handle that converts the unit from stroller to carriage. It is also extremely easy to open or close thanks to side locks that are operated by foot rather than hand, and has a one-touch swivel feature that lets you secure two wheels at once. There is also a three-position reclining seat; thickly padded removable and washable seat cushions with a border to protect the baby's head; a long, closely fitted boot for warmth and protection; an adjustable and removable canopy with a viewing port for the baby; a roomy oversized storage bin under the unit; a footrest; and a three-point harness. Like the Savvy Z, steering this lightweight stroller, which is very stable and solid on the road, is smooth, easy, and fun. It is also extremely elegant with a streamlined design and a choice of two sophisticated fabrics.

Warranty: 1 year (limited)
Manufacturer's Suggested Retail Price: $279
Approximate Low Price: $200-$260

HIGH CHAIRS

A voluntary safety standard created by JPMA exists for high chairs, which basically calls for restraining belts, dependable chair and tray locks, stability, a design with no protruding or sharp edges, and good instructional literature (which covers assembly, maintenance, cleaning, and use). It also addresses issues such as slipping out of the chair under the tray (many models have restraints between the legs that reduce this hazard) and other performance issues. Chairs that meet this safety criteria have a JPMA seal of approval.

FEATURES

Seat-belt latches and tray operation are critical considerations since you will be using this product several times a day. Look for models that allow you to operate the tray with one hand, are sturdy, have no parts that wobble, and have easy-to-use locks on the safety belt. Chairs should also be comfortable for the baby and easy to keep clean (plastic and metal chairs are easiest to wash down).

Special features on high chairs run the gamut. Some fold up, some offer reclining positions for bottle-feeding, and others offer different height positions and convert into booster chairs. Fold-up models are great if space is at a premium, but make sure the legs have sturdy locking mechanisms. Make sure high chairs with different settings are easy to manipulate, or the settings will be too inconvenient to use.

When a child is in a high chair, it is critical to always fasten the seat-belt and never let the child stand in the chair. According to statistics, children under the age of one are most vulnerable to high-chair accidents.

Graco Height-Adjustable
Reclining High Chair 3845

✔**BEST BUY**

Thanks to its sturdy construction and flexibility, this high chair will go the long haul in any household. It reclines in three different positions, so it can be used with very young infants, and it adjusts to six different heights for the ease of the person feeding the baby or to fit under your dining table without using the tray. It also features a deluxe, fully padded leatherette seat pad that's easy to wipe down and keep clean; a T-bar to keep baby from sliding out of the seat; an extra-large wrap-around tray that can be adjusted with a one-hand maneuver; and a removable snack tray. The bottom features A-frame legs that collapse similarly to a folding chair, so the high chair can be stored away easily when not in use.

Specifications: height, 35"-40"; weight, 17.5 lbs.
Warranty: 1 year
Manufacturer's Suggested Retail Price: $70
Approximate Low Price: $50-$65

Cosco Options 5 High Chair 03-286

Budget Buy

From the inventors of the first plastic high chair 50 years ago comes this version that's high on flexibility and style but low on cost. It features seven height adjustments, reclines for infants, has a three-point restraint system and a thickly padded washable seat, and can be used without the tray as a booster seat at the table. The seat can be lowered on the frame for an older child so it becomes an actual chair, or totally removed from the frame and placed on a regular chair for use as a booster. The tray can be set in four different positions. The T-bar design keeps the baby from sliding off the seat, and can be removed or adjusted with one hand. When necessary, the high chair folds up easily for quick and convenient storage.

Warranty: 1 year, parts and labor
Manufacturer's Suggested Retail Price: $49
Approximate Low Price: not available